JUDEOPHOBIA AND THE NEW TESTAMENT

Judeophobia and the New Testament

Texts and Contexts

Edited by

SARAH E. ROLLENS, ERIC M. VANDEN EYKEL,
AND MEREDITH J. C. WARREN

WILLIAM B. EERDMANS PUBLISHING COMPANY
GRAND RAPIDS, MICHIGAN

Wm. B. Eerdmans Publishing Co.
2006 44th Street SE, Grand Rapids, MI 49508
www.eerdmans.com

Book design by Lydia Hall

Printed in the United States of America

30 30 29 28 27 26 25   1 2 3 4 5 6 7

ISBN 978-0-8028-8288-2

Library of Congress Cataloging-in-Publication Data

A catalog record for this book is available from the Library of Congress.

*For Shelly Matthews, who once remarked that a volume
like this could be potentially useful and whose scholarship
helped make a volume like this possible*

Contents

Contents

Contents

Bible Translations Cited

ESV	English Standard Version
NIV	New International Version
NIV-2011	New International Version, 2011 edition
NJPS-1999	New Jewish Publication Society Bible, 1999 edition
NRSV	New Revised Standard Version
NRSVue	New Revised Standard Version, updated edition

Introduction

SARAH E. ROLLENS, ERIC VANDEN EYKEL,
AND MEREDITH J. C. WARREN

Passages from the New Testament are often used to garnish and fuel the screeds and manifestos of Christian supremacists. This is as true today as it has been for centuries. Whether drawing from the more vitriolic John 8:44 (which describes Jesus telling his fellow Jews that they have "the devil" as their father) or Revelation 2:9 and 3:9 (which accuses some Jews of being part of a "synagogue of Satan") or even the more subtle Pauline phrasing that appears to disparage Jewish law in favor of the apparently Christian concept of grace, Judeophobia is, and has been for some time, woven throughout Christian readings of scripture.

In their own original historical and cultural contexts, Judeophobic passages from the New Testament had meanings that were often completely different than what they have been made to mean in their later anti-Jewish contexts; nevertheless, such examples continue to promote animosity and violence against Jews. This is an issue not only with casual or confessional readers of the New Testament, but also, unfortunately, with professional biblical scholars, who (sometimes inadvertently) further Judeophobic ideas in their own work. This book aims to help New Testament scholarship account for such interpretations, take responsibility for them when necessary, and encourage the discipline to push back on rising anti-Jewish rhetoric and violence.

We expect that readers will come to this volume from an array of cultural, religious, educational, and even political backgrounds and will thus encounter and use it in various ways. For that reason, the aim of the introduction is to explain

1

our reasoning for this project, as well as our choice of terminology. We do not expect anything in *Judeophobia and the New Testament* to be the final word on matters related to anti-Jewish rhetoric and the New Testament. But we do hope that it helps to initiate difficult and important discussions, especially in undergraduate classrooms, for this is where we believe that scholars can often reach a larger audience than they might in their more narrowly focused scholarship.

Terminology

The title of this volume—*Judeophobia and the New Testament*—was the topic of more than a few discussions among its editors and contributors. From the earliest stages of the project, we considered a few different options—including "antisemitism" and "anti-Judaism"—before finally deciding on "Judeophobia." Since one of the most frequent questions we received while carrying out this project has to do with our choice of this terminology, we want to address and explain it up front.

There are currently two leading established attempts to define antisemitism for practical purposes. The most prominent definition, although not universally accepted, is the one developed by the International Holocaust Remembrance Association (IHRA). It is brief:

> Antisemitism is a certain perception of Jews, which may be expressed as hatred toward Jews. Rhetorical and physical manifestations of antisemitism are directed toward Jewish or non-Jewish individuals and/or their property, toward Jewish community institutions and religious facilities.[1]

The IHRA provides examples to clarify the intended meaning of this brief paragraph, but this definition is quite general, and for that reason it has received critique from scholars of Judaism and also scholars of genocide.[2] The Association of Jewish Studies notes that various definitions, though they overlap substantially, also disagree with one another, "specifically about when and how antisemitism overlaps with criticism of Israeli policies or Zionism."[3] Among others, a Canadian group, the Jewish Faculty Network, voted not to

---

1. International Holocaust Remembrance Association, "The Working Definition of Antisemitism" (https://tinyurl.com/4awwuu8d).

2. "128 Scholars Warn: 'Don't Trap the United Nations in a Vague and Weaponized Definition of Antisemitism'" (3 November 2022) (https://tinyurl.com/3e8jutpj).

3. Association for Jewish Studies, "A Working Report from the AJS Task Force on Antisemitism and Academic Freedom" (https://tinyurl.com/3ybcfhby).

adopt the IHRA definition.[4] *The Guardian* found that the IHRA definition, which universities in the United Kingdom were forced to adopt or face funding penalties, is regularly being used as a tool to stifle criticism of Israel; a report found that out of forty accusations of antisemitism based on the IHRA definition, thirty-eight were cleared as unfounded.[5]

Many scholars who were uncomfortable with the IHRA definition developed an alternative: the Jerusalem Declaration.[6] This longer and more detailed working definition distinguishes political critique of Israel as a nation state from critique of Israel as representative of Jews. It clarifies that Jews must not be held collectively responsible for Israel's actions; that Jews should not be expected to comment on Israeli state policies simply because they are Jews; that Jews should be assumed to be loyal to their country of citizenship or residence (and not universally loyal to Israel as a nation state); and that Israel as a nation must not be critiqued using antisemitic tropes or images. Assuming that all Jews act the same way, or that they think, believe, or support the same things is an age-old Judeophobic trope that plays into dangerous stereotypes and conspiracy theories. The Jerusalem Declaration also provides topical guidelines for more nuanced application of the definition, which its authors encourage people to also use for interpreting the IHRA definition.

The goal of discussing these two major definitions of antisemitism is not to adopt either one or the other for the purpose of this volume, but rather to demonstrate that defining antisemitism, Judeophobia, or anti-Jewish attitudes and actions is more fraught than it might appear, and that Jews, too, hold diverse opinions about how to define these terms.

An alternative to "antisemitism"—Judeophobia—is proposed by numerous scholars of anti-Judaism and antisemitism. It is this term that we employ for our title, and generally throughout the essays herein. Jonathan Judaken's critique of antisemitism articulates part of why "Judeophobia" makes more sense for him and, consequently, for the purposes of this project. Antisemitism, Judaken argues, "covers everything from personal prejudices to genocide. As is the case with the over-expansive use of the term 'racism,' this equivocation stifles discussion and leads to misunderstandings."[7] Using the term "antisemi-

---

4. Jeremy Appel, "A New Canadian Jewish Faculty Group Opposes the IHRA Definition of Antisemitism" (12 December 2021) (https://tinyurl.com/mr7mstsb).

5. Haroon Siddique, "Antisemitism Definition Used by UK Universities Leading to 'Unreasonable' Accusations," *The Guardian* (13 September 2023) (https://tinyurl.com/55h8kjfc).

6. The Jerusalem Declaration on Antisemitism (https://tinyurl.com/pauh45s3).

7. Jonathan Judaken, "Introduction," *The American Historical Review*, Rethinking Anti-Semitism Round Table, 123.4 (2018): 1122–38 at 1128, https://doi.org/10.1093/ahr/rhy024. See also Yehuda Bauer, "In Search of a Definition of Antisemitism," in *Approaches to Antisemi-*

tism" across all cultural, historical, and political landscapes also creates the potentially misleading impression of a linear, teleological relationship between all examples of anti-Judaism, whether in first-century Rome or twentieth-century Germany; while historians, scholars of religion, and political scientists will certainly draw connections (as, indeed, we do in this volume) between ancient and more contemporary examples of Judeophobia, their unique contexts deserve greater scrutiny than the all-encompassing antisemitism label allows:

> The social forces, political frameworks and institutions, technological mechanisms, and economic conditions that have periodically driven the revival of these persisting myths are not the same in dissimilar contexts. Consequently, different eruptions of Judeophobia require different explanations. For this reason, cyclical eternalism, like its twin, transhistorical anti-Semitism, does not advance our understanding.[8]

In terms of language and categories, the concept of antisemitism itself emerges from the deeply problematic "race science" that was en vogue in nineteenth-century Europe. This "science" sought to classify so-called Semitic people as racially distinct from, and opposed to, so-called Aryans; it reached its horrifying climax in the hands of the Nazis, who deliberately engaged in eugenics to advance the "Aryan" race, which they assumed to be superior. Because this racial classification emerged in this fraught context, some shy away from using it to study the ancient world especially—that is, in a period before categories such as "Semitic" or "Aryan" even existed. Judaken convincingly

---

tism: Context and Curriculum, ed. Michael Brown (New York: American Jewish Committee, 1994), 10–23 at 12.

8. Judaken, "Introduction," 1130–31. See also Matthew Chalmers, "'Anti-Semitism' before 'Semites': The Risks and Rewards of Anachronism" (13 July 2017) (https://tinyurl.com/mrx454ft). Indeed, David Nirenberg (*Anti-Judaism: The Western Tradition* [New York: Norton, 2013]) shows that various cultures that have historically been gathered together under the nomenclature of "the West" have a long history of defining identity in reference to Jews as their "other." Taking his cue from Karl Marx, Nirenberg opts for language of "anti-Judaism," because he is interested in how people rhetorically engage with Judaism, often treated oppositionally, for identity formation. In Marx's writings, Nirenberg explains, Judaism "is not only the religion of specific people with specific beliefs, but also a category, a set of ideas and attributes with which non-Jews can make sense of and criticize their world. Nor is 'anti-Judaism' simply an attitude toward Jews and their religion, but a way of critically engaging the world. It is in this broad sense that I will use the words *Judaism* and *anti-Judaism*. And it is also for this reason that I do not use *anti-Semitism*, a word that captures only a small portion, historically and conceptually, of what this book is about" (3 [emphasis original]).

argues that "Judeophobia" can provide us with more analytical nuance in our examination of anti-Judaism throughout history:

> "Judeophobia" offers a better over-arching term for the field for at least three reasons. First, it defamiliarizes readers. This allows for the conceptual reflection we are calling for. Judeophobia, as I define it, encompasses denigration of Judaism, defamation of the Jewish character, discrimination against Jews, their racialization, and at its extreme, efforts at their destruction. . . . Secondly, "Judeophobia" lends itself more readily to periodization that is attentive to social, political, economic, technological, and cultural shifts. . . . A third reason to adopt the term "Judeophobia" is that it readily links what Frantz Fanon aptly designated "phobogenic" objects itemized in his studies of Negrophobia with instances of Islamophobia, homophobia, or gynophobia. These each name subjects of anxiety or unsubstantiated fear or resentment, but also fascination or even envy.[9]

Like other scholars before us,[10] we wrestled with the best and most productive way to describe the topic of our research. We came to the conclusion, as many have previously in their own work, that "Judeophobia" was an appropriate term for this project.[11] However, our use of "Judeophobia" for this volume is by no means meant to erase or replace antisemitism or anti-Judaism as useful and even preferred categories in some instances. Our goal here is to provide analytical space for various authors to unpack what anti-Jewish animus entails contextually for individual books of the New Testament or within broader methodological categories.

While "Judeophobia" appears prominently in this project's title and also in many of its chapters, contributors to this volume were encouraged to use

9. Judaken, "Introduction," 1131–33. For discussion of antisemitism as anti-Jewish racism, see Abigail B. Bakan and Yasmeen Abu-Laban, "Antisemitism as Anti-Jewish Racism: Reflections on an Anti-Racist Analytic," *Historical Materialism* special issue on "Marxism and the Critique of Antisemitism Today," 32.1 and 2 (2024). Pre-print issue (11 March 2024): https://tinyurl.com/bdfd5ubb.

10. For example, Peter Schäfer, *Judeophobia: Attitudes Toward the Jews in the Ancient World* (Cambridge: Harvard University Press, 1997); David Engel, "Away from a Definition of Antisemitism: An Essay in the Semantics of Historical Description," in *Rethinking European Jewish History*, ed. Jeremy Cohen and Moshe Rosman (London: Littman Library of Jewish Civilization, 2009), 30–53; Zvi Yavetz, "Judeophobia in Classical Antiquity: A Different Approach," *Journal of Jewish Studies* 44 (1993): 1–22.

11. See, contra, Erich S. Gruen, "Was There Judeophobia in Classical Antiquity?," in Gruen's *The Construct of Identity in Hellenistic Judaism: Essays on Early Jewish Literature and History* (Berlin: de Gruyter, 2016), 313–32 (https://tinyurl.com/33ev7vck).

whatever labels and categories they felt were appropriate for them and for their subject matter. They were selected as contributors for their competence as scholars, and so retaining their autonomy and discretion on terminology was important to us. Especially for such a tricky topic where language and word choice can matter so much, we certainly did not want to impose any categories or terminology on them. And so, while we wanted to clarify our language choice here in the introduction, we also wanted to explain why alternative language appears at points throughout this volume's contributions.[12]

12. In the study of ancient Judaism and Christianity, there is considerable debate over another terminological issue: whether the Greek term *Ioudaios* is best translated "Jew" or "Judean." On one hand, some scholars opt for "Judean" in order (1) to emphasize the ethnic dimension of this identity and (2) to acknowledge the ordinary way people in the Roman Empire classified people: certain ethnic groups were known as emerging from a particular region (e.g., Egyptians, Thracians, Dacians). A Judean community in Rome, then, would have been assumed by all other people in the city to be a diaspora group that stemmed from an original ethnic group that lived (or was currently living) in Judea. This perspective is often supported by those who advocate the use of the social sciences for studying the ancient world, for ethnic identity and its construction have been key topics in such scholarship; see Steve Mason, "Ancient Jews or Judeans? Different Questions, Different Answers" (26 August 2014) (https://tinyurl.com/57cbafb9); and Philip F. Esler, "Identity Matters: Judean Ethnic Identity in the First Century CE" (May 2012) (https://tinyurl.com/4829rmjt). However, others argue that such translations gloss over ancient Judaism (rather uniquely) tying religious practice to ethnic identity, in a way that other ethnic groups tended not to (although ancient Judaism still had its share of newcomer adherents [consider such ancient texts as Joseph and Aseneth]). More troubling in the eyes of some is how the term "Judean" erases the presence of Judaism, as a coherent religious tradition, from ancient Christian texts specifically, which, in turn, threatens to downplay the very real antisemitism that has been born out of early Christian literature. Speaking of the Gospel of John in particular, which treats "the Jews" as a negatively marked, stock villain in its story, Adele Reinhartz notes: "To use Judean instead of Jew whitewashes the Gospel of John and relieves us of the difficult but necessary task of grappling with this gospel in a meaningful way"; "The Vanishing Jews of Antiquity" (24 June 2014) (https://tinyurl.com/bddumafj). Reinhartz cites an important statement from Amy-Jill Levine immediately thereafter: "The Jew is replaced with the Judean, and thus we have a Judenrein ('Jew free') text, a text purified of Jews. . . . So much for the elimination of anti-Semitism by means of changing vocabulary" (A.-J. Levine, *The Misunderstood Jew: The Church and the Scandal of the Jewish Jesus* [San Francisco: HarperOne, 2006], 160, 165; see also for a wider discussion of this terminology, Jason A. Staples, *The Idea of "Israel" in Second Temple Judaism: A New Theory of People, Exile, and Israelite Identity* [Cambridge: Cambridge University Press, 2021], 11–24). Thus, we acknowledge that the ethical stakes can be very high even when talking about ancient literature and the identities described therein. As editors, we tend toward "Jew" as the best translation of *Ioudaios*, except where the wording under question specifically means "people located in the Roman province of Judea." Given that this is an ongoing debate among biblical scholars, we did not dictate that contributors use particular terminology on this matter. We note, however,

This volume's work on Judeophobia is indebted to the incisive work of scholars who came before us, some of whom are also contributors to this volume. In particular, it is important to recognize the contributions of scholars whose steadfast work on Judeophobia and the New Testament inspired the present editors to produce this volume. Amy-Jill Levine writes extensively on the ways that Christians have, sometimes with good intentions and sometimes without, reinforced "false and noxious stereotypes" of Jews in their teaching and preaching.[13] It is clear that anti-Jewish ideas permeate much of the way that Christians read their scriptures, including that the Christian concept of grace should be automatically contrasted with the Jewish notion of law; that Judaism's purity laws and general attitudes toward women were misogynist and needed abolishing by Jesus; and that early Jews associated wealth with righteousness and therefore showed no concern for marginalized groups until Jesus came along to set things right.[14] These anti-Jewish stereotypes, Levine observes, are ways that Christian readers position themselves as better than Jews; in this way, such an inaccurate and dangerous misunderstanding of Judaism is reinforced when Christians read the New Testament without understanding the context in which it was written.[15] This book represents a way for Christian readers, as well as those embedded in Christianized secular reading contexts, to reevaluate how they interact with the rhetoric and history of these powerful documents.

Judeophobia in the Current World

We have all watched as violence against Jews has become increasingly more visible in Europe and North America of late. In our undergraduate classrooms, we often discovered that our students, especially but not only those who live in rural areas with rather homogeneous (usually predominantly Christian) populations, do not recognize this swell of hatred or realize the extent of it when they do become aware of incidents.[16] In this section, we want to briefly high-

---

that the majority opted for "Jew" over "Judean," likely because they, too, recognize how these ancient texts can have ethical implications for our world today.

13. Amy-Jill Levine, "Bearing False Witness: Common Errors Made about Early Judaism," in *The Jewish Annotated New Testament*, ed. Amy-Jill Levine and Marc Zvi Brettler (New York: Oxford University Press, 2011), 759–63 at 750.

14. Levine, "Bearing False Witness," 760–61.

15. Levine, "Bearing False Witness," 763.

16. We discussed this issue with respect to our specific institutional contexts in an earlier article: Sarah E. Rollens, Eric Vanden Eykel, and Meredith J. C. Warren, "Confronting Jud-

light some diverse examples of how Judeophobic ideas are expressed explicitly and implicitly in the public sphere, as well as in New Testament scholarship that is supposedly critically and historically grounded.

Most readers are able to recognize more explicit forms of Judeophobia, at the very least because the public outcry against these incidents is often swift and loud. The tragedy that took place in Charlottesville, Virginia, on August 11–12, 2017, illustrates the explicit form that this hatred can take.[17] Under the guise of protesting the removal of a public statue of Robert E. Lee, demonstrators gathered for what became a brazen and impassioned white supremacist assembly, collectively declared as the "Unite the Right" rally. Participants came from recognized white supremacist groups, such as the National Front, the Ku Klux Klan, and Identity Evropa. Numerous forms of prejudice were on display that day, including vivid examples of anti-Jewish hate. Most famously, participants were filmed—again, unabashedly—chanting "Jews will not replace us!" This phrase features prominently in a wider racist conspiracy theory known as the Great Replacement Theory. In this case, these white nationalists were voicing a fear that the "white" race is under threat of being replaced by Jews. Anxiety from the Great Replacement Theory has also been aimed at immigrants from Central and South America in the United States, as well as at Muslim immigrants in the European Union.

Just over a year after Charlottesville, another high-profile antisemitic incident occurred in Pittsburgh.[18] In this horrific event, an armed man entered the Tree of Life Synagogue on November 4, 2018, and murdered eleven people, injuring numerous others. Exploration of the man's social media footprint revealed that he was deeply engaged in Far Right, white supremacist networks. Antisemitism was only one expression of his hate; he also espoused revulsion against immigrants, African Americans, and members of the LGBTQ+ community, among others. Disturbingly, his social media also cited John 8:44 (the verse mentioned at the outset of this introduction) as justification for his actions. The editors of this volume, who all teach in different ways about ancient Jewish and Christian-

---

eophobia in the Classroom," *Journal for Interdisciplinary Biblical Studies* 2.1 (2020): 81–106 (https://tinyurl.com/ykyj9yu7).

17. The tragedy of that day was not simply the blatant racism on display, but also the horrific death of a counterprotester, Heather D. Heyer, who was killed (and many others injured) when James Alex Fields Jr. deliberately drove a vehicle into an assembly of counterprotesters; BBC News, "Charlottesville: One Killed in Violence over US Far-Right Rally" (13 August 2017) (https://tinyurl.com/y3jhrtbw).

18. This is not to say that there were no other incidents in the intervening period. We are simply choosing the most high-profile events that we expect our readers to be most familiar with. The Anti-Defamation League keeps a list of incidents, with the data broken down in numerous interesting ways; see ADL, "Antisemitic Incidents Surge in 2022" (https://tinyurl.com/mtnvfsw7).

identity formation, struggled in the wake of this event to help our students think through his attempt to justify this violence with a verse from the New Testament. We eventually published a cowritten article on dealing with Judeophobia in different kinds of institutional settings.[19] Our work on that article would soon send us down the path to the broader collaborative project found in this book.

Indeed, even after we invited all of the contributors to this volume, we continued to see more and more visible expressions of Judeophobia, made possible in no small part by political leaders who were continuing to give a platform to antisemitism and other forms of hate, often under the cover of dog whistles.[20] The rise of COVID-19 offered a new global anxiety and thus a new discursive sphere in which anti-Jewish prejudices could play out. Many people who were opposed to the COVID vaccine, especially when it was mandated by employers and government institutions, began to liken themselves to persecuted victims of the Holocaust, which, it hardly needs to be said, is enormously offensive to the actual victims of this tragedy. Some even started wearing yellow cloth stars, made to look like what Jews were forced to wear in Nazi Germany, to show their dissent. Such performances seemed absurd to some, but others saw the implicit Judeophobia and harm in these actions. The Anti-Defamation League called this appropriation a "hugely inappropriate use of this enduring symbol of the persecution of Jews by the Nazis during World War II and [it] minimizes and trivializes the experiences of the survivors and victims of the Holocaust."[21]

As we write this introduction (early 2024), the public discourse around the recent Israeli war with Hamas often mobilizes language of antisemitism for various reasons, as well. Without wading into that complex (albeit extremely important) discussion here, it seems essential to point out, even briefly, that *any* discourse attempting to align an identity, thought process, behavior, and so on, with Jewish people based solely on their Jewish identity (e.g., "Jewish people should support X view, simply because they are Jewish" or "all Jewish people are complicit in X, simply because they are Jewish") is deeply problematic and dangerous.

As was the case in antiquity, modern Judaism is diverse in terms of political interests and leanings, moral standpoints, and cultural habits—and this diver-

19. Rollens, Vanden Eykel, and Warren, "Confronting Judeophobia in the Classroom."

20. Aaron Blake, "Trump's Long History of Trafficking in Antisemitic Tropes," *Washington Post* (17 October 2022) (https://tinyurl.com/2nc2v9zu). On dog-whistle politics, see Ian Haney López, *Dog Whistle Politics: How Coded Racial Appeals Have Reinvented Racism and Wrecked the Middle Class* (New York: Oxford University Press, 2015); and Jennifer Mather Saul, *Dog Whistles and Fig Leaves: How Manipulative Language Spreads Racism and Falsehood* (Oxford: Oxford University Press, 2024).

21. ADL, "Anti-Vaccine Protesters Misappropriate Holocaust-Era Symbol to Promote Their Cause" (5 April 2019) (https://tinyurl.com/ysanyhzn).

sity includes a range of perspectives on the state of Israel and its recent actions. Failing to recognize this modern diversity unfortunately often perpetuates older stereotypes—ones that originate in early Christian discourse—that all Jews somehow think and act in the same way. Our hope is that pointing out diverse ways of being Jewish in ancient times, as many of the authors in this volume do, may go some way to supporting the necessary reminder for the present that Jews and Judaism are not monoliths.

Explicit forms of antisemitism and Judeophobia like the Charlottesville rally and the Pittsburgh synagogue shooting are, in many ways, low-hanging fruit. They are easy to recognize and just as easy to condemn as unacceptable in multicultural societies. Yet it is often far more difficult to recognize and call out more *implicit* forms of Judeophobia, which is why we want to offer some examples here too.

Implicit forms of Judeophobia often emerge from places of theological or cultural naivety. Chapters in this volume point out various examples of supersessionist theology, such as Brian Yong Lee's discussion of the interpretation of the law in Romans (chapter 15), or Shayna Sheinfeld's critique of Christian emphases on "belief" or "faith" over and against what they often describe as "empty" Torah observance (chapter 7). From John Chrysostom to Martin Luther to N. T. Wright (see chapter 5), Christian theologians have interpreted Pauline engagement with questions of Torah in a way that drives a wedge between Christianity and Judaism and subsequently disparages Judaism in the service of uplifting Christianity.

As Sarah E. Rollens observes in chapter 4, scholarly resources such as the *Theological Dictionary of the New Testament* often replicate anti-Jewish stereotypes like "Pharisees are lovers of money and consider themselves superior to others." Indeed, it has become common to use the word "Pharisee" to accuse someone of being a hypocrite or holding pretenses of superiority, as Meredith J. C. Warren, Shayna Sheinfeld, and Sara Parks point out in chapter 3. One goal of *Judeophobia and the New Testament* is to shine a light on the multitude of ways that the New Testament and various studies of it have been used in service of propping up Christian supremacy.

Another notable example of implicit Judeophobia is the practice among Christians of holding their own "Christianized" seder meals around the Jewish holiday of Passover. Christians who hold such events often try to argue that they are celebrating an "authentic" Passover, since Jesus was Jewish, and they claim to be honoring Jesus's Jewishness by doing so. However, as many scholars and laypeople observe, this practice is inherently Judeophobic.[22] In connecting contemporary

---

22. Rebecca Cynamon-Murphy, "Why Christians Should Not Host Their Own Passover Seders," *Religion Dispatches* (11 April 2014) (https://tinyurl.com/b4uyz8xs); Alana Vincent, "Christian Seders: Liturgy and Politics," *Medium* (7 April 2019) (https://tinyurl.com/23a

ways of celebrating Passover with the Last Supper and institution of the Eucharist, Christians attempt to replace the significance of the seder for Jews with something that holds theological significance for Christians. Since Passover celebrates God's covenant with Israel, reinterpreting the seder as referring to Jesus and the theological interpretation of his death as sacrifice, Christian-led seders reinforce the notion that Christians (and not Jews) are the true heirs to the covenant.

Perhaps more obviously, it is also problematic that Christian seders mimic *contemporary* Jewish practice, rather than trying to reproduce what kind of meal Jesus and his disciples might have had two thousand years ago. It seems likely that Jesus, as a Jew, celebrated Passover. But he certainly did not celebrate it the way it is celebrated today. Scholars do not even know if the Last Supper depicted in the New Testament gospels was meant to be a Passover meal. If it was, it probably looked different from how it does today. Christianized seders thus erase two millennia of lived, growing, and changing Judaism, and many years of persecution that Jewish people have experienced and continue to experience alongside this growth.

These theological manifestations of Judeophobia seep into the wider cultural milieu as well. Even common ways of talking about the differences between the Hebrew Bible (the Christian Old Testament) and the New Testament regularly express implicit Judeophobia. In popular culture it is frequently assumed that the Hebrew Bible depicts a violent, angry, or irrational God, as opposed to the peaceful, loving, and forgiving God of the New Testament. Such claims ignore that the Hebrew Bible is filled with examples of God's mercy and love. Exodus 34:6, for example, speaks of God's compassion, love, and faithfulness.[23] The false dichotomy between the violent God of the Hebrew Bible and the loving God of the New Testament can be found in rhetoric from across the political spectrum, including opposition to the drive to outlaw abortion in the United States, and in a variety of media, from satire[24] to journalism to film and television.[25] One particularly memorable incident is the rant performed by Peter Venkman (played by Bill Murray) and Ray Stanz (Dan Aykroyd) in 1984's *Ghostbusters* film:

---

jfmht); Yehile Poupko and David Sandmel, "Jesus Didn't Eat a Seder Meal" (6 April 2017) (https://tinyurl.com/44rfzt5c).

23. Other examples include Isa 40:11; Lev 19:34; and Ps 103. Even the famous "love your neighbor as yourself," which is often attributed to Jesus, is actually from the Hebrew Bible (Lev 19:18); Sarah E. Rollens, Eric Vanden Eykel, and Meredith Warren, "The Bible Isn't 'Pro-Life'—and the Old Testament God Isn't 'More Violent' Than the New One," *Independent* (7 September 2021) (https://tinyurl.com/mpwer4u5).

24. BabylonBee.com, "Banned from Playing Violent Video Games, Local Kid Settles for Reading Old Testament" (19 October 2018) (https://tinyurl.com/8f7u78nj).

25. In an episode of *Doctor Who* called "The Witchfinders" (2018) the scriptwriters likewise reinforce the stereotype of the mean Old Testament God, as several scholars pointed out at the time. In this incident, the Doctor invokes "love thy neighbor" as if it were an

PETER: Or you could accept the fact that this city is headed for a disaster of biblical proportions.

MAYOR: What do you mean, biblical?

RAY: What he means is Old Testament biblical, Mr. Mayor. Real wrath-of-God-type stuff. Fire and brimstone coming from the sky! Rivers and seas boiling!

EGON: Forty years of darkness! Earthquakes! Volcanoes!

WINSTON: The dead rising from the grave!

PETER: Human sacrifice, dogs and cats living together, mass hysteria!

James McGrath's chapter 8 in this volume attends in more detail to how this dialogue reflects generalized forms of Judeophobia that exist in our present moment. For now, we note that this seemingly innocuous exchange in an (admittedly) older comedy has gone overlooked by most. Through an academic lens, though, we can easily see the stereotype at work.

It is also particularly ironic that "wrath-of-God-type stuff" is equated with "Old Testament biblical," since some of the most vividly destructive expressions of God's wrath appear in the New Testament's book of Revelation. One actually wonders how much the writers of *Ghostbusters* knew these biblical matters more generally. In another scene when Ray and Winston Zeddemore (Ernie Hudson) chat in a car, we see this exchange:

WINSTON: Hey, Ray. Do you remember something in the Bible about the last days, when the dead would rise from the grave?

RAY: I remember Revelations [*sic*] 7:12. And I looked, as he opened the sixth seal, and behold, there was a great earthquake, and the sun became as black as sackcloth. And the moon became as blood.

WINSTON: And the seas boiled and the skies fell.

RAY: Judgment Day.

WINSTON: Judgment Day.

As numerous scholars point out, these ideas are not, in fact, coming from Revelation 7:12, but rather from (largely) 6:12. Our aim in noting this minor discrepancy is not to be pedantic, but rather to suggest that the writers knew full well of the "wrath-of-God-type stuff" that exists in the New Testament,

---

innovation of the New Testament rather than an example of Jesus quoting the Hebrew Bible. See David Tollerton, "Anti-Judaism in English History and the Strange Moment When *Doctor Who* Appeared to Propagate Biblical Supersessionism," in *Bibles in Popular Cultures*, ed. Rebekah Welton and Zanne Domoney-Lyttle (London: T&T Clark, 2024).

especially Revelation, and still opted to frame it elsewhere as "Old Testament" wrath. As McGrath insightfully concludes in chapter 8: "It should not be overlooked that the joke is at the expense of only the part of the Christian Bible that originated as the Jewish scriptures, while the specifically Christian writings are shielded from this characterization. The scriptwriters created characters who assume these elements are characteristic of Jewish scripture but not the New Testament, when that is not at all the case. They expect those in the film's audience to share this supersessionist assumption."

In addition, one need only look at popular films and television shows to see how this anti-Jewishness is depicted visually. In reviewing the 2016 film *Risen*, which turned out to be not much of a commercial success, one of this volume's editors noted how the movie traffics in typical clichés about ancient Jews:

> The representation of the Jewish leaders, while not as anti-Semitic as *The Passion of the Christ*, nevertheless essentially takes over the stereotypical, polemic representations from the canonical gospels. The Romans refer to them as "fanatics," and Pilate describes Caiaphas as heading "his pack of raving Jews." Caiaphas is also accused of having his "monopoly on piety" threatened by Yeshua. Even more, the Jewish leaders are explicitly portrayed as hypocritically impious as they enter the tomb on the Sabbath to confirm that Yeshua's body is indeed inside before it is re-sealed by the Romans.[26]

We often advise our students to look especially closely at how Jewish people are represented in film portrayal of Jesus's life, because it is in those venues that we often see the implicit—yet nevertheless pernicious—anti-Judaism that pervades our culture, often with many viewers being unaware that they are consuming such imagery.

Finally, Judeophobia is often fostered among biblical scholars who are supposedly engaging in historical critical scholarship. We mention some examples in this introduction, and readers will discover numerous others in the chapters that follow. It can indeed be challenging to be on the lookout for so many forms of Judeophobia in so many cultural pockets. But we hope, at the very least, to expose our students to some of the most common patterns and habits, so as to equip them to identify similar sentiments when they see them "out there" in the real world.

The uncomfortable truth is that many of these explicit and implicit forms of Judeophobia can be traced back to the stereotypical representations of Jewish people in the New Testament gospels. This is especially true for, but unfortunately not limited to, their depictions of Pharisees. As noted, the perpetrator

---

26. MRBlog, "Two Reviews of Risen" (18 February 2016) (https://tinyurl.com/2rbk2x3c).

of the Pittsburgh synagogue shooting cited John 8:44 (which, recall, implies that the Jewish people have "the devil" as their father) on his social media as "evidence" for the transgressions of Jewish people.[27] In that case, the direct line between the polemical representations of Jewish people in Christian scriptures and modern hate crimes could not be more obvious. Even the more general, albeit still problematic, modern stereotypes about Jewish people being "rigid" in their adherence to the law or "stubborn" in their refusals to accept Jesus, which are views that this book's editors regularly hear in undergraduate classrooms, ultimately stem from these negatively marked literary figures in the New Testament. In other words, New Testament scholars have a lot of work to do in showing why these Judeophobic outcomes are not the natural or obvious outgrowths of reading the New Testament. Instead, these prejudices depend on centuries of interpretive habits that have continued to further such polemical stereotypes while being oblivious to (at best) or ignoring (at worst) other ancient evidence. And victims of these stereotypes are not responsible for undertaking all of the hard work of undoing them.

Positionality

Positionality is an important consideration in any scholarly work, but it is especially crucial for a book such as the present volume. Questions about the role of non-Jews in advocacy and allyship around resisting antisemitism lead us to address certain issues in this space. Above all, some might argue that people who do not make public claims of Jewish identity should not be writing about Jewish identity. We believe that it should not be left up to Jewish scholars alone to refute Judeophobia in the discipline, and we constructed this volume with that position in mind. Aside from the so-called insider/outsider problem that is regularly debated in the discipline of religious studies as a whole,[28] we recognize that different positionalities will necessarily yield different data. This is a strength, not a weakness. The editors of this volume strove to include a diverse array of voices, coming together in solidarity with those Jewish scholars who volunteered to contribute their scholarship and voices to this conversation.

27. CBS News, "'Jews Are the Children of Satan' and the Danger of Taking Biblical Passages out of Context" (31 October 2018) (https://tinyurl.com/u3fkvz9v).

28. Russell T. McCutcheon, *The Insider/Outsider Problem in the Study of Religion* (New York: Cassell, 1999). Some even make the claim that scholars of religion should not allow people within the traditions that they study to "define the terms in which they will be understood" or dictate the questions that scholars might ask in the course of their investigation; see Bruce Lincoln, "Theses on Method," *Method and Theory in the Study of Religion* 8.3 (1996): 225–27 at 227.

In recognition of the outsized responsibility that the New Testament and its scholarship have had—and continue to have—in the proliferation of Judeophobia, this volume is dominated by scholars who study the New Testament. As many chapters in the volume will demonstrate in different ways, New Testament scholarship has historically made claims to ownership of Jewish scriptures. While arguing for Christocentric interpretations of those scriptures, New Testament scholars and theologians often promote the implicit (and sometimes explicit!) conclusion that Jewish people were inherently wrong about their own traditions and were unable (or perhaps unwilling) to see how they were fulfilled in the person of Jesus. Indeed, some scholars from Christian backgrounds working today are still unable or unwilling to engage with Jewish critiques of their own scholarship and theology.

Much of this stems from classic supersessionist theology, and this volume hopes to address such claims head-on. But it is precisely that the problem arises *within* New Testament scholarship that we feel we should largely be the ones to own it and fix it. Put simply: making the marginalized tradition (in this case, Judaism) do the heavy lifting of combating anti-Jewishness in New Testament scholarship is unfair and, frankly, unethical. This prejudicial rhetoric needs to be addressed and dismantled by people other than its victims, and it needs to be done with deliberate reference to Christianity's core texts that have historically supplied many of the foundations of Judeophobic attitudes throughout history.

As an analogy, we might look to models of allyship in anti-racism efforts, wherein white allies have a responsibility to advocate for anti-racism in the spaces that they occupy. On this issue, Reni Eddo-Lodge argues compellingly that

> white people who recognise racism have an incredibly important part to play. That part can't be played while wallowing in guilt. White support looks like financial or administrative assistance to the groups doing vital work. Or intervening when you are needed in bystander situations. Support looks like white advocacy for anti-racist causes in all-white spaces. *White people, you need to talk to other white people about race.*[29]

We feel similarly about the need for New Testament scholars (from any cultural background) to do the work of calling out Judeophobia in their midst. In short: New Testament scholarship has historically benefitted from making claims of ownership and authority over Jewish scriptures (whether or not the

---

29. Reni Eddo-Lodge, *Why I'm No Longer Talking (to White People) about Race* (London: Bloomsbury, 2020), 215–16 (emphasis added) (https://tinyurl.com/bdddnjvr).

scholars themselves identify as Christian), and it is thus our responsibility to expose it and call for change.

Origins and Aim of This Project

Judeophobia and the New Testament came about, as is increasingly common in our digital world, from conversations over social media about the implicit and explicit forms of Judeophobia that exist in New Testament scholarship. Shelly Matthews (to whom this volume is dedicated and whose scholarship also appears in its pages) initially noted the absence of any such volume in current scholarship. Matthews makes deliberate efforts to address Christian supersessionism in her own work, and so to see her identify the lack of such a scholarly resource indicated to us how valuable it would be. This volume aims to explore how the formative texts of early Christianity (primarily, but not limited to, the New Testament) are used and sometimes misused to promote Judeophobic violence and rhetoric. Through this long history of interpretation, we now find ourselves at a moment where we can start to expose and undo some of the problematic tropes that have become normalized in many corners of scholarship.

This volume consists of text-based essays that focus on important writings from the formative years of early Christianity. There are essays that engage with all twenty-seven texts in the New Testament. In addition, we included a limited selection of extracanonical texts that, while not part of the New Testament, still engage with important representations of and attitudes toward Jews and Judaism. The Epistle of Barnabas and the Gospel of Peter in particular are included for their troubling ways of relating to Judaism.

Text-based essays form the bulk of this book, but we quickly realized that attention to ancient texts alone would not suffice, and so we decided to include nine thematic essays to help expand some of the important conversations that the text-based essays initiate. For instance, the canonical gospels all feature negative portrayals of the Pharisees, but the text-based chapters could not devote enough time to discussing how these figures have been distorted and caricatured in the last two thousand years of European history. The connection between Pharisees and Judeophobia thus merited its own chapter (chapter 3). Likewise, questions of how ancient Jews interpreted Jewish law crop up in numerous text-based chapters, but a chapter focused singularly on the Torah seemed necessary as well (chapter 7). And, we felt it appropriate to include critiques of the guild's own role in reinforcing Judeophobic interpretations in scholarship; as such, there are chapters on Pauline scholarship (chapter 5), historical Jesus scholarship (chapter 4), and feminist biblical scholarship's responsibilities (chapter 6) regarding anti-Jewish attitudes within theology and biblical studies, as well as some on pedagogy (chapters 1 and 2) and community contexts (chapters 8 and 9).

All of the contributors to *Judeophobia and the New Testament* are reputable and excellent biblical scholars. Quite frankly, we are ecstatic at how many wonderful scholars agreed to be part of this project! Most of their research focuses on religion (primarily Judaism and Christianity) in the ancient Mediterranean world. Despite the impressive body of scholarship that our contributors have produced, we recognize that there is more to scholarship than simply mastering a body of material. Social location and cultural positionality matter as well. For this reason, contributors to this volume represent a range of scholarly voices from a variety of cultural traditions: some identify as Jewish, some as Christian, and some profess no personal religious identity whatsoever. We were also keen to have diversity in terms of gender identity, as well as career stage. No matter the personal positionality of the contributor, all agree that the issue of Judeophobia within early Christian writings must be confronted in the classroom. They bring their own areas of expertise and training to bear on this topic, and we as editors value their scholarship and the diverse range of voices that they bring to this project.

A Note on This Volume's Cover Art

This volume's cover features Albrecht Dürer's *Christ among the Doctors* (1506), a painting that exemplifies the visual rhetoric of Judeophobia in Christian art. The painting depicts a twelve-year-old Jesus engaging in debate with Jewish teachers in the Jerusalem temple, a well-known story that is narrated only in one canonical gospel (Luke 2:41–52). Jesus is depicted as fair-skinned and youthful, exuding calmness and serenity. The Jewish figures around him, by contrast, are portrayed as aged, to symbolize their outdated theology, and with exaggerated and grotesque features—prominent noses, disheveled hair, grimacing expressions, and even a wart.

These visual contrasts are not accidents; rather, they reflect a broader artistic strategy to physically distinguish Jews from Christians, associating them with an "otherness" that goes far beyond theological and ideological differences.[30] In part, they reflect Dürer's goal of depicting Jesus's appearance in line with typical figures in Italian Renaissance paintings, especially since it is known that Dürer took inspiration from Leonardo da Vinci. This stark contrast between Jesus and "the Jews" serves as a metaphor for the perceived

---

30. Ruth Mellinkoff, *Outcasts: Signs of Otherness in Northern European Art of the Late Middle Ages* (Berkeley: University of California Press, 1993).

moral and intellectual superiority of Christianity over Judaism, subtly implying a debasement of Jewish thought and character. The irony and tragedy are
deepened by the fact that the historical Jesus himself was Jewish.

The more subtle and yet troubling aspect of the painting lies in how it embeds these negative stereotypes within what appears to be a "sacred" or "biblical" scene. The image does not need to explicitly reference Jewish identity for
its message to be understood: Jews are here depicted as the adversaries of divine
wisdom, embodying obstinacy and willful ignorance in the face of Jesus's truth.
The real danger of such art is in its ability to normalize harmful ideas by presenting them as natural pieces of the visual landscape of Christian devotion.

For a book dedicated to exposing how the New Testament has been used to
promote Judeophobia, Dürer's painting is a thought-provoking choice for the
cover. It is, undeniably, a Judeophobic image. Yet it is also an ideal choice for this
project because it forces readers to confront the ugliness of anti-Jewish rhetoric
in a nontextual medium. Just as textual interpretations of the New Testament
have perpetuated Judeophobia, visual representations like Dürer's have similarly
shaped Christian and non-Christian perceptions of Jews. We hope that using
this painting encourages readers to reflect critically on how even revered works
of art have contributed to a legacy of hostility, highlighting the ongoing need for
awareness and scholarly engagement with these challenging issues.

How to Use This Book

First and foremost, this book is meant to be used in the classroom. It is also meant
to be paired with the study of primary texts. We envision that professors or teachers will use this book alongside other academic resources such as the *New Oxford
Annotated Bible*, the *Jewish Annotated New Testament*, the *HarperCollins Study
Bible*, or the *SBL Study Bible*. Its chapters can be used piecemeal, or systematically
throughout a course. For instance, one might be teaching an entire semester on
the Pastoral Letters, and thus use the corresponding chapter in this volume. Or,
one might be teaching a survey of the New Testament in a single semester and
might select chapters that resonate with each of the surveyed texts.

In terms of style and accessibility, the chapters were written with undergraduate readers in mind. Complex academic terminology and extensive discussions of scholarly debates are kept to a minimum. In addition, chapters
include discussion questions and sample activities for use in the classroom.
We know that everyone's undergraduate classroom will be different, depending
on institutional and cultural contexts, but we hope that we offer, minimally,

a starting point for how to teach about these topics. Confronting racism and prejudice in the classroom is no easy task, and so having some of that difficult work modeled in these essays can go a long way toward supporting our fellow teachers in their work.

At the same time, we hope that biblical scholars in general will be curious about the pedagogical issues in this volume, even if they do not assign any specific chapters to their students. Many scholars intuitively know the central issues involved in teaching about the anti-Judaism in the New Testament and related writings, but few of us have considered how we could best disrupt these ideologies and stereotypes in our classrooms. While it is admirable for all biblical scholars to be concerned about these problems, we need not all re-invent the wheel to carry out this necessary work. Thus, we offer this resource in the spirit of generosity to our fellow biblical scholars, so that we can help lighten the load of the many tasks that a professor of biblical studies aims to accomplish in their class.

Concluding Remarks

We want to end this introduction by thanking Shelly Matthews, not just for sig-naling so clearly the need for such a volume, but also for providing a model of ethically grounded, historically minded scholarship. Her work reminds us that we can be interested in the historical origins of Christianity at the same time as we recognize that even historical-critical scholarship is not the neutral or objective project that it was originally lauded as. Moreover, as these essays will demonstrate, positions taken in New Testament scholarship often had direct (albeit often unintentional) lines of connection with hate and even violence.

Many of the following essays may be difficult to read, because our contrib-utors worked hard to find particularly insidious cases of Judeophobia in the history of New Testament reception. Indeed, it is clear that anti-Jewish stereo-types from the New Testament and Christian interpretation thereof continue to hold sway in biblical scholarship. From the scholars of the Third Reich[31] to exemplars within biblical criticism today,[32] anti-Jewish rhetoric remains

---

31. See Anders Gerdman, *Roots of Theological Anti-Semitism* (Leiden: Brill, 2008) (https://tinyurl.com/3ydjszpt); Richard Steigmann-Gall, *The Holy Reich: Nazi Conceptions of Christianity, 1919–1945* (Cambridge: Cambridge University Press 2003); Susannah Heschel, *The Aryan Jesus: Christian Theologians and the Bible in Nazi Germany* (Princeton: Princeton University Press 2010).

32. Robert J. Myles and James Crossley, "Biblical Scholarship, Jews, and Israel: On Bruce

influential. Adele Reinhartz notes how scholars are caught up in the Johannine rhetoric surrounding "the Jews," mistakenly supposing that the gospel's vituperative language reflects historical in- and out-groups; in doing so, many scholars reinforce anti-Jewish stereotypes about Jewish isolationism instead of recognizing that "the Johannine *Ioudaioi* are not a specific historical group but rather a rhetorical and theological category."[33]

The notion of a recognizable category of the other, labeled as "the Jews" in John, supported longstanding Christian attempts to self-define in opposition to Jews. Judaism, as Cynthia Baker writes,

> serves as the alpha to the Christian omega; the "Old" to the Christian "New"; the "particular" to the Christian "universal"; grounded and bound materialism to visionary, redeemed spirituality; deicide to self-sacrificial love—at best, the sainted or moribund "ancestor"; at worst, the evil "spawn of Satan" to a godly, good, and triumphantly immortal Christianity. *The Jews*, in other words, serves instrumentally to name the key *other* out of which *and* over against which the Christian *self* was and is constituted.[34]

Likewise, Sara Parks observes in chapter 6 the ways that feminist scholarship around the historical Jesus has made use of anti-Jewish stereotypes in order to prop up a falsely rosy picture of Jesus's interactions with women. Surveying the history of scholarship on the New Testament, chock full as it is with negative depictions of ancient Judaism, is difficult to confront. But it is essential work to do.

We therefore encourage the reader, whether professor, student, or pastor, to read these essays with a mind open to both (1) the reality that forms of Judeophobia have been embedded in biblical discourse over the centuries and (2) the possibilities that emerge when we expose and look behind and beyond such Judeophobic rhetoric. As to where those new possibilities might take us is a project for another time. The present volume is but a first step in that direction.

Malina, Conspiracy Theories, and Ideological Contradictions," *Bible and Interpretation* 2012 (https://tinyurl.com/yckpcvuc); Adele Reinhartz, *Cast out of the Covenant: Jews and Anti-Judaism in the Gospel of John* (Lanham, MD: Lexington/Fortress, 2020), 93–108.

33. Reinhartz, *Cast Out of the Covenant*, 103.

34. Cynthia M. Baker, *Jew*, Key Words in Jewish Studies 8 (New Brunswick: Rutgers University Press, 2017), 4 (emphasis original). See also Nirenberg, *Anti-Judaism*.

Part One

CONTEXTS AND PEDAGOGY

Judeophobia in the Undergraduate Classroom

CHRISTY COBB

I grew up in and around Protestant churches in Appalachia and completed my undergraduate education in a religion department at a small college also in Appalachia. For the first six years of my experience as a professor, I taught undergraduate students at a historically Christian liberal arts university in the rural south. I now teach at a research university in Denver, Colorado. In both of these academic settings, Judeophobia is rampant. I heard it as a child and in classrooms as an undergraduate, yet I was not able to name it or begin to understand it until later in my graduate education. Much of this anti-Jewish rhetoric is rooted in what I view as a misunderstood view of Christian theology as well as what some call a "literal" interpretation of scripture. Whatever the cause or reason, I must confront these views in my undergraduate courses regularly and frequently. The following essay includes a set of assumptions that many students enter the classroom believing. Each myth is briefly countered through references to New Testament passages and/or historical background. Of course, there is much more information that could be added to these brief responses, but this provides a basic and accessible foundation for the larger discussion. I suggest introducing these myths in undergraduate courses during one of the first classes of the quarter/semester in order to counter anti-Jewish rhetoric in class discussions.

Myth #1: Jesus Was the First Christian

Jesus was Jewish. The texts of the New Testament are clear that Jesus was indeed Jewish during his life, ministry, and death. At no point did Jesus abandon

Judaism in order to start a new religion. We see references to Jesus's Jewishness in a number of passages within the canonical gospels. For example, the author of the Gospel of Luke indicates that Jesus "went to the synagogue on the Sabbath day, as was his custom" (4:16 NRSVue). Similarly, Jesus traveled with his family each year to the temple in Jerusalem for Passover (2:41). Jesus also dressed as a traditional Jewish man would dress: both Mark 6:56 and Matthew 9:20 indicate that he wore "fringes," which is comparable to a Jewish *tallit*, or a prayer shawl with fringes at each end. Jesus knew the scriptures of Judaism well and was able to read and study from them. His disciples (who were also Jewish) called him Rabbi, which means teacher. When he taught, he engaged these sacred texts through forms of Jewish teaching, such as midrash and parables (Matt 13:34). Jesus's expectations and teachings about the end times are firmly rooted in Jewish apocalyptic thought. In all four gospels, Jesus goes to Jerusalem to Passover right before his death. He remembers the events of Passover with a traditional Jewish meal with his disciples (the Last Supper). After Jesus dies, his body is prepared in ways that align with the rituals and traditions within Judaism (John 19:40). So, Jesus was not the first Christian. Instead, Jesus was a devout Jew throughout his whole life. Recognizing this begins the work of dismantling anti-Jewish rhetoric within the study of the New Testament.

Myth #2: Jews Killed Jesus and Are Responsible for His Death

All four canonical gospels acknowledge that the condemnation and death of Jesus required the approval of the Roman government, who was in control of the region of Judea during the first century. This can be seen through the scene (or trial) with the Roman governor, Pontius Pilate, who is portrayed sympathetically by the gospel writers but who does order the crucifixion of Jesus following the trial of the Sanhedrin, which functioned like a Jewish court (Mark 15:2–5; Matt 27:11–14; Luke 23:2–7; John 18:28–38) but did not have authority to impose a death penalty. The Gospel of Luke adds to this account a scene with Herod Antipas, who was the tetrarch (or king) of Galilee and Perea. All four gospels also include a scene that indicates that it was customary for Pilate to release one prisoner to the crowd during Passover. Scholars such as Amy-Jill Levine argue that this was not historical; the Roman Empire would not release a political prisoner during this festival, which celebrates the release of the Israelites from slavery. That would be too much of a risk. Therefore, this addition to the gospels is likely fictional, an attempt by the gospel writers to appease and satisfy Rome in their writing. Ultimately, Jesus's condemnation and crucifixion were affirmed by the Sanhedrin in Jerusalem and approved by Rome.

Myth #3: Paul Rejected Judaism in Order to Convert to Christianity

Paul was Jewish and remained Jewish throughout his life and ministry. This is clear throughout all of Paul's letters in the New Testament as well as in the narrative of Paul's journeys found in the book of Acts. In Paul's Letter to the Philippians, he brags about his own Jewishness by noting that he was circumcised, a member of the tribe of Benjamin, a Pharisee, and a devout follower of the law (3:5–6). Paul cites Hebrew scripture from the Torah as well as the Prophets within his letters, revealing his intense study of the sacred texts of Judaism as well as his belief that these scriptures helped him to understand the gospel of Jesus. Acts 9 tells a story about Paul's religious experience on the road to Damascus, but even this fictionalized version of Paul's life is not a conversion scene as many Christian readers tend to understand it today. Paul experiences a vision and has a spiritual experience, such as the one experienced by Heliodoros in 2 Maccabees 3. In the rest of Acts, after this moment, Paul continues to visit Jewish synagogues and quote from the Hebrew scriptures. While he advocates for the inclusion of non-Jews (gentiles) into the religious community and *ekklēsia* ("assembly, church") he is helping to build, he does not reject his own religion and culture of Judaism.

Myth #4: Ancient Jews (Including Pharisees and Sadducees) Were Legalistic and Misguided

Within Second Temple Judaism, several schools of thought were active, including the Pharisees, Sadducees, and Essenes. While we have some information about their views and ideas, we do not have a full understanding of these religious groups. It does seem, though, that only a small number of Jews were a part of these groups, so they do not represent the views of the majority of Jews within this period. In the canonical gospels, Pharisees and Sadducees often function as enemies of Jesus and his disciples. The information that we have concerning the views of these groups comes from the first-century Jewish historian Josephus, the gospels, and later rabbinic literature. This means that what we know of Jewish groups active during the first century was written mostly by outsiders. For example, sources often note that Pharisaic Jews were committed to reading, observance, and interpretation of Jewish law. Sources also mention that the Pharisees strictly observed purity laws such as washing before meals and eating acceptable foods separately to ensure purity. The authors of the canonical gospels include these aspects in the narrative as well but do so in a negative light; gospel authors exaggerate the behaviors and impose inaccurate stereotypes in their portrayals of these groups. Yet these gospels were all written many years after the period in which these religious groups were active. Additionally, the gospel writers were crafting a story about Jesus and his teaching, not attempting to recreate a historical picture of first-century Judaism. Thus, the gospels are not reliable sources for portrayals of sects such as the Pharisees and Sadducees.

Myth #5: Jewish Women Were Not Liberated and Were Drawn to Christianity because of Its Egalitarian Views

This view is inaccurate. In fact, the Hebrew scriptures include stories about women like Deborah, Huldah, Esther, and Judith, all of whom held positions of power. Additionally, Jewish women were recognized as leaders in the ancient synagogue. One scholar, Bernadette Brooten, carefully and undisputedly proves this through analyzing inscriptions from the Roman and Byzantine periods from locations in Palestine, Italy, Asia Minor, and even Egypt. Brooten's work shows that women served in a variety of important roles in synagogues during the period before Jesus as well as the years that document the growth of the religious group that eventually became Christianity. Similarly, many of the women who are noted to be leaders in the New Testament, such as Priscilla, Mary (Acts 12:12), and Junia, were Jewish, and thus their roles as leaders within the religious community of Jesus-followers align with many other Jewish women.

Myth #6: Despite the Many Messianic Prophecies in Scripture, Jews Did Not Recognize Jesus as the Messiah

Some Christians, both historically and today, read the Hebrew Scriptures in light of what they already know about Jesus from the gospels. When they do so, they turn to passages such as Isaiah 53 and find within it prophecies that match the presentation of Jesus from the canonical gospels. The gospel writers likely intended to make these connections through their narratives as the use of scriptures especially from the texts of the Prophets are woven throughout the gospels. This idea of a messianic figure is mentioned in Jewish apocalyptic literature, and it is likely that some Jews in the first century were eager for someone to deliver them from their current situation of oppression and suffering. The historian Josephus names six individuals who were viewed as prophets and perhaps understood by their followers to be a messiah. This was steeped in eschatological ideas as some would hope for a messianic age to begin, which would lead to the resurrection of the dead (another view that was popular by some groups within ancient Jewish community). Yet also, other Jews in the ancient world did not anticipate this type of messianic figure. The Jews who were Jesus's followers, if they viewed him as a messiah, might have expected an imminent resurrection of the dead that would lead to a messianic age (such as what Paul describes in 1 Thess 4:13–17). When this did not occur in the years following his death, Jesus-followers had to wrestle with their theological views and the ways in which they understood and interpreted messianic prophecies. Thus, when the gospels were written, texts from the Hebrew prophets were incorporated that revealed the authors' interpretation of these passages.

Myth #7: Early Christians Rejected Judaism as They Embraced Christianity

In the years after Jesus's death, the majority of his followers remained Jewish, just as they had been during his ministry. According to the letters of Paul and the book of Acts, the move to accept gentiles (non-Jews) into this new religious community was a complicated one. As Paul describes in Galatians 2:11–14, for example, Paul and Peter were in opposition concerning the treatment and inclusion of gentiles. Similarly, early Christ-followers debated if someone who was not Jewish had to become Jewish in order to follow Jesus. Eventually, after several centuries, this new religious group morphed into what we know of as Christianity, which is not Judaism; members of the Christian community were mostly gentile. This was a messy process and not one that can simply be stated, as the myth above, as rejection and conversion. Jesus, Paul, and most of the early followers of Jesus were Jewish. Yet, the religion that eventually emerged from this group of people is not Judaism. In this way, when discussing New Testament and early Christian texts, we must be careful with our word choices and rhetoric. Acknowledging that the texts of the New Testament developed out of its ancient Jewish context is vital. So, too, it is imperative that Christians today not appropriate aspects of Judaism for their own gain, nor view Christianity as a superior religion, which could be perceived as invalidating Judaism. Finally, it is important to recognize that texts from the New Testament have been interpreted as anti-Jewish and have been used to incite violence against Jews for hundreds of years.

Discussion Questions and Activity Suggestions

1. In small groups, add one more myth to this list. Then, write a paragraph that critically analyzes this assumption and offers a different way of understanding the topic. Incorporate scripture and historical references, if possible.
2. If you hear someone repeat a myth such as the ones on this list, how might you respond?
3. What other strategies could be used to deter anti-Jewish rhetoric or Judeophobia?
4. Why is it important for readers of the New Testament to address these myths and reject views that are Judeophobic?

Further Reading

Brooten, Bernadette. *Women Leaders in the Ancient Synagogue: Inscriptional Evidence and Background Issues*. Atlanta: Scholars Press, 1982.

Fredriksen, Paula, and Adele Reinhartz, eds. *Jesus, Judaism, and Christian Anti-Judaism: Reading the New Testament after the Holocaust*. Louisville: Westminster John Knox, 2002.

Levine, Amy-Jill. *The Misunderstood Jew: The Church and the Scandal of the Jewish Jesus*. San Francisco: HarperSanFrancisco, 2006.

Sievers, Joseph, and Amy-Jill Levine, eds. *The Pharisees*. Grand Rapids: Eerdmans, 2021.

2

Judeophobia in the Seminary

TOM DE BRUIN

I keenly remember one of my first days at seminary. A fellow student cornered me in the cafeteria after class to educate me because of something I had said in class earlier that day. I can't remember what I said, but as I had grown up in the Netherlands where the wounds of the Holocaust are still fresh, I must have said something against a Judeophobic reading of the Bible. My colleague felt that I had misunderstood vital theological issues and, worried as he was about my salvation, lectured me at length on how salvation had passed from the Jews to the gentiles after the stoning of Stephen, the Israel of the flesh versus the Israel of the spirit, how the Old Testament laws were a type to Jesus's ministry, and a host of other topics that felt wildly inappropriate to me, especially at the dinner table!

This chapter looks at some of the issues implicit in my colleague's remarks. Studying and later teaching at seminary, I often ran into Judeophobic thinking and theology and noticed many Judeophobic ways the Bible is interpreted in Christian contexts. This chapter explores these issues and highlights some common Judeophobic trends in Christianity and will challenge you to think how you can engage with Judaism and Judeophobia in your faith and ministry.

The Bible, for most Christians, consists of two parts: the Old Testament and the New Testament. Both together are taken as Christian scripture and are, in some way or another, God's inspired revelation to humanity. Neither of these Testaments were written by Christian people, nor for a Christian audience, but rather have become significant for Christian communities as time went on. The Old Testament was produced in pre-Christian, Israelite, and Judahite contexts, while the New Testament was written by ancient Jews.

The term "Old Testament" has a number of drawbacks that Christians need to face. It claims a collection of texts that already were scripture for a group of people as "our own" scripture, and as I will discuss below, this is not always done with enough care. More of an issue is the term "Old" as opposed to "New," which implies that there are two stages of revelation to humanity: an old, and thus outdated and expired, revelation, and a new and improved one. It is easy to read this way of looking at scripture into the New Testament, the most obvious being Hebrews 8:6–13, the last verse of which reads: "By calling this covenant 'new,' he has made the first one obsolete; and what is obsolete and outdated will soon disappear" (8:13 NIV). Other New Testament texts might lead us to similar conclusions (e.g., Luke 22:20; 1 Cor 11:25; 2 Cor 3:6; Heb 8:8; 12:24).

Maybe you have never thought of it in quite this way, but chances are this thinking has influenced you and those around you. Most Christians can think of someone in their faith community who has said something like this: "The Old Testament God is much more violent than the New Testament one"; "The Old Testament is incomplete without the New Testament"; or "The Old Testament prophecies make sense only after you read the New Testament." Even though these statements and others like them are relatively common in Christian churches worldwide, they are seen by many to be Judeophobic. But this does not mean that Christianity or a Christian worldview has to be!

Supersessionism

Let's start with some theological concepts that undergird and reinforce Judeo-phobic readings of scripture. The most obvious is supersessionism, which is the thinking that the church superseded Israel. This thinking is sometimes referred to as "replacement theology," because the church replaces Israel as God's chosen people, or "fulfillment theology," because the Old Testament finds its fulfillment in the incarnation of Christ and the New Testament. Many Christians do not realize that supersessionism is often considered to be Judeophobic.

R. Kendall Soulen suggests that there are three forms of supersessionism, each with different mechanics: punitive, economic, and structural.[1] In all likelihood you have run into all of these. Punitive—or as it is sometimes called "retributive"—supersessionism focuses on Israel's disobedience in the Old Testament and the rejection of Jesus as the Messiah, as portrayed in the New Testament.

---

1. R. Kendall Soulen, *The God of Israel and Christian Theology* (Minneapolis: Fortress, 1996), esp. 28–33.

This view often stigmatizes the Israelite people as a grumbling, stubborn, idol-worshiping nation, which is based on a selective reading of some parts of the Old Testament (e.g., Exod 16, 33; Isa 48; Jer 7; Hos 1). In this view, God rejected them because of these characteristics, and grace moved on to the church.

Economic supersessionism takes a broader view of salvation history, claiming that universal salvation through Jesus Christ was always God's plan. Thus, the righteous figures of the Old Testament—like Noah, Abraham, and David—were a vital step along the way, but their mode of righteousness was never meant to be a permanent feature. The religion of the Old Testament was a placeholder until God's full plan could come to fruition with the incarnation of Jesus Christ. Sometimes people will even argue, as my seminary colleague did, that the Old Testament sacrifices were effective only because they prefigure Christ's death on the cross.

These two types of supersessionism are the easier ones to understand and recognize. Soulen's third type—structural supersessionism—is more subtle. It does not involve explicit teaching that Christianity displaced Judaism. Rather, it's a basic way of reading the Bible where the voice of the Old Testament is diminished or ignored in comparison to the New Testament, and the Jewishness of Jesus and other New Testament characters is downplayed. It should come as no surprise that Christians are often much more interested in how Jesus discusses the law in the Sermon on the Mount than in the original law Moses shared. Or, when Christians describe Jesus or Paul as Jewish, they often do so after removing aspects of Jewishness that are undesirable or incompatible with their own Christian views.[2] Sometimes the focus is so much on the eternal and universal meaning of Scripture that people forget that books of the Old Testament were written for the people in that time. They would have had an original meaning to an original audience, and the Tanak continues to represent the final revelation of God for many Jews today. From a Christian context it is logical to supplement that meaning with another, but it is much less justified to replace it or ignore it completely. In recent decades, many Christian theologians have written postsupersessionist theologies. These argue that the covenant between God and Israel remains, and this enduring covenant is theologically significant for the church in a variety of ways (see below). More

---

2. To get a feel how this looks in practice, I suggest reading these two articles, which give detailed examples of how both Jesus's and Paul's Jewishness is downplayed: James G. Crossley, "The Multicultural Christ: Jesus the Jew and the New Perspective on Paul in an Age of Neoliberalism," *Bible and Critical Theory* 7.2 (2011): 8–16; Stephen L. Young, "So Radically Jewish That He's an Evangelical Christian: N. T. Wright's Judeophobic and Privileged Paul," *Interpretation* 76.4 (2022): 339–51, DOI:10.1177/00209643221107910.

recently, some theologians are building on contemporary discussions of race and racism, to suggest antisupersessionist theologies.

Theology, Worldview, and Revelation

Christian theology varies from church to church and denomination to denomination. So, it's difficult to cover all the theological variations that could benefit from a higher awareness of Judeophobic trends. I will highlight some general issues, which you will have to hold up to your and your faith's traditions and theology. As you read and think about these, you should notice a general trend: they all revolve around a negative view of Judaism.

When some churches divide the biblical history into periods (e.g., dispensationalism, historicism, covenant theology), there is a danger of stigmatizing the period before the New Testament. The Israelites are sometimes portrayed as primitive—intellectually, socially, theologically, ethically—and thus not capable of receiving God's full revelation. Some churches suggest that revelation is progressive, meaning that later sections of the Bible contain a fuller revelation than earlier ones. This idea is inherently supersessionist, and also can lead to more overt Judeophobia. People might claim that Christians are fundamentally better able to understand God than the Israelites were.

In many churches the state or the nation of Israel plays a significant role, especially in their eschatology. Often there is a focus on the restoration of the state of Israel, sometimes as a prophesied event or as a requirement for other eschatological events. Some Christians look forward to a future restoration of Jerusalem or expect the profession of Jesus as Messiah by the nation of Israel (by which they mean all Jews). Most of these interpretations show at the very least evidence of structural supersessionism.

For many Christians it seems difficult, if not impossible, to imagine theology that is completely free of supersessionism. They feel that the incarnation of Jesus Christ must, in some way, indicate that the Old Testament was not the whole story. Yet, antisupersessionist theologians might remind us that God made a covenant with Israel first, that Jesus's primary concern was to minister to the people of Israel, and that Paul portrays gentile believers as grafted onto the first covenant (Rom 11). Thus, Christians might better focus on the grace that is afforded them through Jesus Christ: an invitation to enter covenanted life with God, first established with Israel.[3]

---

3. Daniel Joslyn-Siemiatkoski, "Towards an Anti-Supersessionist Theology: Race, Whiteness, and Covenant," *Religions* 13 (2022): 129, DOI:10.3390/rel13020129.

Talking about Jewish People and Groups

For many Christians and non-Christians, the term "Pharisee" is shorthand for hypocrite, and they are characterized by a slavish adherence to legalism. There are of course many New Testament texts that do say negative things about Pharisees, and when we interpret them we need to realize two important issues: the difference between intra- and intergroup debates, and how generalized language stigmatizes. The first we can illustrate with nationality: imagine a foreigner saying something offensive about your country. Now imagine someone from your country saying the same thing. The words of the foreigner can be seen as discrimination, whereas those of your countryperson are much more likely to be seen as political criticism. Your countryperson is allowed to say things about their own country that a foreigner is not. When Jesus or Paul criticizes aspects of Judaism or some Jewish people, they are doing it as part of the group; but when Christians repeat those words, they are doing it from the outside. This helps us understand why Jesus can call other Jewish teachers "blind fools" (Matt 23:17) or Paul can call them "dogs" (Phil 3:2), but when Christians repeat them they can be considered Judeophobic.

But, from a scholarly point of view, there is an even bigger issue at play here: generalized language stigmatizes. It's good practice to avoid generalizing language whenever possible. A really good way to make generalized language personal is Google autocomplete. Go to google.com, start typing a few words, and Google will give you common suggestions. Try it out with your *own* faith tradition. Type in things like "Why don't Baptists," "Why are Adventists," "Why Catholics"—using the common name for your own denomination—and reflect on these generalized statements. Do you see where they are coming from? Do they reflect your faith identity and practice? Pick one or two that are especially negative, and consider how these statements make you feel. Now, read these New Testament texts and reflect how repeating them stigmatizes (aspects of) Judaism and reinforces Judeophobic readings of the New Testament: Matthew 23:1–15 and John 8:31–47. What options do you see for interpreting these texts without reinforcing Judeophobia?

Discussion Questions and Activity Suggestions

1. Work through "Mean, Angry Old Testament God versus Nice, Loving New Testament God?" in appendix 1.
2. Does your faith tradition or denomination have any doctrines or statements that refer to Judaism or Israel? How do they resonate with concerns raised by this chapter and this book?

3. You have just been asked to preach a sermon series on Judaism and Israel. Plan your series of sermons; which steps will you take to avoid Judeophobia?

4. A prominent church member of yours is sharing increasingly Judeophobic views on social media and in church gatherings. Their opinions are spreading, and some other members have approached you about this. Discuss ways you could address this issue.

5. Read Romans 11:11–32; how does this text enlighten the relation between the church and Israel? Does Paul being a Christ-following Jew affect how we read this passage? Discuss.

6. Discuss what role there could be for Judaism in God's plans and try to answer how the church relates to Israel. Do any of these answers reflect supersessionist thinking? Which type? Can you find theologically useful answers that are not (as) supersessionist?

7. Read Isaiah 7:1–17 and try to discover what Isaiah's words would have meant in their original context. Now read Matthew 1:18–24; how does Matthew reinterpret Isaiah's words? Does the birth of Christ make the original meaning of Isaiah's prophecy invalid, different, or something else? Is there a way to let both meanings coexist?

8. Brainstorm some theological roles that Judaism could play that centers Jewish experience, without replacement or supersession. What new light does centering Judaism in this shine on your faith tradition?

Further Reading

Horrell, David G. "Paul, Inclusion, and Whiteness: Particularizing Interpretation." *Journal for the Study of the New Testament* 40 (2017): 123–47, DOI:10.1177/0142064X17739204.

Joslyn-Siemiatkoski, Daniel. "Towards an Anti-Supersessionist Theology: Race, Whiteness, and Covenant." *Religions* 13.2 (2022): 129, DOI:10.3390/rel13020129.

Skiles, William. "'The Bearers of Unholy Potential': Confessing Church Sermons on the Jews and Judaism." *Studies in Christian-Jewish Relations* 11 (2016): 1–29, DOI:10.6017/scjr.v11i1.9498.

Vlach, Michael J. "Various Forms of Replacement Theology." *Master's Seminary Journal* 20 (2009): 57–69.

3

Judeophobia and the Pharisees

MEREDITH J. C. WARREN, SHAYNA SHEINFELD,
AND SARA PARKS

I t is cliché to begin an essay with a dictionary definition; however, in this instance, the definition reveals a pervasive cultural anti-Judaism surrounding the term "Pharisee." The *Oxford Dictionary of English* defines a Pharisee as "a member of an ancient Jewish sect, distinguished by strict observance of the traditional and written law, and commonly held to have pretensions to superior sanctity." It also includes the following secondary definition: "a self-righteous or hypocritical person."[1] Although this figurative use of "Pharisee" as a slur is problematic, it is the dictionary's job to report on common usage. However, the primary definition is also problematic, just more insidiously so. The phrase "commonly held to have pretensions to superior sanctity" is not accurate. Rather than reflecting historical Pharisees, it uncritically takes over a caricature of Pharisees drawn from ancient political polemics, especially from the New Testament gospels. *Both* definitions perpetuate a use of "Pharisee" as an insult.

Undergirding this insult is a long history of Christian Judeophobia. Although the gospels were written by and about Jews, they were soon read as stories of a "Christian" community actively differentiating itself from surrounding Judaism. Pharisees had been themselves a diverse group among many Jewish groups, but after the loss of the Jewish War against Rome and the destruction of the Jerusalem temple, many Jewish groups were decimated, traumatized, and in flux. At this time, Pharisees began to be used as stand-ins for Judaism as

---

1. Angus Stevenson, ed., s.v. "Pharisee," in *Oxford Dictionary of English*, 3rd ed. (Oxford: Oxford University Press, 2015), DOI:10.1093/acref/9780199571123.001.0001.

a whole. We can see this beginning as early as the writing of the gospels: they begin to lump Pharisees in with scribes, Sadducees, and chief priests, blurring the boundaries between varieties of Jewish thought, status, and practice and erasing the diversity within groups.

The Gospel of John uses Pharisees interchangeably with its signature phrase "the Jews" (see chapter 13) in order to broaden Jesus's interlocutors to more than just that smaller group (e.g., John 9) and drive a rhetorical wedge between Jesus and Judaism (reflecting the separation of nascent Christianity from Judaism at the time of John's authorship). These ancient strategies are encoded in Christian scriptures and read out in churches without context, making it easy for casual Christian hearers and readers to associate Pharisees—and a distorted, negative view of them, at that—with all of Judaism. As Amy-Jill Levine points out, these readers, "implicitly having dissociated Jesus and Paul from 'the Jews,' regard 'the Jews' as either obsessive neurotics who 'tithe mint, dill, and cumin' and neglect 'the weightier matters of the Law: justice and mercy and faith' (Matt 23:23) or complacent legalistic elitists who 'boast in the Law' (Rom 2:23)."[2] Modern usage often presupposes that present-day stereotypes about Pharisees (and about Torah itself) accurately reflect the ancient Pharisees, their beliefs, and their position within ancient Judaism. By extension, and through subconscious supersessionism, these stereotypes often seep into assumptions about Jews today.

When "Pharisee" is used as an insult, it is typically divorced from a particular branch of ancient Judaism and not aimed (directly) at Jews at all. Rather, it is used in Christian cultures to accuse others[3] of being two-faced or arbitrarily legalistic. However, the *implied* meaning is that the accused is "too Jewish."[4] For example, in 2019, a Conservative United Kingdom politician called Labour opponent Jeremy Corbyn a "blinkered Pharisee . . . so convinced of his own rectitude that he sees no contradiction between his pious homilies about racism and equality and a lifetime of support for terrorists, murderers, and racist thugs."[5]

---

2. Amy-Jill Levine, *The Misunderstood Jew: The Church and the Scandal of the Jewish Jesus* (New York: HarperOne, 2007), 123.

3. Frequently, current use of "Pharisee" as a slur is used against fellow Christians; this usage can be traced in part to Martin Luther's and John Calvin's uses of the term to criticize the Catholic Church of their own day. Both reformers viewed the Pharisees as "perverting" scripture toward self-righteous but empty performance of piety and away from Jesus. Randall Zachmann, "The Pharisees in the Theology of Martin Luther and John Calvin," in *The Pharisees*, ed. Amy-Jill Levine and Joseph Sievers (Grand Rapids: Eerdmans, 2021), 200–209.

4. Tweet by @FairYouSee (13 June 2021) (https://tinyurl.com/5n8djeut).

5. Rebecca Taylor, "General Election: Corbyn Is a 'Pharisee' and Johnson Is a 'Liar,' Says

The Man with the Withered Hand (*L'homme à la main desséchée*), 1886–1896, by James Tissot (French, 1836–1902). Publicly owned; image provided by Brooklyn Museum, https://www.brooklynmuseum.org/opencollection /objects/4488

That same year in the United States, then-Democratic Presidential candidate Pete Buttigieg used it to accuse Republican Vice President Mike Pence of being dogmatic about his Christian conservatism on the surface, while selectively overlooking Donald Trump's alleged sexual and financial crimes.[6]

Using "Pharisee" to label one's opponent a hypocrite is common in contemporary politics in culturally Christian regions. Perhaps more frequently, though, the slur is used in Christian confessional contexts. An internet search for "Don't be a Pharisee" returns copious pages of Christian videos and articles, from a variety of denominations. This is by no means limited to evangelical circles. For instance, Jesuit priest and prominent theologian James Martin wrote in a social media post: "Jesus, despite protests from the Pharisees present, heals a man with a 'withered hand' on the Sabbath (Mark 3). For Jesus, helping someone flourish supersedes religious restrictions. Jesus was 'grieved' and 'angered' by the Pharisees' 'hardness of heart.'"[7] Martin included an image entitled *The Man with the Withered Hand* by James Tissot.

Tissot is known for his orientalism and used his studies of modern Mediterranean peoples including Jews living in Palestine, whom he encountered on his visit, to imagine ancient Jews.[8] Here, this orientalism can be recognized in that Jesus is comparably taller and whiter compared to the other Jews depicted; they wear patterns and colors while Jesus wears all white; and while Jesus's head is covered, he does not wear a turban as they do. Their faces are frowning while his is serene.

When brought to task, Martin issued an apology of sorts,[9] but both the

---

Ex-Tory Minister Nick Boles" (12 November 2019) (https://tinyurl.com/3ndxkcm4). There is no evidence for Boles's claims about Corbyn's support for terrorists, murderers, and "racist thugs"; see The Week, "Fact Check: Is Jeremy Corbyn a 'Terrorist Sympathiser'?" (26 April 2019) (https://tinyurl.com/mr2r939u).

6. Ben Sales, "Pete Buttigieg Keeps Calling Mike Pence a 'Pharisee.' Here's Why That Angers Jews" (12 April 2019) (https://tinyurl.com/yfjd3wa7).

7. James Martin, "The Man with the Withered Hand" (19 January 2022) (https://tinyurl.com/4uz7mkt5).

8. For discussion of Tissot's orientalism and the continuing anti-Jewish myth of the "accuracy" of his representations of Jews, see Katie Turner, *Costuming Christ: Re-Dressing First-Century "Christians" and "Jews" in Passion Dramas*, Library of New Testament Studies (London: T&T Clark, forthcoming).

9. The apology name-drops Amy-Jill Levine as a prominent influence for Martin, which he frames in such a way as to attempt to excuse his use of "Pharisee" in this way (https://tinyurl.com/544stefh). As of 30 July 2024, the original tweet remains online; the apology has fourteen retweets while the original has sixty-nine. The tweet is consistent with other references by Martin to Pharisees (https://tinyurl.com/ys9mjk33), and to that specific pericope (https://tinyurl.com/5e44vjy7).

image and the tweet itself remain emblematic of Christian usage of Pharisees as stubborn and unreasonably legalistic foils to Jesus's ("non-Pharisaic" and even, incorrectly, "anti-Torah") kindness, generosity, and flexibility. The tweet was especially problematic in that it was posted only two days after yet another armed attack on a Jewish community in their place of worship.[10]

Likewise, in her otherwise powerful and important book *White Evangelical Racism*, Anthea Butler writes: "Evangelicals are being judged for not keeping to the very morality they asked others to adhere to. They have been found wanting. Evangelicals comfort themselves in the arms of power, in symbols that Jesus disdained. They are the Pharisees."[11]

The qualities Butler attaches to Pharisees (hypocrisy, religious conservatism, power, and violent prejudice) are then worked into her critique of white evangelicals. The critiques are valid, but Butler's analogy to Pharisees follows in a long tradition of Christian "othering" of Jews. While seeking to highlight the oppression of one group, Butler's use of this trope fails to support another racialized and minoritized community, who also suffer from the violence of white supremacy.

Rachel Mikva observes that in cultures where these negative images are used, people absorb anti-Jewish prejudices without realizing it: "My students . . . are surprised when they realise how much of the New Testament's anti-Pharisaic polemic they have absorbed and how it has shaped their understanding of Judaism. Even though they know better, they catch themselves denigrating 'the law' . . . and suggesting that ancient Judaism was too parochial."[12]

When figures from Catholics to Protestants, and from priests to politicians, use "Pharisee" as a slur, does this mean ancient Pharisees were actually a massive bunch of hypocrites? If not, how have people come to think this to the extent that their name is so widely used as an insult? To historians, one thing is clear: this depiction of ancient Pharisees in Christian texts is not accurate; rather, it arose from polemically charged literature (mostly the canonical gospels) where Pharisees were *used rhetorically*. Because the gospels aim to distinguish Jesus from everyone else, they often use his *closest* colleagues in Torah interpretation, Pharisees, as a foil. Different gospel authors slot in different interlocutors for Jesus depending on their aims and audiences, switching out "crowds" for "Pharisees" for "Scribes and Pharisees" for "Jews" in the same passage, so we can hardly

---

10. Haroon Siddique and Oliver Laughland, "Texas Synagogue Siege: Hostage-Taker Named as 44-Year-Old Briton," *The Guardian* (16 January 2022) (https://tinyurl.com/4x8tvvh7).

11. Anthea Butler, *White Evangelical Racism: The Politics of Morality in America* (Chapel Hill: University of North Carolina Press, 2021), 145.

12. Rachel S. Mikva, *Dangerous Religious Ideas: The Deep Roots of Self-Critical Faith in Judaism, Christianity, and Islam* (Boston: Beacon, 2020), 4.

know which group may have been around the historical Jesus several decades earlier. The depiction of Pharisees in these texts is rhetorical.

The gospels arose within a diverse and sometimes tense Jewish milieu, but once Christianity became a separate religion, Christians began to read these texts in Christian-centric (or even Christian-supremacist) ways that have lasted to the present. However, using "Pharisee" as a slur is not just inaccurate historically; it is also insensitive to the present-day impact it has on Jews. Maligning Pharisees continues to have serious negative consequences for real Jewish people, ranging from discomfort and discrimination all the way down to violence, murder, and even genocide.

The Quest for the Historical Pharisees

So who *were* the Pharisees? Aside from the letters of Paul, Pharisees did not leave any writings, so we must read between the lines of other sources that mention them. Outside the New Testament, their most explicit descriptions come from the first-century Jewish historian Josephus. The earliest settings in which Josephus mentions them are the Hasmonean (Jewish) monarchies of Jonathan (160–143 BCE) and John Hyrcanus (134–104 BCE). They may also have been mentioned as opponents of the Dead Sea Scrolls community.[13] Finally, many scholars think that Pharisees have some continuity with the rabbinic Judaism that developed after the destruction of the Jerusalem temple.[14]

Put together, what the ancient sources tell us is that Pharisees were one of various Jewish groups in the sociopolitical landscape of late Hellenistic and early Roman Judaism. The gospels might make it seem like Pharisees were among the most prominent, if not *the* most prominent, Jewish group; but our other sources mention them only briefly, and it's more likely the vast majority of ancient Jews didn't belong to any named subgroup. The groups that did exist were not official card-carrying organizations, but more like worldviews or schools of thought. Nevertheless, we can see that over several centuries of Mediterranean antiquity, Pharisees enjoyed popular (and sometimes royal) support within Jewish communities, and at times had heated differences with other groups or among themselves.

---

13. The "seekers after smooth things" in 4Q169 are often associated with Pharisees; Anthony Saldarini, *Pharisees, Scribes, and Sadducees in Palestinian Society: A Sociological Approach* (Grand Rapids: Eerdmans, 2001), 279.

14. Gunter Stemberger, "The Pharisees and the Rabbis," in *The Pharisees*, ed. Amy-Jill Levine and Joseph Sievers (Grand Rapids: Eerdmans, 2021), 159–68 at 165.

While they were popular and sometimes acted as social leaders, they were a people's movement; in other words, their influence came from people's confidence in their interpretations of the Torah, not from any consistent political authority. What tied them loosely together was their belief in a flexible oral tradition of Torah interpretation that was as ancient as written Torah and their liberalizing shift of responsibility for ritual and piety away from elite priests and into the hands of everyday people. Additionally, Josephus describes their beliefs in a combination of fate and free will, in the immortality of the human soul, and in postmortem resurrection and judgment.

In fact, the more carefully we observe these beliefs, the more we can see their overlap with the two most famous characters in the New Testament—Jesus and Paul. Even by the New Testament's own polemical accounts, the Pharisees share more commonalities with Jesus than differences. For example, both Jesus and the Pharisees . . .

- attend synagogue (Matt 4:23; Luke 11:43)
- wear phylacteries and fringes on their garments (Matt 9:20; 23:5)
- anticipate a resurrection after death (Mark 12:24–27; Acts 23:8; Josephus, *Jewish War* 2.8.14 §§162–163)
- wash before a meal (Mark 7:1–8; cf. Luke 11:38)
- expect a portion of income to go to charity (Matt 6:2–4; 23:3)
- are careful to wash dishes for ritual purity (Luke 11:39)
- prefer the title "rabbi" (Mark 9:5; Matt 23:7)
- hold to the "Greatest Commandment" (Matt 22:34–40; Mark 12:32–33; Deut 6:5; Babylonian Talmud, tractate *Shabbat* 31a)
- live a frugal lifestyle (Mark 10:21; Josephus, *Antiquities* 18.1.3 §12)
- enjoy support from women (Matt 26:6–13; Luke 8:1–3; Josephus, *Jewish War* 1.5.2 §§110–112; *Antiquities* 17.2.4 §§41–43)
- believe in divine judgment after death (Acts 23:8)
- engage in debate on divorce within Jewish law (Mark 10:2–12)
- respect elders (cf. Luke 14:26; Josephus, *Antiquities* 18.1.3 §12)
- share a meal with "sinners" (Mark 2:16)

Although the New Testament sometimes shows Pharisees plotting against or fighting with Jesus, as we will discuss below, it also shows them trying to save Jesus's life (Luke 13:31) and following Jesus (John 3:2; Acts 15:5).

The most well-known Pharisee who followed Jesus (albeit after Jesus's death) was Paul. He is also the *only* ancient self-proclaimed Pharisee who left writings. While he didn't write much about Pharisaism directly, his undisputed letters offer a glimpse into his beliefs and practices as a Pharisee. As was the case with other Pharisees, the eschatological resurrection of the dead and the final judgment were important to Paul. When he describes himself as "with regard to Torah, a Pharisee" (Phil 3:5), it is in the context of a list of things that he feels could be boasted about. He does not speak of his Pharisaism as though it were in the past. In Acts 23:6, Paul is brought in front of a tribunal, made up of both Pharisees and Sadducees. To get out of hot water, Paul gives a speech designed to get the two groups fighting with each other: "I am a Pharisee, a son of Pharisees. I am on trial concerning the hope of the resurrection of the dead" (NRSVue). This controversial topic gets the jury fighting, and Paul escapes. The author of Acts explains why this worked: Sadducees are against supernatural beliefs in resurrection, angels, and souls, and Pharisees embrace them (23:8).

Of course, Paul's belief in Jesus as returning eschatological messiah was not typical of Pharisaism, but Pharisees could have wide-ranging beliefs on specific matters, and so the two are not mutually exclusive. Paul's other beliefs, which he teaches to the Christ assemblies he corresponds with in Asia Minor, all align with the beliefs of the Pharisees.[15] That is, aside from Jesus's messianic/divine status, the beliefs that the early followers of Jesus took as their own align with many of the beliefs of the Pharisees.

All of this goes to show that the modern and historical depiction of Pharisees as entirely negative, and the use of the name as a slur is not grounded in careful observation of the New Testament (see appendix 2). Instead, it requires overriding a number of positive texts to focus on the negative ones that sparked the horrible reputation of Pharisees in Christian cultures. One particular presentation of the Pharisees in the New Testament is used in support of Christian Judeophobia.

Case Study: Matthew 23:2–3

Matthew 23 opens after Jesus arrives in Jerusalem and enters the temple precinct to address crowds and followers and engage in Torah debate with Sadducees and fellow Pharisees (Matt 21–22). One of his speeches is: "The scribes and the Pharisees sit on Moses' seat; therefore, do whatever they teach you and follow it; but do not do as they do, for they do not practice what they teach" (23:2–3 NRSV). He then pronounces a series of "woes"—that is, sayings that

---

15. In cases where Paul discourages Torah observance, it is for a non-Jewish audience only. See Mark Nanos and Magnus Zetterholm, eds., *Paul within Judaism: Restoring the First-Century Context to the Apostle* (Minneapolis: Fortress, 2015).

are used to pronounce curses on specific actions, attitudes, or people. These sayings are predominantly addressed to Jewish elites ("woe to you, scribes and Pharisees, hypocrites!"), and they critique a list of actions that are meant to *look* pious to the casual observer but, according to Matthew's Jesus, are not.

As one of the key passages used to depict the Pharisees as hypocrites, Matthew 23 supports the negative definitions of Pharisees we examined at the start of this chapter. But these verses are perplexing; does Jesus approve of the Pharisees or not? While Jesus says not to imitate these Pharisees' behavior, he clearly upholds the interpretive authority of the Pharisees and instructs his disciples to follow their teachings. Later Jewish texts, such as the Babylonian Talmud, are likewise wary of any teachers who say one thing and do another (e.g., tractate *Yoma* 72b). Interpretations of Matthew 23 tend to use the Pharisees as examples of how not to practice one's religion, making sure instead that one's word and actions match. However, while Matthew's Jesus is critical of specific Jewish leaders who teach one way and practice another, later Christian interpretations misunderstand the context and instead paint not only all Pharisees, but all Jews as doing religion wrong. Pharisees, standing in for all Jews, become the way to point out modes of "deficient Christian piety,"[16] while reinforcing anti-Jewish sentiment.

It is possible to read Jesus's objections to the Pharisees in the context of his earlier diatribe against them in Matthew 5, where he claims they are too soft on issues of the law, and in light of a tendency among some schools of legal thought to attempt to make Torah[17] more compassionate. While many Christian interpreters of the gospels take pains to portray Jesus as radically compassionate in comparison to the Pharisees, this is not what the New Testament evidence suggests. Instead, Jesus is frequently depicted as stricter in interpreting law when compared to the Pharisees. For example, while the Pharisees permit divorce, Jesus forbids it in any context (5:31–32; 19:3–9). Pharisees forbid murder, but Jesus goes so far as to forbid anger (5:21–22). He even declares the extreme view that amputation is preferable to sin (5:29).

We don't have access to any other Pharisaic debates, but it's clear that diversity of opinion flourished for centuries. Matthew's Jesus and the Pharisees

---

16. Warren Carter, "Matthew," in *Fortress Commentary on the Bible: The New Testament*, ed. Margaret Aymer, Cynthia Briggs Kittredge, and David A. Sanchez (Minneapolis: Fortress, 2014), 127–72 at 165.

17. On what might be meant by "Torah" or "law" in this period, see Shayna Sheinfeld's essay in this volume (chapter 7), and Shayna Sheinfeld, "From *Nomos* to *Logos*: Torah in First-Century Jewish Texts," in *The Message of Paul the Apostle within Second Temple Judaism*, ed. František Ábel (Lanham, MD: Lexington/Fortress, 2020), 61–74.

are depicted as having many similar interpretations of Jewish law and a few divergences—precisely the kind of difference of opinion recorded at length in earlier texts (e.g., Dead Sea Scrolls and other noncanonical texts) and in later texts (e.g., rabbinic texts like the Mishnah and the Talmuds). Jesus participates in this tradition of debate in these highly rhetorical verses; we should not be so quick to read his diatribe as wholly oppositional to Pharisaic opinions. Taking Matthew's polemical representation of these Pharisees as historically accurate, and concluding that all Pharisees are hypocrites, ignores Jesus's participation in the normal diversity of Jewish law and practice among Pharisees.

As we have seen above, it's likely that Jesus and Paul placed themselves in close proximity to Pharisaic Torah interpretation. This is supported in part by these verses: Jesus states that the Pharisees sit "on Moses' seat" (23:2)—a place of authority, whether this is interpreted as a literal or metaphorical seat. He therefore places his stamp of approval on their actions and interpretations in some sense. Matthew's Jesus is critical of some Jewish leaders, certainly, but not all Jews, or all Pharisees, and certainly not of Torah. In fact, Matthew's Jesus errs on the side of caution to be fastidiously Torah observant.[18] So while certain Pharisees are labeled hypocrites either by the historical Jesus or perhaps by the author of Matthew, their hypocrisy has to do with a specific occasion; it is not a reflection of all Jews, or even of all Pharisees, and should not be used to draw conclusions about whole groups or appropriated by non-Jews as an insult. What the debates do reinforce is something that Christians often overlook: Jesus was passionate about accurate Torah interpretation and observance.

Conclusion

The New Testament is one of our most important sources for the Pharisees, but we have to read between the lines of rhetoric and heated debate. When we do, we learn that Pharisees' beliefs align remarkably close with those of Jesus and Paul, that Paul counts himself as a Pharisee and sees this as something to be proud of, and that not all references to Pharisees in the New Testament are negative. We also learn that some of the depictions of Pharisees are deliberately exaggerated, nasty, or falsified, and that it is these negative depictions, never

---

18. See Matthew Thiessen, *Jesus and the Forces of Death: The Gospels' Portrayal of Ritual Impurity within First Century Judaism* (Grand Rapids: Baker Academic, 2020), to better understand Jesus's care for Jewish and specifically Pharisaic concerns, such as accurate Torah interpretation, correct temple leadership, and especially ritual purity.

the positive ones, that have been culturally perpetuated by Christians through the centuries. When unsure about whether it is appropriate to use the word "Pharisee," this tweet offers a good test:

> It's like the word "Jew"
> My friend can say "don't give him pork, he's a Jew"—not offensive.
>
> An antisemite can say "Shut up, Jew"—offensive.
>
> In fact in general, if you're going to say Pharisee, replace it with the word "Jew." If that makes it sound antisemitic, it always was. (https://tinyurl.com/yw3s375a)

Given that we are currently in a political climate where, in some places, a new generation of neo-Nazis and white supremacists are emboldened to come out publicly as such with impunity, the way we use "Pharisees" in classrooms and churches is one area where we do not want to be lazily reinscribing harmful caricatures; such laziness has and will continue to be used to promote violence against Jews. Instead, we want to show solidarity with students and citizens whose safety and wellbeing are endangered by religious and racial stereotypes. We can do this by being ethical and mindful about how we teach and use the concept of Pharisees. As a bonus, we will also be doing much better work as scholars.

Discussion Questions and Activity Suggestions

1. Can you think of an example from recent politics/culture where someone has used a slur like "Pharisee" that does potential harm to a group of people? (Hint: try searching social media for examples.) What is the rhetorical force of such an example in its own context? Does that help situate the New Testament's use of "Pharisee"?
2. Read John 9 (the healing of a man born blind) and think about the ways that the text's rhetoric and its description of Pharisees might have generated anti-Jewish sentiment. Come up with at least three observations with references.
3. Brainstorm some other ways to draw attention to hypocrisy without contributing to Judeophobia. Where else might you find culturally impactful metaphors for thinking about hypocrisy? Take a look, for example, at Aesop's fable about the fox and the woodsman, or create your own.

Further Reading

Levine, Amy-Jill. *The Misunderstood Jew: The Church and the Scandal of the Jewish Jesus*. New York: HarperOne, 2007.

Reinhartz, Adele. *Cast out of the Covenant: Jews and Anti-Judaism in the Gospel of John*. Lanham, MD: Lexington/Fortress, 2020.

Schiffman, Lawrence H. "Pharisees." Pages 619–22 in *The Jewish Annotated New Testament*. Edited by Amy-Jill Levine and Marc Zvi Brettler. 2nd edition. Oxford: Oxford University Press, 2017.

Sievers, Joseph, and Amy-Jill Levine. *The Pharisees*. Grand Rapids: Eerdmans, 2021.

4

Historical Jesus Research and Judeophobia

SARAH E. ROLLENS

O ne of the most troubling sites of Judeophobia in contemporary biblical scholarship is that which focuses on the historical Jesus. Historical Jesus scholarship is interested in probing what we can know about the life of Jesus as a real person in the first century, as opposed to what Christians believe about him as the object of confessional belief (i.e., that he was the Son of God, the Son of Man, the Messiah, the Lord, etc.). Scholars have engaged in the pursuit of the historical Jesus for roughly two centuries, and even in this relatively short time period, we can already start to discern certain habits in historical Jesus scholarship, many of which are directly related to questions about the Jewishness of Jesus and his cultural, religious context. And like most trends in scholarship, they often reflect the historical and cultural settings, as well as the interests, of the scholars involved.

The modern study of the historical Jesus is typically divided into three "quests," largely taking place within European and North American institutions. The First Quest began in the late nineteenth century and lasted (roughly) until World War One. The period during the World Wars is sometimes called the "No-Quest" period, because European scholarship was significantly disrupted by wartime events (though we will see momentarily that German scholars had a significant, lasting impact on New Testament scholarship during these years). The Second (or New) Quest began circa 1950 and focused on situating Jesus in his Greco-Roman environment. And some four decades later, the Third Quest was initiated with the aim of highlighting the Jewishness of Jesus.[1]

---

1. When this volume was in its early stages, a rejuvenation of historical Jesus scholarship

Judeophobia and the Historical Jesus

Unfortunately, it is uncomfortably easy to identify explicit instances of Judeophobia in historical Jesus scholarship in certain periods. As noted above, although scholars regularly say that historical Jesus scholarship in Europe paused during the World Wars, this is not entirely true. Not only was influential scholarship on Jesus and his social setting being produced in this period, but it was also being produced by people with overt Nazi sympathies—sometimes with actual Nazi party affiliation. As has been the case throughout the quests, ideas about Jesus and his relationship to Judaism were directly influenced by the scholar's political leanings. We will briefly consider two examples: Walter Grundmann and Gerhard Kittel.

Walter Grundmann was a German theologian, New Testament scholar, and member of the Nazi party. He wrote an influential book on the historical Jesus and his relationship to his contemporary Jews entitled: *Jesus der Galiläer und das Judentum (Jesus of Galilee and Judaism)*. Grundmann's scholarship offers an excellent example of how seemingly critical, objective scholarship about Jesus's ancient context can be wielded for Judeophobic ends. Most strikingly, he did not believe that Jesus should be considered Jewish, either racially or culturally.[2] He supported this view by using archeological and papyrological data to argue that the population of Galilee in the first century was racially different than the population of Judea.[3] This line of reasoning is still present

---

was simultaneously underway. Chris Keith and James Crossley initiated a collaborative project that they deemed the "Next Quest," which would be dominated, not by a particular or singular interest (such as demonstrating the Greco-Roman context of Jesus or mastering the perfect criteria of authenticity), but rather by foregrounding a number of topics—some of which, like apocalypticism and martyrdom, are long-explored in historical Jesus studies, while others, such as social networks and disability, chart relatively new territory—and demonstrating how those topics must be "accounted for" by scholars before they can conclude anything concrete about the historical Jesus. See further, including the present author's contribution: James Crossley and Christ Keith, eds., *The Next Quest for the Historical Jesus* (Grand Rapids: Eerdmans, 2024).

2. It is common to speak of Judaism today as both a religion/culture and an ethnicity. I use language of race here, because Nazi scholars were employing nineteenth-century "race science." Though these theories are discredited today, at the time they were taken by some to be objective "science."

3. In the first century, Galilee was a Roman province located in the north of what was once ancient Israel. The province of Judea, within which the city of Jerusalem was located, overlapped with what was once the southern portion of ancient Israel. Almost all of Jesus's activity in the gospels takes place in Galilee and Judea. These geographical distinctions will be important for this and later discussions of ethnic differences in these regions.

in slightly different form in contemporary scholarship, so we will return to it below. For now, we can observe that innocuous scholarship about ancient ethnic identities was deployed by Grundmann to ensure that Jesus was seen as distinct from the ordinary Jews in the Roman Empire.

Gerhard Kittel was a German theologian who "found National Socialism attractive."[4] As a German Lutheran, he was interested in the historical Jesus, whom he, unlike Grundmann, at least acknowledged to be Jewish. Kittel was the editor of the *Theologisches Wörterbuch zum Neuen Testament* (*The Theological Dictionary of the New Testament*, abbreviated *TDNT*), which became an important reference work for New Testament studies. Yet Kittel was also deeply interested in the contemporary Jewish population within the Third Reich. Toward that end, he wrote *Die Judenfrage* (*The Jewish Question*) to think about a solution to this "problem." While he did not call for explicit violence against Jews, he did advocate legal discrimination, which was justified by his theological belief that Jews deserved punishment for rejecting the gospel of Jesus. In this vein, he further argued that Christians should target contemporary Jews for conversion and that if they didn't convert, they would always be outsiders in German society. In fact, biblical scholar William F. Albright even argued: "In view of the incredible viciousness of his attacks on Judaism and the Jews, which continued at least until 1943, Gerhard Kittel must bear the guilt of having contributed more, perhaps, than any other Christian theologian to the mass murder of millions of Jews by the Nazis."[5] Especially because he produced such an important reference work for New Testament studies, one might be tempted to try separate his writings in support of National Socialism from his writings about Jesus and ancient Christianity. However, I argue that these two things are necessarily connected.

Let us briefly consider a few examples to see how Judeophobic rhetoric entered into this influential scholarly resource. For instance, while discussing the Greek term *ekmyktērizō* ("to sneer/scoff"), the *TDNT* considers its use in Luke 16:14. The entry explains: "While the Pharisees are lovers of money, they can hardly be scoffing at the fact that Jesus, although poor, teaches about poverty and wealth, or at the idea that wealth and piety are incompatible. . . . They are expressing an attitude of conceited superiority which *a priori* rejects

---

4. Robert P. Ericksen, "Theologian in the Third Reich: The Case of Gerhard Kittel," *Journal of Contemporary History* 12.3 (1977): 595–622.

5. W. F. Albright, "The War in Europe and the Future of Biblical Studies," in *The Study of the Bible Today and Tomorrow*, ed. Harold Willoughby (Chicago: University of Chicago Press, 1947), 162–74 at 165.

the bearer of revelation."[6] Here we see two common Judeophobic tropes: "lovers of money" and "conceited superiority." Elsewhere, when discussing the term *misthos* ("reward") in ancient Jewish usage, the *TDNT* again reproduces longstanding stereotypes about Jews being overly legalistic: "While salvation will ultimately depend on God's forgiveness, the stress on human achievement introduces a common note of uncertainty and leads in some circles to the legalistic piling up of merits in order to counterbalance offenses."[7] A final example makes clear how the *TDNT* also uses supersessionist language to interpret theological claims in the New Testament; in the entry for *dikaiosynē* ("righteousness/justification/virtue"), the discussion explains that in Paul's letters "an act of grace replaces ordinary legal procedure."[8] This reflects a widespread Judeophobic tendency to juxtapose the grace or mercy of Christianity with the rigid legalism of Jewish law and, indeed, to argue that grace *replaces* Jewish law. As other chapters in this volume show, supersessionism is not the only way to interpret Pauline theology.

The *TDNT* remains extremely influential today. It is lauded on the website of Logos Bible Software, which is one of the most common digital resources for biblical scholars today. On their website, the *TDNT* is referred to as a "monumental reference work . . . considered by many scholars to be the best New Testament Dictionary ever compiled. . . . One of the most widely-used and well-respected theological dictionaries ever created, *TDNT* is indispensable for studies in the Greek New Testament and theology."[9] Similarly, on the personal website of William D. Mounce, renowned scholar of biblical Greek who has produced essential biblical language instruction resources,[10] we read that the *TDNT* "has long been the standard for serious [Greek] word studies."[11]

Grundmann and Kittel are no doubt dramatic, cut-and-dry examples of how insidious Judeophobia—in their cases, explicit racism—can exist in mod-

---

6. *Theological Dictionary of the New Testament*, ed. Gerhard Kittel and Gerhard Friedrich, trans. Geoffrey W. Bromiley, abridged in one volume by Geoffrey W. Bromiley (Grand Rapids: Eerdmans, 1985), 549.

7. Kittel and Friedrich, *Theological Dictionary of the New Testament*, 538.

8. Kittel and Friedrich, *Theological Dictionary of the New Testament*, 154.

9. Logos, "Theological Dictionary of the New Testament | TDNT (10 vols.)" (https://tinyurl.com/2z9r8vx9).

10. Mounce authored the popular *Basics of Biblical Greek* textbooks and related resources published in the Zondervan Language Basics Series.

11. Bill Mounce, "Theological Dictionary of the New Testament (10 Volume Set)" (https://tinyurl.com/yzjsme6k). Ironically, on the same page Mounce cautions his evangelical readers: "Beware of the theological bias of many of the writers; they were not generally evangelical."

ern scholarship on the historical Jesus and his social and cultural context. Unfortunately, there are also much more implicit, indeed inadvertent, characterizations of the historical Jesus that have unintentionally Judeophobic effects. I emphasize that the following instances of scholarship *do not represent explicit racism or antisemitism* that rises to the level of Grundmann, Kittel, and the like.[12] Furthermore, I have no reason to think that the scholars responsible for the theories discussed below hold any negative views about contemporary or ancient Jews. The discussion will suggest, rather, that many of these the trends in scholarship reveal assumptions about essential religious or ethnic difference or distinction, which *could* perpetuate Judeophobic ideas even when the scholars do not intend it.

The quests for Jesus, discussed above, were concerned with the concept of authenticity and developed criteria for evaluating it. These criteria included such things as the criterion of multiple independent attestation (a tradition about Jesus is most likely to be authentic to Jesus if it appears in multiple, independent texts, as opposed to a single reference in one text) and the criterion of historical plausibility (a tradition about Jesus is most likely to be authentic to Jesus if it makes sense in the historical, social, and cultural contexts of Galilee and Judea before circa 30—this should be juxtaposed with traditions that clearly reflect the contexts of a later period). The criterion of difference (or dissimilarity) is especially relevant to the present topic. Its logic maintains that any teaching of Jesus that was *dissimilar* from the Judaism of Jesus's day was more likely to be authentic to Jesus than something that fit perfectly within what Jews were already believing and practicing. The Judeophobic assumption behind such reasoning should be evident: it implicitly claims that Jesus's teachings could not derive from Judaism, despite the fact that he himself was Jewish. In the hands of some commentators, it could also voice supersessionist views: Jesus's teachings are *beyond* or *better than* the Judaism of his day. William Arnal sharpens this critique even more, when he argues that this approach "often entails some serious distortion . . . by characterizing 'Judaism' in such rigid and prejudicial way that it becomes much easier for nearly any well-rounded figure to 'transcend' it."[13]

Happily, many scholars now recognize the bizarre and prejudiced logic that animates this criterion, and indeed, more recent historical Jesus scholarship

---

12. See Susannah Heschel's *The Aryan Jesus: Christian Theologians and the Bible in Nazi Germany* (Princeton: Princeton University Press, 2010) for a wider discussion of biblical scholars with Nazi sympathies.

13. William E. Arnal, *The Symbolic Jesus: Historical Scholarship, Judaism, and the Construction of Identity*, Religion in Culture: Studies in Social Contest and Construction (London: Equinox, 2005), 12–13.

seeks to center and reclaim Jesus's Jewishness, instead of trying to show how he stood apart from or transcended it.[14]

Yet this enthusiasm immediately brought about a new and related problem: what, in fact, did it mean to be Jewish in Jesus's day? How many characteristics did Jesus need to have to equate him with the "typical Jew" in his environs? Indeed, what happens if Jesus is so thoroughly styled as Jewish that there is no longer anything unique about him? Can we imagine him inaugurating a new social movement if he's just like everyone else in his time? These anxieties have clearly manifested in more recent historical Jesus scholarship that essentially revolves around the question: "How Jewish was he?"[15] We will look at two examples: Jesus's attitude toward the Torah and (once again) the ethnic composition of ancient Galilee.

Jesus's Attitude toward the Torah

Jesus's relationship to the Jewish law has long been a topic for debate (see chapters 3 and 7). The New Testament is clear that Jesus had *something* to say about the Jewish law (e.g., Matt 5–7). Unfortunately, this is an area in contemporary scholarship where Judeophobia rears its ugly head, as numerous scholars promote the idea that Jesus was "correcting" problematic legal codes or "softening" the supposed austere legislation that regular Jews lived by. We saw this above in the *TDNT*'s representation of the Pharisees and their attitudes toward the law. The underlying Judeophobic logic is clear: there was something inherently problematic about ancient Judaism, and Jesus was the "solution." Needless to say, it is easy for modern readers to project these Judeophobic ideas out into their own world and to thus think of contemporary Judaism as a problem in need of a solution.

Such a view about Jewish law as "wrong" and in need of fixing is evident in a recent blog post by Michael LeFevre.[16] LeFevre situates Jesus alongside

14. James Crossley, "The Context: Judaism and Christianity; Israel and the West," in his *Jesus in an Age of Terror: Scholarly Project for a New American Century*, BibleWorld (London: Routledge, 2008), 145–72.

15. James G. Crossley, "Jewish . . . but Not That Jewish," in *Jesus in an Age of Terror*, 173–94.

16. Michael LeFevre, "Jesus Restored the Original Purpose of the Law in the New Testament," Center for Hebraic Thought (20 October 2021) (https://tinyurl.com/ycydntc2). Interestingly, an editor's note on this particular post states that "some language in this article was revised on 10/28/21 to address concerns that the original version (published 10/20/21) suggested supersessionist views. The author did not intend to imply that he endorses su-

numerous other Jewish teachers and intellectuals in ancient Judea and Galilee. Exemplifying the Judeophobic tendencies I discussed above, Jesus comes out transcending all of his contemporaries, who appear to be doing Judaism wrong: "Unlike many of his contemporaries, Jesus actually read Scripture in a 'Hebraic', Torah-sensitive way."[17] This essay also embodies the old Judeophobic stereotype that Jews used the law transactionally in order to earn salvation: "The Law was never intended to be a how-to manual for making oneself righteous, as mistaken by Greek-influenced rabbis of the late Second Temple era. In contrast to them, Jesus took his stand on the Law in the New Testament as understood in its original context."[18] With this final sentence, we can see a modern, supersessionist strategy of depicting Jesus as a "solution" to Judaism, since Jesus's contemporary Jews were carrying out their religion all wrong.

It is important to note that many of these stereotypical views on Second Temple Judaism (Jews as rigidly legalistic, Jews as trying to earn salvation through performing the law, etc.) come from the New Testament itself, which is trading in negative stereotypes for rhetorical effect. Thus, Judeophobic conclusions about what Jesus taught about the Jewish law often follow, unfortunately, from scholars' lack of knowledge about Second Temple Judaism and lack of critical awareness of how the gospels carry out their rhetorical projects.

The Ethnic Composition of Ancient Galilee

The question of the ethnic composition of Galilee also has implications for the discussion of Judeophobia and the historical Jesus. We saw earlier that Nazi scholars wielded this discussion to show that Jesus was not Jewish. A variation of this discussion still exists today: in a nutshell, when trying to reconstruct the historical Jesus, many people try to explain his ideas and teachings by asking about the *kind of people* that lived in the Galilee. There are two interrelated debates. The first debate concerns whether the population of Galilee was predominantly Jewish or gentile.[19] There is some evidence that some parts

---

persessionism." However, as of April 18, 2023, the quotations I included in the body of this essay are still found in the post linked here.

17. LeFevre, "Jesus Restored the Original Purpose of the Law."

18. LeFevre, "Jesus Restored the Original Purpose of the Law."

19. Jonathan L. Reed, *Archaeology and the Galilean Jesus: A Re-examination of the Evidence* (Harrisburg, PA: Trinity Press, 2000), 23–61 at 24–25.

of Galilee were known for their gentile population.[20] However, most scholars today maintain that the majority of the population was Jewish; the archeological evidence for settlements in this period mirrors settlements of the Jewish population in Judea, evincing classic ethnic markers such as *mikvoth* (stepped pools for Jewish purity practices), synagogues, and absence of pork bones.[21] Certainly, most inhabitants in the towns and villages that Jesus is depicted as visiting in Galilee (Chorazin, Capernaum, Nazareth, Bethsaida, etc.) should be understood as Jews. When Jesus does encounter gentiles, he is in cities outside of the Galilee, such as Tyre, Sidon, and cities in the Decapolis.[22]

A second and related question is *what kind of Jews* lived in Galilee. This is a more nuanced question that, in some formulations, allows Judeophobia to sneak into the discussion. There are two major positions in this debate. The first argues that the Jewish population in Galilee was essentially continuous with the Jewish population in Judea. The reasoning for this goes all the way back to the period of the monarchy in ancient Israel. After the reign of Solomon, the unified kingdom of Israel split into the Northern Kingdom (essentially ten of the twelve tribes) and the Southern Kingdom (the two remaining tribes). In circa 740 BCE,[23] the Assyrian army attacked Israel and eventually decimated the Northern Kingdom; many cities were destroyed and the majority of the population seems to have never been heard from again, likely because those that were not killed were deported to Assyria and assimilated to Assyrian society.[24] Indeed, archeological data shows that the settlement patterns in Galilee and the surrounding regions basically cease in this period. They do not resume until the Hasmoneans (a political dynasty that ruled Judea in 140–37 BCE) expanded into the region in the mid-second century BCE.[25] The population in Galilee was rebuilt, so the argument goes, as Judeans Jews from the south expanded northward under the protection of the Hasmonean

20. Isa 9:1, for instance, refers to it as "Galilee of the nations" (NRSVue), which is the term that Jewish texts use for gentiles.

21. Reed, *Archaeology and the Galilean Jesus*, 43–53.

22. An exception would be the centurion in Capernaum in Matt 8:5–13 // Luke 7:1–10.

23. The Assyrians carried out a series of attacks against Israel from circa 740 BCE to 720 BCE.

24. The Northern Kingdom is referred to now as the so-called Lost Ten Tribes of Israel. There have been a number of elaborate modern hypotheses for what happened to them, but historically speaking, the most plausible answer is that they were either killed or deported to Assyria.

25. The Hasmonean expansion in the first and second centuries BCE is well attested by texts, archeology, and coinage; see many helpful essays in Andrea M. Berlin and Paul J. Kosmin, eds., *The Middle Maccabees: Archaeology, History, and the Rise of the Hasmonean Kingdom*, Archaeology and Biblical Studies 28 (Atlanta: SBL Press, 2021).

armies. The consequence for Jesus's identity is that his ancestors are essentially the same as those of the Judeans in the south (this almost makes arguments for his Davidic lineage easier). In other, perhaps more blunt, words, Jesus, the Pharisees, Sadducees, and scribes are all "the same kind of Jews."

But there is another view. Focusing on that same historical situation, some argue that a small population of northern Israelites was left in and around Galilee after the Assyrian conquest. This population was largely peasant farmers who lived off the land and managed to regenerate their population over time. Not only were they disconnected from the Judean Jews due to their experience with the Assyrians, but they also did not experience the Babylonian conquest, a traumatic event in 586 BCE that destroyed Jerusalem and the first Jewish temple and took the majority of the Judean population into exile for approximately forty years. The Judean exiles were eventually liberated and were able to return home and rebuild Jerusalem and the temple, but the experience of exile had an overwhelming influence on their understanding of Judaism from then on.[26] Scholars who support this second view essentially argue that the remnants of the Galilean population after the Assyrian conquest developed in isolation from Judean Jews (and their formative experience of exile) for nearly six hundred years. When the Hasmoneans expanded northward, they found a rebellious population that had no interest in submitting to authorities in Jerusalem.[27] On this view, Jesus is still "Jewish," in that he could trace his ancestors back to the kingdom of Israel, but he was born into a population of Galilean Jews who had departed both culturally and religiously from their Judean counterparts. The Judeophobic logic is thus: Jesus is ethnically and culturally different from Judean Jews (such as Pharisees and Sadducees), and thus, everything he said and did was inherently at odds with religious leaders in Jerusalem. In other words, Jesus was fundamentally distinct from the Jews in Judea.

This latter view is unfortunately similar to the reasoning that Grundmann used nearly a century ago when he argued that Galilee was ethnically distinct

---

26. A significant portion of texts in the Hebrew Bible were written in the wake of the Babylonian exile and reflect on the theological problem of how God could allow his sacred city and temple to be destroyed and his chosen people to be taken from the land he had given them. There are too many examples to name, but the beautiful poetry in Lamentations is a personal favorite.

27. One of the most vocal proponents of this view is Richard Horsley. In his scholarship, this understanding of the Galilean population serves his interest of seeing Jesus voicing the "Little Tradition" (popular, folk traditions in northern Galilee), which is in opposition to the "Great Tradition" fostered by elite figures associated with the Jewish temple in Jerusalem. See, for instance, Richard A. Horsley, *Archaeology, History, and Society in Galilee: The Social Context of Jesus and the Rabbis* (Harrisburg, PA: Trinity Press, 1996).

from Judea. His goal, if one recalls, was to separate Jesus entirely from Judaism. Proponents of more modern incarnations do not have the explicit racist goals in mind when advocating for the modern variations of this theory, but the structure of the arguments is strikingly parallel. For the purposes of this essay, it is not important to level accusations at any particular scholar, especially because they likely do not personally have nefarious ends at all. Rather, we should observe the unstated assumptions in having this debate at all. It is essentially a question about *what kind of Jew* Jesus was. Why should such heated debates about ethnicity of Galileans matter? We can think about the Galilee being culturally distinct from Judea even without weaponizing that possibility against Judean Jews. The ink spilled over this topic in historical Jesus scholarship is thus indicative of broader anxieties about how to place Jesus ethnically and culturally, which I argue, can often make space—however unintentional—for Judeophobic attitudes.

Conclusion

The most common way of understanding the historical Jesus today—at least among historical-critical scholars—is that Jesus was thoroughly embedded in Second Temple Judaism and was not trying to start a new religion. All of his teachings about contemporary Judaism make sense in the diverse field of religious competition and experimentation within Second Temple Judaism itself. To be a "Christ-follower" initially meant to follow a form of Judaism defined by a teacher known as Jesus of Nazareth. Indeed, for decades after Jesus's death, his followers were likely indistinguishable from other Jews from the perspective of outsiders. Numerous scholars persuasively show that rabbis, followers of Jesus, church leaders, and other cultural producers were in dialogue with each other for centuries as they tried to work out the distinct identities that we now call "Jewish" and "Christian."[28] The explicitly antisemitic scholarship from the mid-twentieth century is rightly questioned today, but there are still areas of scholarship that are strangely concerned with "how Jewish" Jesus was or "what kind of Jew" he was. While often these discussions are related to a variety of other conversations in New Testament scholarship, the issue of Jesus's Jewishness, Arnal observes, is a "screen onto which other, more

---

28. See, for instance, Daniel Boyarin, *Borderlines: The Partition of Judaeo-Christianity*, Divinations: Rereading Late Ancient Religion (Philadelphia: University of Pennsylvania Press, 2004).

current, and unresolved matters are being projected."[29] And while there are important historical and cultural questions bound up in such discussions, we have to take care to ensure that our discussions do not embody Judeophobic or supersessionist assumptions.

Discussion Questions and Activity Suggestions

1. This rather elaborate activity could take the better part of a fifty-minute class. The goal is to problematize the self-evident nature of the category "the Jews" in teachings attributed to Jesus. It focuses on the Gospel of John, because that text is known for making sweeping statements about "the Jews" in the story of Jesus:

   - Ask volunteers to read the following passages out loud: John 7:11–13; 8:31–32; 9:22; 4:7–9; 8:42–44. (I recommend discussing them in the order listed here and, importantly, treating 8:42–44 last, since its rhetoric against the Jews is the harshest.)
   - After each one, ask students what information we learn about the category "the Jews" from the passage (and from only that passage!). There are both positive and negative uses in these examples.
   - Give the students a contextual framework within which to grapple with these references, including the following facts:
     - The historical Jesus, his family, and his disciples were all obviously Jewish.
     - Christianity does not become an identity until much later—all the people in the gospel stories thought that they were properly expressing Judaism with Jesus as the long-awaited Messiah.
     - The way these references to "the Jews" in John is historically unlikely, namely, an entire group of people acting or speaking with a common voice—John was obviously creating a stereotypical stock character.
   - After all this, suggest that "the Jews" is not a historical description, but rather, a placeholder for something else, a way to mark outsiders and deviant figures. It is meaningful in the stories of Jesus's life, but it was never meant to refer to all Jewish people in all times and places.

2. What textual evidence could you use to prove that Jesus was seen as one of many authoritative teachers in Second Temple Judaism?

---

29. Arnal, *Symbolic Jesus*, 19.

3. Imagine that you are a gentile reader in Rome and you come across the gospels of Jesus. Which aspects of Jesus's description in the gospels would signal to you that Jesus was a Jewish person? Think about the topics he was talking about, the practices he was depicted doing, and the ways other people reacted to him.

4. What do you think it implies about Second Temple Judaism that Jesus, the Pharisees, and other people in the gospels are regularly discussing how to best interpret the Torah?

Further Reading

Arnal, William E. *The Symbolic Jesus: Historical Scholarship, Judaism, and the Construction of Identity*. Religion in Culture: Studies in Social Contest and Construction. London: Equinox, 2005.

Crossley, James G. "Jewish . . . but Not That Jewish." Pages 173–94 in his *Jesus in an Age of Terror: Scholarly Project for a New American Century*. BibleWorld. London: Routledge, 2008.

Fredriksen, Paula, and Adele Reinhartz, eds. *Jesus, Judaism, and Christian Anti-Judaism: Reading the New Testament after the Holocaust*. Louisville: Westminster John Knox, 2002.

Levine, Amy-Jill. *The Misunderstood Jew: The Church and the Scandal of the Jewish Jesus*. New York: HarperCollins, 2007.

Vermès, Géza. *Jesus the Jew: A Historian's Reading of the Gospels*. Minneapolis: Fortress, 1981.

5

Pauline Scholarship and Judeophobia

MATTHEW R. ANDERSON

After Jesus, Paul is the most influential figure at Christianity's roots. Of the many letters attributed to him in the New Testament, almost all scholars agree on the authenticity of seven: 1 Thessalonians, 1 Corinthians, 2 Corinthians, Philippians, Philemon, Galatians, and Romans. There is disagreement about whether Paul actually wrote 2 Thessalonians, Colossians, and Ephesians. Most critical scholars agree that 1 Timothy, 2 Timothy, and Titus are pseudonymous, that is, that they may bear his name but were not written by Paul. Nonetheless, between his undisputed letters, later letters written in his name, and the book of Acts, Paul's importance is clear from about half of the New Testament's books being by, about, or attributed to him. It is also not an overstatement that Paul's writings or, more accurately, Christian misuses of them since the second century, are behind much Christian anti-Judaism. This chapter earmarks three important ways in which Paul has been viewed:

- The Traditional Perspective or the anti-works-righteousness reading:[1] the Reformation era for the most part doubled down on ancient Christian anti-Jewish interpretations of Paul.[2] It reinforced readings that resulted in prejudice and hatred against Jews.[3]

1. So Matthew Thiessen, who notes that this is sometimes, unhelpfully, called "the Lutheran perspective"; Thiessen, *A Jewish Paul: The Messiah's Herald to the Gentiles* (Grand Rapids: Baker Academic, 2023), 4.
2. For more see Krister Stendahl, "Paul and the Introspective Conscience of the West," in Stendahl's *Paul among Jews and Gentiles, and Other Essays* (Philadelphia: Fortress, 1976), 78–96.
3. Brooks Schramm and Kirsi I. Stjerna, *Martin Luther, the Bible, and the Jewish People:*

- The New Perspective: the mid-to-late-twentieth century saw a chastened re-examination of readings of Paul in response to the Holocaust. Many Christian scholars attempted with various degrees of success to better understand first-century Judaism and place Paul within it, so as not to be complicit in more acts of violence against Jews.[4]
- Paul-within-Judaism or the Radical New Perspective: building on initiatives that began decades earlier a wave of scholars from the late 1990s began to re-read Paul armed with better and more complete knowledge of the varieties of Second Temple Judaism (Judaism that existed from about the 500s BCE to about 100 CE) and its writings.[5] These scholars realized that by focusing on Paul's supposed universalism and contrasting it against a caricatured past,[6] and often limiting their examinations to canonical texts, the New Perspective was still not seeing Paul within his Jewish context. Although the Paul-within-Judaism approach is increasingly accepted by scholars, this third phase of interpretation[7] is still criticized by those who for ideological reasons, usually of Christian self-identity, insist on seeing Paul through a later Christian lens as addressing some kind of "Jewish dilemma" (that is, there was *something* wrong with Judaism that Jesus and later Paul set

---

A Reader (Minneapolis: Fortress, 2012). An example of the kind of anti-Judaism that arises from reading Paul against his context is Ernst Käsemann, *Commentary on Romans*, trans. G. W. Bromiley (Grand Rapids: Eerdmans, 1980). See Matthew V. Novenson, "Anti-Judaism and Philo-Judaism in Pauline Studies, Then and Now," in *Protestant Bible Scholarship: Antisemitism, Philosemitism, and Anti-Judaism*, ed. Arjen F. Bakker et al. (Leiden: Brill, 2022), 106–24 at 113–14.

4. The foremost example is James D. G. Dunn, *The New Perspective on Paul*, rev. ed. (Grand Rapids: Eerdmans, 2008). E. P. Sanders, *Paul and Palestinian Judaism: A Comparison of Patterns of Religion* (Philadelphia: Fortress, 1977), is often included in this category but in fact fits it poorly. See Novenson, "Anti-Judaism and Philo-Judaism," 114–15.

5. The following is an illustrative but hardly complete list: Gabriele Boccaccini and Carlos A. Segovia, *Paul the Jew: Rereading the Apostle as a Figure of Second-Temple Judaism* (Minneapolis: Fortress, 2016); Pamela Eisenbaum, *Paul Was Not a Christian: The Original Message of a Misunderstood Apostle* (San Francisco: HarperOne, 2009); John G. Gager, *Reinventing Paul* (Oxford: Oxford University Press, 2000); Mark Nanos, "Paul and Judaism: Why Not Paul's Judaism?," in *Paul Unbound: Other Perspectives on the Apostle*, ed. Mark D. Given (Grand Rapids: Baker Academic, 2010); and Paula Fredriksen, *Paul: The Pagans' Apostle* (New Haven: Yale University Press, 2017).

6. For example, James D. G. Dunn, "Who Did Paul Think He Was? A Study of Jewish-Christian Identity," *New Testament Studies* 45.2 (1999): 174–93, esp. 181–83.

7. Thiessen, *Jewish Paul*, 4, adds the category of "apocalyptic" as a fourth approach. I disagree.

out to rectify),[8] or that Paul's message and his communities represent and represented a discontinuous and fundamentally different religious system than Judaism.[9]

Like Jesus, Paul lived and died a Torah-observant Jew (Rom 11:1; 2 Cor 11:22).[10] Yet shortly after Paul's death, his writings began to be drastically misinterpreted and weaponized against Jews. Paul's undisputed letters contain desperate arguments to keep the few non-Jews who had turned to Israel's God safe in what Paul believed would be the soon-coming judgment (Rom 3:29; 4:16–17; 1 Thess 1:9–10). But within a century, early Christians drew a conclusion that was 180 degrees opposite to what Paul had written. They began to teach that Paul was the originator of a rejection-replacement scheme where God privileged Christianity and abandoned Judaism forever (based on noncontextual readings of passages like Rom 3:19–20; 9:8; 11:7; 2 Cor 3:14–16; etc.).

The idea that Paul taught that Jews were replaced by Christians as the people of God has long been at the core of Christianity. It is called supersessionism. Supersessionism goes beyond incorrect stereotypes; it can lead to systemic discrimination and to white supremacy and violence. It paved the way for genocide against the Jews. (For instance, the Nazis used Martin Luther's sixteenth-century supersessionist tracts advocating violence against Jews as white nationalist, ideological support.)[11] Supersessionism is neither ethical nor historically accurate. The only conscionable historical approach to Paul is to begin by reading him as much as possible within his first-century, Jewish context.

---

8. An exception (that is, a *scholarly* critique of Paul-within-Judaism) can be found in Terence L. Donaldson, "Paul within Judaism: A Critical Evaluation from a 'New Perspective' Perspective," in *Paul within Judaism: Restoring the First-Century Context to the Apostle*, ed. Mark D. Nanos and Magnus Zetterholm (Minneapolis: Fortress, 2015).

9. Mark D. Nanos, "Paul and Judaism: Why Not Paul's Judaism?," in Given, *Paul Unbound*, 117–60 at 117.

10. Nanos addresses those who propose Paul as a "flexible" practitioner in "Why Not Paul's Judaism?," 121–22.

11. "Doubtless, the most painful response came in November 1938 in a pamphlet written by the Lutheran bishop of Thuringia, Martin Sasse, who saw the burning of the synagogues in the Kristallnacht as the long-last realization of Luther's advisories"; Hans Joachim Hillerband, "Commentary: About the Jews and Their Lies: 1542," in *Christian Life in the World*, vol. 5 of *The Annotated Luther*, ed. Hans Joachim Hillerband (Minneapolis: Fortress, 2017), 442. See also Susannah Heschel, *The Aryan Jesus: Christian Theologians and the Bible in Nazi Germany* (Princeton: Princeton University Press, 2008).

Poster at the exhibit "Luther's Image of the Jews and Its Long Shadow: 1933 to 1946," Eisleben, Germany. Photo by Matthew R. Anderson, 16 May 2016. The poster's text translated is "Martin Luther on the Jews: Get rid of them!"

Unfortunately, Paul's views on Torah and his statements on salvation can be misread in subtle and structurally anti-Jewish ways, even by the well-intentioned.[12] As with Jesus, there is the historical figure behind Paul's letters, but there is also what could be called "the Paul of faith"—Paul as he has been read, heard, repeated, and understood throughout history. Most people know only this "received" Paul. They view the first-century figure through the lens of pop culture, Sunday School, church, or tradition. For instance, the movie *Paul, Apostle of Christ* represents an ahistorical, almost Euro-American Paul familiar to many.

What can add to Judeophobic readings of Paul is that his letters are confusing, as the New Testament itself says in 2 Peter 3:15–16.[13] Even if we limit ourselves to the seven letters scholars agree were definitely written by Paul, these seem to say conflicting, almost diametrically opposite things about Judaism and Paul's Jewish identity. In some passages, he seems to vilify Torah, while in others he praises it (compare Gal 3:10 and 2 Cor 3:15–16 to Rom 7:12). In some of his writings Paul decries the practice of circumcision, calling its advocates "dogs" and "mutilators of the flesh" (Phil 3:2 NIV). Yet he also states in Romans 3:1–2a: "Then what advantage has the Jew? Or what is the value of circumcision? Much, in every way" (NRSV). Examples of such seeming contradictions abound.

Until recently, most readers and scholars of Paul have not been able to reconcile these inconsistencies. John G. Gager points out that some people deal with the contradictions by diagnosing Paul as hopelessly mired in his

---

12. See Charles H. Cosgrove, "Paul and Ethnicity: A Selective History of Interpretation," in Given, *Paul Unbound*, 71–98 at 74–75.

13. See Thiessen, *Jewish Paul*, 2–3.

An American and an English actor play Luke (Jim Caviezel) and Paul (James Faulkner), in *Paul, Apostle of Christ* (2018).

own psychological conflicts, some propose that the most difficult passages are interpolations added later, and some throw up their hands and say there is no reconciling the opposite opinions Paul expresses.[14] However, the most common solution is to minimize the pro-Torah passages and (often unconsciously) focus on those that appear to be anti-Israel, thereby affirming the supersessionist, "Christian" Paul.[15] This is the most common reading. Consider this tweet that agrees with many Christians in seeing Paul in opposition to his Judaism:

> The Apostle Paul came out of a highly controlled religious sect. He had a lot of rethinking to do after learning that Jesus was God.
>
> Yes, he started street-preaching immediately (Acts 9:20), but other than that he did not jump right into apostolic ministry. (https://tinyurl.com/4th5xyvd)

Gager's list of the traditional ways of reconciling Paul's inconsistencies roughly parallels the three trends in Paul's reception identified above. For most of history, Christians embraced the millennia-old rejection-replacement reading: namely, that Paul "converted" to Christianity and subsequently taught that God had abandoned Jews. In this perspective, "Jew" is emptied of its rich and diverse first-century historical meaning. Instead, it becomes a slur and a

14. Gager, *Reinventing Paul*, 7.
15. Gager, *Reinventing Paul*, 9.

synonym for "unbelief" convenient for whomever one's opponents happen to be. A good example of this is Luther's 1543 tract "About the Jews and Their Lies." There Luther wrote that the Jews of his generation had "lost God and his word and now no longer have any understanding of the Scriptures."[16] Luther goes on to discuss the pope and monastic orders as if "Jews" and "Papists" (that is, all who disagreed with Luther) were more or less the same thing, proving that rhetorically, for him, they were.[17] The anti-Judaism of Luther's polarized and emotionally undifferentiated approach is obvious. It resulted in pogroms, murder, other forms of persecution, and wholesale genocide. Luther's tracts against the Jews are so horrific that his English translators introduced some as being for "scholarly assessment only" and simply refused to include others in early editions of his works.[18]

From the 1960s through the 1980s, scholars like E. P. Sanders, Krister Stendahl, and others began to examine Pauline scholarship in the postwar shadow of the Holocaust and the complicity especially (but not only) of German Protestantism. Stendahl, a Lutheran scholar and bishop, questioned continuing to read Paul through Luther's and Augustine's "introspective consciences."[19] Against the traditional reading of Judaism as some form of unspiritual, legalistic "works righteousness," Stendahl pointed to Paul's claims that he was, "as to righteousness under the law, blameless" (Phil 3:6 NRSVue). James D. G. Dunn coined the term "New Perspective" for a broad range of scholarly work seeking to reposition Paul within a more knowledgeable picture of first-century Judaism.[20] Perhaps the greatest contribution of this scholarship was to cease the caricature of Judaism ancient and modern as "legalism" and to understand Torah in a more joyful and accurate sense as a mutual sign of the covenant of love between Israel and its God.[21]

In this interpretive framework, when Paul *commends* circumcision, it comes from this understanding of covenant as grace. When Paul *condemns* circumcision, it does not apply to fellow Jews, but only to situations where it was used as a marker of identity to enforce ethnic distinction between Jew and non-Jew (gentile). Here, however, the New Perspective seems to trade older

---

16. Luther, "About the Jews and Their Lies," 479.

17. Luther, "About the Jews and Their Lies," 486–87, 490.

18. Hillerband, in "Commentary: About the Jews and Their Lies: 1542," 442–43; and Brooks Schramm, "Luther's Schem Hamphoras," *Dialog* 56.2 (2017): 151–55 at 151–52.

19. Stendahl, *Paul among Jews and Gentiles*. For a gentle critique of Stendahl's approach as antihistorical, see Novenson, "Anti-Judaism and Philo-Judaism," 116–17.

20. Dunn, *New Perspective on Paul*.

21. See especially the classic work of Sanders, *Paul and Palestinian Judaism*.

criticisms of Judaism as legalistic and works-dependent for softer critiques of an ethnic exclusivism.[22] Where the Traditional Perspective saw Christianity as a radical break from Judaism, the New Perspective saw Christianity in continuity with Judaism. Notably, however, this perspective usually frames Paul as innovating a widely expansive, universal improvement over narrower, parochial Judaism.[23] In the end, this still constitutes supersessionism.[24]

The contemporary approach that views Paul-within-Judaism (formerly known as the Radical New Perspective) began in earnest in the late 1990s with the work of Pamela Eisenbaum, Lloyd Gaston, Mark Nanos, and Paula Fredriksen, among others. This approach is marked by the research and writing of increasing numbers of Jewish and women New Testament scholars. It incorporates wide knowledge of Second Temple Jewish texts outside of the Bible. It then uses those insights to fill in a picture of a Paul who can be quite alien to contemporary readers, even if he is more at home in his own time. For some Paul-within-Judaism scholars, when Paul discouraged Torah observance, it was *exclusively* directed to non-Jews and for a completely Jewish reason: Paul held an apocalyptic Jewish expectation that the "eschaton" or end of days might be hastened, if some earlier Jewish prophecies that non-Jews would turn to the God of the Jews at the end were fulfilled. Strands of this eschatological timeline sometimes indicated that the nations would turn to Israel's God but *remain gentile*, so that they could fulfill scriptural prophecies of the "coming in of the nations" (Isa 18:7; 45:14; 60:6–7, 11; Sibylline Oracles 3:772–773).[25] While other early Jesus movements would require non-Jewish Jesus-followers to convert to Torah-abiding Judaism, Paul was convinced that his pagan followers had to turn to the God of Israel and away from their own gods, but remain in their state as gentiles *in order for the Jewish prophecies to be fulfilled*. In this framework, Paul's contradictory language concerning Torah makes sense, because his differing opinions are aimed at differing *audiences*: for Jews he affirms

---

22. See Cosgrove, "Paul and Ethnicity," 80–83.

23. Dunn, "Who Did Paul Think He Was?," 181–83.

24. See Paula Fredriksen, *Paul: The Pagans' Apostle* (New Haven: Yale University Press, 2017), 110. This idea of Christianity replacing Judaism's "ethnocentrism" is found in N. T. Wright's statement that by contrast to his contemporary Judaism, Paul preached "grace, not race"; *The Climax of the Covenant: Christ and the Law in Pauline Theology* (Minneapolis: Fortress, 1992), 194, 247.

25. Fredriksen, *Paul: The Pagan's Apostle*, 164. Scholars within the Paul-within-Judaism school tend to disagree about whether Paul believed in a "two ways" (or *Sonderweg*) salvation, one for Jews and a completely different one, based on faith in Christ, for gentiles. See Thiessen, *Jewish Paul*, 150, 156–57.

Stained glass of Paul holding a Christian Bible with the Alpha and Omega symbols referenced in the book of Revelation. Jordan Station United Church in Jordan Station, Ontario. Photo by Matthew R. Anderson.

Torah and circumcision as life-giving gifts; for non-Jews who will inevitably fail at following Torah, circumcision is a failure and becomes a curse; for gentiles to convert by completely following Torah also works against the biblical prophecies of the end of days as Paul interpreted them.

This type of Paul-within-Judaism perspective thus situates Paul squarely (and *only*) in the eschatologically charged 50s and early 60s of the first century. The approach sacrifices any easy applicability of Paul's Christ teachings to contemporary audiences.[26] (This may be why some Paul scholars writing for Christian audiences dislike it.) In essence, in this perspective, Paul was an apocalyptic preacher who got it wrong. The inclusion of non-Jewish Christ-

---

26. See Novenson, "Anti-Judaism and Philo-Judaism," 120.

followers was a temporary solution that became an exclusive and permanent brand Paul never imagined nor of which he would have approved.

I assume that anyone consulting this volume wishes to avoid anti-Judaism in their learning, research, and writing about Paul. It is important nonetheless to be careful of subtle and structural Judeophobic tendencies that can creep into our work. To avoid anti-Judaism, students and researchers into Paul should be careful of binaries, especially around the notion of Paul's identity. These may include contrasting Paul's Jewishness to his identity as a subject of Rome, or against his cultural "Greek-ness" as a Greek-speaking and culturally Greek inhabitant of the eastern Mediterranean who also lived his life in the midst of that culture and its philosophies and social organizations. In this way at least, Paul can helpfully be compared with us: we do not have to choose among binaries. Paul's identity consisted of multiple, overlapping layers, in the same ways our identities do. To insist only on his Jewishness (as opposed to his Roman identity), or only on his Greek cultural identity (as opposed to his Jewishness), is to misrepresent not only Paul, but the intersectionality of identity in all times and places.

To avoid perpetuating anti-Judaism, we should be proactive in refuting several popular misconceptions of the historical Paul:

- Paul never "converted." Paul never once describes his vision of Christ (compare Gal 1:13–17 and Acts 9) or his taking up of the mission to the non-Jews as conversion. Since Christianity did not yet exist as a religion, what would he have been converting to? Rather, to describe the radical change in his life, Paul used the language of a prophetic *call* like Jeremiah's (Gal 1:15–16), well known from earlier Jewish writings.
- Paul was not the first Christian. Christianity didn't begin to exist as a separate religion from Judaism until well after Paul's death. The Jesus movement was one Jewish group among many in first-century Judaism.
- Paul's letters are not to Jews. Paul wrote almost exclusively to non-Jews, whom we know made up his assemblies. The letters mirror his concern about them, and their concerns as non-Jews. What happens to "the Jews" in the last days takes up some (see especially Rom 9–11), but remarkably little, of Paul's letters; it takes up much more space, textually, among Paul scholars.
- The "opponents" Paul rails against are not "the Jews." Most likely Paul had different individual or ideological opponents in different places. In any case, his opponents were not "the Jews" at large but competing missionaries of the same small movement (2 Cor 11:13–14). They were possibly non-Jewish Christ worshipers who had been circumcised and now urged the same on "Paul's" people (Gal 6:12).

- Paul's letters are not a sustained critique of "the law." Rather, Paul's letters all have different purposes, particular to the historical situations he is addressing, and many uphold various aspects of the Jewish law. As discussed above, he praises the Torah for Jews and condemns it as a necessity for non-Jews (since observing Torah would amount to conversion, and his message is that at the resurrection the gentiles will turn to the God of the Jews and welcome Jesus as Messiah precisely in their condition as gentiles).

What *do* historians know of this important figure? Paul was a first-century Jesus-follower who only joined the movement after Jesus's death (Gal 1:11–12; 1 Cor 15:8–9) and who rarely used the name "Jesus" without attaching the messianic title "Christ" (what God had done with Jesus up to and after his death was apparently more important to Paul than what Jesus did or taught during his life; 2 Cor 5:16). Paul's emphases on a messiah, a general resurrection, the judgment, the day of the Lord, and the "turning" of the nations to the God of the Jews are not in any way Christian inventions. Rather, they were elements of Jewish religious belief already well established in strands of Second Temple Jewish thought and practice (2 Maccabees 7:9; Psalms of Solomon 17.24, 28, 31; 2 Baruch 72.2–6; Isa 60:8–9, 12).

Paul was a Pharisee trained to apply Torah to daily life.[27] Like other Pharisees, he believed in a resurrection of the dead and a judgment at the end of time, which he expected immediately. Paul was Torah-observing, proud of his status and heritage, and confident of his righteousness before the Jewish God. Although he wrote almost exclusively to non-Jews and counseled them specifically not to take on all aspects of Judaism, he himself remained proud of his level of observance and his accuracy of interpretation (Phil 3:4–6; see also Gal 1:14–15).

Paul grew up in, and moved easily within, the wider Mediterranean world; nevertheless, he held Jerusalem and the Jerusalem temple (which in his day still existed) in high regard. Paul saw himself as an eschatological figure, a "last days" prophet drawing his urgent timeline of impending judgment from Jesus tradition and from his and his Christ-community's interpretations of their Jewish scriptures. Paul was different from other Jewish messengers of Christ because he was unusually focused on, even obsessed with, the role and place of non-Jews (gentiles) in the final events that would precede the reign of the Jewish God over all humanity and the vindication of the Jews as that God's chosen people. Paul was a city dweller and cosmopolitan craftsperson with

---

27. See Eisenbaum, *Paul Was Not a Christian*, 125–31.

overlapping, nested identities. He was a subject of the Roman Empire, culturally Greek, celibate, ascetic, a craftsperson who worked with his hands and spread his message while working, and mobile enough to travel, with stops, sometimes for significant periods, along the major Roman thoroughfares of the eastern Mediterranean.

Evidence of who Paul was should be taken from the seven letters known to be written by Paul (again, 1 Thessalonians, 1 Corinthians, 2 Corinthians, Philippians, Philemon, Galatians, and Romans), alongside the Jewish writings that were likely influential to him—those found in the Septuagint and Apocrypha and other early Jewish apocalyptic and ascetic texts. New Testament letters outside Paul's undisputed letters, and (arguably) the New Testament book of Acts, do not teach us about the historical Paul. Instead, they teach us about Paul's *reception*. That is, they tell us about later, sometimes much later, Jesus-followers doing "damage control," trying to shift away from Paul's embarrassingly apocalyptic and ascetic sayings.[28]

Learning about or teaching Paul without falling into Judeophobia means seeing him first in his world, and letting the strangeness of that world sink in.[29] It means paying attention to the presuppositions we bring to words like apostle, freedom, justification, salvation, saint, church, Christ, faith, law, and even Jew, gentile, and God. It means that even though Paul's letters ended up in a sacred canon of a new religion, they must be read not only historically, but ethically. This avoids appropriating Paul's Judaism in a way that perpetuates violence. It means attempting to situate these concepts, along with our image of Paul, in his own first-century world, not our own.[30]

Discussion Questions and Activity Suggestions

1. New religions and cultures never pop out of a vacuum; it is only natural that they are responding and related to previous and surrounding cultures. However, cultural appropriation occurs when a dominant culture borrows from (and benefits from) something created by an oppressed culture, but without giving the oppressed culture any credit (and while continuing to participate in the oppression of the original culture). Could cultural appro-

---

28. For instance, contrast a reading of 1 Cor 7:7–9, 26–31 against 1 Tim 4:1–6.

29. The first chapter of Thiessen's *Jewish Paul* is appropriately titled "Making Paul Weird Again."

30. See Novenson, "Anti-Judaism and Philo-Judaism," 120–21.

priation be a useful lens for understanding how later Christians created a New Testament using letters written by an apocalyptic Second Temple Jew like Paul? Why or why not? Is there an ethical way for Christians to read Paul without participating in cultural appropriation?

2. Pretend you were describing this chapter to a friend. How would you title Paul? On the surface, the term "apostle Paul" is not anti-Jewish. This is how he has been known for millennia and to billions. Does it change your usage to know that "apostle" was a title Paul fought for, against others who denied it of him, including the writer of Acts? How can we avoid retrojection of a later Christian status and authoritative *gravitas* on to our study of this first-century figure? In a similar vein, for the first few Christian centuries, Paul was better known as a martyr than as a theologian or apostle.[31] Is calling him an apostle when discussing him in his first-century context automatically importing later anti-Jewish understandings of who he was? Does calling him an apostle without reflection allow Paul the writer to control the historical narrative or judgment about his life? What options do we have? What other words might we need to be careful of?

3. Make three signs with the following headings:
    - Traditional View of Paul
    - New Perspective on Paul
    - Paul-within-Judaism

Now print the following six statements on separate slips of paper. Ask the participants to place—and discuss—the statements in the perspective that they think is the best fit:
    - Paul believed he observed Torah extremely well and was proud of this to the point of bragging about it.
    - Jews ancient and modern have a life-giving relationship with God but an ethnic narrowness (that is, "we're the only people of God") that Paul helped to open up to the larger world.
    - Paul's emphasis on grace, as opposed to works, helped liberate the faith of Jesus from its narrow Old Testament confines to become the universal religion it is today.
    - "All have sinned and fall short of the glory of God" applies equally well to both Jew and non-Jew and shows that Paul's gospel was the same for all people.

---

31. David L. Eastman, *Paul the Martyr: The Cult of the Apostle in the Latin West* (Atlanta: Society of Biblical Literature, 2011), 187.

- The opponents Paul had so much trouble with in the cities where he preached were the local Jews.
- The opponents Paul had so much trouble with in the cities where he preached were competing Christ missionaries, often non-Jewish Christ-adherents who had fully converted to Judaism and felt Paul's people should do the same.

(Note for leaders: because of the overlap between perspectives, especially the New Perspective and the Paul-within-Judaism school, and also that no single perspective is monolithic, some of these statements will need discussion in light of the chapter.)

4. Compare Galatians 1:13–17 and Acts 9, where Paul's call is variously described. One is in Paul's own words (Galatians) and the other is not. Note any similarities and differences between the accounts. Then read Jeremiah 1:1–12, where Jeremiah's prophetic call occurs. Again, note any similarities and differences. Examine the lists you've made, and discuss how this impacts the common framing of Paul's experience as conversion.

5. Ask a Generative AI program such as ChatGPT or Google Gemini to summarize Paul's views of the law. What do you notice in its answer? Does it fit in any of the perspectives (e.g., Traditional, New Perspective, Paul-within-Judaism) outlined in this chapter? Based on what you've read in this chapter, analyze and critique the response. Try pushing back with some questions to the AI and see if you can get it to nuance its response. Reflect on what this activity reveals about common understandings of Paul.

Further Reading

Fredriksen, Paula. *Paul: The Pagans' Apostle*. New Haven: Yale University Press, 2017.

Nanos, Mark D., and Magnus Zetterholm. *Paul within Judaism: Restoring the First-Century Context to the Apostle*. Minneapolis: Fortress, 2015.

Thiessen, Matthew. *A Jewish Paul: The Messiah's Herald to the Gentiles*. Grand Rapids: Baker Academic, 2023.

6

Feminist New Testament Scholarship
and Judeophobia

SARA PARKS

W e usually don't like to hear bad things about those we admire—a celebrity we love, a politician from our preferred party, a cherished author. If we adhere to a religious tradition, we like its founding figures to come across looking good. Christians share memes about Jesus "turning the other cheek" (Matt 5:39; Luke 6:29) or sharing with those in need (Matt 19:21), not memes of him cursing a tree because he's hangry (Mark 11:13–14) or calling anyone who's not Jewish a "dog" (Matt 15:26). This impulse to associate our heroes with only *good* stories also exists in some feminist studies of the New Testament. This chapter focuses on how certain feminist work on Jesus has had the unintended consequence of fostering anti-Judaism.

In the twentieth century, feminist movements pushed society to address gender discrimination. As the wider world struggled toward women's equality, Christians did too. In searching the Bible to lend authority to the cause, they found a champion in Jesus. Through careful reading of the gospels, we learn that:

- Jesus traveled around not just with twelve male disciples but with a core group that included "many women" (Mark 15:41; Matt 27:55).
- Women provided the financial backing for Jesus's movement (Luke 8:1–3).
- Jesus taught in a uniquely inclusive style that ensured women were represented.[1]

---

1. Sara Parks, *Gender in the Rhetoric of Jesus: Women in Q* (Lanham, MD: Lexington/Fortress, 2019).

- He sent women disciples to baptize and preach.[2]
- When he endured torture and execution, he was supported almost exclusively by close women followers.[3]
- His postcrucifixion movement was launched by women.[4]

From Elisabeth Schüssler Fiorenza[5] to Hisako Kinukawa,[6] historical Jesus scholars and feminist theologians uncovered a remarkably gender-egalitarian Jesus who was there in the texts all along.

In contexts where Christian women are encouraged to see themselves as subordinate to men,[7] any affirmation that key New Testament figures valued women and entrusted them with powerful roles can be life changing. Highlighting the overlooked importance of women in the Jesus movement benefits historians too by improving accuracy. But the process of correcting past errors can be two steps forward, one step back. Just so, in the case of the feminist Jesus, there has been a frequent error—one just as harmful as using Christianity to disparage women in the first place: when some New Testament interpreters write about the ways that Jesus (or Paul) valued women as coworkers, apostles, prophets, disciples, patrons, and full human agents with worth and dignity, they frequently use a seemingly innocent but deadly phrase: "unlike other Jews at the time."

From an Inclusive Jesus to Those Terrible Jews

Studying Jesus through a lens of gender is a worthy aim, but it too often comes with the unfortunate assumption that Jesus was *unique* in his gender inclu-

---

2. Joan Taylor, "Male-Female Missionary Pairings among Jesus' Disciples: Some Further Considerations," in *Patterns of Women's Leadership in Early Christianity*, ed. J. Taylor and I. L. E. Ramelli (Oxford: Oxford University Press, 2021), 11–25; cf. 1 Cor 9:5.

3. See Jane Schaberg with Melanie Johnson-Debaufre, *Mary Magdalene Understood* (New York: Continuum, 2006), 98–126.

4. Despite the many differences in the crucifixion and resurrection accounts across all four gospels, the tradition of women (sometimes exclusively) supporting Jesus at his death, and being first or sole witnesses to the resurrection, is a constant.

5. Elisabeth Schüssler Fiorenza, "'You Are Not to Be Called Father': Early Christian History in a Feminist Perspective," *Cross Currents* 29.3 (1979): 301–23.

6. Hisako Kinukawa, *Women and Jesus in Mark: A Japanese Feminist Perspective* (Maryknoll, NY: Orbis, 1994).

7. Some modern Christian denominations rely heavily on the later Pastoral Epistles and their Roman household codes (see chapter 24) to structure relationships among women and men hierarchically.

sivity. In order to highlight ways that women were important in the earliest Jesus movements, some interpreters drive a wedge between Jesus and other Jews in order to make him appear different.[8] This chapter will focus on why that wedge is both false and dangerous.

Since around the 1970s, some thinkers have pointed out that people who do feminist analysis of the gospels keep pitting Jesus against Judaism, and that this move is neither honest nor ethical.[9] As Amy-Jill Levine says, the "prevailing hypothesis" is that women in ancient Christianity were emancipated, but women in ancient Judaism were hopelessly trapped in patriarchy.[10] Judith Plaskow was one of the first to warn that feminist New Testament scholarship was liberating Christian women at Jewish people's expense.[11] Katharina von Kellenbach points out that Judaism keeps popping up as a "scapegoat for patriarchy."[12] Elisabeth Schüssler Fiorenza cautions that when people "draw 'Jesus the feminist' against the patriarchal background of Judaism," they are "reproducing . . . anti-Jewish tendencies."[13] And Levine calls the trope of Jesus rescuing women from terrible Jews "both bad history and bad theology."[14]

These and many other critics warn that contrasting Jesus starkly against patriarchy, and then equating ancient patriarchy with Jews (rather than with the ancient Mediterranean at large), is poor scholarship that has negative consequences. To demonstrate, let us turn to some New Testament texts that are used to show Jesus as an ally to women, and then break down how things are a little more complicated than they may seem.

---

8. For more on separating Jesus from Judaism (especially by exaggerating his differences from fellow Pharisees), see chapter 3.

9. For overviews, see Susannah Heschel, "Anti-Judaism in Christian Feminist Theology," *Tikkun* 5.3 (1990): 25–28, 95–97; and Hanna Liljefors, "The 'Old Testament' as the Origin of the Patriarchy," *Nordisk judaistik/Scandinavian Jewish Studies* 34.1 (2023): 82–98.

10. Amy-Jill Levine, "Second-Temple Judaism, Jesus, and Women: Yeast of Eden," in *A Feminist Companion to the Hebrew Bible in the New Testament*, ed. A. Brenner (Sheffield: Sheffield Academic, 1996), 302–31 at 303–7.

11. See, e.g., Judith Plaskow, "Christian Feminism and Anti-Judaism," *Cross Currents* 33 (1978): 306–9; Plaskow, "Anti-Judaism in Christian Feminist Interpretation," in *Searching the Scriptures: A Feminist Introduction*, ed. Elisabeth Schüssler Fiorenza (New York: Crossroad, 1993), 7–29.

12. Katharina von Kellenbach, *Anti-Judaism in Feminist Religious Writings* (Atlanta: Scholars Press, 1994), 107–20.

13. Elisabeth Schüssler Fiorenza, *Jesus, Miriam's Child, Sophia's Prophet: Critical Issues in Feminist Christology* (New York: Continuum, 1995), 70–71.

14. Amy-Jill Levine, "The Word Becomes Flesh: Jesus, Gender, and Sexuality," in *The Historical Jesus in Recent Research*, ed. J. D. G. Dunn and S. McKnight (Winona Lake, IN: Eisenbrauns, 2005), 516.

Case Studies

The gospels contain many things that feminist scholars point to as proof that Jesus was progressive. We will look at just one set of texts: those that highlight women disciples and supporters. Various passages in the Synoptic Gospels reveal that women were a much larger and more important part of the core group that traveled with Jesus than we tend to think of at the words "Jesus's disciples." For instance:

> These [women] used to follow him and provided for him when he was in Galilee; and there were many other women who had come up with him to Jerusalem. (Mark 15:41 NRSV)

> Many women . . . had followed Jesus from Galilee and had provided for him. (Matt 27:55 NRSV)

> [Jesus] went on through cities and villages, proclaiming and bringing the good news of the kingdom of God. The twelve were with him, as well as some women . . . who provided for them out of their resources. (Luke 8:1–3 NRSV)

The gospel authors do not seem particularly favorably disposed to women, and in some ways they even work to diminish them.[15] Yet they include the tradition of a substantial female cohort within Jesus's core group, as though they have no choice but to admit it was women who supported the group financially. You might assume that "providing for" Jesus meant something like fixing snacks for the "real" (male) disciples, but there is no hint in the Greek text that it means anything other than bankrolling. These verses form one textual cluster out of several that researchers point to when demonstrating that Jesus's movement was powered by women.

It is natural that theologians take such scripture verses and extrapolate lessons for today; this is what Christian feminist scholarship and Christian preachers do. They rightly posit that if Christ was inclusive of women, then the church today should be as well. After all, if Jesus is meant to be the ultimate

---

15. Jane Schaberg and Sharon Ringe demonstrate just how hard Luke seems to have worked to model women's subordination in "Gospel of Luke," in *Women's Bible Commentary, 20th Anniversary Edition Revised and Updated*, ed. Carol Newsom, Sharon Ringe, and Jacqueline Lapsley (Louisville: Westminster John Knox, 2012), 493–511.

example for modern Christians, then Christians should take seriously that the Jesus in the gospels was surrounded by women whom he trusted, whom he specifically catered to in his teaching style, in whom he confided, and whom he sent out as workers, essentially ignoring gender as a criterion for inclusion or exclusion. The problem comes when, from the pulpit on a Sunday morning or in scholarly writing, the concept that "Jesus was good to women *unlike other Jews at the time*" is claimed, without any supporting evidence from Judaism (except perhaps selective negative examples from much later rabbinic writings, which are allowed to stand in for all of ancient Judaism). I will not call out specific scholars or religious leaders for making this kind of argument because it is so ubiquitous and longstanding. I imagine that any Christians reading this chapter will have heard such narratives.

The problematic tendency of constructing a simplistic scenario where women had universally terrible lives until a dazzlingly feminist Jesus saved the day is wrong on two counts. First, it does not reflect the diversity of ancient Judaism and the complexity of ancient Jewish women's experiences. Second, it does not take into account the connection between Jesus's treatment of women and his apocalyptic Jewish expectations.

To tackle the first problem: if we examine the actual evidence for ancient Jewish women, it becomes difficult to claim that Jesus was the only or the first ancient Jew to treat women as full human beings. Jewish women in the time of and before Jesus appear in a range of roles. The savvy and long-reigning Jewish Queen Salome Alexandra[16] and the Herodian Queen Berenice[17] both ruled during the late Second Temple period. We find the contemplative Therapeutrides mentioned by Philo, and the wealthy female patrons mentioned by first-century historian Josephus, such as Fulvia and Pheroras's wife.[18] In the roughly contemporaneous writings of the Apocrypha we find noble and courageous literary characters like Judith, Susannah, Sarah, and the martyred mother in 2 Maccabees 7. And we find in inscriptions and nonliterary documents many real-life Jewish women who donated to synagogues, owned businesses, prac-

16. Read about Salome Alexandra and the ancient sources for her in Tal Ilan, "Shelamziyyon Alexandra," *Shalvi/Hyman Encyclopedia of Jewish Women* (Jewish Women's Archive, 1999) (https://tinyurl.com/38zau2pf).

17. We can learn about Berenice from several ancient sources like Josephus (*Antiquities*), inscriptions, Acts 25–26, rabbinic authors, and Roman authors. See Sara Parks, Meredith J. C. Warren, and Shayna Sheinfeld, *Jewish and Christian Women in the Ancient Mediterranean* (London: Routledge, 2022), 133–34.

18. To learn more about all of these women, see the chapter "Ancient Judaism" in Parks, Warren, and Sheinfeld, *Jewish and Christian Women*, 118–50.

ticed philosophy, served as religious officiants, or wrote eloquent correspondence.[19] Yes, Mediterranean antiquity was patriarchal in general, but within that patriarchy, some Jewish women—like some Roman women—could be influential, intellectual, and active participants in religion and society. So if Jesus treated women well, catered to them in his teaching style, and included them in his movement, it was as *yet another example* of a Jewish community in which women featured prominently.

To tackle the second problem: that Jesus involved women in his movement, as did John the Baptist before him, and Paul after him (see Rom 16), does not automatically mean these male leaders deserve the title "feminist." We must consider their contexts. John, Jesus, and Paul were all part of a specific worldview within Judaism that has been called "apocalypticism." This means that they believed the "day of the Lord" or the "end of days" was close or already happening (1 Thess 4:17; Matt 16:28), and as a result they were living in urgent and socially volatile times. Such movements could proactively begin to live out utopian social arrangements they believed would soon come to pass. Thus when such movements featured enslaved persons eating together with slave owners, or women in roles they didn't always occupy, this was not because the movement was setting out to smash the patriarchy. It was more a case of "all hands on deck." When we see Jesus and Paul relying on women patrons and prophets, it is less because they were "feminist" on principle, and more because they were members of a movement that urgently saw God's social future already beginning, and that required flexible leadership to prepare itself.[20]

For feminist pastors and theologians to draw lessons from empowered New Testament women for their religious communities today is normal; it's how people creatively use their sacred texts to make the world a better place. However, if they portray Jesus as positive to women by perpetuating negative and untrue claims about Jews, it is irresponsible, inaccurate, and harmful. The cliché of the feminist Jesus is complicated by his reasons for including women,

---

19. Many such examples can be found in Kathy Ehrensperger and Shayna Sheinfeld, eds., *Gender and Second-Temple Judaism* (Lanham, MD: Lexington/Fortress 2020), such as Angela Standhartinger's "Female Officiants in Second Temple Judaism" (219–40). See also Laura S. Lieber, "Jewish Women: Texts and Contexts," in *A Companion to Women in the Ancient World*, ed. S. L. James and S. Dillon (Chichester: Blackwell, 2012), 329–42; and Philip A. Harland, "Familial Dimensions of Group Identity (II): 'Mothers' and 'Fathers' in Associations and Synagogues of the Greek World," *Journal for the Study of Judaism* 38 (2007): 57–79.

20. See Cecilia Wassen and Tobias Hägerland, *Jesus the Apocalyptic Prophet*, trans. Cian J. Power (Edinburgh: T&T Clark, 2021).

which came more from necessity than from combatting patriarchy. In this sense his inclusion of women was only one example among many of how he and others were preparing for what they thought would soon be history's end and the reign of Israel's God over all humanity.[21]

Conclusions

In the Judaism before and around Jesus, there is evidence for a range of attitudes toward, and roles for, women—some more patriarchal, some more agentic, from queens to patrons to protagonists. There is no evidence (nor is there any rhetorical need) to vilify Judaism when analyzing Jesus's attitude to gender. Any gospel materials that point to Jesus as somehow gender-egalitarian are examples of one Jewish individual among others being decent to women in antiquity; in the case of the early Jesus movement this must also be linked to apocalyptic urgency. Understanding this means there is no warrant for contrasting Jesus with his Jewish environment. If anything, as the early Christians realized that the end of history was *not* happening anytime soon, and as Christianity developed and shifted *away* from majority Jewish membership, the situation of women actually became much *worse.*[22]

It is a shame that so many theologians and pastors over the years who have used Jesus to try and make the world safer for women ended up making it less safe for Jews. Thanks to scholars like Heschel, Levine, Schüssler Fiorenza, von Kellenbach, and Plaskow, this error has been challenged, and it is our job to continue to correct it in our classrooms and our world.

Discussion Questions and Activity Suggestions

1. Read John 4:1–42 (the woman at the well or the Samaritan woman). In small groups, come up with a feminist reading of the passage. Share your inter-

---

21. See Bart Ehrman, *Jesus: Apocalyptic Prophet of the New Millennium* (Oxford: Oxford University Press, 1999); Paula Fredriksen, "Paul and Judaism," *Bible Odyssey* (https://tinyurl.com/3m9d5bp9).

22. Women were leaders in earlier Jesus movements but were systematically suppressed over the following centuries. See Ute Eisen, *Women Officeholders in Early Christianity: Epigraphical and Literary Studies* (Collegeville, MN: Liturgical Press, 2000); K. J. Torjesen, *When Women Were Priests: Women's Leadership in the Early Church and the Scandal of Their Subordination* (New York: HarperOne, 1995).

pretations with the larger group; note whether each other's readings might perpetuate anti-Jewish stereotypes. Develop solutions for less harmful readings. For more ideas, see the open-access article by Meredith Warren: "Five Husbands: Slut-Shaming the Samaritan Woman," *Bible and Critical Theory* 17.2 (2021): 51–70.

2. Does it change your view of the importance of gender equality today if you learn that the historical Jesus was more (or less) gender egalitarian than you once believed? Why or why not?

3. For every passage in the New Testament that can be interpreted as misogynist or gender hierarchical, there is a passage that can be interpreted as feminist or gender egalitarian. In other words, there is no single overarching view of gender in the New Testament, but a number of views in tension (compare Gal 3:28 with Eph 5:22–23). What are some strategies for interpreting sacred texts ethically on an issue when the texts themselves hold conflicting visions?

Further Reading

Kellenbach, Katharina von. *Anti-Judaism in Feminist Religious Writings*. Atlanta: Scholars Press, 1994.

Melcher, Sarah J. "The Problem of Anti-Judaism in Christian Feminist Biblical Interpretation: Some Pragmatic Suggestions." *Cross Currents* 53 (2003): 22–31.

Plaskow, Judith. "Anti-Judaism in Christian Feminist Interpretation." Pages 7–29 in *Searching the Scriptures: A Feminist Introduction*. Edited by Elisabeth Schüssler Fiorenza. New York: Crossroad, 1993.

———. "Christian Feminism and Anti-Judaism." *Cross Currents* 33 (1978): 306–9.

7

Torah, the Law, and Judeophobia

SHAYNA SHEINFELD

The question of Jewish law, and Jesus's relationship with it, colors many
New Testament readings. Much of Protestant theology assumes that the
law is irrelevant, "obsolete" (Acts 10), or even "dead" (Gal 2:19; Rom 7:4); many
readers end up disparaging torah[1] through inaccurate readings of first- and
second-century texts, from Jesus's "temple tantrum"[2] and healings[3] to Paul's
warnings to his gentile communities.

Christian theology's discomfort with the law is not only an academic matter,
that is, an inaccurate interpretation of New Testament texts. It has also led to
people using the concept of law as an *insult*—that Christians who focus on a list
of dos and don'ts are somehow similar to Jews (and are therefore doing theology
wrong). This has obvious implications for stereotyping present-day Jews, who
are in dynamic relationship with torah and with working out what the mitzvot
(that is, the commandments found in Jewish law) mean for daily life.

On social media, for example, some Christians critique others who are not
doing Christianity correctly as being legalistic. This stems from a pervasive
(largely Protestant) assumption that religion can be defined by faith and/or

---

1. In this essay "torah" generally refers to that amorphous category called Jewish law.
Because of its potentially varied meanings, I use lowercase "torah" for the word except when
writing specifically about the first five books of the biblical canon.

2. Paula Fredriksen, *From Jesus to Christ: The Origins of the New Testament Image of
Jesus*, 2nd ed. (New Haven: Yale University Press, 2000), xxi.

3. Readers often assume Jesus deliberately heals those who suffer from ailments that render them ritually impure in order to make a statement against the purity system, rather than
assuming it is to render them able to participate fully again in a system about which Jesus
cares deeply. See Matthew Thiessen, *Jesus and the Forces of Death: The Gospels' Portrayal
of Ritual Impurity within First-Century Judaism* (Grand Rapids: Baker Academic, 2020).

belief in certain dogmatic claims, over and against ethical behavior or ritual practice. This assumption emerges from a desire to take what Protestantism deems important and make it normative for all religions. In reality, both historically and currently, the majority of human religious expression prioritizes action over belief (including much of Protestantism, despite its claims to the contrary).[4] In the post-Reformation period, Protestant rhetoric sets up faith, belief, or a relationship with Jesus/God as antithetical to works or law. This dichotomy creates a situation where non-Christian religions, in particular Judaism, are therefore understood to be inadequate, false, or empty. This idea of law as antithetical to belief is then read back into the New Testament texts.[5]

Torah or Law in the First Century?

What, exactly, is torah? What do the gospel writers mean when they talk about law? What does Paul mean? The vocabulary of torah and law are often left undefined, and therefore it is assumed that the reader knows what is meant. But a survey of these terms within the first century—as well as both before and after it, even into the contemporary world—highlights their diverse meanings. Torah may be a set of texts (the first five books of the Bible) but often also refers to all sacred Jewish texts, including oral traditions, or to allegorical interpretation of Jewish scriptures, such as is found in Jewish philosopher Philo of Alexandria (circa 20 BCE–50 CE); likewise Jewish law may indeed refer to the commandments found in the Pentateuch, but more often includes diverse interpretations and traditions that may or may not be associated with written commandments. In other words, the meanings of "torah" and "law" depend on context and, if left undefined, are a way of nodding toward Jewish identity without providing readers with any real specificity of meaning.

For example, the first-century Jewish historian Flavius Josephus writes about three distinct Jewish groups: Pharisees, Sadducees, and Essenes. Josephus clearly identifies all three of these groups as Jewish, but notes that they

---

4. Even evolutionary science suggests that religious commitments are not achieved through rational contemplation of explicit propositions, but instead through ritual participation; see Richard Sosis and Jordan Kiper, "Religion Is More Than Belief: What Evolutionary Theories of Religion Tell Us about Religious Commitments," in *Challenges to Moral and Religious Belief: Disagreement and Evolution*, ed. Michael Bergmann and Patrick Kain (Oxford: Oxford University Press, 2014), 256–76.

5. See Bernadette Brooten, "Is Belief the Center of Religion?," in *Religious Propaganda and Missionary Competition in the New Testament World: Essays Honoring Dieter Georgi*, ed. Lukas Bormann, Kelly Del Tredici, and Angela Standhartinger (Leiden: Brill, 1994), 471–79.

each approach their explanations of Jewish law differently. While Josephus does not give us details as to how they differ, his comments highlight that different ways to understand Jewish law are all legitimate.[6] This approach—of recognizing the potential for diversity and *not* stagnation—is key to reading about torah and law in the New Testament.

What Does Paul Think about Jewish Law?

Pauline teachings contain both pro- and anti-torah messages (see chapter 5). For example, in Galatians 3:10, Paul writes negatively about the law: "For all who rely on the works of the law are under a curse; for it is written, 'Cursed is everyone who does not observe and obey all the things written in the book of the law'" (NRSVue). Romans 7:12, on the other hand states that "the law is holy, and the commandment is holy and just and good" (NRSVue). There have been numerous attempts at understanding Paul's seemingly inconsistent message about the law.

In the Traditional Perspective on Paul, Paul's anti-torah message is aimed at everyone, Jew and non-Jew alike, and verses that praise the law are downplayed or completely ignored by traditionalist scholars. Paula Fredriksen notes that in this approach "'Torah' comes to serve as the antipode to 'Christ,' 'Law' to 'grace,' 'Judaism' to 'Christianity.'"[7] Fredriksen shows how direct the path is from misunderstanding Paul as anti-torah, to disparaging torah as oppositional to God, to its logical conclusion: Judaism as a failure in its rejection of Christ. Regardless of intent, reading Paul as propping up a dichotomy between law and grace, where the former is rejected in favor of the latter, likewise sets up Christianity in opposition to Judaism in a hierarchical, anti-Jewish relationship.

Instead, Paul's teaching on law should be read within the framework in which he preached: as a Jewish Christ-adherent who sought to bring non-Jews into salvation through this Jewish messiah. Paul's teachings on the law are addressed *only* to his non-Jewish audience, as these non-Jews are not supposed to first become Jews before worshiping the God of Israel. This approach embeds Paul within early Judaism, understanding Paul's positionality as a diaspora Jew in the first century sharing his apocalyptic message of Jewish salvation to

---

6. Shayna Sheinfeld, "From *Nomos* to *Logos*: Torah in First-Century Jewish Texts," in *The Message of Paul the Apostle within Second Temple Judaism*, ed. František Ábel (Lanham, MD: Lexington/Fortress, 2020), 61–74.

7. Paula Fredriksen, *Paul the Pagan's Apostle* (New Haven: Yale University Press, 2017), 121.

non-Jews. When Paul seems to disparage the law, then, he is doing so only to convince his gentile audience they do not need to observe Jewish law in order to benefit from this Jewish messiah; he does not mean that Jews should not maintain their diverse, living, and ancestral practices, even if they are now also Christ-followers.

What Does Jesus Think about Jewish Law?

"Do not think that I have come to abolish the Law or the Prophets; I have come not to abolish but to fulfill" (Matt 5:17 NRSVue). Many readers misread Jesus's criticisms of his intellectual sparring partners as criticisms of the law itself. Frequently, though, Jesus argues for more stringent applications of legal practices; far from abolishing torah, Jesus doubles down on it. For example, in Mark 10:1–12 (cf. Matt. 19:2–9), Jesus takes the Mosaic law of divorce—that a man can divorce his wife—further and states that neither a man nor a woman should divorce their spouse, and if they do, they are committing adultery. In several other places, Jesus also expands or intensifies torah—taking a written law and making it stricter (e.g., Matt 5:28, 43–44). In the quotation above, Matthew's Jesus owns his full participation in the law and its variegated history.

A particular example of how readers often misinterpret Jesus's relationship to torah is found in the Gospel of Mark. In Mark 3:1–6, Jesus heals a man on the Sabbath, a time when work is supposed to cease. In all three gospels where this story occurs (cf. Matt 12:9–14; Luke 6:6–11), just prior to this story, Jesus has been with his disciples who have been plucking grain, another activity that could ostensibly be considered work and therefore not appropriate for the Sabbath. In response to some Pharisees questioning this activity, Jesus responds: "The Sabbath was made for humankind and not humankind for the Sabbath" (Mark 2:27 NRSVue). In the next pericope, Jesus enters a synagogue, a marked Jewish space, and encounters a man with a visible disability (literally a dried-up hand) that might have affected his life and livelihood:

Again he entered the synagogue, and a man was there who had a withered hand. They [the Pharisees] were watching him [Jesus] to see whether he would cure him on the Sabbath, so that they might accuse him. And he said to the man who had the withered hand, "Come forward." Then he said to them, "Is it lawful to do good or to do harm on the Sabbath, to save life or to kill?" But they were silent. He looked around at them with anger; he was grieved at their hardness of heart and said to the man, "Stretch out your hand." He stretched it out, and his hand was restored. The Pharisees went out and immediately conspired with the Herodians against him, how to destroy him. (Mark 3:1–6 NRSVue)

This passage is often used to point to Pharisees as sticklers of the law to the point of cruelty; they are portrayed as objecting to the healing (see chapter 3). However, Jesus is not arguing over whether one *should* observe the Sabbath— it is clear that he himself observes it and considers it important—but what is permissible on the Sabbath, for example: When is healing allowed on the Sabbath? When can food be collected and prepared on the Sabbath? Questions such as these, which ask what is included or excluded in God's commandment to observe the Sabbath, were points of discussion and debate among Jews in the first century and before—and still are today among different streams of Judaism. Taking Mark's polemical representation of the Pharisees as sticklers over and against Jesus ignores this diversity of opinion on Sabbath observance in the first century. While we do not have access to any Pharisaic debates, diversity of opinion on Sabbath observance flourished before and after the encounter described in Mark. Jesus and the Pharisees are depicted as having different readings of acceptable behavior on the Sabbath; it is precisely the kind of difference of opinion recorded at length in later rabbinic literature,[8] as well as earlier in the Dead Sea Scrolls and other Jewish literature.[9] Scholarship on this passage often depicts Jesus as radically compassionate in comparison to the Pharisees, although the question was never about whether the man should be healed, but whether Jesus was being intentionally provocative by choosing to break the Sabbath rather than wait the few hours until it was over. Had the situation been about saving a life, the Pharisees would likely also have broken the Sabbath to do so—healing on the Sabbath would not only be acceptable in that case, but actually a requirement of Jewish law. Jesus's choice here is about power dynamics, not about compassion in contrast to the law.

The disagreements portrayed in the gospels between Jesus and Jewish leaders, especially the Pharisees, over matters of law are interpreted by both lay leaders and scholars as reflecting the Pharisees' obsession with law and Jesus's rejection of it. But even within the gospels, it is not the *law* that is the problem for Jesus, but rather "correct" interpretation of it. The law is used to

8. For example, Mishnah, tractate *Yoma* 8.6; Babylonian Talmud, tractate *Yoma* 85b; Mekilta d'Rabbi Yishmael 31:13; etc.

9. E.g., Damascus Document, 4QHalakha A, 4QMiscellaneous Rules, 2 Maccabees, etc.

demonstrate Jesus's passion for (his interpretation of) proper torah observance, correct temple management, and challenges to power structures; he is by no means challenging the relevance of the law.

Why Is This Dangerous?

J. Gresham Machen (1881–1937), founder of Westminster Theological Seminary, wrote *The Origin of Paul's Religion*, where he argued that

> unquestionably post-exilic Judaism was devoted to the Law. The Law was found in the Old Testament, especially in the books of Moses. But around the written Law had grown up a great mass of oral interpretations which really amounted to elaborate additions. By this "tradition of the elders" the life of the devout Jew was regulated in its minutest particulars. Morality thus became a matter of external rules, and religion became a credit-and-debit relationship into which a man entered with God.[10]

As is evident in this example, identifying Jews with a legalist approach to their religion creates a straw man narrative of first-century Judaism that Jesus and Christianity can then come in and "save." Not only does Machen cast aspersions on oral torah by labeling it "a great mass of oral interpretations," simultaneously implying that it is both superfluous and illegitimate, and neglecting to note that Jesus participates in it, but he also conjures up a longstanding anti-Jewish trope of Jews as greedy, exacting, and unscrupulous in financial dealings. By labeling torah observance as "a credit-and-debit relationship" with God, Machen suggests that Jews' relationship with God is one that relies on extracting profit based on a system of arbitrary rules. Barbara Meyer reminds us that Christian anti-Judaism "does not need to refer to Jews or Judaism explicitly" to be problematic.[11] Regardless of Machen's intent to invoke this trope, its persistence is dangerous and is the cause of violence against Jews; this demonstrates how quickly misinterpretations (deliberate or otherwise) of New Testament material as being against torah descend into outright Judeophobia. It is the responsibility of all readers to guard against such readings.

10. J. Gresham Machen, *The Origin of Paul's Religion* (New York: Macmillan, 1925), 178.
11. Barbara U. Meyer, *Jesus the Jew in Christian Memory* (Cambridge: Cambridge University Press, 2020), 51.

Discussion Questions and Activity Suggestions

1. Write two letters that describe how you celebrate your favorite religious holiday (e.g., Easter, Eid al-Fitr, Solstice) to invite two different people to celebrate with you. Write the first letter to someone who knows nothing about that holiday, an outsider to your religion. Write the second letter to a friend who also practices the same religion as you. Include as many details as you think necessary. What differences are there between the letters? Come up with one or two ways this exercise sheds light on Paul writing specifically to non-Jews in his epistles.

2. Read Matthew 21:12–17; Mark 11:15–19; Luke 19:45–48; John 2:14–17—passages often used to suggest that Jesus opposed temple sacrifice. Reading carefully, what is Jesus actually concerned about? Does anything in any of the accounts tell us about Jesus's opinion about temple worship?

Further Reading

Fredriksen, Paula. *Paul: The Pagan's Apostle*. New Haven: Yale University Press, 2017.

Henze, Matthias. "Did Jesus Abolish the Law of Moses?" Pages 115–46 in *Mind the Gap: How Jewish Writings between the Old and New Testament Help Us Understand Jesus*. Minneapolis: Fortress, 2017.

Meyer, Barbara U. *Jesus the Jew in Christian Memory*. Cambridge: Cambridge University Press, 2020.

Sheinfeld, Shayna. "From *Nomos* to *Logos*: Torah in First-Century Jewish Texts." Pages 61–74 in *The Message of Paul the Apostle within Second Temple Judaism*. Edited by František Ábel. Lanham, MD: Lexington/Fortress, 2020.

Thiessen, Matthew. *Jesus and the Forces of Death: The Gospels' Portrayal of Ritual Impurity within First-Century Judaism*. Grand Rapids: Baker Academic, 2020.

8

Judeophobia in Contemporary Culture

JAMES F. MCGRATH

A book on Judeophobia is obviously necessary in an era in which a politician can blame wildfires in California on space-based weapons funded by the famous Jewish banking family the Rothschilds. What may be less obvious is the place of a chapter on contemporary culture in a book specifically about Judeophobia in the *New Testament*. Yet certain New Testament ideas, and indeed the notion of a "New Testament" itself, regularly appear in close conjunction with antisemitic conspiracy theories in their contemporary forms. Since by its definition the contemporary quickly becomes the historical, many points explored here deserve to be considered not only as contemporary examples of the Bible featuring in popular culture, but also as part of the history of Judeophobia in contemporary European and North American culture, tracing the themes and patterns to see which contemporary expressions are longstanding and how they have evolved over time. In the absence of such considerations, one may miss, for instance, that in a bygone era the church (despite its prohibition in Lev 25:36–37) problematically associated usury (lending money with interest) specifically with Jews, condemning it on the basis of Luke 6:35, which commands followers of Jesus to lend without seeking anything in return. This, in turn, allows us to recognize that in our time, when the practice of lending with interest is all but universally embraced by Christians in the English-speaking world, it is ironic and disturbing that the stereotype of Jews as greedy bankers remains with us.[1]

One persistent means of disparaging Judaism is through contrasts between Jewish and Christian scriptures. An example can be found in the 2018 *Doctor*

---

1. Frank Felsenstein, *Anti-Semitic Stereotypes: A Paradigm of Otherness in English Popular Culture, 1660–1830* (Baltimore: Johns Hopkins University Press, 1995), 33.

Who episode "The Witchfinders." When the character Becka invokes the Bible, saying, "As King James has written in his new Bible, thou shalt not suffer a witch to live," the Doctor responds by saying: "In the Old Testament. There's a twist in the sequel. Love thy neighbor." Although referred to as a "sequel" the implication is that the New Testament overrides and negates elements of the "Old Testament." Most ironic, of course, is the Doctor attributing the command to "love your neighbor" to the "sequel" when it is from Leviticus 19:18.[2] The false antithesis between Old and New Testament, and errors about what is found in each or in both, abound in contemporary culture. If one goes back a few decades earlier to the 1984 movie *Ghostbusters* there is a telling bit of dialogue offered as "clarification" of what is meant by a "disaster of biblical proportions." Various members of the Ghostbusters team speak in turn:

> RAY: What he means is Old Testament biblical, Mr. Mayor. Real wrath-of-God-type stuff. Fire and brimstone coming from the sky! Rivers and seas boiling!
> EGON: Forty years of darkness! Earthquakes! Volcanoes!
> WINSTON: The dead rising from the grave!
> PETER: Human sacrifice, dogs and cats living together, mass hysteria!

We may set aside the dogs-and-cats scenario that appears nowhere in the Bible. The boiling rivers and seas are only distantly related to imagery used in Job 41:31 and Isaiah 57:20. Rivers and seas being transformed in some way as divine judgment on the Earth, on the other hand, is found in both Jewish and Christian scripture, not surprisingly since the plagues of Exodus are the inspiration for the plagues predicted in the book of Revelation. The wrath of God is found in both Testaments, as are fire and brimstone (with volcanoes only ever implicitly the source).[3] The dead rising from their graves is to be found more in the New Testament than the Old (one thinks in particular of Matt 27:52–53). In neither Testament is the reference to a zombie apocalypse (although Ezek 37:1–14 may sound a bit like one, until one reaches the part that makes clear the dry bones coming to life are a symbol of national resto-

---

2. Adding to the irony is Leviticus being considered a "sequel" to Exodus, the source of the statement that a witch is not to be permitted to live. Note as well that the Doctor uses the older English form "thy" in the quotation from the King James Bible, which was then brand new and used such forms because they were current in that time. Yet the Doctor and her companions do not use them in their ordinary speech with the people of that time.

3. A search for "brimstone" reveals that precisely seven references are to be found in each Testament.

ration). Neither Jewish nor Christian scripture has forty years of darkness, but forty is a biblical number that occurs in both Testaments, and periods of darkness are likewise common to both, as are earthquakes. It would be easy to write this segment of the movie off as mere silliness in the interest of humor. However, it should not be overlooked that the joke is at the expense of only the part of the Christian Bible that originated as the Jewish scriptures, while the specifically Christian writings are shielded from this characterization. The scriptwriters created characters who assume these elements are characteristic of Jewish scripture but not the New Testament, when that is not at all the case. They expect the film's audience to share this supersessionist assumption.

In both these examples the terminology of "Old Testament" deserves to be highlighted. Within the New Testament writings one may encounter the terminology "new covenant," a concept that stems from Jeremiah 31:31–34 and thus from what Christians label the "Old Testament." This way of referring to the Jewish scriptures as part of the Christian Bible is nowhere found within the Bible itself, and the use of this terminology plays a significant role in turning what were simply "the scriptures" for the authors of the New Testament into something that is of secondary status to their own writings, which at the time they composed them were not yet scripture. It is indicative of just how pervasive these views are that they appear in works whose creators and intended audiences are not allied in any meaningful way with the Christian religion.

Those of us who teach biblical studies regularly encounter Judeophobic use of the New Testament in relation to the Jewish scriptures, for instance when our Christian students read Genesis and refer to *Jesus* creating the world, or when they refer to the Jerusalem temple as a "church." If we wait to address these things when they come up in student assignments it may lead to students offering defensive responses because they feel their own views and assumptions are being attacked, even if their specific assignment is not singled out in the classroom discussion. As an alternative, I suggest that scenes from television and film be shown to students, asking them to identify and evaluate the assumptions about the Bible that the characters in the clips express. It is frequently easier to spot the issues when they are expressed by a third party, in particular when the one articulating them is a fictional character. The surprise at a clip (whether the examples from *Ghostbusters* or *Doctor Who*, the goblins in *Harry Potter*, or *The Handmaid's Tale* when discussing Gen 30:1–3) appearing in a course on the Bible can also be disarming, whether on its own or as a precursor to showing a clip in which a politician or other public figure gives voice to similar views and assumptions. Because of the history of these specific franchises, the use of these examples can also serve to bring up the relevance of the popular culture concept of "retconning" to biblical interpretation. ("Retcon" is short for "retroactive continuity" and reflects continuity errors that inevitably arise in a franchise as writers come up with ideas for plot details later on that contradict the narrative thus far.) Applying this concept may help students to shift away from the frequent Christian claim that the Jews had misunderstood who the Messiah would be according to their scriptures, and to realize instead that Christians redefined the idea of messiah in light of Jesus. Jesus is retconned by Christians into the Jewish scriptures, and those scriptures themselves are retconned when they are categorized as the "Old Testament" when the existence of a "sequel" is not granted from a Jewish perspective.[4] The concept of fandom may itself be helpful for students who find themselves wrestling with whether they can still be "fans" of Christianity and of Jesus while being honest about the way Jesus is retconned as the fulfillment of ancient Israelite prophecy.

Discussion Questions and Activity Suggestions

1. Find out whether your favorite movie, TV, or literary franchise contains allusions to the Bible. Analyze whether supersessionism is detectable, and share what you find with the class.
2. What was your impression of the meaning of "Pharisee" in the past? After reading at least one academic article about them, how has your understanding changed?
3. How has academic study of the Bible made you more aware of how Jews and Christians are stereotyped and treated differently in works of popular culture? Which academic authors have provided you with the most helpful tools for detecting more subtle instances and for taking a stance against supersessionist and other problematic uses of biblical texts?

Further Reading

Dodds, Alice Rose. "Star Trek: Are the Ferengi an Anti-Semitic Stereotype?" *Game-Rant*, 1 March 2022. https://tinyurl.com/22evzyen.

---

4. It is probably advisable to avoid analogies that might be controversial in their own right, such as when some fans of *The Matrix* insist that it did not have sequels.

Freedman, Aaron. "If You Prick Watto, Does He Not Bleed?" *Jewish Currents*, 14 June 2019. https://tinyurl.com/583eccy8.

Garcia, Jorge J. E., ed. *Mel Gibson's Passion and Philosophy: The Cross, the Questions, the Controversy*. Chicago: Open Court, 2004.

Levine, Amy-Jill. "First Take the Log Out of Your Own Eye: Different Viewpoints, Different Movies." Pages 197–210 in *On the Passion of the Christ: Exploring the Issues Raised by the Controversial Movie*. Edited by Paula Fredriksen. Berkeley: University of California Press, 2006.

Mandell, Lyric, and David L. Stamps. "Oy Vey, the Shtick: Exploring the Relationship between Audience Consumption of Jewish Television Characters and Attitudes toward Jewish Populations." *Howard Journal of Communications* 34.5 (2023): 443–59. DOI:10.1080/10646175.2023.2199685.

Reinhartz, Adele. "Jesus of Hollywood." Pages 165–80 in *On the Passion of the Christ: Exploring the Issues Raised by the Controversial Movie*. Edited by Paula Fredriksen. Berkeley: University of California Press, 2006.

9

Interreligious Dialogue and Judeophobia

ALANA M. VINCENT

I n the context of interreligious dialogue, Judeophobia is most frequently expressed as a distrust of—and occasionally hostility to—claims regarding Jewish particularity, the idea that the Mosaic covenant applies specifically to Jews, rather than providing a basis for a universal system of ethics. Such claims are considered antithetical to the universalist nature of dialogue programs, which tend to present differences in practice or understanding as subjects through which robust dialogue can reveal a deeper underlying commonality that is then taken to point toward the universal truth that dialogue aims to reveal. Taking seriously the understanding of Judaism as a particular set of covenantal obligations, most of which do not apply to any group of people other than Jews, is therefore already antithetical to such projects, and there is considerable incentive for Judaism to be represented in dialogue contexts as a more generic form of "ethical monotheism."

A universalizing presentation is more congenial to some branches of Judaism than others. The Jewish representatives at the 1893 Parliament of the World's Religions were all involved in the American Reform movement, which particularly at that moment was already strongly committed to a universalist, ethical understanding of Judaism. But this commitment itself resulted from previous contestations, both in America and in Europe, and both within Jewish communities and between Jews and non-Jews, over whether Jewishness could be recognized as a legitimate form of religious difference (akin to the difference between Protestant and Catholic) within a secularizing Christian society. The Reform movement responded to those debates by constructing a deliberately Christianized form of Judaism, in which the elements of Jewish practice that were most apt to attract Judeophobic critique were first declared to be nonessential and then revised out of existence. The 1885 Pittsburgh Platform, which laid out the foundational principles of American Reform, is the apotheosis of this tendency.

The Pittsburgh Platform opens with an articulation of Judaism within the framework most likely to be recognized by participants in dialogue programs such as the Parliament of the World's Religions:

> We recognize in every religion an attempt to grasp the Infinite, and in every mode, source or book of revelation held sacred in any religious system the consciousness of the indwelling of God in man. We hold that Judaism presents the highest conception of the God idea as taught in our Holy Scriptures and developed and spiritualized by the Jewish teachers, in accordance with the moral and philosophical progress of their respective ages. We maintain that Judaism preserved and defended midst continual struggles and trials and under enforced isolation, this God idea as the central religious truth for the human race.[1]

Having declared Judaism simply one among many "attempt[s] to grasp the Infinite," the platform moves on to disavowing particular practices that have historically been understood as sources of Jewish distinctiveness, declaring that "all such Mosaic and rabbinical laws as regulate diet, priestly purity, and dress originated in ages and under the influence of ideas entirely foreign to our present mental and spiritual state." The apparent ease[2] with which Reform representatives issued these disavowals served to reinforce understandings of religion as properly concerned with universal truth, rather than particular practices, heightening the degree of Judeophobia directed at non-Reform Jews who may wish to assert the value of particularism.

The tendencies already present in nineteenth- and early-twentieth-century dialogue movements also informed the approach taken by post-Holocaust Jewish-Christian dialogue. The International Conference of Christians and Jews, which is the main umbrella organization for groups engaged in this particular form of interreligious dialogue, was founded in 1946, in response not just to the Holocaust itself, but also to the self-perception of Christian

---

1. Central Conference of American Rabbis (CCAR), "Declaration of Principles: The Pittsburgh Platform, 1885" (https://tinyurl.com/2jksevb4).

2. Note that "apparent" is doing a great deal of work in this sentence; the history of contestation that led to this point is long and complex and well worth careful study, but it does not appear to have been visible to many people not involved in Jewish communities.

theologians that Christian teachings had promoted and enabled the racialized antisemitism that found its full expression in the Holocaust. This understanding of Jewish-Christian dialogue as a distinct project removes it from the wider field of interreligious dialogue, which both erases the longer history of Jewish participation in dialogue with traditions other than Christianity, around issues other than antisemitism, and also removes from view questions of Judeophobia arising in the wider field of dialogue. However, it is still the case that Jewish assertions of religious particularism, and particularly attempts to maintain boundaries around both the performance and interpretation of particular rituals, are often construed as inimical to the reparative goal of Jewish-Christian dialogue.

This has been particularly evident in disputes over Christian appropriation of the Passover seder. Beginning in the 1960s, the Catholic Church, drawing on the account of the Last Supper from the Gospel of Mark, began to promote the practice of holding seder meals on Holy Thursday as a way of emphasizing Jesus's Jewish background and prompting Catholics to learn about and appreciate Judaism. The practice has since spread to many other Christian denominations. It has also been the focus of critique, on the following grounds:

1. The modern Passover ritual was not in existence at the time of Jesus. Presenting Jewish practice as though it has not changed over the course of two thousand years is itself a perpetuation of a Judeophobic trope, carrying implications of Jews as uniquely stubborn, rule bound, and resistant to or constitutionally incapable of participation in modernity.

2. Christians performing Passover rituals tend to superimpose christological meanings on the ritual, rather than engaging with and learning to appreciate Judaism as it is currently practiced.

Within the context of a dialogue process that is aimed at interreligious reconciliation, such critique can be, and has been, received as a rejection of the intentions behind the action. Interpreting a valid critique of ritual appropriation as a refusal to accept or engage in a process of reconciliation is yet another way to perpetuate images of Jews as difficult, stubborn, and not open to cooperation or coexistence.

Interreligious dialogue is essential to peaceful coexistence in the religiously diverse world we now inhabit. It is important, however, to ensure that dialogue does not simply reinscribe the prejudices it is intended to overcome. In the case of Jewish-Christian dialogue, in particular, balancing between acknowledgment of a shared history and maintaining boundaries that respect the autonomy of all parties within the dialogue is a difficult, but essential, task.

Discussion Questions and Activity Suggestions

1. While a great deal of Judeophobic treatment of Judaism within interreligious dialogue stems from a preference for universal framings of religion that appears to favor Reform Judaism, most formal, institutional dialogue programs—for example, the Vatican Commission on Religious Relations with the Jews—focus almost exclusively on dialogue with Orthodox Jews. Why do you think that is? What do you think the outcome of this choice is likely to be in terms of promoting or alleviating Judeophobia?

2. Framing Jewish-Christian dialogue as specifically a project of post-Holocaust reconciliation positions Christians as the initiators or the "hosts" and Jews as "guests." How do you think that positioning changes the way that each group approaches the other?

3. What practical steps do you think could be taken to avoid promoting Judeophobic stereotypes in interreligious dialogue?

4. Divide the room into two groups. Group 1 will be extremely committed—at least for the purposes of this exercise—to the proposition that pizza is pie. Group 2 will be committed to the proposition that pies must have both a top and a bottom crust as well as a sweet filling. You must discuss the design of a menu for the celebration of Pi Day (March 14). Your task is not to agree on a menu—if you manage to agree, then you are not taking your commitments to the definition of pie seriously enough—but to pay attention to how you carry out the discussion. How easy is it for Group 2 to insist on limiting the menu to items that fit their definition of pie without excluding Group 1? How easy is it for Group 1 to argue for the inclusion of their pie preferences without dismissing the concerns of Group 2? (Hint: this is not actually about pie!)

Further Reading

Kellenbach, Katharina von. "Guilt and the Transformation of Christian-Jewish Relations." *Studies in Christian-Jewish Relations* 15.1 (2020): 1–21.

Rutishauser, Christian. "The 1947 Seelisberg Conference: The Foundation of the Jewish-Christian Dialogue." *Studies in Christian-Jewish Relations* 2.2 (2007): 34–53.

Soloveitchik, Joseph. "Confrontation." *Tradition: A Journal of Orthodox Thought* 6.2 (1964): 5–28.

Vincent, Alana. "Convergence and Asymmetry: Observations on the Current State of Jewish-Christian Dialogue." *Interreligious Studies and Intercultural Theology* 4.2 (2020): 201–23.

Part Two

Texts in the New Testament and Beyond

10

Gospel of Matthew

NATHAN L. SHEDD

The Gospel of Matthew is one of four texts in the New Testament that narrate the life of Jesus of Nazareth. The majority of scholars think that the author composed this gospel sometime around 80–90. Several considerations seem to point in this direction: (1) the destruction of the Jerusalem temple (70) is talked about in Matthew as a foregone conclusion (22:7; 23:38–24:2); (2) the comments "to this day" in 27:8 and 28:15 assume that a significant amount of time has passed since Jesus's crucifixion and purported resurrection; (3) the standard scholarly opinion is that Matthew utilized the Gospel of Mark (circa 70) as a literary source; and (4) Ignatius of Antioch (*To the Smyrnaeans* 1:1; cf. Matt 3:15) and the Didache show familiarity with Matthean tradition. Together, these pieces of evidence suggest a date of composition between the destruction of the Jerusalem temple in 70 and the death of Ignatius in 110. Scholars typically narrow this range to 80–90 to account for the time required for (1) the Gospel of Mark to gain literary currency (and thus to be harnessed as a source for the Gospel of Matthew) and (2) the Gospel of Matthew also to gain literary currency and thus to become familiar in Syria by the early second century (cf. Matt 4:24).

The actual author of the Gospel of Matthew is unknown. Patristic tradition ostensibly associates the text with the disciple Matthew (Eusebius, *Ecclesiastical History* 3.39.16), but most critical scholars doubt the veracity of this tradition.[1] The superscription of the gospel—"according to Matthew"—is likely

---

1. Mikael Winninge, "The Gospels and the Acts of the Apostles," in *Jesus, the New Testament, and Christian Origins: Perspectives, Methods, Meanings*, ed. Dieter Mitternacht and Anders Runesson (Grand Rapids: Eerdmans, 2021), 245.

not original, but a secondary addition in later manuscripts. Many scholars, moreover, find it implausible that a supposed eyewitness (Matthew) to the life of Jesus would rely so heavily on a non-eyewitness (Mark) to construct his account and, relatedly, would take over the calling story of someone else ("Levi" in Mark 2:13–14) to recount his own calling (Matt 9:9).[2] This essay will refer to the author as "Matthew" as a convenient shorthand, but without the implication of true Matthean authorship.

Evaluations of Gospel of Matthew's Anti-Jewishness

Biblical scholars debate not only whether the Gospel of Matthew is anti-Jewish, but also how to categorize its apparent anti-Jewish characteristics. The question of its anti-Jewishness hinges in large measure on how experts envision the social location in which the text was produced and distributed. On one end of the scholarly spectrum are those who understand the text to be the product of a gentile (i.e., non-Jewish) Christ-follower addressing other gentile Christ-followers. According to this position, the relationship between non-Christ-following Jews/Judaism and the Matthean community "behind" Matthew's text is an *external* one between two groups as opposed to an internal one within a single group. The parting between Judaism and Christianity has already occurred and gentile Christians are now looking to forge a path forward as the true Israel over and against Jews/Judaism after the destruction of the Jerusalem temple. Such a strong distinction between Matthew's largely gentile audience and non-Christ-following Jews seems to be implied from the sharp language of "their synagogues" and "their scribes" in Matthew 4:23 and 7:29, respectively.

From the vantage point of this paradigm, the Matthean text itself is fundamentally anti-Jewish. Matthew's rhetoric consists of utilizing Jews and Jewish symbols as a negative foil to construct "Christian" identity and guide behavior. The Matthean Jesus's vitriolic rhetoric against the scribes and Pharisees in Matthew 23, for example, functions as a warning to the Matthean community not to fall prey to their dubious behavior. These opponents of Jesus function to cast a negative light on the Pharisaic leadership that emerged over the Jew-

---

2. For further discussion of the composition, date, and audience of the Gospel of Matthew, see, e.g., Matthias Konradt, "Gospel of Matthew," in *The Reception of Jesus in the First Three Centuries*, vol. 1, *From Paul to Josephus: Literary Receptions of Jesus in the First Century CE*, ed. Helen K. Bond (London: T&T Clark, 2020), 107–10; Winninge, "Gospels and the Acts of the Apostles," 245–49.

ish people after the destruction of Jerusalem's temple. The scribes and Pharisees—and those who mimic them—stand in a cultural lineage of those who murdered God's prophets:

- "You testify against yourselves that you are descendants of those who murdered the prophets" (Matt 23:31 NRSV)
- "Jerusalem, Jerusalem, the city that kills the prophets and stones those who are sent to it!" (Matt 23:37 NRSV)

The vitriol culminates with the questionable historical claim in 27:20, 25 that the Jewish crowds in Jerusalem, under the influence of the Jewish leadership, accepted the responsibility for Jesus's death. Further, although the good news of the kingdom of heaven was initially limited to the Jewish people exclusively (1:21; 10:5–6; 15:24), its postcrucifixion epicenter is now located outside the Jewish world, among "all the gentiles" (28:19).

On the other end of the scholarly spectrum are those who understand the text to be the product of a Jewish Christ-follower addressing other Jewish Christ-followers. The relationship between non-Christ-following Jews and the Matthean community "behind" Matthew's text is, in this paradigm, an *internal* one. John Kampen summarizes one iteration of this position by claiming that Matthew's Jewish audience "was a deviant group within the Jewish community who engaged in bitter and vitriolic debate with other portions of that same group."[3] The sharp language of "their synagogues" and "their scribes" in Matthew 4:23 and 7:29 and the polemicizing against the scribes and Pharisees in Matthew 23, from this perspective, reflect an internal Jewish conflict between Jewish Christ-followers and the Pharisees in Matthew's social context who had assumed predominant leadership over Jewish synagogues in the aftermath of the temple's destruction.[4]

---

3. John Kampen, "The Problem of Christian Anti-Semitism and a Sectarian Reading of the Gospel of Matthew: The Trial of Jesus," in *Matthew within Judaism: Israel and the Nations in the First Gospel*, ed. Anders Runesson and Daniel M. Gurtner (Atlanta: SBL Press, 2020), 378. Kampen's language of "the Jewish community" here is problematic insofar as it suggests that the Christ-following community was a deviant group of a unified or monolithic entity. It is more likely that the Jesus movement was *one* variant among multiple variations of Judaism during this time.

4. Those who situate the Gospel of Matthew primarily as a Jewish text in this regard point to the Jewish modes of thought throughout Matthew's discourse. Jesus is conceptualized as the Son of David who will save his people (Matt 1). Matthew portrays Jesus as a new Moses figure, who like Moses—for example—escapes death as a child (2:13–23) and ascends a mountain and delivers teaching (5:1–2). For further connections between Jesus

From this vantage point, the Matthean text's anti-Jewishness is questionable. Terence Donaldson, for instance, makes the following prototypical claim:

[If we understand that] the Gospel [of Matthew] was written in and for a Jewish sect or renewal group still existing within the world of Judaism and participating in its structures and institutions, even if standing in critical opposition to the current Jewish leadership; and that the polemic was directed solely against the Jewish leaders with the aim of encouraging the rest of the Jewish people to choose Jesus as their teacher and leader instead—then the Gospel is neither antisemitic nor anti-Judaic and may not even be supersessionistic.[5]

Amy-Jill Levine, however, cautions against the logical traction of the assertion that the Jewish identity of the author and audience absolves the Matthean text from the charge of anti-Jewishness. An appeal to Matthew's polemic as conventional among first-century models of discourse—and therefore tolerable—she argues, "does not keep that discourse from being abusive. It may be conventional to imprecate one's opponents, but if there is no indication of reconciliation to be found, if the presentation is entirely one sided, and if the targets of the rhetoric are eventually described as killing the speaker, the matter of its typicality is irrelevant."[6] Levine goes on to observe that the targets of the Matthean Jesus's invective in 21:45–46 do not find his polemic tolerable; they rather wish to arrest him. She thus asks: "If the characters in the Gospel do not find the rhetoric tolerable, then why should those outside the Gospel?"[7]

---

and Moses in Matthew's discourse, see, Dale C. Allison Jr., *The New Moses: A Matthean Typology* (Eugene, OR: Wipf & Stock, 1993). Not only does Matthew conceptualize Jesus using Jewish imagery and symbols, his ethical code is based on a concern with keeping the Torah: "Do not think that I have come to abolish the Law or the Prophets; I have come not to abolish but to fulfill. For truly I tell you, until heaven and earth pass away, not one letter, not one stroke of a letter, will pass from the law until all is accomplished" (5:17–18 NRSV). The Matthean Jesus's Sermon on the Mount, moreover, intensifies the requirements of the law (e.g., lusting after a woman breaks the commandment against adultery; 5:27–28).

5. Terence L. Donaldson, *Jews and Anti-Judaism in the New Testament: Decision Points and Divergent Interpretations* (Waco, TX: Baylor University Press, 2010), 54.

6. Amy-Jill Levine, "Anti-Judaism and the Gospel of Matthew," in *Anti-Judaism and the Gospels*, ed. William R. Farmer (Harrisburg, PA: Trinity Press, 1999), 16–17. Similarly, Levine, "Matthew, Mark, and Luke: Good News or Bad?," in *Jesus, Judaism, and Christian Anti-Judaism: Reading the New Testament after the Holocaust*, ed. Paula Fredriksen and Adele Reinhartz (Louisville: Westminster John Knox, 2002), 88.

7. Levine, "Anti-Judaism and the Gospel of Matthew," 18.

Plenty of variation exists in scholarly discussions between the two poles outlined in the previous pages. As mentioned above, in terms of the gospel's anti-Jewishness, much seems to depend on scholarly reconstructions of Matthew's origins—his Jewish or non-Jewish identity, his community's relationship to the Jewish synagogue system, and so on. Recent scholarship, moreover, casts influential historical-critical paradigms regarding the origins and location of the gospels in dubious display. Some scholars, for example, are beginning to question the legitimacy of even talking about a "community" standing "behind" the gospels.[8] The impact of such scholarship on the question of the Gospel of Matthew's anti-Jewishness has yet to be adequately theorized. Regardless of how one nuances the Gospel of Matthew's interface with anti-Judaism in terms of the gospel's origins, what is demonstrable is that the reception history of this gospel is marked by clear anti-Jewish characteristics.

Anti-Jewish Trope: The Jews as the Killers of Christ and God's Prophets

The Gospel of Matthew establishes cultural patterns of thinking that subsequent readers of the gospel have seamlessly morphed into anti-Jewish ideology, ideology that has had a profoundly negative and harmful impact on the lived experience of Jews for nearly two millennia. One scholar aptly writes: "Wherever [Matthew] has been read, anti-Judaism erupts—not from all readers, to be sure, but from a significant number in a significant variety of cultural contexts and geographical locations."[9] This recognition is nowhere more apparent than in the promulgation of the trope that "the Jews" are responsible for the death of Christ and God's prophets. The dubious basis for this trope comes from Jesus's trial scene in Matthew 27 after Pontius Pilate is portrayed as giving the Jewish crowds a choice between two prisoners to release: Jesus or Barabbas. The chief priests and the elders of the Jewish people convince the crowds to choose Barabbas and have Jesus crucified. The scene then unfolds with the Jewish crowds accepting the blame for Jesus's impending crucifixion: "The

---

8. See, e.g., Robyn Faith Walsh, *The Origins of Early Christian Literature: Contextualizing the New Testament within Greco-Roman Literary Culture* (Cambridge: Cambridge University Press, 2021); Sarah E. Rollens, "The Anachronism of 'Early Christian Communities,'" in *Theorizing "Religion" in Antiquity*, ed. Nickolas Roubekas, Studies in Ancient Religion and Culture (Sheffield: Equinox, 2019), 307–24.

9. Levine, "Anti-Judaism and the Gospel of Matthew," 35.

people as a whole [*pas ho laos*] answered, 'His blood be on us and on our children!'" (27:25 ESV).

William Farmer refers to the interpretive history of this verse as the classic example in which Christian anti-Judaism has been fueled.[10] Similarly, Kampen avers: "In terms of derogatory and vicious treatment of Jews throughout Christian history, the bloodguilt of Matt 27:25 has been most ubiquitous. No other verse in the New Testament has been so influential in promoting the development of anti-Semitic activity."[11] In Matthew's narrative, 27:25 is more than just polemic against the local Jewish crowds in Jerusalem. Matthew positions Jesus's crucifixion along a cultural framework of Jewish leadership actively opposing and killing God's prophets.

We can see the fault lines of this cultural apparatus throughout Matthew's discourse. As scholars have long noticed, for example, Matthew's iteration of John's beheading foreshadows Jesus's crucifixion (cf. Mark 6:14–29; Luke 9:7–9).[12] At Matthew 14:5, Herod Antipas, the ruler who oversaw Galilee and Perea, "wanted" (*thelō*) to kill John the Baptist but feared the crowd "because they regarded him a prophet." Similarly, at 21:46, the chief priests and Pharisees wanted to arrest Jesus, but they feared the crowds "because [the crowds] regarded him as a prophet" (NRSVue). By the time of Jesus's trial, however, the chief priests and Jewish elders convince the crowds to "want" (*thelō*) Jesus crucified (27:15–23). Elsewhere, Matthew situates Jesus as (1) a prophet (21:11), (2) the fulfillment of the prophets' oracles (e.g., 1:22; 2:17, 23; 8:17; 12:17; 13:35; 21:4; 26:56), and (3) the upholder of the Law and Prophets (5:17; 22:40). By contrast, Matthew casts the scribes, Pharisees, and Jerusalem as the "descendants" of those who killed God's prophets (23:31, 37; cf. 5:12). Even the "children" of the local Jerusalem crowd in 27:25 share the guilt of Jesus's crucifixion.

The upshot of these maneuvers is that Matthew maps the opposition John the Baptist and the prophets encountered onto Jesus's opposition, and vice versa. Jesus and John the Baptist stand in an *transgenerational* lineage of the persecuted and killed prophets; their opponents likewise join a legacy of those who rivaled and murdered the heroes of Israel's ancestral past. The close connection Matthew draws between Herod Antipas, the chief priests, scribes, Pharisees, elders, and Jerusalem crowds in this vein led Christian interpreters across the centuries to activate these Matthean figures as descriptions of all

---

10. William R. Farmer, "Introduction," in *Anti-Judaism and the Gospels*, ed. William R. Farmer (Harrisburg, PA: Trinity Press, 1999), 5.

11. Kampen, "Problem of Christian Anti-Semitism," 372.

12. For further connections between John's beheading and Jesus's crucifixion in Matthew, see Nathan L. Shedd, *A Dangerous Parting: The Beheading of John the Baptist in Early Christian Memory* (Waco, TX: Baylor University Press, 2021), 99–104.

Jews in their own lifetimes—to the detriment of many.[13] Here I primarily focus on three examples of interpretation that utilized Matthew's cultural framework to brand Jews in their own cultural contexts.

The first example comes as early as the mid-second century, in Justin Martyr's *Dialogue with Trypho*. In this text, Justin—a Christian—recounts an alleged conversation between himself and a Jew named Trypho. Importantly, Trypho introduces himself to Justin as a Hebrew refugee of the relatively recent Bar Kokhba Revolt (1.3). Second-century Jews "faced horrific postrevolt consequences, including banishment from Jerusalem and the land of Judea."[14] Later in the *Dialogue*, Justin goes so far as to claim that the Jewish custom of circumcision was designed to mark out the Jews exclusively for these traumas:

> Indeed the custom of circumcising the flesh, handed down from Abraham, was given to you [Jews] as a distinguishing mark, to set you off from other nations and from us Christians. The purpose of this was that you and only you might suffer the afflictions that are now justly yours; that only your land be desolate, and your cities ruined by fire; that the fruits of your land be eaten by strangers before your very eyes; that not one of you [Jews] be permitted to enter your city of Jerusalem. (*Dialogue with Trypho* 16)[15]

Justin then immediately proceeds to justify these horrific conditions:

> Nor do I believe that any of you will attempt to deny that God either had or has foreknowledge of future events, and that He does not prepare before-

---

13. Similarly, Adela Yarbro Collins, "Polemic against the Pharisees in Matthew 23," in *The Pharisees*, ed. Joseph Sievers and Amy-Jill Levine (Grand Rapids: Eerdmans, 2021), 168: "It is likely that the scribes and Pharisees in Matthew 23 represent the leaders of the Jewish communities with whom the evangelist and his fellow leaders competed for power and influence. It is certain that, over the centuries, Christian readers and auditors of this passage connected its scribes and Pharisees with the Jews of their own times and cultures. This occurred at times directly, as teachers and clergy applied the language of Matthew 23 to Jews in their cultural contexts. It also happened indirectly, as it did in my childhood and youth, when teachers and clergy let the text stand without challenging it as a characterization of Jews in general. Furthermore, such perceptions of this text no doubt instilled considerable prejudice against Jews among many who read or heard it."

14. Shedd, *Dangerous Parting*, 131.

15. *Justin Martyr: The First Apology, The Second Apology, Dialogue with Trypho, Exhortation to the Greeks, Discourse to the Greeks, The Monarchy or the Rule of God*, trans. Thomas B. Falls, Fathers of the Church 6 (Washington, DC: Catholic University of America Press, 2008; reprint), 172.

hand what everyone *deserves*. Therefore, the *above-mentioned tribulations* were justly imposed upon you [Jews], *for you have murdered the Just One, and His prophets before Him*; now you spurn those who hope in Him, and in Him who sent Him, namely, Almighty God, the Creator of all things; to the utmost of your power you dishonor and curse in your synagogues all those who believe in Christ. (*Dialogue with Trypho* 16)[16]

At this juncture, Justin employs the framework of the Jews as the killers of Jesus and the prophets to legitimize the violent conditions the Jewish populace is experiencing in the aftermath of the Bar Kokhba Revolt, including Trypho's status as a refugee. Simultaneously, Justin closely aligns non-Christ-following Jews in his contemporary context to the crucifixion of Jesus. Their supposed actions—as the instigators of perceived Christian persecution in Jewish synagogues—is thereby made to resemble those who supposedly murdered Jesus and the prophets in Jewish history.

The second example is Origen, the third-century Christian allegorist whose continued influence down to the present on Christian biblical interpretation is difficult to overestimate. In one of his final exegetical works, *The Commentary on Matthew*, Origen repeatedly morphs the opponents of Jesus and John the Baptist in Matthew's narrative into descriptions of third-century Jews. For instance, in his comments on the beheading of John the Baptist (Matt 14:1–12), Origen writes:

And notice further that Herod does not murder John boldly, but secretly and in prison. For even *the present Jewish people* do not boldly deny the prophecies, but implicitly and secretly they deny them and are convicted of this by their disbelief in them. For just as it is true that if they had believed Moses, they would have believed Jesus, so it is true that if they had believed the prophets, they would have accepted the one prophesied. But when they do not believe in him, they also do not believe in the prophets and decapitate them, having confined "the prophetic word" in prison, and they consider it to be dead, divided, and by no means sound, because they do not understand it. But we have Jesus complete, since the prophecy which says of him, "not a bone of him will be broken," has been fulfilled. (*Commentary on Matthew* 10.22)[17]

---

16. *Justin Martyr*, trans. Falls, 172 (emphasis added).

17. Ronald E. Heine, ed., *The Commentary of Origen on the Gospel of St Matthew*, 2 vols. (Oxford: University Press, 2018), 1:57–58 (emphasis added). For an analysis of this passage, see Shedd, *Dangerous Parting*, 161–63.

In short, Origen draws a direct line between Herod Antipas's beheading of John in prison and Origen's Jewish contemporaries. He likens the actions of the former according to his philosophical conceptualization of the latter as a people who fundamentally misunderstand the Law and the Prophets. Doing so allows him to assert the superiority of Christian teaching and the inferiority of Jewish pedagogy.

Later in the same work, Origen harnesses the Jerusalem crowd's blood cry in Matthew 27:25 to claim that the Jews—writ large—hold responsibility for the shedding of Jesus's blood: "Therefore, the blood of Jesus has been imputed not only to those who were alive at that time, but also to every subsequent generation of Jews up to the consummation. Therefore, to the present time, their house has been abandoned to them empty" (*Commentary on Matthew*, series 124).[18] He thereby frames the destruction of the Jerusalem temple within the framework of Jewish guilt in the death of Jesus. Highly indebted to the work of Origen, Jerome made the following claim about 14:11 a century later in his own *Commentary on Matthew*: "But down to the present day we discern in the head of the prophet John the fact that the Jews destroyed Christ, who is the head of the prophets."[19] Similarly, Jerome avers regarding the blood cry: "This imprecation upon the Jews continues until the present day. The Lord's blood will not be removed from them. . . . The Jews have left the best heritage to their children, saying: 'His blood be upon us and on our children'" (*Commentary on Matthew* 27.25).[20]

The final example is a twenty-first-century white supremacist group—named Kingdom Identity Ministries—that operates out of Harrison, Arkansas. They describe themselves as a Christian nonprofit organization that manufactures various media to offer solutions to the problems confronting the white race and nation. Their doctrinal statement offers their rationale—if one can even call it that with a straight face—for their white supremacist ideology and antisemitism.[21] They believe, for instance, that the biblical Adam is the ancestor of the white race exclusively and that God gave Adam a superior form of consciousness that exceeds the consciousness of any other race on earth. Because they believe that the white race is God's true people, they insist that they are divinely chosen to be separate from other races, and thus believe in segregating from nonwhite races. They expressly forbid interracial relations;

18. Heine, *Commentary of Origen*, 2:737.

19. *Jerome: Commentary on Matthew*, trans. Thomas P. Scheck, Fathers of the Church Patristic Series (Washington, DC: Catholic University of America Press, 2014), 169.

20. As quoted in Kampen, "Problem of Christian Anti-Semitism," 372–73.

21. For the full doctrinal statement of Kingdom Identity Ministries, see https://tinyurl.com/ms7e4tuw.

race mixing, as they call it, is a satanic ploy aimed at destroying God's elect. They claim that God has outlawed the Jews from holding authority over the white race. To be crystal clear: it is necessary as a biblical scholar to point out that, despite their efforts, no single biblical text makes anything close to these white supremacist claims.

In their ideology, furthermore, the Jews are the racial seed of Satan. They are a demonic force that actively opposes these "true" possessors of the Law and Prophets. In other words, the organization aligns itself to Jesus and the prophets while simultaneously categorizing the Jewish race entirely in diametric opposition to Jesus, the prophets, and their supposed white compatriots. Kingdom Identity Ministries anticipates the eventual termination of the Jewish race. They justify this outcome by explicitly interpreting 27:25 (and 23:35) as a racial pronouncement on the Jewish people as a whole: "This evil race . . . bear[s] the blood of our [white] Savior (Matt. 27:25) and all the righteous slain upon the earth (Matt. 23:35)." They insist that this fate of the Jewish race is divinely sanctioned and approved.

The Gospel of Matthew's cultural schematic—wherein the Jewish leadership is actively hostile to Jesus and God's prophets—was an integral component in the formation of an even broader cultural ideology that located Jews of all times and places at the center of guilt in the death of Jesus. As Levine observes, it was not until 1965 that the Roman Catholic Church rejected "this teaching of permanent, inherited guilt."[22] As this brief and limited survey shows, the trope of the Jews as killers of God's Messiah and prophets has been perpetuated to legitimize the trauma of second-century refugee Jews, to frame and justify the destruction of the Jerusalem temple, to characterize Jewish behavior in various times and social contexts, to paint a picture of Christian superiority to Judaism in terms of comprehending scriptures, to sanction the termination of the entire Jewish race, and to solidify white supremacist lines of thinking more broadly—including segregation and the prohibition against interracial relations—in twenty-first-century America.

Discussion Questions and Activity Suggestions

1. In light of the survey in this essay of various readers understanding Matthew's rhetoric of Jewish figures as descriptions of contemporary Jews, what are some reading strategies we can adopt to combat anti-Jewish patterns of thinking?

---

22. Amy-Jill Levine, *The Misunderstood Jew: The Church and the Scandal of the Jewish Jesus* (New York: HarperOne, 2006), 101.

2. Does emphasizing the reception history of the Gospel of Matthew relieve it from charges of anti-Jewishness? Why or why not?

3. Some scholars suggest that Matthew's vitriolic rhetoric against the scribes and Pharisees in Matthew 23 is designed to mimic the function of similarly harsh rhetoric of the prophets in the Old Testament / Hebrew Bible—to lead Israel to repentance. If this is indeed the aim, does this clear Matthew from the charge of anti-Jewishness? Why or why not?

4. This essay observes several ways that the idea of the Jews as Christ-killers has been used to justify harm against Jews throughout history. Can you think of additional ways that the death of Jesus has been harnessed in anti-Jewish directions?

5. As a group, discuss precisely why blaming "the Jews" for the death of Jesus is anti-Jewish. Think here in terms of (1) the local portrayal of Jesus's trial in Matthew's text, (2) the historical context of Matthew's portrayal, and (3) how subsequent readers have expanded Matthew's account to describe Jews in other times and places.

6. Read and compare the following Matthean passages: Matthew 2; 14:1–12; 21:1–39; 23; 27. Pay particular attention to how Matthew characterizes certain Jewish figures (like the scribes and Pharisees), political figures (such as the Herodian family and Pontius Pilate), and place-names (especially the capital, Jerusalem). Observe specific language that is repeated across these passages. Which figures are portrayed as resembling one another? What is the significance of these connections in terms of the history of Christian interpretations of Matthew? Can you summarize one specific way that these figures have been read as descriptions of other Jews in other cultural contexts? Now, analyze how Matthew characterizes several Jewish women and the Jewish man Joseph of Arimathea in 27:55–66 in particular. Does Matthew align them with Jesus? How do these observations subvert the idea that 27:25 is a condemnation of all Jews?

Further Reading

Donaldson, Terence L. *Jews and Anti-Judaism in the New Testament: Decision Points and Divergent Interpretations.* Waco, TX: Baylor University Press, 2010.

Gale, Aaron M. "The Blood Cry." Page 62 in *The Jewish Annotated New Testament.* Edited by Amy-Jill Levine and Marc Zvi Brettler. 2nd ed. Oxford: Oxford University Press, 2017.

Kampen, John. "The Problem of Christian Anti-Semitism and a Sectarian Reading of the Gospel of Matthew: The Trial of Jesus." Pages 371–97 in *Matthew within Judaism: Israel and the Nations in the First Gospel.* Edited by Anders Runesson and Daniel M. Gurtner. Atlanta: SBL Press, 2020.

Levine, Amy-Jill. "Anti-Judaism and the Gospel of Matthew." Pages 9–36 in *Anti-Judaism and the Gospels.* Edited by William R. Farmer. Harrisburg, PA: Trinity Press, 1999.

———. "Matthew, Mark, and Luke: Good News or Bad?" Pages 77–98 in *Jesus, Judaism, and Christian Anti-Judaism: Reading the New Testament after the Holocaust.* Edited by Paula Fredriksen and Adele Reinhartz. Louisville: Westminster John Knox, 2002.

Yarbro Collins, Adela. "Polemic against the Pharisees in Matthew 23." Pages 148–69 in *The Pharisees.* Edited by Joseph Sievers and Amy-Jill Levine. Grand Rapids: Eerdmans, 2021.

11

Gospel of Mark

SARAH EMANUEL

The Gospel of Mark is one of four canonical gospels within the New Testament. Although Mark is the second gospel within the canon—that is, after Matthew and before Luke and John—most scholars agree that Mark was written first. Reasons for this range from historical detail to Mark's use of grammar—Mathew and Luke, for instance, have cleaner Greek versions of Markan stories, indicating that they may have each relied on a copy of Mark to craft their narratives and polished Mark's grammar in the process. Overall, however, we do not have much information regarding the "who, what, and where" of this text. The original gospel, for example, did not have an author's name attached to it ("Mark" was added by later Christ-followers in the second century, likely in an attempt to provide the gospel legitimacy; see Acts 12:12; Col 4:10; Phlm 24).[1] The text does not claim to be written from any particular place. And it does not claim to be written at any particular time. Scholars thus rely on textual clues to make hypotheses about authorship, dating, and writing location.

Fortunately, there are some clues. In terms of dating, there are textual indications that Mark was written in the wake of the Jewish-Roman war in 66–70. In Mark 13, for example, Jesus's description of war, famine, and destruction within Jerusalem is reminiscent of the pains surrounding the Jewish-Roman war, especially the destruction of the Jewish Second Temple in 70. While it remains unknown where this gospel was written (see below), it is evident that

---

1. For brevity, I will continue to call this gospel and its author "Mark." All Bible translations in this chapter are my own in consultation with the NRSV. When in agreement with the NRSV, this will be noted.

the author has an eye toward Jerusalem. It is also clear he has an eye toward Jewish communal loss and Jesus's place within that loss.

Despite Mark's interest in Jerusalem, his writing location seems less clear. In fact, most scholars agree that Mark did not write his gospel in Jerusalem—or anywhere in Roman Palestine—because he illustrates a general lack of knowledge regarding the area's geography. As far as the author's name, we really have no idea. As noted above, the name "Mark" was attributed to the author long after the text was written. What we *can* say is that, in all likelihood, the author was an educated male (because most authors were male), and to be able to read and write in antiquity meant that you were educated more than most. The author was clearly influenced by the early Jesus movement, likely crafted his story from oral traditions passed down to him, and likely also included his own storied interpretations to showcase his own perspective and communal needs.

Jesus the Jew in the Gospel of Mark

Jesus's Jewishness in Mark is evident from the start. In the first sentence, the author writes: "This is the beginning of the gospel of Jesus Christ" (1:1). This is a Jewish statement about a Jewish figure. For example, if we were to translate "Jesus" from the original Aramaic (*Yeshua*) into English, and therefore bypass the Latinization of Jesus's name, Jesus's name would be "Joshua," meaning "God is deliverance." In short, Jesus is a Jewish name. Christ, too, is Jewish. By calling Jesus "Christ," Mark is making a claim that Jesus is *the* Christ—that is, *the* Messiah (Greek *Christos*). To call someone Christ in ancient Jewish context meant to believe that that person was the Jewish king who would deliver a new world order in which Jewish suffering—such as the suffering of the Jewish-Roman war— would stop. Jews, according to this belief, would finally live in a world in which their ideologies would prevail and in which all people would finally see that their God—the God of Israel—is the one true God. From the start, Mark invites readers into a story that centers on Jewish belief with a Jewish protagonist.

Jesus's Jewishness continues throughout Mark's story. Shortly after Mark's affirmation of Jesus's messianic status, a Jewish prophet named John ritually purifies Jesus in the Jordan River (1:6–8). Although English Bibles call this purification "baptism," which is a transliteration of the Greek word *baptizō*, the Greek is a translation of the Hebrew word, *mikveh*. Jesus, in short, is doing something Jewish. He is participating in a Jewish purification ritual that takes place in natural flowing water, such as the Jordan River.

Jesus's ministry begins shortly thereafter. First, he announces that the kingdom of God is arriving soon. In ancient Jewish context, the kingdom of God referred to the Jewish messianic new world—the world in which the God of Israel would be the God of all people (see, e.g., Zech 14:9; 1 Chron 29:10–12; Dan 4:3). After making this claim, Jesus travels around Roman Palestine, sharing his Jewish ideologies with different groups of Jewish listeners. From start to finish, he converses with other Jews (Mark 1:21; 2:18), discusses Jewish theologies (1:15, 21), quotes traditional Jewish sources (2:10; 7:9–10), participates in Jewish ritual practices (1:9; 14:35), and is repeatedly named, in addition to the Christ (1:1), both Son of God (a Jewish title highlighting one's closeness to the God of Israel; see Mark 1:1; cf. Exod 4:22; 1 Chron 28:6) and Son of Man (a Jewish title used for messianic figures; Mark 2:10; cf. Dan 7; 1 Enoch 71:14). Jesus's followers are also Jewish, and when Jesus dies, they are the ones who mourn his death. Some even wish to provide him a proper Jewish burial (Mark 16:1).

Jesus the Anti-Jew in the Gospel of Mark

Most ideas about anti-Judaism in the Gospel of Mark stem from three major textual concerns: (1) Jesus disagrees harshly with Jews around him; (2) Jesus shows discontent toward the Jerusalem temple; and (3) Jews wish for Jesus's death.

Let us start with the first. Throughout Mark's Gospel, Jesus debates with Jews about forgiveness of sins (2:6–7), messianism (12:35–37), and Jewish practices (2:1–3:6; 7:1–23). In Mark 2, for example, Jesus rebukes the Pharisees, a known Jewish group of the time—a group who are depicted as believing that they had a more appropriate interpretation of Jewish text, law, and ritual than other Jewish groups—for not understanding the role of the Sabbath. For most Jews, including Pharisees, the Sabbath was a day for rest—that is, a day for not working. Jesus, however, picks grain and heals the wounded on the Sabbath, which are two forms of work. When the Pharisees tell Jesus that he is being unlawful, Jesus tells them that *he* has the right interpretation and that *they* misunderstand their own Jewish rituals.

This kind of reproach continues into Mark 7. Here, Jesus berates Jews for their way of keeping *kashrut* (kosher laws). First, a group of Pharisees ask Jesus why he does not have his disciples wash their hands before eating. The scene escalates quickly, as Jesus responds by calling the Pharisees hypocrites. He then says that there is no need to purify before eating because "there is nothing outside a person that can defile going in. It is the things that come out that defile" (7:15). Mark then adds that Jesus "declared all foods clean" (7:19 NRSV).

According to traditional interpretation, Jesus is claiming that *kashrut* is unnecessary, which denounces not just the Pharisaic way but also the entire Jewish practice of keeping kosher. Jews, according to this interpretation, constructed a lifestyle that is simply wrong.

The discomfort continues. In Mark 11, Jesus visits the Jerusalem temple during the Passover celebration. But instead of participating in the standard custom of changing money for an animal to sacrifice, Jesus curses those who work at the temple, including those who are handling the money and sacrificial animals (he flips over their table and chairs! 11:15). This curse comes immediately after another: Jesus declares that a nearby fig tree should never bear fruit again (11:13–14). Contextually speaking, declaring the fig tree's destruction meant to declare God's judgment upon the Jewish people (Isa 34:4; Jer 5:17). Jesus then enacts that destruction by destroying temple property.

Finally, Mark announces that the Pharisees and Herodians are plotting to kill Jesus. This begins in Mark 3:6, but is later supported by the temple elite in Mark 14–15: "The chief priests and the entire Jewish council were looking for evidence against Jesus to put him to death" (14:55). Shortly thereafter, Jesus is crucified. The last words we hear from Jesus are shrieks of agony: "My God, my God!! Why have you forsaken me?" (15:33).[2] Jesus then lets out an incomprehensible death scream (15:37). With that, he dies.

Because Jesus is the protagonist of Mark's story—the celebrated Messiah, moreover—readers are influenced to support Jesus and thus (1) be in pain when Jesus dies, and (2) be against those who wished him harm. Those who wished him harm, as noted, are Jews. Crucifixion was a specifically Roman punishment for this time period, so even if there were some Jews within the temple center who supported Jesus going to trial, they are not the ones who had the power to kill him. Mark is thus doing something through narrative; he is persuading readers to associate Jesus's death not with Rome, but rather with Jews. He is training them to project their pain and anger onto the shoulders of Jewish characters and, in turn, on Jewish people beyond the text.

Many interpreters understand these issues as indicative of Mark creating separation between Judaism and Jesus-followers. Jesus's activities on the Sabbath, his dismissal of *kashrut*, his curses, the tone with which he rebukes Jews, and the wider Markan setup to ban against Jews who wish Jesus harm leads some readers to believe that Mark was trying to showcase how the historical Jesus—that is, not just Mark's version of Jesus, but the actual man—was

---

2. These words are in Aramaic, which juxtaposes painfully Jesus's own Jewishness with other Jews wanting him dead.

disgusted by Judaism. Given Jesus's harshness throughout the gospel, he has been viewed as *anti*-Jews and, more, anti-Jewish broadly. This type of reading became essential for Christian supporters of the Nazi movement in the mid-twentieth century.[3] In 1939, when the Study and Eradication of Jewish Influence on German Church Life was established, leaders combed the gospels for proof that Jesus hated Jews. Stories such as Mark's were used to give the institute's anti-Jewish agenda divine sanction.

Making Mark's Anti-Jewish Jesus a Very Jewish Jesus

According to more recent scholarship, however, there is no way Jesus would hate Jews or Judaism if he truly understood himself to be a Messiah. In other words, if Jesus saw himself as a Messiah, he must have seen himself as Jewish and must have respected Jews and Judaism, as messianism at its core was a Jewish theology. Surely, scholars argue, there must be another way to understand Jesus's words and actions.

And another way there is. A very Jewish way, in fact. By reading more closely New Testament texts alongside contemporaneous Jewish sources, scholars find that the types of differences and debates we see within the New Testament are actually *part* of ancient Judaism. By the time Jesus was born in 4 BCE, in fact, there were many different schools of Jewish thought that had varying ideas about how best to be Jewish. Practitioners of Judaism would enter heated debates about their theological convictions and would use hyperbole and harsh rhetoric to disarm their opponents. Such argumentation was common for not just Jews of the first century but also their Greco-Roman neighbors. Oration was art, yes, but it was also game, and verbal sparring was part of every match.[4]

When situating Mark within an ancient context, we can see Jesus and the Markan narrator leaning into this type of oration. When Jesus discusses his ideas of Jewish dietary practices, for example, he is not discounting Judaism. Instead, he is arguing with other Jews about how best to be Jewish, using hyperbole, insult, and invective to help support his claims. In fact, we must recognize that Jesus isn't even saying that he disavows *kashrut*. Instead, he is disagreeing with a specific *Pharisaic* way of keeping kosher: the washing of

---

3. See the Hitler quotation later in this chapter.

4. Verbal sparring was gendered, too, in that oration—or, more rightly, *persuasive* oration—was connected to wisdom and excellence, and was therefore also considered a masculine virtue.

foods, hands, and containers prior to eating kosher foods.[5] Nowhere in the Torah does it say that kosher foods can become impure and thus defile the body if the food is not washed; that idea is added by the Pharisees with whom Jesus is speaking. It is precisely *that* addition—the washing—that Mark's Jesus is combatting.[6] Moreover, even though Jesus disagrees with this particular Pharisaic interpretation, he is still entering the conversation in a remarkably Pharisaic way, in that he contends, as the Pharisees do about themselves, that he has the right interpretation of Jewish law and practice!

The Markan narrator also uses hyperbole. For example, when Mark writes that Jewish groups plot to kill Jesus, we should not assume that this is not the idea of *all* Jews—not even all Pharisees or all Herodians.[7] New Testament scholar Amy-Jill Levine urges us to be mindful of Mark's exaggerations.[8] Jewish groups differed from each other on various theological topics, but even participants *within* those groups—such as Pharisees or Herodians or even temple elites—carried conflicting views from each other. Not every Jew or every Pharisee or every Herodian or every Jewish scribe or every temple-goer followed the Sabbath or kept kosher in the same way. When Mark or Mark's Jesus make big declarations toward various groups of people, we have to keep in mind their invocation of conventional oration. When they say things about the Pharisees, including their plot to kill, they are clearly not talking about *every single Pharisee* (and certainly not every single Jew). The proof of this is within the text itself. We must remember that, in the end, it is still Jews who are following Jesus, perhaps even some who identify as Pharisaic. Jews are the ones crying at the foot of his cross, weeping over his death and their loss.

Mark the Anti-Jew in the Gospel of Mark

Still, we have a problem. Thus far, we have been discussing the Markan Gospel as if it is providing a historically accurate picture of Jesus and Jesus's Judaism,

---

5. Mark adds that "all the Jews" (see 7:3) wash their hands before eating, but this is ahistorical and thus likely either a misunderstanding of Judaism or an intentional use of hyperbole.

6. Daniel Boyarin, *The Jewish Gospels: The Story of the Jewish Christ* (New York: New Press, 2012), chap. 3.

7. Even though Mark mentions "Herodians," we don't really know who they were, other than having some sort of connection with the Herodian family and its various networks.

8. Amy-Jill Levine, *The Misunderstood Jew: The Church and the Scandal of the Jewish Jesus* (New York: HarperOne, 2006), 81.

and as if Mark himself is situated within Jesus's own historical moment. But if we follow the claim that Mark was written around the year 70, which is indeed the scholarly consensus, it is possible that much of Jesus's Jewishness has been lost. A major reason for this is because, by the time Mark wrote his gospel, the Jesus movement had spread to include more than just Jews. The apostle Paul is perhaps the most well-known figure to usher gentiles into the movement, and he was doing this in the 50s—that is, long before Mark's Gospel. By the time we get to 70, differences and debates have skyrocketed. Jesus-followers, akin to Jews, are arguing about how best to be Jesus-followers. Some are insisting that the best way to follow Jesus is to be Jewish. Others are insisting that the best way is to be gentile. Others still are arguing that a mix of both is fine.[9]

If we read Mark as gentile, this does not mean that his gospel misses Jesus's Jewishness. But it does raise the possibility. Although gentiles were welcomed to participate in Jewish conversation, many remained unfamiliar with the intricacies of Jewish customs. Some even wanted to separate the Jesus movement from Jesus's original Judaism. The problem, however, is that we don't know how Mark felt. He doesn't tell us. He doesn't even tell us his name. While it is certainly plausible that Mark—or rather "Mark"—sought to position Jesus within his own Judaism, it is equally possible that he sought to separate Jesus from Judaism. Maybe the above understanding is wrong. Maybe Mark's Jesus *is* attempting to abrogate Jewish law.

Given what we know about the Jesus movement in the mid-first century, we have the following options:

1. Mark is a Jew crafting a story of a Jewish Jesus.
2. Mark is a Jew crafting a story of a Jewish Jesus who can appeal to non-Jews.
3. Mark is a gentile crafting a story of a Jewish Jesus.
4. Mark is a gentile crafting a story of a Jewish Jesus who can appeal to non-Jews.
5. Mark is a gentile crafting a story of a Jesus separating himself from Judaism.[10]

As the scholarship stands currently, there is no consensus regarding which option is most historical, although the first and fourth have perhaps gotten

9. For insights into these debates, see Paul's letters to the Galatians and Corinthians.

10. This is the least likely option, as the follow-up question becomes: "to join what?" There is no replacement for Judaism other than paganism(s), but given Jesus's conversation topics, this move seems unlikely. We must remember that there is no Christianity at the time in which Jesus lived or the time in which the gospels were written. If Jesus in Mark believes in the God of Israel and the power of the Torah and the Prophets, the only theological choice is Judaism.

the most attention in recent years (and the fifth the least). Regardless, con-tra Adolf Hitler's approach ("the art of reading and studying consists in re-membering the essentials and forgetting what is not essential"; *Mein Kampf*), scholars remain open to the nuances within the text and the understanding that multiple interpretations, depending upon one's focus, may develop. There is no cherry-picking. The "art" of reading Mark rests in multiple interpretive possibilities.

Mark's Anti-Jewish Afterlife

Again, we don't know which option is historical fact. We may never know. But what we do know is that this gospel was in its afterlife—that is, in the thousands of years of post-70 interpretation—removed from a Jewish context. As the gentile Jesus-following movement spread and became more popular, the Jewish aspects of both the historical Jesus's life and the texts written about him were forgotten.[11] Even the gospels written shortly after Mark add more hostility between Jesus and other Jews, indicating a potential gentile-oriented rewriting of Mark by way of separating Jesus from Judaism (or further sep-arating, depending on how one reads Mark).[12] Potentialities aside, however, what we know for sure is that Jesus's debates with Jewish groups, in both Mark and later gospels, have been *interpreted* as proof that Jesus discounted Judaism. Jesus's cursing of the fig tree and temple workers, paired with the Markan narrator's insistence that Jewish groups wanted Jesus dead, bolstered the *interpretation* that Jesus was against Jews, and that we as readers should be too. The Jewish characters who want Jesus to die in Mark have been granted center stage—as if they are a historical representation of all Jews at the time of Jesus's ministry—while the Jewish mourners and supporters of Jesus are cast aside. It is up to us as readers to bring them back into the story.

Concluding Thoughts

Mark's Jesus is not the historical Jesus. Mark's Pharisees, Herodians, scribes, temple elite, and Jesus-followers aren't the historical ones Jesus encountered either. But even if we conclude that, gospel stories aside, the *historical* Jesus was

---

11. Think about this alongside the Hitler quotation above.
12. See especially Matt 23; Luke 2:32 (paired with Acts 2:35; 3:14–15; 7:52); and John 8.

a Jew deeply embedded in his own Judaism, that is not enough. In fact, even if we conclude that Mark's Gospel is not historically anti-Jewish, but rather a narrative situated firmly within ancient Jewish difference and debate, that too is not enough. Interpretation tells us that Mark has been *used* to support anti-Judaism and later antisemitism. This gospel, regardless of authorial intent, has been *read as* having a Jesus who gives permission to condemn Judaism and to treat Jews with hostility. Mark has a place in anti-Jewish history. Let us not forget it.

Discussion Questions and Activity Suggestions

1. Think of a time in which you got into heated arguments. Have you ever used verbal takedowns to disarm your opponent(s)? Do you tend to use greater hyperbole against those with whom you are closer (e.g., parents, siblings, or friends as opposed to teachers, neighbors, or strangers)? If so, does Jesus's use of harsh language with Jewish groups showcase his closeness to (and perhaps care for) them?

2. Consider the five Markan options listed above. Do you find one in particular to be convincing? Why or why not? Does your answer matter when considering the interpretive impact of Mark's Gospel on anti-Judaism and antisemitism? Why or why not?

3. How would you describe the essential components of Mark's Gospel? How might essentialized readings of texts become dangerous? Why might pushing back against Hitler's reading strategy—in addition to or even aside from it being endorsed by Hitler—be important?

4. Assign groups of students a different passage from Mark in which Jesus talks about the Jewish law. Ask them to identify what basic issue from the torah is under discussion, and then assess how Jesus responds to this basic issue. Encourage them to note if any of the passages show Jesus stating that Jewish law was no longer important or that it should no longer be discussed by Jesus or his followers.

Further Reading

Donaldson, Terence L. *Jews and Anti-Judaism in the New Testament: Decision Points and Divergent Interpretations.* London: Baylor University Press, 2010.

Fredriksen, Paula, and Adele Reinhartz, eds. *Jesus, Judaism, and Christian Anti-*

Judaism: Reading the New Testament after the Holocaust. Louisville: Westminster John Knox, 2002.

Heschel, Susannah. *The Aryan Jesus: Christian Theologians and the Bible in Nazi Germany.* Princeton: Princeton University Press, 2008.

Levine, Amy-Jill. *The Misunderstood Jew: The Church and the Scandal of the Jewish Jesus.* New York: HarperOne, 2006.

Wills, Lawrence M. "Mark." Pages 67–106 in *The Jewish Annotated New Testament.* Edited by Amy-Jill Levine and Marc Z. Brettler. 2nd ed. Oxford: Oxford University Press, 2017.

12

Gospel of Luke

MEIRA Z. KENSKY

The Gospel of Luke is the only gospel to have a sequel, the Acts of the Apostles. It looks like it was originally a two-volume work; the preface to Acts talks about "the first book" (Acts 1:1), and the two works heavily parallel each other thematically, episodically, and structurally.[1] David Aune argues that Luke was separated from Acts early in the second century to combine it with the other gospels.[2] Scholars usually date Luke to the period of 85–95 and suggest that Luke was highly educated and wrote in an urban environment. Mark Allan Powell draws our attention to Luke's rich vocabulary and familiarity with both Hebrew scripture and classical literature, arguing that Luke in particular "integrates Old Testament concepts and patterns into his work, often using allusions and imagery that go beyond simple citation of individual verses."[3] Since Acts contains several passages written in the first person plural in the context of Paul's travels, Acts was thought to be written by someone close to Paul. Early church leaders named this author "Luke," because "Luke the physician" was a traveling colleague of Paul mentioned in Colossians 4:14 (also 2 Tim 4:11; Phlm 24), and the gospel was also assigned to this author.

Scholars often argue that Luke was a gentile who wrote for a predominantly gentile audience. However, Luke's gospel is very Jewish: steeped in Jewish texts and tradition, and Septuagintal in its storytelling, particularly in the opening

---

1. For extensive discussion of the literary parallels between Luke and Acts, see Robert Tannehill, *The Narrative Unity of Luke-Acts*, 2 vols. (Minneapolis: Fortress, 1989–1991).

2. David Aune, *The New Testament in Its Literary Environment* (Philadelphia: Westminster, 1987), 77.

3. Mark Allan Powell, *Introducing the New Testament* (Grand Rapids: Baker Academic, 2009), 151.

chapters.[4] Luke's gospel begins and ends in the Jerusalem temple and is filled with allusions to and quotations of Jewish scripture. Jesus is Jewish in Luke's Gospel. His family makes pilgrimage to the temple when he is a boy, he teaches publicly in synagogues, and his parables draw heavily on Jewish values and traditions, particularly when it comes to treating your neighbor as yourself and demonstrating true hospitality. Luke presents Jesus as the absolute heir to Jewish history, prophecy, and tradition, the fulfillment of Isaianic prophecy in particular, whose death and resurrection is able to be understood only through Jewish scripture.

The Gospel of Luke contains some of the most positive portrayals of righteous Jews and Jewish religious practice in the corpus of early Christian literature. At the same time, however, the gospel portrays all of these righteous Jews and their practices as located squarely in a lost past, connecting the loss of that past to the Jewish rejection of Jesus and God's decision to bring the saving message to the gentiles. Though not as overtly anti-Pharisaic and anti-Jewish as is the leadership in the Gospel of Matthew, who edits Mark to remove all positive portrayals of Jewish leadership, and not as pointed as the Gospel of John's repeated condemnation of "the Jews," throughout both Luke and Acts the author builds a portrait of Jews as participating in their own rejection and thus left out—at least for now—of God's plans. For these reasons, Lloyd Gaston asserts that Luke-Acts is "one of the most pro-Jewish and one of the most anti-Jewish writings in the New Testament."[5] From Jesus's first public teaching in Luke 4, Luke insists that God is passing over the Jews in favor of the gentiles, an assertion that builds steam throughout the gospel and comes to the foreground in Acts. In his pioneering study *Anti-Semitism in the New Testament*, Samuel Sandmel famously describes Luke as engaging in "a frequent subtle, genteel anti-Semitism."[6] This often takes the form of supersessionism; Luke repeatedly portrays Jesus as the ultimate fulfillment of the prophecies of the Hebrew scriptures (particularly those of Isaiah), closing the door on any other ways of interpreting the Jewish texts. Those who do not see Jesus as the fulfillment of the Suffering Servant prophecies are thus on the wrong side,

4. This leads some scholars to suggest that Luke had a more Jewish orientation. Loveday Alexander suggests that Luke was writing for Diaspora Jews, while Michael Wolter argues for a full Jewish background. For discussion, see Barbara E. Reid and Shelly Matthews, *Luke 1–9*, Wisdom Commentary 43A (Collegeville, MN: Liturgical Press, 2021), xlviii–xlix.

5. Lloyd Gaston, "Anti-Judaism and the Passion Narrative in Luke and Acts," in *Anti-Judaism in Early Christianity*, ed. Peter Richardson and David Granskou (Waterloo: Wilfred Laurier University Press, 2006), 127.

6. Samuel Sandmel, *Anti-Semitism in the New Testament* (Philadelphia: Fortress, 1978), 73.

only capable of rejection and—in Acts especially—murder. Luke portrays the gentiles as the true inheritors of God's promises, a reading that sets the scene for the explicitly supersessionist portrayal of Christians as *verus Israel* ("true Israel") in the centuries that follow.[7]

In what follows, I will trace out some of the ways this "subtle, genteel anti-Semitism" manifests itself in the Gospel of Luke, focusing our attention on several key elements of the gospel: the way Jerusalem appears throughout the gospel, the way Jesus's first sermon lays out the central theme of the gospel moving from the Jews to the gentiles, and the supersessionist and replacement elements of some of the parables. For the most part, I will concentrate my analysis on those materials that are unique to Luke and leave the discussion of Acts to chapter 14 in this volume.[8]

"Jerusalem, Jerusalem, the City That Kills the Prophets and Stones Those Who Are Sent to It" (Luke 13:34)

Jerusalem plays a central role in the Gospel of Luke, more so than in any other gospel. The gospel begins in the city, where we meet a host of righteous Jews who are devoted to God and to Israel. Jesus visits the capital city as a child, where he meets religious leaders from whom he learns and who listen to him attentively (2:41–49). The rest of the gospel is studded with mentions of Jerusalem. In Luke's version of the temptation narratives (material originally thought to be from Q), the three temptations climax with Jesus being taken to Jerusalem, to the pinnacle of the temple (4:9), reflecting the centrality of the city in the religious life of first-century Judea. Jerusalem continues to be a key focal point in the gospel; though he structures his gospel according to Mark, Luke reorganizes the narrative so that Jesus's journey to Jerusalem takes center stage (9:51–19:27). Unlike other gospels, which do not spend a lot of time on this trip, Luke makes it the centerpiece of his account. This journey is notoriously difficult to plot on a map, but Luke keeps reminding his readers that they are on the road to Jerusalem, making at least eleven references to this

---

7. For this reason, Reid and Matthews consider Luke to be "protosupersessionist"; *Luke 1–9*, lx–lxi.

8. I thus do not spend a lot of time on the Lukan passion narrative. For full discussion of the anti-Jewish elements of the passion narrative, see Gaston, "Anti-Judaism and the Passion Narrative"; Peter Rice, "The Rhetoric of Luke's Passion," *Biblical Interpretation* 21 (2013): 355–76; Reid and Matthews, *Luke 10–24*, Wisdom Commentary 43B (Collegeville, MN: Liturgical Press, 2021), 558–99.

in the course of these eleven chapters. Luke thus constantly orients the reader toward Jerusalem. This orientation, however, prepares readers for Jerusalem to be the space of ultimate conflict. As Keith Nickle explains: "The expanded journey narration serves Luke's interest in depicting Jesus as doing his utmost to prepare his followers for the fearful fate awaiting him on his arrival in Jerusalem—his arrest and trial."[9] Jerusalem is anticipated as the space of final conflict, the space where Jesus will confront the current realities of Jewish and Roman leadership and will be "taken up."

The portrayal of Jerusalem in the Gospel of Luke starts out positively, as the location of righteous Jewish leaders and the space of Jewish religious practice designed to serve God. After the prologue to Theophilus (1:1–4), Luke begins by taking us to a Jerusalem of the past, where we meet a host of pious and law-observing Jews who are celebrated for their fidelity to God and Jewish religious practice. We meet Zechariah and his wife Elizabeth, Mary and her husband Joseph, Simeon the righteous, and Anna the prophet, all of whom demonstrate love for and loyalty to God and faith in his plans for Israel. No other gospel includes such positive portrayals of Jewish religious practice and righteous Jews. Joseph Tyson underscores this point, writing that "the infancy narratives in Luke 1–2 present us with images of Jewish piety unlike any other descriptions in early Christian literature."[10] However, all of this is set "in the days of King Herod of Judea" (1:5),[11] in other words, in a place and time that is no longer. This introduction has a "once upon a time" quality, much like the book of Ruth, which also begins in a lost past, "in the days when the judges judged" (Ruth 1:1).

The description of Zechariah and Elizabeth evokes a biblical past, and the language and style is similar to that of the Septuagint. Tyson highlights this, noting that "not only is there a multitude of quotations and allusions to a wide variety of texts from the Hebrew Scriptures in their Greek translation, but the linguistic style itself appears to be a conscious imitation of Septuagintal language."[12] This evocation of the Septuagint, though, especially in comparison to the rest of the gospel, has the effect of distancing this set of circumstances from everything else that happens in Jesus's lifetime. The unparalleled depic-

---

9. Keith F. Nickle, *The Synoptic Gospels: An Introduction* (Louisville: Westminster John Knox, 2001), 137.

10. Joseph B. Tyson, *Images of Judaism in Luke-Acts* (Columbia: University of South Carolina Press, 1992), 45.

11. All scripture quotations in this chapter are from the NRSVue unless otherwise noted.

12. In particular, Tyson points to the work of Henry Cadbury, who notes distinctive elements of the syntax here. For discussion see Tyson, *Images of Judaism*, 46.

tions of righteous Jews and Jewish religious practice are thus firmly located by Luke in an unrecoverable past—a time and space that is no longer accessible or able to be recreated.

The first character we meet is a priest named Zechariah, who, we are told, is from the priestly order of Abijah and is married to Elizabeth, a descendant of Aaron. These are characteristics that would give them both a distinguished lineage among Jews. Moreover, Luke tells us that "both of them were righteous before God, living blamelessly according to all the commandments and regulations of the Lord" (1:6 NRSV).[13] Elizabeth, however, is barren, and both are advanced in years (1:7). This setup locates Elizabeth among biblical matriarchs like Sarah, Rachel, and especially Hannah, the mother of Samuel (1 Sam 1). These evocations set the reader up for the annunciation that is to follow, where a heavenly figure (here the angel Gabriel) announces the impending birth of a son.

The annunciation happens in the inner sanctuary of the temple. Luke, continuing to evoke a biblical past, tells us that "once," when Zechariah was serving as a priest, "he was chosen by lot, according to the custom of the priesthood, to enter the sanctuary of the Lord and to offer incense" (1:8–9). While Zechariah is offering the incense, the whole assembly is praying outside (1:10), even though this has not been marked by Luke as a particular festival holiday, just "once." The temple is thus portrayed as a space of faithful religious practice, both by the priests and the people as a whole. Zechariah sees an angel standing by the censor and is afraid, but the angel tells him not to fear, promising a manifold destiny for John within God's plans for Israel (1:13–17).

The angel, who identifies himself as Gabriel in 1:19, tells Zechariah that this son, John, will be "great in the sight of the Lord" (1:15) and is set apart for a particular purpose, to "turn many of the people of Israel to the Lord their God" (1:16). He thus must refrain from alcohol (1:15), language that recalls the vow Hannah makes to God in 1 Samuel 1, and with the spirit of Elijah he will turn the hearts of children to their parents (Luke 1:17), fulfilling the predictions of Malachi 4:5–6. Zechariah responds not dissimilarly to the way Abraham does (Gen 17:15–21), asking questions and expressing doubt: "How will I know that this is so? For I am an old man, and my wife is getting on in years" (Luke 1:18 NRSV). In response, Gabriel identifies himself but then strikes Zechariah mute, telling him he will regain the ability to speak when these things are fulfilled (1:20). When John is finally born, Zechariah is able

---

13. Reid and Matthews note that Elizabeth is the only woman called "righteous" in the New Testament; *Luke 1–9*, 6–7.

to speak again (1:64), demonstrating the connection between prophecy and fulfillment that will be so important throughout the gospel.

The story of the annunciation to Zechariah is followed by the story of the annunciation to Mary (1:26–38), setting the scene for the great praises of God sung by Mary (1:46–55) and Zechariah (1:68–79). All of these characters demonstrate righteous and pious responses to God's actions, attributing what has happened to them to God's plans. In Mary's song, Mary recognizes the special favor that God has shown her, connecting her to God's larger plans (1:47–55). Mary's song highlights some of the major themes of Luke, including Luke's special emphasis on God's favor to the poor and the presentation of Israel as God's servant. Singing this song of God's praise, Mary places herself within God's plans for Israel, going all the way back to the initial promise to Abraham (1:55). Luke thus develops an early understanding of Jesus's birth as fulfilling God's plans, part of the larger story of God's salvific actions when it comes to Israel as a whole.

These same emphases are developed further in the song of Zechariah, which he utters after finally being able to speak again. The first half of the song blesses God for fulfilling his prophecies of redeeming Israel (1:68–73). Just as Mary connected herself to the larger story of God's promises to Israel, so too does Zechariah, emphasizing how Jesus fulfills the promises God made to "our ancestors" (1:72–73). Zechariah proleptically looks to the birth of Jesus as God fulfilling his plans to send a savior from the House of David (1:69) to save the people from their enemies (1:71, 74). This redemption and salvation will allow the people to serve God in holiness and righteousness (1:74–75). Throughout this song, Luke continues to develop his understanding of the role Jesus plays within salvation history, the history of how God saves the people. While Mary's song focused on the way God overturns the inequities of the status quo, Zechariah's song focuses on God's promises being fulfilled in the coming of the promised Davidic savior.[14]

Both Zechariah and Mary are exceptional representations of righteous Jews, faithfully observing the law and recognizing God's hand in history. They connect themselves to the history of Israel and respond to God in what the narrative understands to be the correct way: by praising God for the favor he has shown them and a recognition of God's power and mercy.

Following the narrative of the nativity, where the angel confirms Jesus's identity as the prophesied Davidic savior (2:11), Luke's positive portrayal of

---

14. In the second half of the song, Zechariah focuses on the role his son will play in God's plans (1:76–79).

Jewish religious practice continues. First, Joseph and Mary are presented as pious, law-abiding Jews. After his birth, they circumcise Jesus and then present him at the temple "according to the law of Moses," offering sacrifice on behalf of their firstborn son (2:22–24). We are also told that they made pilgrimage to Jerusalem every year for Passover, bringing Jesus with them to celebrate the festival (2:41).

This second chapter of the gospel introduces us to Simeon and Anna, two more prophetic figures who bless Jesus and recognize the unique role he plays in fulfilling God's plans for Israel. When Joseph and Mary bring Jesus in to be presented at the temple, Simeon recognizes Jesus as the fulfillment of the prophecy that he would not die until he had seen the Lord's Messiah (2:26). He praises God, saying that "my eyes have seen your salvation, which you have prepared in the presence of all peoples, a light for revelation to the gentiles and for glory to your people Israel" (2:30–32). For Luke, Jesus's coming fulfills God's prophecies, particularly the prophecies of Isaiah. As has long been noted, Simeon's song of praise "borrows heavily from the Isaianic vision of the advent of God's consolation and the mission of the Servant in Isaiah 40–66."[15] Isaiah is a critical resource for Luke throughout both the gospel and Acts, as he portrays Jesus as the ultimate fulfillment of Isaianic prophecy. Moreover, Simeon also sees the conflict ahead, as he predicts that the child will be greatly opposed and lead many in Israel to fall and rise (Luke 2:34–35). More clearly than others, Simeon's proclamation envisions what it means for God to fulfill his plans in this way.[16] Jesus's identity will reveal the inner thoughts of many (2:35), a revelation that does not sound promising.

In the opening chapters of Luke, the author thus introduces us to a choir of voices of righteous Jews faithfully following God's plan. However, as Amy-Jill Levine reminds us, though this is a highly positive picture of Jews and Jewish practice, it is confined by Luke to the past, a time that is unrecoverable. She also asks us to look again at the infancy material: "It's all good. It's also a lovely memory of a time that is no more. Following the nativity material in the first two chapters, the sacred quality of Israel, Jerusalem, and the temple is gradually eroded. Once readers encounter this erosion, they will find, when they return to the infancy material, subtle critiques throughout."[17] Levine points

---

15. Joel Green, *The Gospel of Luke*, New International Commentary on the New Testament (Grand Rapids: Eerdmans, 1997), 144.

16. Reid and Matthews highlight the ominous nature of Simeon's words, connecting the predicted "falling" of many in Israel to the way Luke understands the destruction of Jerusalem; *Luke 1–9*, 88–89.

17. Amy-Jill Levine, "Anti-Judaism in the Gospel of Luke," *Interpretation* 68 (2014): 393.

out, for example, that though the temple is the site of Zechariah's initial reve-lation, "it is also the place where the priest is struck mute (1:8–20). The temple and its priesthood, in effect, have nothing more to say."[18] Zechariah's son will not minister in the temple; he moves to the banks of the Jordan to proclaim his message to the crowds. Likewise, "Simeon, the righteous one in the temple, is now ready to die. His generation will not be repeated."[19] Moreover, Simeon's prophecy previews the Lukan theme of Jesus as a light for revelation *to the nations*, a theme that Luke will immediately develop in his opening presenta-tion of Jesus's public teaching (see next section). By highlighting the conflict ahead and the presentation of Jesus as a light to the nations, Luke prepares the readers for what is to come, when Jesus will be rejected by those who should have accepted him, and his special emphasis on Jesus fulfilling the prophecies of Isaiah.

As the gospel progresses, Jerusalem takes on a much more ominous as-sociation, as the space where prophets die (13:34), and thus where Jesus will meet his end. The central section of Luke, the journey to Jerusalem, begins in 9:51, where we are told that "when the days drew near for him to be taken up, he set his face to go to Jerusalem." This phrase "set his face" is repeated in 9:53 and implies a clear intention for the journey. However, it also implies a grim determination; Jesus is ready to face Jerusalem, including whatever awaits him there. In Luke 13, Jesus tells his followers that he must be on his way, "because it is impossible for a prophet to be killed outside of Jerusalem" (13:33). He laments over the city: "Jerusalem, Jerusalem, the city that kills the prophets and stones those who are sent to it! How often have I desired to gather your children together as a hen gathers her brood under her wings, and you were not willing!" (13:34). This sorrowful exclamation redefines Jerusalem not as the space of righteous Jews and sincere religious practice, but as a space of death. Not only is Jerusalem the space of Jesus's death, Jesus is part of a series of Jerusalem-based deaths, a series that continues in Acts.[20]

---

18. Levine, "Anti-Judaism in the Gospel of Luke," 393.

19. Levine, "Anti-Judaism in the Gospel of Luke," 393. Levine also points to Anna as one-half of a type of widow diptych with the widow who puts her whole life into the temple treasury (Luke 21:4). Though not explicitly stated, Levine reads the two widows as appar-ently childless, arguing that they "symbolize the fate of the institution: there will be no next generation to continue temple piety."

20. Jesus makes his fate clear to the disciples in Luke 18:31–33: "Then he took the twelve aside and said to them, 'See, we are going up to Jerusalem, and everything that is written about the Son of Man by the prophets will be accomplished. For he will be handed over to the gentiles, and he will be mocked and insulted and spat upon. After they have flogged

Moreover, it is also a dead space. By the time Luke writes his gospel, the temple has been destroyed and the city reduced to rubble. Luke does not blame the Romans for this, however; he places the blame squarely on the shoulders of the Jews, connecting this destruction to Jesus's story. When Jesus finally gets to Jerusalem and sees it, he weeps over it, recognizing its fate: "As he came near and saw the city, he wept over it, saying, 'If you, even you, had only recognized on this day the things that make for peace! But now they are hidden from your eyes. Indeed, the days will come upon you when your enemies will set up ramparts around you and surround you and hem you in on every side. They will crush you to the ground, you and your children within you, and they will not leave within you one stone upon another, because you did not recognize the time of your visitation'" (19:41–44). Here Luke has Jesus predict Jerusalem's destruction, connecting its ultimate fate at the hands of the Romans to what is about to happen to Jesus. Moreover, Jesus here places the blame for the destruction of Jerusalem squarely on the Jewish rejection of Jesus and their failure to recognize "the time of [their] visitation." As Barbara Reid and Shelly Matthews explain: "The lament embodies the theology that Jerusalem deserved its destruction by the Romans because it rejected Jesus as Messiah and mirrors the rationale given for the slaughter of the resentful citizens in the parable of the pounds. In this way, the lament aligns with what will become a standard explanation in subsequent centuries for the transfer of God's favor from the Jews to the Christians."[21]

The Jerusalem of Zechariah, Elizabeth, Mary, Simeon, and Anna, the Jerusalem of Luke 1–2 and even Luke 24, no longer exists and is unrecoverable. Pious Jews are no longer to be found in the narrative, and worse, Luke implies that pious Jews no longer exist—or at least that the only pious Jews are those who turn to Jesus.

Luke 4: Violent Rejection in the Synagogue

After the temptation narratives, Luke begins his presentation of Jesus's public ministry with a brief summary statement: "Then Jesus, filled with the power of the Spirit, returned to Galilee, and a report about him spread through all the surrounding country. He began to teach in their synagogues and was praised

---

him, they will kill him, and on the third day he will rise again.'" While the disciples do not understand (18:34), the readers are prepared for what is to come.

21. Reid and Matthews, *Luke 10–24*, 520.

by everyone" (4:14–15 NRSV). This positive portrayal of Jesus's reception in synagogues, however, is immediately undercut by the subsequent narrative of Jesus's teaching in the synagogue at Nazareth (4:16–30), a narrative filled with hostility and violence, which sets the scene for the rest of the gospel (and Acts). In this opening to Jesus's ministry, Luke highlights the eventual rejection of Jesus by Jews, the movement of God's salvific actions from Jews to gentiles, and the desire of Jews to eradicate Jesus through violence. The positive portrayal of pious Jews working in the temple and praising God for his mercies is abruptly replaced by a negative portrayal of Jews as stubborn, willfully hostile, and violent. While the *temple* (which only exists in the unrecoverable past) might have been a place of piety, the *synagogue* (which exists in Luke's present) is certainly not.

Scholars often draw our attention to the way 4:14–30 reveals and highlights key themes in the rest of the gospel (and Acts). As Rosemary Radford Ruether explains: "By weaving in the saying that 'no prophet is acceptable in his own country' and then describing the synagogue's reaction to Jesus's midrash as one of angry ejection from the city and attempted murder, Luke makes the story of Jesus's first preaching of salvation into a paradigm of the rejection of unbelieving Israel and the election of the Gentiles."[22] This story begins with Jesus going to the synagogue on the Sabbath, "as was his custom" (4:16). This opening paints Jesus as a faithful member of the local Jewish community. Samuel Sandmel draws our attention to the placement of this story at the start of Jesus's public ministry, and to its key themes:

> The incident as it is presented in Luke (4:28–30) suggests that Jesus was rejected by the Jews right at the start of his career and that already then the Jews tried to kill him; also at that very early time it was publicly announced that the benefit to arise from the activities of Jesus was destined for Gentiles. One needs to notice that Jesus is again seen "customarily" attending the synagogue on the Sabbath. The fidelity to Judaism of Luke's Jesus is in contrast to the imputed Jewish infidelity of the Jews themselves.[23]

Standing up in the synagogue, Jesus reads the opening of Isaiah 61: "The Spirit of the Lord is upon me, because he has anointed me to bring good news to the poor. He has sent me to proclaim release to the captives and recovery of

---

22. Rosemary Radford Ruether, *Faith and Fratricide: The Theological Roots of Anti-Judaism* (New York: Seabury, 1974), 86.

23. Sandmel, *Anti-Semitism in the New Testament*, 77.

sight to the blind, to set free those who are oppressed, to proclaim the year of the Lord's favor" (Luke 4:18–19). Closing the scroll, Jesus tells the congregation that "today this scripture has been fulfilled in your hearing" (4:21). Saying this, Jesus identifies himself as the prophetic speaker, anointed by God for a particular mission.[24] This quote from Isaiah functions as a guide to the reader, telling the reader that the key to understanding who Jesus is lies in Isaiah. Luke intersperses quotations from Isaiah throughout the infancy narratives and returns time and again to the book of Isaiah to demonstrate that Jesus is the fulfillment of prophecy.[25]

The crowd is "amazed" at Jesus's words, saying, "Isn't this Joseph's son?" (NIV). This seems to suggest that they are (reasonably!) having a hard time reconciling the boy next door with the anointed prophet of Isaiah 61. Jesus, however, reacts harshly, predicting that they will mock him in the future and demand signs from him (Luke 4:23) and that "no prophet is accepted in his hometown" (4:24). While in its immediate context, this refers to Jesus's reception at Nazareth, it also proleptically looks forward to the larger scope of the gospel: that Jesus will not—or cannot—be accepted by Jews (the "hometown").

This is made abundantly clear by the examples Jesus brings forth to illustrate his claim, one from the career of Elijah and one from that of Elisha. First, Jesus reminds the congregation that there were many widows in Israel during the great drought, but Elijah wasn't sent to any of them; he was sent instead to the widow at Zarephath in Sidon, outside the boundary of Israel (4:25–26). Likewise, there were plenty of Israelite lepers, but Elisha didn't heal any of them, only Naaman the Syrian (4:27). The implication is clear: if the hometown doesn't accept the prophet, the prophet will go elsewhere. In Luke-Acts, this is the way God's plans unfold: the good news is rejected by the Jews, but will instead be accepted by gentiles. The message is clear to the congregation, who are filled with rage, drive Jesus out of the town, and attempt to throw him off a cliff (4:28–29), thus illustrating the lesson for Luke's readers. Jesus here is shown as provoking his own reaction: the message he teaches, a message of scriptural fulfillment, particularly the prophecies of Isaiah, in which he proclaims the good news, will lead to a violent rejection by Jesus's Jewish contemporaries.

---

24. This quotation from Isa 61 in Luke 4:18 functions as a kind of program for the way Luke presents the life of Jesus, with different aspects of the verse pointing forward and backward in the gospel. For example, the opening "the spirit is upon me" harkens back to Jesus's baptism (3:22), while the recovery of sight to the blind looks forward to 18:35–43.

25. In the gospel, this culminates in Jesus's explicit quotation of Isa 53:12 at Luke 22:37, which functions as a sort of bookend to 4:18–19.

Anti-Jewish Tendencies in the Parables

These key themes of Luke—the movement from the Jews to the gentiles, Jesus as the fundamental fulfillment of Jewish scripture, and the infidelity and violence of the Jews—continue throughout the gospel and into Acts, Luke's second volume. Several of Luke's parables—including those that are unique to Luke—highlight these themes either implicitly or explicitly.

One of Luke's most famous parables is the parable of the Good Samaritan (10:30–37), which Jesus tells in response to a hostile question from a lawyer about inheriting eternal life. When the lawyer asks who is meant by "neighbor" in the commandment to love one's neighbor as themselves (10:29), Luke's Jesus tells the story of a man returning from Jerusalem on the Jericho road, who is beaten and left for dead. After being ignored by both a priest and a Levite, the man is treated with exceptional hospitality by the third person who comes along, namely a Samaritan—a non-Jew—who is truly the one who treated the man as a neighbor. This parable explicitly emphasizes that the Samaritan behaved with more fidelity to the law than either of the two Jewish leaders in the parable, Jews who are supposedly especially dedicated to serving God and humans. One could argue that this parable is not anti-Jewish, per se, it is anti-Jewish leadership. However, in her book on the parables, Levine reminds us that priest and Levite are first two members of a classic triad of Jewish characters: the priest, the Levite, and the *Israelite* (i.e., an ordinary Jew).[26] Hearers of this parable in the first century would probably have expected, once they saw the priest and the Levite behaving poorly, for it to be an Israelite to show them up in the parable's climax. Luke's choice to make the third person a Samaritan—a non-Jew—subverts the hearer's expectations. This parable reflects Luke's theme of the gentiles as the true inheritors of God's plans. This is as opposed to *all* Jews, not just Jewish leaders like priests and Levites.[27]

The theme of the rejection and replacement of the Jews sounds repeatedly throughout Jesus's journey to Jerusalem, the central section of Luke. In the teaching on the narrow door, Jesus tells those assembled that "there will be weeping and gnashing of teeth when you see Abraham and Isaac and Jacob and all the prophets in the kingdom of God, and you yourselves thrown out"

---

26. Amy-Jill Levine, *Short Stories by Jesus* (New York: HarperCollins, 2014), 96.

27. The same dynamic seems to be at play in the healing of the ten lepers (Luke 17:11–19), where the only leper who turns back to praise God is a Samaritan (17:16).

(13:28). Instead, "people will come from east and west, from north and south, and take their places at the banquet in the kingdom of God" (13:29). Likewise, in the parable of the great banquet (14:15–24), those who are invited to the banquet make excuses for not coming, leading to their ultimate exclusion from the meal, in favor of others who were not initially invited.

Though Luke has been sounding these themes throughout the gospel, they are, as in Mark and Matthew, given their most explicitly supersessionist formulation in the parable of the tenants (Luke 20:9–19). In all three gospels, Jesus teaches this parable in the temple, in response to questions from the chief priests, scribes, and elders about the authority behind his actions (Mark 11:28; Matt 21:23; Luke 20:1–2). What provokes the question is slightly different in each gospel. While Mark says that Jesus was walking in the temple, and Matthew says he was teaching in the temple, Luke specifically says that Jesus was teaching and proclaiming the good news (Luke 20:1). Luke thus not only highlights the proclamation of the gospel as leading to the questioning, but also portrays Jesus as teaching the gospel at the center of Jewish power.

Luke's version of the parable is similar to that of Mark and Matthew. Unlike Mark and Matthew, he does not elucidate the ways the owner cared for the vineyard before leasing it out to the tenants (Mark 12:1 // Matt 21:33), jumping right in instead to what happens when the owner sends the slave to collect the share of the produce. Instead of giving him the share, they beat him and send him away empty-handed (Luke 20:10). This happens twice more, before the owner sends his beloved son, thinking that they will respect him (20:13). The tenants, though, recognize that he is the heir, kill him, thinking that they will get his inheritance (20:14). Jesus finishes the parable: "What then will the owner of the vineyard do to them? He will come and destroy those tenants and give the vineyard to others" (20:15–16).

This parable most explicitly lays out the synoptic understanding of how the actions of the tenants directly lead to their replacement. As has long been recognized, the parable builds on Isaiah's image of Israel as the beloved vineyard of God (Isa 5:1–7). Each character in the parable clearly represents someone else. The owner is God, while the tenants are those who currently have stewardship over the people of Israel (the Jewish leadership). The tenants beat the slaves (the prophets), but when the owner of the vineyard sends his beloved son (clearly representing Jesus in the parable), the tenants recognize who he is and decide to kill him precisely so they can have his inheritance. This action directly leads to their destruction by the owner, who hands over the care of the vineyard to others. This parable foresees the termination of Jewish leadership and the rise of new authorities over the people, a story that Luke continues to tell in the book of Acts. Because of the Jewish leadership's plan to murder the true heir, they will be destroyed and replaced.[28]

This parable, coming when it does and where it does, infuriates its hearers. Here Luke deviates from the Markan tradition in order to highlight the audience's reaction to the parable. The people (not just the leaders), hearing the parable, react negatively, exclaiming, "Let it not be so!" (Luke 20:16). It is not immediately apparent what they are hoping will not come to pass. Is it the actions of the tenants? Or the replacement of the tenants with others? Most commentators understand it as the latter; the hearers immediately recognize that he told the parable about them (which is explicitly stated in 20:19). In response, Luke tells us that Jesus "looked at them and said, 'What then does this text mean: "The stone that the builders rejected has become the cornerstone"? Everyone who falls on that stone will be broken to pieces, and it will crush anyone on whom it falls'" (20:16–18).[29] Luke adds these graphic depictions of bodily harm to the Markan teaching about the cornerstone. The imagery of falling stones and crushing bodies may also allude to the destruction of the temple and the city (21:6), further connecting this historical event with the theology of Jewish culpability. Jesus's words infuriate the hearers. who wish to arrest him immediately, but don't, because they are "afraid of the people" (20:19 NIV).

This parable thus sets the scene for how to interpret everything that follows in Jerusalem. Though crucifixion is a Roman imperial punishment, carried out by Pontius Pilate, Luke instructed his readers to see this as the Jewish leadership (the tenants) murdering the Beloved Son. In Luke, Jerusalem is about to live up to its reputation as the city that kills the prophets (13:34), the space of the final moment that seals the fate of the people. Luke prepared his readers for this throughout the entire gospel, giving them the hermeneutical keys to interpret the events of Jesus's passion as the inevitable, necessary fulfillment of scriptural prophecy, when Jesus will fulfill his role as the suffering servant of Isaiah 52–53, suffering and dying for the people despite his innocence, which is proclaimed over and over again in the trial scenes.

---

28. Jack Sanders suggests that in its Lukan context, this parable is not just about the destruction of Jerusalem, but relates to "God's final rejection of the Jews," given the reaction of the people, arguing that "Luke probably thinks of Jews and Jerusalem going down together"; *The Jews in Luke-Acts* (Philadelphia: Fortress, 1987), 62.

29. Ruether (*Faith and Fratricide*, 92) argues that the christological reading of Ps 118:22 must have been very early, because it is taken for granted by Paul in Rom 9:33.

Conclusion

Though not as overtly anti-Jewish as other gospels, the Gospel of Luke contains a pernicious attitude toward the Jews as responsible for the death of Jesus along with other prophets and thus willing contributors to their own destruction. His positive portrayals of Jewish practice and righteous Jews are limited to a period that is no longer possible, and he appropriates Jewish scripture so that it points only toward Jesus, foreclosing all other Jewish readings of scripture. He portrays the entire crowd as united in their desire to have Jesus crucified, and he paints the synagogue, a Jewish space that still exists at the time of his writing, as a space of hostility and violence. His anti-Jewish tendencies are both subtle and overt throughout the gospel, his first volume, and his story of Jewish rejection of Jesus and God continues in his second volume.

Discussion Questions and Activity Suggestions

1. How does the author of Luke use texts from the Hebrew Bible? Does he use them in different ways, or is he consistent throughout the gospel?
2. This chapter argues that Luke's Gospel contains supersessionist tendencies, portraying Christianity as the true fulfillment of God's promises. How is this theme developed in the gospel, and what examples from the text support this claim?
3. Examine the depiction of the Pharisees in Luke. How does this gospel depict their connection to and engagement with Jesus?
4. Look at the parable of the pounds in Luke 19:11–27, which Jesus narrates "because he was near Jerusalem and because they supposed that the kingdom of God was to appear immediately" (19:11). How does this parable set the stage for what happens in Jerusalem? How does it contribute to the anti-Jewish tendencies in Luke's Gospel overall?
5. Read Luke 22:1–25. Who among the Jews does Luke portray as being responsible for the death of Jesus? How does this compare to Mark's version of the story?

Further Reading

Levine, Amy-Jill. "Luke and the Jewish Religion." *Interpretation* 68 (2014): 389–402.
Reid, Barbara, and Shelly Matthews. *Luke 1–9.* Wisdom Commentary 43A. Collegeville, MN: Liturgical Press, 2021.

———. *Luke 10–24*. Wisdom Commentary 43B. Collegeville, MN: Liturgical Press, 2021.

Sanders, Jack. *The Jews in Luke-Acts*. Minneapolis: Fortress, 1987.

Tyson, Joseph. *Images of Judaism in Luke-Acts*. Columbia: University of South Carolina, 1992.

13

Gospel of John

ADELE REINHARTZ

The Gospel of John, often referred to as the Fourth Gospel, is one of the most beloved books in the Christian scriptures. The gospel's lofty Christology—describing Jesus as the preexistent Word (John 1:1), commanding believers to "love one another as I have loved you" (15:12),[1] and reassuring them that they will join Jesus in his Father's house (14:2)—has consoled and sustained countless Christians over the centuries. At the same time, the gospel's vilification of the *Ioudaioi* (best translated "the Jews") as the spawn of Satan (8:44), its repetition of the deicide charge (e.g., 11:53), and its references to the exclusion of Christ-confessors from the synagogue (9:22; 12:42; 16:2) have allowed the Fourth Gospel to become fodder for Judeophobia and Judeophobes. It is no accident that the Gospel of John was a favorite among the German New Testament scholars who sympathized with and even actively supported the Nazi program to eradicate the Jewish people.[2]

Like the gospels of Matthew, Mark, and Luke, the Fourth Gospel took its present form after a period of oral transmission, during which stories and traditions about Jesus's words and deeds were told, retold, and eventually shaped into a continuous narrative that was edited and written down. The identities of the author(s) and/or redactor(s), however, remain unknown, as do the date, place, and the circumstances in which the gospel took its present shape.

The evangelist (as the authorial voice is often referred to), or, more precisely, the implied author, was probably not named John; this attribution occurred

---

1. All scripture quotations in this chapter are from the NRSV unless otherwise noted.

2. See Susannah Heschel, *The Aryan Jesus: Christian Theologians and the Bible in Nazi Germany* (Princeton: Princeton University Press, 2008).

during the process leading to the Fourth Gospel's inclusion in the Christian canon in the centuries following its composition.[3] The implied author is often described as a Jewish Christ-believer, possibly the head of the local Christ-confessing church or community. Most of these points cannot be proven, however; any answers to these questions are speculative, based on inferences drawn from (specific readings of) the gospel itself. The exception concerns the dating of the gospel. Although we cannot date it precisely, we know that it had to have been written down by the 160s, as it is apparently quoted in the *Epistula Apostolorum*, dated to approximately 160–70.[4]

Similar uncertainty pertains to the place and circumstances in which the gospel took shape. Many scholars argue that the gospel's final redaction was completed in an urban location such as Ephesus, in circumstances that involved tension or even hostility with or from the leaders of the local Jewish community. Due to the absence of external evidence, these claims can be neither proven nor disproven.[5]

The Gospel's Aim

We are on slightly more solid ground when it comes to the gospel's purpose. Like the other evangelists (whose identities are also unknown), the implied author no doubt wrote this gospel at least in part in order to set down his version of Jesus's life story. He probably knew or knew of other versions of Jesus's biography and may even have known all or part of the gospels attributed to Matthew, Mark, and/or Luke.[6]

But we do know that recording this story was not John's only aim. The gospel itself tells us that its account of Jesus's "signs" was written in order to

3. The implied author is the image of the author that readers construct as they read a text. In many books, including the Gospel of John, the implied author is also the narrator. For discussion, see R. Alan Culpepper, *Anatomy of the Fourth Gospel: A Study in Literary Design*, Foundations and Facets: New Testament (Philadelphia: Fortress, 1983), 16.

4. For detailed discussion of the second-century knowledge of the Fourth Gospel, see Charles E. Hill, *The Johannine Corpus in the Early Church* (Oxford: Oxford University Press, 2004), 76 (see 75–183 for detailed discussion).

5. On the association of the Gospel of John with Ephesus, as well as the problems of historicity, see Paul R. Trebilco, *The Early Christians in Ephesus from Paul to Ignatius* (Tübingen: Mohr Siebeck, 2004), 237–63.

6. The theory that the author(s) of the Gospel of John knew the Gospel of Mark is now widely though not universally accepted. See the essays in Eve-Marie Becker, Helen K. Bond, and Catrin H. Williams, eds., *John's Transformation of Mark* (London: T&T Clark, 2021).

persuade its audience "that Jesus is the Messiah, the Son of God, and that through believing you may have life in his name" (20:31). Whether these words were addressed to those who already believed in Jesus or to those who were sitting on the fence—interested but not yet fully on board—it is clear that the evangelist wanted his book to have a transformative impact on those who heard or read his gospel. In this regard, we can describe the Fourth Gospel as having a rhetorical, that is, persuasive, intent.

Belief (Greek *pistis*) is an important but slippery term. Although it may refer to a purely intellectual exercise, it often also has spiritual and emotional components. All these elements are present in the Gospel of John. John presents various proofs, such as stories of Jesus's miracles or signs, that are meant to demonstrate his relationship to God and his identity as the Messiah and Son of God. He also describes eternal life—a highly desirable prospect for most people—as a consequence of, or perhaps reward for, faith in Christ. For the implied author, Christ is the only channel through which humankind can relate to, and be in relationship with, God.

Judeophobia in John

For the Fourth Gospel, however, belief requires not only an adjustment of intellectual ideas and emotional and spiritual actions but also concrete ones: joining together with others as "one flock" (10:16) or as the branches of one "vine" (15:5). The gospel employs what I refer to as a rhetoric of affiliation to encourage believers to join together, and a rhetoric of disaffiliation to distance them from the *Ioudaioi*, Jews who do not believe. The gospel's hostile or negative statements about or to *Ioudaioi* contribute to its rhetoric of disaffiliation.

The presence of so many hostile statements about a group labeled "the Jews" raises the question of whether the gospel itself is anti-Jewish, or whether it has only been read that way by generations of interpreters. This is a highly sensitive question, given the gospel's status as part of the Christian canon. Some Christian interpreters insist that it is the history of interpretation that is anti-Jewish, not the gospel itself.[7] Others, however, face the challenge, the

---

7. See, for example, Paul N. Anderson, "Anti-Semitism and Religious Violence as Flawed Interpretations of the Gospel of John," in *John and Judaism: A Contested Relationship in Context*, ed. R. Alan Culpepper and Paul N. Anderson (Atlanta: SBL Press, 2017), 265–312.

paradox, if you will, of a gospel that espouses the love of "one another" and yet demonizes an entire group of people.[8]

Part of the problem concerns the difficulty of defining anti-Judaism, or Judeophobia, itself. Without denying other possibilities, I work with the understanding that Judeophobia is distinct from antisemitism.[9] Whereas antisemitism is generally ethnically based—based on a particular ancestry, for example—John's Judeophobia pertains specifically to the *Ioudaioi* who do not believe in Jesus as Messiah and Son of God. Within the gospel, ethnically Jewish characters who follow and believe in Jesus, such as the disciples, are not referred to as *Ioudaioi*. There is no evidence to suggest that the evangelist intended or foresaw the detrimental impact of his statements about the *Ioudaioi*, or that he would have condoned the vilification and denigration of Jews, or actions of verbal and physical violence against Jews.

I do, however, consider the gospel to be anti-Jewish (or, more precisely perhaps, anti-*Ioudaioi*) insofar as it uses those it labels *Ioudaioi* as the negative pole of its rhetoric, therefore assigning a rhetorical, if not necessarily physical, separation from the *Ioudaioi* an important place in its persuasive program. Believers, John argues, should not only band together with other believers, but they should also distance themselves from *Ioudaioi*.

The problematic role of the *Ioudaioi* in John's rhetoric has long loomed large for Johannine interpreters, particularly in the post-Holocaust era. Since the mid-twentieth century, several literary and historical explanations are suggested. One solution is to argue that John's *Ioudaioi* are not the Jews as a religious or ethnic group, but rather one or more specific subgroups, such as the Jewish leaders, or as the group that returned from Babylonian exile to Judea.[10] Some who adopt this perspective suggest that the precise referent of the word *Ioudaioi* in each passage must be determined from the immediate context.[11]

---

8. See, for example, Anthony Le Donne, "Reading John with Reinhartz: Reception of and Reflections on *Cast out of the Covenant*," *Journal of the Jesus Movement in Its Jewish Setting* 7 (2020): 141–50. Cf. Adele Reinhartz, "The Grammar of Hate in the Gospel of Love: Reading the Fourth Gospel in the Twenty-First Century," in *Israel und seine Heilstraditionen im Johannesevangelium: Festgabe für Johannes Beutler SJ zum 70. Geburtstag*, ed. Michael Labahn, Klaus Scholtissek, and Angelika Strotmann (Paderborn: Schöningh, 2004), 416–27.

9. Although many scholars differentiate between anti-Judaism and antisemitism, the point can be debated. See Robert Morgan, "Susannah Heschel's Aryan Grundmann," *Journal for the Study of the New Testament* 32 (2010): 431–94; Susannah Heschel, "Historiography of Antisemitism versus Anti-Judaism: A Response to Robert Morgan," *Journal for the Study of the New Testament* 33 (2011): 257–79.

10. See Adele Reinhartz, *Cast out of the Covenant: Jews and Anti-Judaism in the Gospel of John* (Lanham, MD: Lexington/Fortress, 2018), 94–98.

11. For detailed discussion of reference and translation matters, see Ruth Sheridan, "Is-

For the past half-century, many have been persuaded by the hypothesis presented by J. Louis Martyn, that the gospel was written for a community of Jewish believers in Christ who were excluded from the synagogue on account of their faith.[12] From this perspective, the hostile comments about the *Ioudaioi* are a natural reaction to the community's trauma.

Furthermore, John's Jesus makes what many perceive as an unequivocally positive statement in 4:22, in which Jesus tells the Samaritan woman that "salvation is from the Jews."[13] Finally, some scholars argue that because the Johannine Jesus (that is, the Jesus presented in John's Gospel) promises eternal life to everyone regardless of ethnic or other identities, it cannot be anti-Jewish: Jews too have been invited to become "children of God" on the same basis—faith in Jesus as the Messiah and Son of God—as everyone else.[14]

These various explanations are not mutually exclusive. Nor are they all necessarily wrong. It is true that in certain passages, the term *Ioudaioi* seems to refer to Jewish leaders rather than the Jewish people as a whole, and that the damning description of Jews as children of the devil (8:44) may be directed specifically at Jews who had once believed but no longer did. It is always possible that some Jewish believers in Christ were maligned or otherwise mistreated by some Jewish leaders who did not share their belief, though there is no solid evidence that this is the situation underlying John's Gospel. The statement in 4:22 can mean various things; but even if taken as entirely positive, one must consider whether this one statement outweighs the fifty-four verses in which *Ioudaioi* are described in negative, often hostile, terms.

And of course it is historically true that Jesus and his disciples were Jews. There are "good" Jews in this gospel, as many commentators point out. These Jews, including the disciples, Nicodemus, and the Bethany siblings, are Jews who believe in Jesus. It is striking, however, that these characters, with the possible exception of Nicodemus, are not explicitly labeled *Ioudaioi* despite their obvious Jewishness. Even Jesus, whose Jewishness is unmistakable, is not labeled a *Ioudaios* except by the Samaritan woman (4:9). This pattern of labeling shows that the term is reserved primarily for Jews who do not believe.

Scholars present these points as explanations of, or excuses for, John's treatment of the *Ioudaioi*. What holds them together, however, is the view of John

---

sues in the Translation of οἱ Ἰουδαῖοι in the Fourth Gospel," *Journal of Biblical Literature* 132 (2013): 671–95.

12. J. Louis Martyn, *History and Theology in the Fourth Gospel* (Louisville: Westminster John Knox, 2003). Earlier editions were published in 1968 and 1979.

13. Andrew J. Byers, review of *Cast out of the Covenant: Jews and Anti-Judaism in the Gospel of John*, by Adele Reinhartz, *Review of Biblical Literature* 6 (2019): 3–4.

14. Anderson, "Anti-Semitism and Religious Violence," 266.

as a sacred text that, by virtue of its sacredness, cannot also be anti-Jewish. Rather than face the problem of John's hostile statements honestly and directly, they explain it away.

Most troubling is the claim that the gospel cannot be anti-Jewish because its message of faith in Christ is open to Jews. This claim is itself anti-Jewish, and supersessionist, in that it presumes that Jews must look to Christ in order to be in right relationship with God. Judaism itself, a faith not based on following Christ, is not enough. The same is implicit in the assertion that John is not hostile to Jews because it shows that many Jews believe in Christ. What is wrong with the *Ioudaioi*, apparently, is that they continue to view the Jewish beliefs and practices they engaged in before Jesus's coming as good, sufficient, and in accordance with the divine will. If, on the other hand, they adopt this new belief system, then they are "good." This does not equate, however, to a positive attitude toward Jews, as it pertains only to those Jews who become Christ-confessors, and for that reason it still is redolent of implicit anti-Judaism.

The gospel includes over fifty hostile references to the *Ioudaioi*. These passages, taken as a group, leave the gospel open to the charge of Judeophobia. The issue is to find ways to discuss them in ways that challenge or even counteract the Judeophobia to which a straightforward literal reading might lead, without at the same time denying the gospel's evident hostility toward the *Ioudaioi*. In what follows I attempt this type of discussion with respect to three important passages: 8:44; 4:22; and 9:22.

John 8:44

We begin with the most notorious of John's hostile passages. In 8:44, John's Jesus tells a group of *Ioudaioi*: "You are from your father the devil, and you choose to do your father's desires. He was a murderer from the beginning and does not stand in the truth, because there is no truth in him. When he lies, he speaks according to his own nature, for he is a liar and the father of lies."

This startling claim appears in the midst of a lengthy back-and-forth. The discussion begins with a challenge that Jesus issues "to the Jews [*hoi Ioudaioi*] who had believed in him: 'If you continue in my word, you are truly my disciples; and you will know the truth, and the truth will make you free'" (8:31–32). The *Ioudaioi* counter with three claims: they are Abraham's descendants (8:33, 39), they have never been enslaved (8:33), and they have God as their father

(8:41). Jesus has rebuttals for each point; his statement in 8:44 is his refutation for the third claim made by the *Ioudaioi* concerning their divine parentage.

Jesus's accusation must be read in the context of the genealogical claim made by the *Ioudaioi* in 8:41: "We have one father, God himself." This claim can be supported from the Jewish scriptures. In Exodus 4:22–23, for example, God coaches Moses on what to say to the Pharaoh as he tries to secure Israel's release from slavery: "Then you shall say to Pharaoh, 'Thus says the LORD: Israel is my firstborn son. . . . Let my son go that he may worship me.'" In Deuteronomy 14:1, God tells the Israelites: "You are children of the LORD your God." The term also appears in Second Temple Jewish literature (e.g., Wisdom 5:5; Baruch 4:37; 5:5; 3 Maccabees 6:28; 7:6) and is also implied in the use of "Abba," a familiar Hebrew term for father ("daddy"), to refer to God, evoking the emotional attachment of fathers and children and other elements of the father-child relationship.[15]

To this Jesus responds: "If God were your Father, you would love me, for I proceeded and came forth from God; I came not of my own accord, but he sent me" (John 8:42 [my translation]). The association of Jews and the devil is a persistent theme in antisemitic discourse. Some interpreters dismiss the negative impact of this verse by suggesting that the evangelist didn't mean it to be taken seriously. Rather, it is suggested, calling Jews the devil's children should be heard as a conventional accusation, akin to the name-calling one might hear in a school playground.[16] This point seems to be more of an excuse than a historical explanation. Schoolyard slander may seem innocent to the perpetrators or even to onlookers, but not to their victims. Indeed, many a child has been traumatized by such bullying.[17]

This type of explanation not only fails to defuse the impact of the verse but it also does not do justice to the Fourth Gospel. John 8:44 is far from peripheral or tangential to the discourse in 8:31–59. Rather, it functions as the climax of the Johannine Jesus's rebuttal of the covenantal claims made by the *Ioudaioi*.

In teaching this passage, care must be taken to avoid interpreting 8:44 as a truth claim about the Jews, or as the actual words uttered by the historical

---

15. "Abba" was an appellation for God in Second Temple Jewish texts, including the Dead Sea Scrolls. See Eileen M. Schuller, "The Psalm of 4Q372 1 within the Context of Second Temple Prayer," *Catholic Biblical Quarterly* 54 (1992): 67–79.

16. Luke Timothy Johnson, "The New Testament's Anti-Jewish Slander and the Conventions of Ancient Polemic," *Journal of Biblical Literature* 108 (1989): 419–41.

17. On the traumatizing impact of schoolyard bullying, see Thormod Idsoe et al., "Bullying Victimization and Trauma," *Frontiers in Psychiatry* 11 (14 January 2021): 480353.

Jesus. Rather, the passage makes sense only when we interpret it in the context of the gospel's rhetorical program. Viewing it as an element of the gospel's rhetoric of disaffiliation, designed to impugn Jews who did not believe in Jesus as the Christ and Son of God and thereby to encourage its audience to distance themselves from such individuals.

Of course, rhetorical statements can also be factual. This statement, however, is patently untrue about Jews, or any human beings, and it is inconceivable as a statement that Jesus would have made. But it contributes, if in troubling ways, to the gospel's rhetoric aimed at persuading its audience to believe, or continue to believe, in Jesus as the Christ and Son of God, and to affiliate with others who do the same.[18]

John 4:22

According to John 4:1–30, Jesus met a Samaritan woman near the Samaritan city of Sychar, as he was resting at Jacob's well on his way from Jerusalem to the Galilee via Samaria. In contrast to the scenes in the Jewish scriptures in which Israelite men, or their surrogates, meet their future brides at wells, Jesus and the Samaritan woman do not flirt but rather immediately engage in deep theological conversation.[19]

The conversation begins with Jesus asking the Samaritan woman for a drink of water. She is surprised: "How is it that you, a Jew, ask a drink of me, a woman of Samaria?" (4:9a). The narrator explains that "Jews do not share things in common with Samaritans" (4:9b). John 4:9 is the only verse in which Jesus is called a *Ioudaios*. While he does not deny this label, he does not repeat it. Rather, he corrects the woman's understanding of his identity. He immediately redefines himself as a "gift of God," the giver of eternal water (4:10), and, later, as the one who fulfills the Samaritans' expectations of the coming Messiah.

---

18. The Greek of 20:31 has a textual variant. Some manuscripts have the aorist subjunctive *pisteusēte*, which has a future sense, as indicated by the NRSV's "you may come to believe." This variant suggests that the gospel's intended hearers are not yet believers. But there is also strong textual evidence for the present subjunctive *pisteusēte*, which implies "that you may continue to believe," suggesting that the hearers are already believers. For further discussion, see Donald A. Carson, "Syntactical and Text-Critical Observations on John 20:30–31: One More Round on the Purpose of the Fourth Gospel," *Journal of Biblical Literature* 124 (2005): 693–714.

19. See Lyle Eslinger, "The Wooing of the Woman at the Well: Jesus, the Reader, and Reader-Response Criticism," *Literature and Theology* 1.2 (1987): 167–83.

In the course of their conversation, Jesus tells the Samaritan woman: "You [Samaritans] worship what you do not know; we worship what we know, for salvation is from the Jews" (4:22). The precise meaning of this declaration, however, is unclear. Is Jesus referring here to "we Jews"? Or is he speaking in the name of the narrator, in which case he may be referring to "we" who affirm that relationship with God is only through Christ?

Throughout the passage, the Samaritan woman relates to Jesus as a Jew and contrasts Jewish and Samaritan practices. In 4:20 she points out that "our ancestors worshiped on this mountain, but you [Jews] say that the place where people must worship is in Jerusalem." As he does in 4:10, the Johannine Jesus moves the discourse beyond the Jew-Samaritan dichotomy. In 4:21 he promises that in the future such differences will be irrelevant, because "the hour is coming when you will worship the Father neither on this mountain nor in Jerusalem."

In 4:22a, however, he seems to pick up on the woman's polarizing perspective: "You worship what you do not know; we worship what we know." In the Fourth Gospel, knowledge is generally a reference to knowledge of God, and the same appears to be true here. Some scholars therefore suggest that this is a positive statement about Jews, as those who know God (see note 13 on p. 141). Some go one step further to suggest that this positive statement should be seen as a counterbalance to the hostile or negative statements about the *Ioudaioi* elsewhere in the gospel.[20]

Whether one verse can outweigh the more than fifty negative references to the *Ioudaioi* is debatable. But certainly one can infer that Jesus's positive words concern the *Ioudaioi* as the ones who know God; this reading makes sense in the context of the Samaritan woman's identification of Jesus as a *Ioudaios* and in the fact that Jesus does not provide an alternative antecedent for the verbs in the clause that states, "We worship what we know."

Yet there are grounds on which to question whether this statement in fact refers to Jews' knowledge of God. Elsewhere in the gospel, the Johannine Jesus insists that the *Ioudaioi* do *not* know God. In 3:11, he tells Nicodemus, a leader of the Jews (3:1): "Very truly, I tell you, we speak of what we know and testify to what we have seen; yet you do not receive our testimony." Later he castigates the *Ioudaioi*, who claim to know him: "You know me, and you know where I am from.

---

20. For a detailed survey, see Gilbert Van Belle, "'Salvation Is from the Jews': The Parenthesis in John 4:22b," in *Anti-Judaism and the Fourth Gospel: Papers of the Leuven Colloquium, 2000*, ed. R. Bieringer, Didier Pollefeyt, and F. Vandecasteele-Vanneuville (Assen: Royal Van Gorcum, 2001), 370–400.

I have not come on my own. But the one who sent me is true, and you do not know him. I know him, because I am from him, and he sent me" (7:28–29). And in 8:19, he tells the *Ioudaioi* that "you know neither me nor my Father. If you knew me, you would know my Father also." Only those who know Jesus to be the Christ can know the Father, as he tells the disciples: "If you know me, you will know my Father also. From now on you do know him and have seen him" (4:17). Indeed, those who have such knowledge will experience the life promised in 20:31: "And this is eternal life, that they may know you, the only true God, and Jesus Christ whom you have sent" (17:3). Given this strong emphasis, it would seem anomalous for Jesus to be referring to the *Ioudaioi* who "worship what we know."

The difficulty in interpreting 4:22 rests in great measure on the meaning of "from" in the phrase translated "salvation is from the Jews." The Greek preposition translated "from" is *ek* (sometimes *ex*). This preposition can mean "of" as in "a part of" or "can be found within." It can also mean "out of" or "emerging from."

Those who read 4:22 as the positive counterbalance to the negative portrayal of the Jews interpret "salvation is from the Jews" as "belonging to or reserved for Jews only." But in Greek the phrase can just as easily be read "salvation emerges from the Jews." John's point here is not to emphasize that the Jews are the origin of salvation but that Jesus is the one through whom salvation comes. In other words, Jesus, the Jew who, by rights, should not have been speaking to a Samaritan woman, is the salvation that comes from the Jews. This analysis supports the idea that, while *Ioudaioi* is a positive term here, the point of the verse is not to stress Jesus's Jewish origins so much as to draw attention to Jesus himself.

It may seem that an interpreter keen to avoid Judeophobic readings of this passage might do well to focus on the positive resonances of John 4:22 and downplay the christological and rhetorical elements of the verse in its context within the gospel. Taking this route, however, amounts to an apologetic reading that, perhaps paradoxically, may reinforce the anti-Judaism it is attempting to avoid. A more successful, as well as more critically defensible, approach is to situate this passage within its literary and theological context in John's Gospel. Doing so allows us to see that 4:22, like 8:44, contributes to the gospel's rhetorical program.

John 9:22

Unlike the letters of Paul, the gospels do not provide explicit information about the circumstances within which and for which they were written down. This has not prevented scholars from generating hypotheses to address these issues. In Johannine scholarship, the most widespread hypothesis is that first published by Martyn in his 1968 book *History and Theology in the Fourth Gospel*.[21]

According to Martyn, the gospel was written within and for a particular group of Christ-believers, often referred to as the "Johannine community." On the basis of three verses—9:22; 12:42; 16:2—that refer to a person who is outside the synagogue (an *aposynagōgos*), Martyn argues that a group of Jewish Christ-confessors, the so-called Johannine community, was expelled from the Jewish community ("the synagogue") on account of their confession of Jesus as the Christ. The gospel, including its hostile references to the *Ioudaioi*, was written in response to this traumatic experience. Martyn finds external corroboration for the expulsion hypothesis in the curse on the heretics (*Birkat Haminim*, the "blessing" concerning the heretics) that was added to the daily liturgy. On the basis of a sixth-century story in the Babylonian Talmud, Martyn argues that this curse was added in the late first century as a way of flushing Jewish Christ-confessors out of the worship service and thereby from the community.[22]

Popular as it is, the expulsion hypothesis is flawed on numerous grounds.[23] Detailed studies of *Birkat Haminim* show that it was not incorporated into the liturgy until the third century at the earliest.[24] Furthermore, there is no evidence for an established Johannine community in the late first century, nor is there evidence that Jewish Christians were excluded from synagogue worship, let alone from the community as a whole. On the contrary, the well-documented theological diversity within first-century Judaism makes it unlikely that Jews would have been excluded from the synagogue for believing Jesus to be the Messiah. Similar claims were made for Simeon Bar Kosiba in the period 132–35 and attributed to the prominent Rabbi Akiva, whose status

---

21. The most recent edition was published in 2003.

22. Martyn, *History and Theology in the Fourth Gospel*; Raymond Edward Brown, *The Community of the Beloved Disciple* (New York: Paulist, 1979).

23. For detailed discussion, see Adele Reinhartz, "The Johannine Community and Its Jewish Neighbors: A Reappraisal," in *What Is John?*, ed. Fernando F. Segovia (Atlanta: Scholars Press, 1998), 2:111–38.

24. Ruth Langer, *Cursing the Christians? A History of the Birkat Haminim* (New York: Oxford University Press, 2011); Reuven Kimelman, "Birkat Ha-Minim and the Lack of Evidence for an Anti-Christian Jewish Prayer in Late Antiquity," in *Jewish and Christian Self-Definition* (Philadelphia: Fortress, 1981), 2:226–44; Steven T. Katz, "Issues in the Separation of Judaism and Christianity after 70 CE: A Reconsideration," *Journal of Biblical Literature* 103 (1984): 43–76.

within rabbinic Judaism did not suffer as a result.[25] While the historicity of this rabbinic tradition cannot be verified, it casts some doubt on the claim that belief in Jesus as the Messiah would have generated such a strong response.

This verse, like 8:44, is part of John's rhetoric of disaffiliation. From a rhetorical perspective, the references to expulsion contribute to a rhetoric of fear that John used along with other strategies to construct a boundary between Christ-confessors and the *Ioudaioi*. By portraying characters who fear expulsion due to their faith, the gospel conveys the message that Christ-confessors have good reason to stay away from the Jews. Whether Christ-confessors experienced persecution at the hands of Jews or their authorities cannot be demonstrated. From a rhetorical perspective, however, the fear of such persecution can be powerful, even in the absence of any historical referent.

Conclusion

The presence of anti-Jewish or Judeophobic passages in John's Gospel presents a challenge especially to those for whom this gospel is a sacred, beloved, and inspirational text. Meeting that challenge, however, is not accomplished by an apologetic mode of interpretation. John's hostile statements about the *Ioudaioi* cannot be interpreted out of the text, nor can they be wished away. But they can be understood, and their Judeophobic potential disarmed, at least to some extent, by setting them in the context of John's overall rhetorical program. In doing so, we can view them not as the authoritative words of Jesus, meant to be normative for all Christians in all eras, but as the efforts of a late-first-century person or group using the various modes and devices of Greco-Roman rhetoric to persuade their audience to "believe that Jesus is the Messiah, the Son of God" (20:31), to affiliate with others who so believe, and to distance themselves from those who do not.

Discussion Questions and Activity Suggestions

1. There is a striking contrast between the sublime language and theology expressed especially in the lengthy discourses that the evangelist scripts for the character of Jesus and the hostility toward the *Ioudaioi* that is expressed in

25. Adele Reinhartz, "Rabbinic Perceptions of Simeon Bar Kosiba," *Journal for the Study of Judaism* 20.2 (1989): 171–94.

some of the statements by the narrator and Jesus. Do you think that readers should just accept the contrast, negotiate between, or somehow bring these two poles into alignment, and if so, how?

2. We do not know the precise identity of the person or people who contributed to the content, language, and structure of the Gospel of John as we now have it. A majority of Johannine scholars, however, believe that the author(s) was/were ethnic Jews. If correct, does or should such an identification affect how we interpret the gospel's hostile statements about the *Ioudaioi*?

3. In John 5:18, the narrator explains that one reason the *Ioudaioi* persecuted Jesus was that he was "calling God his own Father, thereby making himself equal to God." Is this accusation borne out by the rest of the gospel? Possible answers: Yes; no; yes and no.

4. The gospel presents itself as a narrative written from the perspective of a follower of Jesus, perhaps even the so-called Beloved Disciple himself (19:35; cf. 13:23), whom we might refer to as the narrator as well as the implied author of this book. The implied author presents a clear perspective on Jesus's identity and mission and stresses that eternal life—an undefined but positive state of being—is possible only by having faith in Jesus as the Messiah and Son of God. This perspective is presented forcefully throughout the gospel, and the gospel, through its rhetoric, strongly encourages its audience to agree with the implied author's views about Jesus and eternal life and also, one might suggest, about the *Ioudaioi* who do not believe. For this exercise, imagine how listeners or readers who do not (yet) share these views might respond to the Fourth Gospel. How might this gospel be heard by those who are Jewish and interested in the gospel's message, Jewish and rejecting of the gospel's message, Samaritans who may or may not be inclined to believe the gospel's truth claims, and gentiles (non-Jewish participants in Roman worship of various types)?

Further Reading

Bieringer, R., Didier Pollefeyt, and F. Vandecasteele-Vanneuville, eds. *Anti-Judaism and the Fourth Gospel: Papers of the Leuven Colloquium, 2000*. Assen: Royal Van Gorcum, 2001.

Culpepper, R. Alan. "Anti-Judaism in the Fourth Gospel as a Theological Problem for Christian Interpreters." Pages 68–91 in *Anti-Judaism and the Fourth Gospel: Papers of the Leuven Colloquium, 2000*. Edited by R. Bieringer, Didier Pollefeyt, and F. Vandecasteele-Vanneuville. Assen: Royal Van Gorcum, 2001.

Reinhartz, Adele. *Cast out of the Covenant: Jews and Anti-Judaism in the Gospel of John.* Lanham, MD: Lexington/Fortress, 2018.

———. "The Johannine Community and Its Jewish Neighbors: A Reappraisal." Pages 111–38 in *What Is John?* Vol. 2. Edited by Fernando F. Segovia. Atlanta: Scholars Press, 1998.

Wilson, Tom. *Jesus and the Ioudaioi: Reading John's Gospel with Jewish People in Mind.* Newcastle upon Tyne, UK: Cambridge Scholars Publishing, 2020.

14

Acts of the Apostles

SHELLY MATTHEWS

Acts narrates events among followers of "the Way," from the time of Jesus's ascension to Paul's imprisonment in Rome. While the traditional ascription, the Acts of the Apostles, may lead readers to expect accounts of each of the individual apostles, the narrative focuses attention first upon Peter, who functions as chief spokesperson for the Twelve in Jerusalem (Acts 1–8, 10–12); and then upon Paul who, after his conversion, transverses regions of the northeastern Mediterranean proclaiming Jesus as Messiah before facing arrest in Jerusalem, trial in Caesarea, and transport to Rome under military surveillance (Acts 9, 13–28).[1]

Christian tradition ascribes both the Third Gospel and Acts to the same author: Luke "the physician" and traveling companion of Paul (compare Luke 1:1–4 and Acts 1:1 for indications that the same author is writing both volumes for his patron, Theophilus; see Col 4:14 and 2 Tim 4:11 for references to a certain Luke as Paul's companion). Current scholarly consensus holds that both volumes were produced by the same author. But the view that he was a contemporary of Paul and a physician is no longer widely held for several reasons. The so-called we-passages in Acts (16:10–17; 20:5–15; 21:1–18; 27:1–28:16) were once regarded as the author's eyewitness testimony, but are now considered as literary embellishment. Suggested dates for the composition of Acts range from 85 CE to the early decades of the second century, dates well beyond Paul's death. Once the rug is pulled out from under the claim that Paul's com-

---

1. Philip (8:26–40) and James (15:13–21; 21:17–26) have cameo roles. Though he is a deacon, not an apostle, the Stephen episode is also prominent (6:1–8:1).

panion wrote Luke and Acts, so also falls the claim that the companion is the physician named in Colossians 4:14.[2]

Acts is not a historical work, at least not according to modern sensibilities concerning historical narrative. While moderns expect histories to reflect past events "accurately," ancient historians regarded history writing as an exercise in elite ideology—as a means of instilling in its readers the values they should emulate. From this perspective, since elite heroes are by definition virtuous, they should be depicted in histories and biographies as speaking virtuously and doing virtuous deeds. Conversely, villains should be described in language that signals their repellence. A common ancient rhetorical form, known from Greek school handbooks, was the *chreia*, a Greek word meaning "use" or "service." *Chreiai* were pithy anecdotes composed to highlight the exemplary or disreputable deeds of named figures from the past, for the purpose of instructing readers/hearers on how and how not to behave. Ancient narratives, including histories, novels, biographies (and gospels!), are chock full of *chreiai*, a literary form guided less by questions of historical accuracy than by concerns of usefulness in teaching virtue.[3]

The preface to Luke-Acts shows that the author shares these concerns (Luke 1:1–4). He aims to compose "an orderly account," providing for his elite patron Theophilus security or reassurance (Greek *tēn asphaleian*, often translated "truth"; cf. NRSV Luke 1:4). To provide such order and reassurance to an elite patron, Luke showcases virtuous speeches and deeds of the movement's protagonists. He also establishes clear boundaries between the movement's heroes on the one hand and evildoers, rabble-rousers, and seditious plotters on the other.

The Heroic Paul

The clearest beneficiary of Acts' program to reassure Theophilus, by bringing order to the events involving Jesus-followers and by idealizing its protagonists according to Roman understandings of virtue, is Paul. Once Paul converts from persecutor to chief spokesperson for the movement, his nobility and

2. For a classic refutation of the proposal that Luke-Acts contains specialized medical vocabulary signaling the author's status as physician, see Henry J. Cadbury, "Lexical Notes on Luke-Acts II: Recent Arguments for Medical Language," *Journal of Biblical Literature* 45 (1926): 190–209.

3. For a brief introduction to the *chreia* form and its relevance to the gospels, see David B. Gowler, "The Chreia," in *The Historical Jesus in Context*, ed. Amy-Jill Levine, Dale C. Allison Jr., and John Dominic Crossan (Princeton: Princeton University Press, 2006), 132–48.

virtue radiate from the pages. In modern parlance, we might say Acts is an instance of Pauline "fan fiction."

Paul is portrayed as a Roman citizen, a standing he merits through birth rather than through the less prestigious route of purchase (22:27–28; cf. 16:37). He is also a citizen of the preeminent city of Tarsus (21:39). Furthermore, he is a Pharisee, and not just any Pharisee, but one who learned at the feet of the esteemed Gamaliel (22:3). (Paul's status as Roman citizen, something he does not mention in his own letters, likely owes to Luke's idealizing program, rather than to historical accuracy. The suggestion that he is both a citizen of a leading Greek city—a status requiring immersion in polytheistic city liturgies—and a devotee of Gamaliel also strains credulity.)

Acts depicts Paul as a man of astounding achievements. Paul converts the Roman proconsul of Cyprus, Sergius Paulus, by his effective curse of Elymas (13:7). Roman proconsuls, appointed by the emperor to govern provinces, were drawn from the most rarefied layer of the imperial elite. Thus, Acts attributes to Paul the conversion of the highest Roman government official to Christ belief until the time of Constantine. Paul's physical endurance resembles that of the "Energizer Bunny" from modern American television commercials promoting reliable batteries. Left for dead after a stoning at Lystra (14:19–20), he springs up to undertake his missionary journey without any recharging necessary. Paul heals disease by the mere touch from his handkerchiefs (19:12), raises the dead (20:10), commandeers terrified sailors during a tempest (27:21–38), and survives a snake bite on Malta that would have killed an ordinary mortal (28:3–6).

Most of all, Paul offers speeches—eloquent speeches concerning the role of Jesus in the plan of the God of Israel, perfectly crafted for each audience he faces. During the time Acts was composed, oratory was the battleground on which elite Roman manhood was achieved. Skilled oratory required both intellectual and physical prowess: considerable schooling, the strength to perform under the weight of a heavy toga, projecting the voice in large open-air settings without technical aids for amplification, managing expected gestures gracefully, and reacting deftly to unscripted audience response. The classicist Maude Gleason refers to oratory in this time period as the "calisthenics of manhood."[4] Though Paul in his letters admits to physical infirmity, bodily weakness, and contemptible speech (e.g., 2 Cor 10:10; Gal 4:13–14), Acts presents Paul as orator exemplar, the epitome of elite Roman manhood.

---

4. Maude Gleason, *Making Men: Sophists and Self-Presentation in Ancient Rome* (Princeton: Princeton University Press, 1995), xxii.

In spite of Paul's virtues, he is repeatedly charged with criminal activity. Paul endures beating and imprisonment in Philippi (Acts 16:19–40), stands before a Roman tribunal in Corinth on charges of lawbreaking (18:12–16), barely escapes being caught up in disturbances concerning "the Way" in Ephesus (19:21–40), and is finally arrested for charges of subversion in Jerusalem (21:28). Yet, as the narrator and several prominent spokespersons make clear time and again, the charges against Paul are always false. Philippian magistrates apologize to Paul for his mistreatment (16:39); the Roman proconsul Gallio proclaims Paul's innocence (18:14–15); the Asiarchs of Ephesus (exceedingly high-placed governmental officials) advocate on his behalf (19:31); Roman centurions bend over backward to rescue and protect him (23:25–35; 27:1, 3, 43); Roman governors and Jewish kings acknowledge his innocence (23:29; 25:25; 26:31). Charges that Jesus-believers were criminal would have been of particular concern to a reader like the "most excellent Theophilus." Acts acknowledges that such charges were made, but then redirects them onto another social group, to which we now turn.

The Nonbelieving Jews/*Hoi Ioudaioi*

Standing in stark contrast to the heroic Paul of the Acts narrative are Jewish groups who do not believe in Jesus, often designated simply as "the Jews" (Greek *hoi ioudaioi*).[5] While Acts' idealization of the postconversion Paul is relatively straightforward, its treatment of "the Jews" is more complex. There are three aspects of that complexity:

1. In the case of individual Jews, to be a Jew (*Ioudaios*) can be regarded as a positive identity marker. The best example of this is, once again, the heroic Paul. Twice, in self-defense, Paul identifies himself as a Jew, using the emphatic formula *egō eimi* ("I am") as he does so (Greek *egō eimi Ioudaios*; 21:39; 22:3). Individual missionaries for the Jesus group, such as Apollos, are introduced as Jews (18:24). The Pharisee Gamaliel is portrayed as learned and prudent, even though he does not confess Jesus as Messiah (5:34–39).

2. Groups of Jews (*Ioudaioi*) can be regarded positively, especially if they are spokespersons for the movement or come to believe in Jesus. The Jewish-

---

5. Curiously, when Acts depicts this group as hostile to the Way, it seldom uses the qualifier "*some of* the Jews," but prefers the plural noun form with the definite article: "The Jews/*hoi Ioudaioi*."

ness of neither the Jerusalem apostles nor the deacons appointed to assist them (6:1–7) is questioned or criticized; all of the spokespersons and missionaries of the Jesus group are Jews. The coming to belief of myriads of Jews in Jerusalem is a cause for celebration (21:20).

3. Members of the Jesus group engage in the signature practices of Jewish piety—prayer, temple worship, sacred vows, and reverence for scripture. The Jerusalem apostles congregate at the temple (3:1; 5:12–16). Paul himself is vigorously defended as a strict adherent of the law (21:20–24).

Because of the positive valence that a single *Ioudaios*, or some *Ioudaioi*, or Jewish practices of piety can have in Acts, some interpreters argue that (Luke-) Acts mitigates anti-Jewish hostility—at least in comparison to the Gospels of Matthew (with its harsh polemic against Pharisees and other Jewish leaders; Matt 23) and John (with its explicit denunciation of "the Jews" as children of the devil; John 8:44). But we argue here that (Luke-)Acts does not so much soften anti-Jewish polemic as to embed anti-Judaism on a different plane than the Gospels of John, Matthew, or Mark. Instead of denigrating Jewish piety, Jewish institutions such as temple or law, or Jewish leaders such as the Pharisees, Acts' anti-Judaism is largely in the realm of sociology—Roman imperial sociology to be precise.[6]

Consider Acts' negative depictions of nonbelieving groups of Jews.[7] The Jews who deny Jesus as Messiah, or who oppose Jesus's earthly representatives, are depicted as the story's villains. Their villainy does not come into focus so much in the realm of ideas—that is, through their inadequate arguments, or what we might call "bad theology"—but rather as a matter of horrendous deeds. These deeds stand in defiance of ideal Roman social protocols. The Romans valued dutiful and obedient subjects, civic restraint, orderly legal proceedings, piety toward the gods. "The Jews" in Acts violate these values

---

6. Shelly Matthews, *Perfect Martyr: The Stoning of Stephen and the Construction of Christian Identity* (Oxford: Oxford University Press, 2010); see also Lawrence Wills, "The Depiction of Jews in Luke-Acts," *Journal of Biblical Literature* 110 (1991): 631–54.

7. As I argued previously, the instance of Apollos nicely illustrates the tension in Acts between individual Jews with positive valence and "the Jews" as a negative foil. Apollos is introduced in Acts 18:24–28 as "a certain Jew" from Alexander. Apollos is of considerable value to the movement because he powerfully "refutes the Jews" in public debate, through proving from scripture that Jesus is the Messiah. The identification of "a Jew" who refutes "the Jews" captures the tension that is frequently found in Acts' employment of the singular and plural forms *Ioudaios/hoi Ioudaioi*. See Matthews, *Perfect Martyr*, 7.

at nearly every turn in their incessant pursuit of violence toward followers of the Way.

The trial and stoning of Stephen is a programmatic case (6:8–8:1). Jews from a wide variety of regions engage in a host of improper legal procedures as they bring Stephen to trial: they procure false charges, stir up opposition, and set up false witnesses (6:11–14). What begins as a sham trial ends in a chaotic murder, as Stephen is dragged out to be stoned. While Romans devised many means by which to punish evildoers, they avoided the practice of stoning in legal procedures, regarding stoning as a mob action, symptomatic of bad social order. Acts demonstrates precisely this bad order on the part of "the Jews" by showing how Stephen is killed.

This horrendous behavior of nonbelieving Jewish groups is highlighted both in speeches emphasizing the role of "the Jews" in the killing of Jesus and in narratives concerning attempts to kill Paul, considered below. Here we note in more general terms how the bad behavior that leads to the stoning of Stephen is replicated across the Acts narrative. Peter, Stephen, and Paul accuse various groupings of Jews of having killed Jesus.[8] In his preconverted state, Paul/(Saul) "breathes threats and murder" upon followers of the way (9:1) and is complicit in Stephen's killing (8:1, 3; 22:19–20). Once he is converted, Paul becomes the constant target of lawless attempts on his life. These attempts begin in Damascus immediately after his conversion, where "the Jews" are said to patrol the city gates "day and night" in their plot to murder him (9:23–24). "The Jews" stir up mobs (17:5; 21:27), hurl stones (14:19), scream for Paul's death (21:36), and vow to kill him (23:12, 14, 21).

In short, while the author of Acts is skilled enough to include variation of detail as his narrative unfolds, the basic schema nevertheless holds: Jews who believe in Jesus demonstrate virtue; any charges of sedition or lawlessness on their part are false; their persecution is undeserved. "The Jews"/*hoi Ioudaioi* who do not believe in Jesus are lawless and bloodthirsty; their behavior in Acts conforms to the worst of ancient anti-Jewish stereotypes, which depict the Jews as a people who violate Roman/(human) norms and who are perpetually engaged in sedition (cf. the harsh assessment of the Jews by Roman historian Tacitus, *History* 5.4–12).

This twofold depiction in Acts of Jesus-believers as "good Jews" and Jesus-renouncers as "bad Jews" is likely a rhetorical strategy born of its author's anxious circumstance. If the early Christian apologists reflect a circumstance

---

8. For elaboration on these accusations, see below and also Matthews, *Perfect Martyr*, 58–60.

similar to the one faced in Acts (and we believe they do), many followers of Jesus in this time were ridiculed as superstitious, gullible, antisocial, and possibly seditious.[9] Consider the charges laid against believers in Thessalonica, that they "turn the world upside down" and "act contrary to the decrees of the emperor" (17:6–7; cf. 16:20–21; 24:5). While Jews at this time were also thought by many to be antisocial and seditious (as noted above with respect to Tacitus), Jews still had a relatively greater measure of social capital than Christians, owing to their antiquity, reverence for Moses as an ancient lawgiver, and their integration into the major cities of the Mediterranean region.

In light of the hostility faced by his own group, and the (slightly) more positive assessment of the Jews across the Roman Empire, the author of Acts splits the difference between attitudes toward Jews in his narrative. On the one hand, the law-abiding and respectable Jews follow the Way and accept Jesus as Messiah. They read the scriptures rightly, observe Jewish law, and do not engage in disorderly conduct. On the other hand, those who deny Jesus as Messiah embody the negative social traits associated with Jews.

Acts and Judeophobia

Violence against Stephen Justifies Violence against Jews

The earliest use of Acts by Christians to justify violence against Jews may date to 418, on the Island of Minorca. In a letter of this date attributed to the Christian bishop Severus, the story unfolds that Christians of the island destroyed a Jewish synagogue by setting it on fire and then proceeded to terrorize the island's Jews in hopes of converting them. The impetus for the attack is the arrival of St. Stephen's relics to the island, relics that cause great upset to the Christians. The upset may have owed to recollection of Stephen's martyrdom at the hands of the Jews, the story preserved in Acts noted above.

Caveats are necessary. First, while the *relics* of St. Stephen are said to ignite the religious fervor that leads to the hostilities, the story of Stephen's martyrdom in Acts is not referenced in the letter and Stephen is not featured prominently as Severus details the synagogue's burning and subsequent forced

---

9. For an example of pagan critique of Christians, see Minucius Felix, *Octavius*. For commentary, see Shelly Matthews, *The Acts of the Apostles: Taming the Tongues of Fire*, Phoenix New Testament Guides (Sheffield: Sheffield Phoenix, 2013), 45–47.

conversion.[10] Second, while the recent critical edition of Severus's letter assumes the event's historicity, the letter may serve not as historical record, but rather as a "how-to manual" for bringing about mass conversion.[11] Caveats aside, the letter constructs the peaceful Christians and the violent Jews similarly to the way that Acts does: "We brought books in order to instruct; you brought swords and clubs to commit murder. We wish to increase; you desire to destroy . . . you thirst for blood while we thirst for your salvation."[12] Further, whether historical or not, the document endorses violence for the purpose of conversion: burning and looting the synagogue and then terrifying the surviving Jews with violent threats.

While this may or may not be the earliest recorded use of Acts for violent ends, a most recent citation of Acts to justify killing Jews is not ambiguous. The shooter who murdered a woman and injured several others at the Poway Synagogue in California, in April 2019, wrote a screed against Jews to explain his deed that includes the murder of Stephen among the justification for his violence. He argued that the violence and killing of Jews is deserved owing to "their persecution of Christians of old (including the prophets of ancient Israel—Jeremiah, Isaiah, etc. [sic]), members of the early church (*Stephen—whose death at the hands of the Jews was both heart-wrenching and rage-inducing*) . . . [and] their role in the murder of the Son of Man—that is the Christ."[13]

Acts Depicts Jews as Violent and Conspiratorial

The larger harm of Acts' depictions of "the Jews" may not lie in explicit instances where someone engaged in Judeophobic violence first points to a specific passage from this book to justify violence. Its larger harm may owe to its influence in shaping the deeper structures of Western consciousness. Acts is the single narrative of postresurrection apostolic activity in scripture, one revered and studied by countless Christians across time. Its repeated accusation that Jews killed Jesus and then plotted in large numbers to kill the chief repre-

---

10. Severus of Minorca, *Letter on the Conversion of the Jews*, ed. and trans. Scott Bradbury, Oxford Early Christian Texts (Oxford: Clarendon, 1996), 43–45.

11. Bernard S. Bachrach, review of *Severus of Minorca: Letter on the Conversion of the Jews*, ed. and trans. Scott Bradbury, *Speculum* 73.4 (1998): 1167–69.

12. Severus of Minorca, *Letter on the Conversion of the Jews* 12.9–10.

13. DTTTM, "The Anti-Jewish Manifesto of John T. Earnest, the San Diego Synagogue Shooter" (15 May 2019) (https://tinyurl.com/4ckhbwm3) (emphasis added).

sentatives of Jesus among his followers likely frames Christian understanding of Jews to an extent that is impossible to measure.

I was first writing this chapter in the immediate aftermath of an antisemitic incident in my local community—Dallas-Fort Worth, Texas—that received global attention: on January 21, 2022, Malik Faisil Akram, a British national, traveled to the United States and held hostage members of the Beth Israel synagogue in Colleyville, Texas. He demanded that they work to free Aafia Siddiqui, a high-profile Pakistani woman from a federal prison in neighboring Fort Worth. As Yair Rosenberg, a contributor to the *Atlantic* magazine, noted about the incident:

> After Akram pulled a gun on the congregation, he demanded to speak to the rabbi of New York's Central Synagogue, who he claimed could authorize the release of Aafia Siddiqui. . . . Obviously, this is not how the prison system works. "This was somebody who literally thought that Jews control the world," Beth Israel Rabbi Charlie Cytron-Walker told *The Forward*. "He thought he could come into a synagogue, and we could get on the phone with the 'Chief Rabbi of America' and he would get what he needed."[14]

Contemporary analysts of the nature of the antisemitism fueling this hostage taker's actions point to the widespread antisemitic belief that the Jews, even though they compose a tiny fraction of the world's population, somehow conspire to control the world.[15]

This hostage taker does not, of course, ground his conspiratorial outlook in the Acts of the Apostles. But our broader point is that someone holding such conspiratorial views would not be dissuaded of those views by reading Acts. While violent agents against the Jews are often fueled by fringe internet websites, the Acts of the Apostles is read from church lecterns and studied in Sunday schools around the world. The wicked behaviors assigned to nonbelieving Jews in Acts align with the wicked behaviors that continue to be attributed to Jews today. This wickedness has been continually pointed to in order to justify violent acts against them.

14. Yair Rosenberg, "Why So Many People Still Do Not Understand Anti-Semitism," *Atlantic*, 19 January 2022 (https://tinyurl.com/ypxjzryu).

15. In addition to the citation to Rosenberg in the previous note, see also Laura E. Adkins, "The Myth That Jews Are All-Powerful Is the Biggest Threat to Jewish Lives," *Washington Post*, 20 January 2022 (https://tinyurl.com/368xmns6).

Jews as "Incomplete" Christians

Before turning to examine two passages in Acts in which the wickedness of "the Jews" is depicted starkly, we pause to consider a different sort of Judeophobic understanding that a reader of Acts might draw—one not predicated on violent depictions of Jews. As noted previously, all representatives for the Jesus group in Acts are Jewish, and Jews who convert to Jesus belief are celebrated. This feature of Acts sets it apart from traditional forms of antisemitism, in which Jewishness is considered as an inferior racial essence that cannot be eradicated, even through conversion. Some biblical scholars go so far as to argue that Acts is not anti-Jewish because Jewish conversion is celebrated in this way.

But still, celebrating Jews only if they are converts, or potential converts, to belief in Jesus as Messiah is also a form of Judeophobia. It is a classic Christian conceit to imagine that "true Jews" are those who convert to Christianity. To hold this hope is to assume that Judaism as an identity apart from Christ belief is inadequate. The imagined conversion of Jews in Acts is an early expression of that longstanding Christian hope. For example, prayers for the conversion of the Jews on Good Friday in many Christian traditions were prayed for millennia and are sometimes still prayed today. These prayers do not reflect good will toward Jews *as Jews*, but rather the desire of Christians for Jews to confirm the truth of Christianity.

The Christ-Killing Charge in the Speeches in Acts

The justification of antisemitic violence on the grounds that "the Jews" killed Jesus is widely known and typically associated with the passion narratives of the gospels. This charge is mitigated in the gospels, to greater or lesser extent, through the concession that Roman officials were involved in this crucifixion. In each canonical gospel, the Roman governor Pilate takes a chief role in administering the verdict, and Roman soldiers nail Jesus to the cross. The concession in the gospels that Romans were involved reflects the historical fact that crucifixion was a Roman punishment. It hints at the historical likelihood that the Roman authorities governing Judea subjected Jesus to this cruel punishment for the crime of sedition. But in Acts the charge that *Jews* killed Jesus is heightened, distilled, and repeated multiple times: in the speeches of Peter (2:22–23, 36; 3:12–15a; 4:8b–10a, 28–29; 5:30; 10:39—seven times total), Stephen (once, at 7:51–52), and Paul (once, at 13:27–28). The effect of these multiple charges is that Roman agency in the death all but disappears.

Acts 4:27–30 includes Pilate with Herod and the gentiles with the people of Israel in a global conspiracy to kill Jesus.[16] That Jerusalemites must work through Pilate to get Jesus killed is acknowledged in 13:27–28. The remaining seven speeches in Acts that recount the death of Jesus assign responsibility to Jewish groups alone. The accusations ring stark:

- "This Jesus whom you crucified" (2:36 NRSV)
- "You rejected the Holy and Righteous One and asked to have a murderer given to you, and you killed the Author of life, whom God raised from the dead" (3:14–15 NRSV)
- "You stiff-necked people, uncircumcised in heart and ears, you are forever opposing the Holy Spirit, just as your ancestors used to do. Which of the prophets did your ancestors not persecute? They killed those who foretold the coming of the Righteous One, and now you have become his betrayers and murders" (7:51–52 NRSV)

In two passages, the Roman cross becomes a Jewish "lynching tree":

- "The God of our ancestors raised up Jesus, whom you had killed by hanging him on a tree" (5:30 NRSV; cf. 10:39).

All accusations are addressed to Jewish audiences. No Roman audience (for example, the Roman centurion Cornelius addressed by Peter in Acts 10 or the Roman governor Felix addressed by Paul in 24:10–21) hears accusation that Romans played a part in killing Jesus.

In a remarkably unfortunate sign of Christian unity, Orthodox, Catholic, and Protestant lectionaries coincide in assigning these stark speeches from Acts accusing Jews of killing Jesus, during the liturgical season of Easter. For example, in the Common Lectionary, which assigns scripture readings over a three-year cycle, readings from Acts are substituted for readings from the Hebrew Bible during the seven Sundays of Easter. In every year of the three-year cycle, at least one of the speeches noted above is assigned for Sunday lectionary reading, and in some years these accusatorial speeches appear over two consecutive Sundays. It is left to Christian priests, ministers, and others

---

16. For more on this passage, see Matthews, *Perfect Martyr*, 59.

who offer sermons on these holy days to decide whether to address the problem these passages create.

In these accusations of Christ killing, the groups responsible are never said to be "the Jews"/*hoi Ioudaioi*. They are rather "residents of Jerusalem," "rulers," "Israelites," and sometimes "you"—the Jewish groups listening to Peter, Paul, and Stephen speak. Because the specific agents accused in these speeches can vary, some argue that Acts restricts blame for the killing of Jesus to a subgroup of Jews, rather than to the Jews as a whole. It is more difficult to argue that Acts limits depictions of nonbelieving Jews as acting murderously to a subgroup, if one considers how Jewish groups in Acts continue to plot against Jesus's representatives, apart from the crucifixion—this is the case with the plot to kill Paul in 23:12–35.

The Plot to Kill Paul in Cold Blood in Acts 23:12–35

While Paul is under arrest in Jerusalem, Acts tells how "the Jews"/*hoi Ioudaioi* conspire to kill him. We know this is an important story to the author of Acts, for as with other signature episodes, the details are reported three times (23:12–13, 14–15, 20–21).[17] The passage lays out clearly who the agents of murder are, using the term *Ioudaioi* three times (23:12, 20, 27). The number of plotters is specified: "more than forty." With respect to biblical numerology, forty is not a random number. Rather, it represents completeness, and thus can stand for the whole. To say that more than forty *Ioudaioi* are complicit in the plot is to suggest the involvement of all *Ioudaioi*. Lest the culpability of the group as a whole remain in any doubt, Acts reports that plotters work in cooperation with the leaders of *hoi Ioudaioi* (23:14–15, 20).

The wickedness of the deed is underscored by the multiple use of terms for oath taking—*anathematizō* and *anathema* (23:12, 14, 21). As virtually every contractual agreement in the ancient Mediterranean world was sealed by a sacred oath ritual, ancient readers would have been widely familiar with the significance of oath taking. Questions of the piety or impiousness of various oath takers was a stock scene in ancient drama and literature. Readers of scenes in which oath taking occurs would recognize that those who foreswear oaths are inviting divinely initiated execution (consider the fate of Ananias

---

17. Other episodes that are recounted three times in the Acts narrative include the conversion of Saul/Paul (9:1–19; 22:1–21; 26:9–23) and Cornelius's vision concerning Peter (10:1–6, 23–32; 11:13–14).

and Sapphira; 5:1–11). As Albert Harrill notes, the pledge to kill Paul inverts the function of the sacred oath, rendering them as "functional atheists who do not fear that the Lord will act on foreswearing. Their plot of murder and lawlessness reveal their unbelief in divine judgment."[18]

As with the Christ-killing charge made in the speeches, so the story of the plot against Paul positions nonbelieving Jews in a negative light. Unfortunately, these depictions of "the Jews"/*hoi Ioudaioi* as lawless murders and of Jesus-believers as innocent victims deflect from a historical situation that would have been much more complex. Violence under the Roman Empire would have had a number of perpetrators and a number of kinds of victims. Many Jews—Jesus-believers or not—suffered under empire. We may imagine that sometimes the violence was intra-Jewish, as various groups competed for a measure of security in a situation of precariousness. Further, we may imagine that Jews devoted to Jesus sometimes acted in solidarity with Jews who did not accept messianic claims for him, or that Jesus-believers themselves sometimes initiated violence against others. But to employ such historical imagination requires that one step away from the Acts narrative that offers up, with few exceptions, this binary of Jewish persecutor / Christian victim.

Discussion Questions and Activity Suggestions

1. As noted above, many Christians throughout history have held out hope that Jews might prove the truth of Christianity by converting. Is it necessarily a bad thing to hope for others to convert to one's own faith? Identify some strategies for how Christians might better understand Judaism as a religion *on its own terms.*

2. Admittedly, the argument of this essay that the depiction in Acts of nonbelieving Jews/*Ioudaioi* as killers has embedded itself into Western consciousness is difficult to prove. Do you think the more well-known depictions of the role of Jews in the passion narratives of the gospel play a larger role in Christian understandings of Jews than Acts? How would you assess the influence of Acts with respect to questions of Judeophobia, in comparison to the influence of the gospels? Or of the Pauline letters?

3. This essay suggests that Acts is not concerned with historical accuracy in the way that modern readers might expect. Does such an assertion trouble you?

18. Albert Harrill, "Divine Judgement against Ananias and Sapphira (Acts 5:1–11): A Stock Scene of Perjury and Death," *Journal of Biblical Literature* 30 (2011): 351–69 at 365.

How would you support your own views on questions of the New Testament and historicity? What sources might you turn to in order to understand the history of the early Jesus movement?

4. While depictions of nonbelieving Jews as violent are typical in Acts, there are exceptions. For example, Gamaliel advocates on behalf of the apostles before the council (5:34–39), and Paul reaches out to Pharisees (23:6–9). How important are exceptions such as these in assessing Acts' treatment of "the Jews"?

5. Divide the book of Acts into four or five sections (depending on the size of the class), and assign groups to each section to analyze the nature of violent episodes within. What are the proper names associated with perpetrators? With victims? What is the nature of the violence? Chart results in the classic form used by journalists: who, what, where, when, and why?

6. Explore the lectionary readings from the book of Acts assigned by various Christian groups (e.g., Catholic, Protestant, Orthodox), especially during the liturgical season of Easter. Identify passages that lay blame at the feet of various Jewish groups for Jesus's crucifixion. Discuss whether it would be possible to influence the church's use of such readings in liturgical settings (whether on a local or a more centralized level).

Further Reading

Matthews, Shelly. *The Acts of the Apostles: Taming the Tongues of Fire*. Phoenix New Testament Guides. Sheffield: Sheffield Phoenix, 2013. Reissued as *The Acts of the Apostles: Introduction and Study Guide; Taming the Tongues of Fire*. London: T&T Clark, 2017.

———. *Perfect Martyr: The Stoning of Stephen and the Construction of Christian Identity*. Oxford: Oxford University Press, 2010.

Smith, Dennis E., and Joseph B. Tyson. *Acts and Christian Beginnings: The Acts Seminar Report*. Salem, OR: Polebridge, 2013.

Wills, Lawrence. "The Depiction of Jews in Luke-Acts." *Journal of Biblical Literature* 110 (1991): 631–54.

15

Romans

BRIAN YONG LEE

M any educators will recognize this pattern. Students nod their heads when confronted with the historical facts: Jesus was a Jew, Paul was a Jew, Christian teaching does not reject the vast majority of torah. But, to our great frustration, at the end of the semester one still hears from students reasoning and interpretation grounded in assumptions and tropes long used in the construction of anti-Jewish stereotypes and nowhere found in the Bible: the many commandments of the Jewish law lead to a forgetfulness of God's mercy and grace, invite human arrogance, reduce faith to a mechanical application of rules, and engender a merciless moralism and rejection of the sinner. These homiletic tropes are solidly engrained in Christian thinking, because the New Testament tended to use other first-century forms of Judaism, with which Christ-following Judaism was in competition, as a foil for explaining Jesus's message. In Sunday morning sermons, early Christian rhetoric tends to become anachronistically construed as a binary, essentialist, truism: *the pursuit of (Christian) virtue entails the denunciation of (Jewish) vice.* For the educator, it can often feel that no amount of historical reasoning introduced in our courses can make a dent in this anti-Jewish framework shared by so many of our well-intentioned students (and now, writing almost three months after October 7, 2023, I fear that this problem has grown even more complex, and yet ever more urgent).

The unexamined fallacy underlying the widespread essentialist view is that Judaism and Christianity were separate, categorically opposed, religions in the first century. Paul's letters have historically played a key role in this anti-Jewish construction of the New Testament. The Letter to the Romans, in particular, which focuses on explaining Paul's understanding of "justification by faith apart from works of the law" (Rom 3:28) is often seen as a linchpin in the anti-Jewish interpretation of Paul.

In recent years the historical-critical work of rereading Paul's letters in their first-century context has done much to demonstrate the need to critically interrogate the deeply Protestant reading instincts of academic Pauline studies and the falsity of the anti-Jewish Paul. This essay seeks to offer guidance through this scholarship by identifying texts, concepts, and arguments key to the debates. I will argue that Paul's statements on the law should be seen as intra-Jewish rather than supersessionist discourse,[1] that Paul's intended readers should be identified as gentiles, and that situating Paul's letters in these terms helps to dismantle Judeophobic readings of Paul's letters.

Starting from Consensus: From Treatise to Letter

Matthew Novenson quips that "never are Protestants more Protestant, we might say, than when they are reading Paul."[2] This centrality of Paul for Protestant theology, Novenson suggests, means that just as Jews and Judaism function as a foil for Jesus's message in Paul, through Paul, they do so also for Christian self-understanding.[3] From Reformation founder Martin Luther to twentieth-century German Lutheran scholar Ernst Käsemann,[4] the antagonist to Paul's

---

1. Where some scholars characterize Paul's theology as supersessionist I would categorize it as belonging to intra-Jewish claims to normatively define Jewish identity, teaching, and practice. In my view, using the term "supersessionism" to refer to intra-Jewish claims to normatively define Judaism is imprecise and gets in the way of accurately representing and differentiating early Christian claims before and after "the parting of the ways." While I grant that Paul's two-ages apocalyptic worldview, which differentiates between his faith-centered gospel and law-centered Judaism as "what was set aside" and "the permanent" (2 Cor 3:11) and describes the churches of God as a new creation (5:17), represents a particularly strong form of intra-Jewish claim to redefine normative Judaism, I still insist on a categorical difference between Paul's understanding of the difference between faith and law in the first century (or Qumran apocalyptic sectarianism) and later Christian interpretation of Paul after Christianity and Judaism came to see themselves as two separate religious systems.

2. Matthew Novenson, "Anti-Judaism and Philo-Judaism in Pauline Studies, Then and Now," in *Protestant Bible Scholarship: Antisemitism, Philosemitism, and Anti-Judaism*, ed. Arjen F. Bakker et al., Journal for the Study of Judaism Supplement 200 (Leiden: Brill, 2022), 106-124 at 109.

3. As someone with teaching experience in a Catholic university as well as a Catholic seminary, I can say with confidence that this issue is alive and well in Catholic educational contexts as well.

4. As Ernst Käsemann ("Justification and Salvation History in the Letter to the Romans,"

doctrine of justification is the Jew; but "the Jew" for Luther stands for all those who reject "justification by faith alone," whether "Jews or Turks or papists or sectarians,"[5] and becomes a psychological archetype in Käsemann: "Israel has exemplary significance for [Paul]; in and with Israel he strikes at the hidden Jew in all of us, at the man who validates rights and demands over against God."[6]

Paul's Letter to the Romans holds a particular pride of place in this tradition, because it was long viewed as a privileged window onto Pauline theology. Late medieval, Renaissance, and Reformation writers in particular often characterized Romans as a dogmatic treatise, from Philip Melanchthon's "summary of all Christian doctrine" to Günther Bornkamm's "last will and testament of the Apostle Paul." Read as such, the document's binary contrasts between "the works of the law" and "faith" easily lend themselves to later supersessionist understandings of the relationship between Christian faith and Jewish law.

Contemporary historical-critical interpretation of Pauline letters, on the contrary, does much to demonstrate that long-traditional interpretations of Romans require significant revision when the historical circumstances of its production are brought into clearer focus. Uniquely among Paul's seven undisputed letters, in Romans Paul writes to persons he does not yet know and to a community he himself has never visited. Paul must provide his addressees with an account of his "gospel" because it represents an understanding of the implications of salvation for gentiles that was highly controversial in its time. This does not mean, however, that Romans is an ahistorical summary of Pauline doctrine, as it was read for centuries. Specific historical circumstances motivate his explication.

A Critical Interpretive Question: The Audience of Romans

At the forefront of many of the interpretive questions that drive the historical-critical interpretation of Romans is the issue of the "implied reader" or in-

---

in *Perspectives on Paul* [London: SCM, 1971], 70; quoted by Novenson, "Anti-Judaism and Philo-Judaism," 111) puts it: "The apostle's message of justification is a fighting doctrine, directed against Judaism."

5. On the acute influence of Pauline soteriology for Luther's anti-Judaism, see Gregory Miller, "Luther's Views of the Jews and Turks," in *The Oxford Handbook of Martin Luther's Theology*, ed. Robert Kolb, Irene Dingel, and L'ubomír Batka (Oxford: Oxford University Press, 2013), 427–34.

6. Ernst Käsemann, "Paul and Israel," in *New Testament Questions of Today* (London: SCM, 1969), 186; quoted by Novenson, "Anti-Judaism and Philo-Judaism," 113.

tended audience of Romans. While many scholars conclude that the letter is written to a mixed audience of gentiles and Jews on the basis of Suetonius's account of the expulsion of Jews from Rome under Claudius (*Claudius* 25), there are many problems with this reconstruction.[7] Moreover, whether or not the actual makeup of the Roman community of Jesus-followers included ethnic Jews,[8] there are numerous indications from the letter itself that its *intended* audience was gentile. The audience is addressed as such; for example, in 1:5-7, where Paul identifies himself as apostle to the gentiles, "including yourselves" (1:6 NRSV), and in 1:13-15, where Paul mentions that he has "often intended to come to you . . . [to] reap some harvest among you, as . . . among the rest of the gentiles" (1:13 NRSVue; cf. 15:15-16). Paul discusses the failure of ethnic Israel to believe in Jesus Christ in Romans 9-11 in part as a warning "to you gentiles" (11:13) against arrogance. Finally, that Paul assumes knowledge of Jewish law and customs[9] does not require the presence of Jews among his audience. In fact, it likely tells us something important about what kind of gentiles Paul understood himself to be addressing: a familiarity with central elements of Judaism could be presumed among gentile Christ-followers who were already associated to some degree with Jewish communities in Rome: "These are not just any gentiles, but gentiles who are relatively familiar with—and attracted to—Jewish customs."[10]

---

7. For two contrasting approaches to these problems: Richard N. Longenecker, *Introducing Romans: Critical Issues in Paul's Most Famous Letter* (Grand Rapids: Eerdmans, 2011), 55-91; Mark Nanos, "Some Problems with Reading Romans through the Lens of the Edict of Claudius," in *Reading Romans within Judaism*, vol. 2 of *Collected Essays of Mark D. Nanos* (Eugene, OR: Cascade, 2018), 23-39.

8. While Paul refers to the names of Jewish Christ-followers in his greetings in Rom 16, that he asks his intended readers to greet them suggests that they were not expected to be among the initial audience of the letter; Runar M. Thorsteinsson, Matthew Thiessen, and Rafael Rodríguez, "Paul's Interlocutor in Romans: The Problem of Identification," in *The So-Called Jew in Paul's Letter to the Romans*, ed. Rafael Rodríguez and Matthew Thiessen (Minneapolis: Fortress, 2016), 1-37 at 15.

9. E.g., Paul's discussion of the patriarch Abraham in Rom 4, with references to Jewish law throughout.

10. Thorsteinsson, Thiessen, and Rodríguez, "Paul's Interlocutor in Romans," 14. Influential for contemporary arguments for a gentile audience for the Letter to the Romans is the seminal work of Stanley K. Stowers, *A Rereading of Romans: Justice, Jews, and Gentiles* (New Haven: Yale University Press, 1994). More broadly, the work of Terence Donaldson (e.g., *Paul and the Gentiles: Remapping the Apostle's Convictional World* [Minneapolis: Fortress, 1997]) was an important study of the gentile proselytes to Judaism as relevant for understanding Paul's gentile believers.

Paul's Theology: From Supersessionism to Intra-Jewish Discourse

Identifying the intended audience of Romans as gentile Christ-followers attracted to Jewish theology and the customs imbued with its meanings and values can significantly impact how one interprets Paul's statements regarding Judaism and Jews in the letter. Paul's statements about Jews and gentiles in Romans 2 illustrate some of the major shifts in interpretation of Paul's theology.

The contrast between justification through faith in Jesus Christ and justification through observance of the Jewish law takes a central place in Paul's letters to the Romans and to the Galatians. In what is often referred to as the "Lutheran" or "traditional Protestant" interpretation of Paul, Paul is understood to say that the "law," the core of late Second Temple Judaism, cannot make Jews right with God, or in Paul's terminology, "justify" them, because of its tendency to encourage the legalistic attitude that salvation is earned by one's observance of legal obligations, often understood to include the expectation of *perfect* fulfillment of all the requirements of the law. In contrast, Paul asserts that faith in Jesus alone "justifies" because it entails due recognition of one's sinful nature and the anti-legalistic belief that the grace of God alone, granted through Jesus's sacrificial death, can save one from one's sins. According to this reading, Paul contrasts a Christian *sola fide* ("faith alone") position with Jewish legalism and sees Judaism as superseded by Christianity.

Much of this reconstruction is understood to be rooted in the logic of Paul's Letter to the Romans and relies, for example, on interpreting passages such as Romans 2 as Paul's attack on hypocrisy as a psychological feature of Jewish legalism,[11] the inevitable product of a religion that impossibly requires perfect obedience. This reading involves assuming, for example, that the person Paul addresses in 2:17, "you call yourself a Jew and rely on the law and boast of your relation to God" (NRSV) refers to a typical Jew, one whose reliance and boasting in God is taken in a negative sense, whom Paul goes on to criticize for their hypocrisy and transgression of the law: "You, then, that teach others, will you not teach yourself? While you preach against stealing, do you steal?

---

11. Against this view, see, e.g., Krister Stendahl's classic argument against the psychologism of the Lutheran reading that argues that Paul's agonizing over sin and the impossibility of doing God's will in Rom 7 should be understood as the voice of a gentile, expressing Paul's concern with the problem of gentile inclusion given the depth of their alienation from God, rather than the voice of Paul, here understood as a representative of non-Christ following Judaism; "The Apostle Paul and the Introspective Conscience of the West," *Harvard Theological Review* 56 (1963): 199-215.

. . . You that abhor idols, do you rob temples?" (2:21–22 NRSV). When Paul continues in 2:25–26, he is typically understood to be condemning all Jews, insofar as their inevitable failure to observe the law perfectly can only dishonor their God.

In the twentieth and twenty-first centuries, reading Paul's work in light of Judaism offers various interpretations that at times reinforce and at other times counter anti-Jewish readings of Romans. E. P. Sanders is among the first to contextualize Paul's writings among Second Temple Jewish and rabbinic literature. He points out that law observance, rather than being negatively associated with legalism, almost always in fact functions within the context of "covenantal" grace.[12] But he nevertheless understands Paul's theology in Romans 2 as speaking about Jews generally and therefore as privileging "Christianity" as uniquely capable of offering salvation. James D. G. Dunn instead suggests that Paul's affirmation of faith in Christ is not a solution to legalism but rather to the exclusion of gentiles from the covenantal people of God (unless they become Jews by being circumcised and adopting the ancestral laws). Dunn, still reading the exemplary Jew in Romans 2 as a stand-in for all Jews, sees much of Romans as Paul's critique of the ostensibly ethnocentric features of Jewish covenant theology.[13]

More recently, scholars belonging to the Paul-within-Judaism school argue that the assumption that Paul is criticizing Judaism *at all* in his letters, whether the "anti-legalist" reading of Paul or Dunn's anti-ethnocentric reading of Paul, is a misunderstanding of Paul's rhetoric unduly influenced by early Christian writers whose reading of Paul was colored by their own efforts to create a Christian identity distinct from Judaism.[14] Instead, for such scholars, it is important that one reads the letters of Paul, the apostle to the gentiles (1:5), in their original historical context—that is, as the messages of the herald of a Jewish messiah addressed to *gentiles*. As such, Paul's statements on the "works of the law" are understood to represent criticisms not of Judaism but of the efforts of gentile Christ-followers to adopt Jewish practices such as circumcision,

---

12. E. P. Sanders, *Paul, the Law, and the Jewish People* (Minneapolis: Fortress, 1983), 128–29.

13. James D. G. Dunn, "The New Perspective on Paul: Paul and the Law," in Dunn's *The New Perspective on Paul*, rev. ed. (Grand Rapids: Eerdmans, 2008), 150. In *Romans 1–8*, Word Biblical Commentary 38A (Dallas: Word, 1998), 91–92, Dunn sees the stereotypical image of the "hypocritical Pharisee" represented in Rom 2.

14. Matthew Thiessen, *Paul and the Gentile Problem* (Oxford: Oxford University Press, 2016), 8. See also Adam H. Becker and Annette Yoshiko Reed, eds., *The Ways That Never Parted: Jews and Christians in Late Antiquity and the Early Middle Ages* (Minneapolis: Fortress, 2007).

or to "Judaize." Matthew Thiessen, for example, rightly points out that Paul's criticism of the so-called Jew, described in 2:17 as someone who relies on the law and boasts of their relationship to God, cannot represent a criticism of Judaism since it is clear that Paul thinks that boasting in God is not only perfectly legitimate, it is a theological ideal (cf. 5:11; 1 Cor 1:31; 2 Cor 10:17). Thiessen argues that Romans 2 makes more sense as a criticism of the Judaizing gentile claiming to be a Jew but still tied to gentile sin, and he concludes that Paul does not accuse Judaism of hypocrisy and transgression of the law.[15]

Our examination of scholarly debate over Romans 2, which has often been seen as among the strongest evidence in support of a supersessionist or anti-Jewish Paul, is representative of our broader claims: before the "parting of the ways," Paul's letters must be read as intra-Jewish literature, advancing recognizably Jewish, not supersessionist, claims. The problem, of course, is that Paul is no longer read, at least in any normative theological sense, in this manner. The "ways" have been "parted" for some time now. Christianity no longer sees itself "within" Judaism.

Reception History: From Tensions to Irresolvable Contradictions

What was a profound tension in the thought of Paul and his first readers becomes the source of profoundly contradictory views as received by later Christian interpreters. After the parting of the ways, Christian reading of Paul no longer operates within an intra-Jewish context, thus creating a type of meaning stubbornly resistant to closure in any clearly pro-Jewish or anti-Jewish sense. This phenomenon is perhaps most tragically, and paradigmatically, demonstrated among the Christian interpreters of Paul's letters under the Third Reich.

Many Christians under the Nazis found Paul's statements on the Jewish law (as interpreted through the Lutheran reading) useful for their purposes,

---

15. Matthew V. Novenson ("The Self-Styled Jew of Romans 2 and the Actual Jews of Romans 9–11," in Rodríguez and Thiessen, *The So-Called Jew in Paul's Letter to the Romans*, 133–62) rightly notes that the charge of hypocrisy and transgression of the law (theft, adultery, sacrilege, transgression of the law) in Rom 2 is very different from the criticisms of the "faithlessness" (*apistia*) of Israel in Rom 9–11. The former has to do with transgression of the Jewish law, whereas the latter "has to do entirely with the apostolic announcement, the gospel" (161). Neither represents a criticism of Judaism per se: Rom 2 criticizes the Judaizing gentile while Rom 9–11 criticizes Jews for their failure to "obey the gospel" (10:16) and for "enmity with respect to the gospel" (11:28).

but a full integration of Paul and his theology proved consistently challenging. Many scholars of this period argued for a non-Jewish Jesus or a Jesus who transcended his Jewish origins and asserted that the deeply Jewish worldview of the New Testament must have originated with the Judaizing influence of Paul.[16] Such claims were often accompanied by calls for the removal of Paul from theology or de-Judaizing Paul. Christian racist Walter Grundmann's *The Message of God* in 1940, for example, eliminated Paul's autobiographical references, as in Galatians 1, and other selected passages from his letters in order to present a consistent Pauline rejection of Judaism. Although Grundmann asserted that "a German faith cannot be based upon Paul, because it would be deformed by his Jewish system of coordinates,"[17] he was never able to fully exorcise Paul from theological discussion of the institute (i.e., The Institute for the Study and Eradication of Jewish Influence on German Church Life) despite his efforts up to the end of World War Two. When, for example, Hugo Pich called for removing the "Jew Scha-ul [Saul]" altogether to focus on Jesus, who had died "in battle against Judaism"[18] to uphold faith in God, he was roundly criticized by members of the institute. Paul's status was highly ambivalent for many theologians and biblical scholars seeking to support Nazi ideology: Paul was foundational for Martin Luther and all Lutherans (and as is well known, Luther's 65,000 word treatise "On the Jews and Their Lies," penned three years before his death, illustrates how far Luther's anti-Jewish sentiments could go), and yet, as a self-proclaimed Jew and even Pharisee, Paul was often used to explain how Jesus's teachings could take on such Jewish expression in much of the New Testament.

On the other hand, Paul, particularly in Romans 9-11, supplied the Confessing Church with inspiration to resist such anti-Jewish theological positions, even if their Paul was still ultimately understood in supersessionist terms. After the Kristallnacht pogrom (9–10 November 1938), Dietrich Bonhoeffer wrote to his students: "In the last few days, I have thought much about Ps. 74, Zech. 2:8, Rom. 9:4-5, and 11:11-15. That leads deeply into prayer." Eberhard Bethge suggested that despite the few references to Jews in Bonhoeffer's later writings, these scripture passages drove Bonhoeffer's "turning point" after the

16. A few examples: the German philologist Paul de Lagarde argued that Paul perverted Christianity by Judaizing it (Susannah Heschel, *The Aryan Jesus: Christian Theologians and the Bible in Nazi Germany* [Princeton: Princeton University Press, 2010], 37); similarly, the pastor Martin Slotty (50); Reinhold Krause in November 1933 denounced Paul as a Jewish theologian to thunderous applause from a crowd of twenty thousand at a Berlin rally (69).

17. Heschel, *Aryan Jesus*, 145.

18. Heschel, *Aryan Jesus*, 146.

pogrom that eventually led him to join the military conspiracy against Hitler,[19] "stimulating a complete theology of Israel in contrast to the time, and communicating his own involvement as well."[20] At the same time Bonhoeffer famously penned "The Church and the Jewish Question," an essay that reflects some surprising sympathy and insights, yet calls on the church to defend Jewish victims of Nazi persecution in a manner that reflects a supersessionist interpretation of Romans 9–11: "The history of the suffering of this people, loved and punished by God, stands under the sign of the final homecoming of the people of Israel to its God . . . and this homecoming happens in the *conversion* of Israel to Christ."[21] While Paul in Romans 9–11 does indeed believe that Israel will eventually be saved by recognizing Jesus as the Davidic Messiah, he does not envision a "conversion" from Judaism to Christianity. This, once again, would be anachronistic to Paul's own views. The historical Paul would, I suspect, likely be bewildered, probably deeply saddened, by the suggestion that modern Jews should join today's Christian churches. He envisioned no such separation of two religions that saw themselves as incommensurable, essentially different, entities.

Conclusion

Paul's critiques of the law in Romans (1) were likely directed toward Judaizing gentiles, (2) should be understood in their rhetorical context of arguing that God's Spirit (rooted in Second Temple Jewish covenant discourse) is the main agent of salvation, and therefore (3) should be read, particularly in light of Paul's affirmation of Jewish election in Romans 9–11, as a fundamentally Jewish theology. After the parting of the ways, likely beginning in late antiquity but becoming magnified in the medieval and Reformation periods,[22] what

---

19. Cf. Eberhard Bethge, "Dietrich Bonhoeffer and the Jews," in *Ethical Responsibility: Bonhoeffer's Legacy to the Churches*, ed. John D. Godsey and Geffrey B. Kelly (Lewiston, NY: Mellen, 1982), 43–96 at 75–77.

20. Eberhard Bethge, "One of the Silent Bystanders? Bonhoeffer on November 9, 1938," in *Friendship and Resistance: Essays on Dietrich Bonhoeffer*, ed. Eberhard Bethge (Grand Rapids: Eerdmans, 1995), 58–71 at 65. See further, Andreas Pangritz, "Bonhoeffer and the Jews," in *The Oxford Handbook of Dietrich Bonhoeffer*, ed. Michael Mawson and Philip G. Ziegler (Oxford: Oxford University Press, 2019), 91–107.

21. Dietrich Bonhoeffer, "The Church and the Jewish Question," in *No Rusty Swords: Letters, Lectures, and Notes, 1928–1936* (New York: Harper & Row, 1965), 226 (emphasis added).

22. See the account of the development of anti-Judaism and antisemitism in Robert

was a profound tension in Romans became the source of profoundly contradictory views as received by later Christian interpreters—never allowing for either absolutely pro-Jewish or anti-Jewish readings—but at the same time providing an abiding motive (at least for Christians) to continue to pursue Jewish-Christian dialogue.

Discussion Questions and Activity Suggestions

These classroom exercises are designed to develop an active historical imagination, one that facilitates the critical reading of biblical texts and, specifically, the ability to critically interrogate anti-Jewish Christian bias in the interpretation of early Jewish and Christian literature.

1. What kind of metaphors does Paul use to describe the relationship between Jews and gentiles in Romans?
2. What does the suggestion that the presumed audience of Romans was "Judaizing gentiles" tell us about Judaism throughout the Roman Empire? Does imagining a different kind of audience on the other side of this letter change how we understand it?
3. Why is it important to study the Protestant Reformation in the fifteenth century to understand modern interpretations of Paul, and especially Romans?
4. Explore the Jewishness of Paul's ideas, assumptions, and language. Whether they realize it or not, many first encounter early Jewish discourse through Christian texts like Paul's letters. Paul's language, phrases, images, and ways of arguing in relation to scripture sound "churchy" and "Christian," and in contrast to modern ways of thinking and communicating, they seem mysterious and resistant to critical interrogation and historical contextualization. These exercises aim to help students "make Paul weird again" (to quote Matthew Novenson) and to make Paul Jewish again.
5. Contextualize Paul's "negative anthropology," that is, his radically dichotomous language of "flesh" and "spirit," within late-Second Temple Judaism by having students read, for example, the Hodayot (1QH^a). What similarities and differences do you find between this text and Paul's letters?
6. Compare Paul's themes of the unmerited gift of God's spirit and the justification it entails to prophetic expectations of a future renewal of the peo-

---

Chazan, *From Anti-Judaism to Anti-Semitism: Ancient and Medieval Christian Constructions of Jewish History* (Cambridge: Cambridge University Press, 2016).

ple of Israel through moral transformation, often described as a kind of democratization of prophecy, in Deuteronomy 30, Jeremiah 31, Ezekiel 36, Joel 2, and so on.

7.   Reenact the New Testament as an intra-Jewish debate. Paul's Letter to the Galatians makes it clear that he was controversial in his time. Much scholarship is devoted to exploring possible tensions, conflicts, and indebtedness between other New Testament literature and Paul, whose letters make up the earliest texts in the New Testament canon. This exercise encourages students to develop an active historical imagination by speculating on the relationships of early Christian texts to Paul's thought and the way in which the ideas, genres, rhetoric, and practices of early Christian texts function in relation to one another as intra-Jewish forms of discourse. Split students into three to five groups and have them present on texts like Matthew, Revelation, Luke-Acts, James, Mark, John, and so on, in relation to Paul. Have each group try to draw out aspects of their assigned text that seem best designed to challenge and contest Paul's ideas, practices, and rhetoric, to reinforce Paul's authority, and/or to identify ideas and practices shared between their text and Paul's letters. Encourage them to search for patterns of correlation between concepts/rhetoric and possible social function in the service of reconstruction of early Christian history.

Further Reading

Heschel, Susannah. *The Aryan Jesus: Christian Theologians and the Bible in Nazi Germany*. Princeton: Princeton University Press, 2008.

McKnight, Scot, and B. J. Oropeza, eds. *Perspectives on Paul: Five Views*. Grand Rapids: Baker Academic, 2020.

Novenson, Matthew. "Anti-Judaism and Philo-Judaism in Pauline Studies, Then and Now." Pages 106–124 in *Protestant Bible Scholarship: Antisemitism, Philosemitism, and Anti-Judaism*. Edited by Arjen F. Bakker et al. Journal for the Study of Judaism Supplement 200. Leiden: Brill, 2022.

Rodríguez, Rafael, and Matthew Thiessen, eds. *The So-Called Jew in Paul's Letter to the Romans*. Minneapolis: Fortress, 2016.

Thiessen, Matthew. *A Jewish Paul: The Messiah's Herald to the Gentiles*. Grand Rapids: Baker Academic, 2023.

16

1 Corinthians

EKAPUTRA TUPAMAHU

The so-called First Letter to the Corinthians is likely Paul's second letter to this congregation. First Corinthians 5:9 suggests that he had written at least one other to the Corinthians previously. In short, there are several letter exchanges between Paul and the Corinthians, although we have only two surviving letters from these interactions, now known as 1 Corinthians and 2 Corinthians. Scholars today commonly date 1 Corinthians to around the mid-50s, making this one of the earliest documents in the New Testament.

Although scholars often question the historical validity of Acts because of its *tendency* to be Paul's apologist, the book of Acts recounts that after Paul went to Athens, he visited Corinth and stayed there for one and a half years (Acts 18:11). According to Acts, Paul's enemies in Corinth were "the Jews" who attacked and dragged him in front of a Roman proconsul named Gallio (18:12–16). Various nineteenth- and twentieth-century scholars of the New Testament pick up this story of conflict in order to vilify the Jews as the archenemy of Pauline church, and thus Christianity. Acts does not say a word about Paul's letters to the Corinthians. Thus, the exact literary and historical connections between Acts and 1 Corinthians remain open to scholarly speculation.

In the opening part of the letter, Paul calls the Corinthians "the *ekklēsia* [Greek assembly] of God" (1:2). He says that he heard from "those of Chloe" (1:11) that this community is in conflict with each other and full of many problems. Whether Paul's description of the Corinthians is correct is open for debate. Some scholars think that he may have misunderstood the Corinthians and their situations. Nevertheless, based on Paul's representation of them, the Corinthians do seem to be in a messy conflict. There are serious divisions (1:10) and quarrels (1:11) among them, Paul writes. Some of the Corinthian Christians argue that they "belong" to Paul, others to Apollos, others to Cephas, and others to Christ (1:12). Paul spends at least the first four chapters of his letter addressing this issue. And at the end of his discussion on this matter of divisions, he threatens to return to Corinth with a "stick" to beat them (4:21).

There are other contentious issues in addition to the divisions and quarrels in the beginning of 1 Corinthians. In chapter 5 he discusses human sexuality, and in chapter 6 the topic is matters that are brought to a civic court outside of the congregation. He switches his attention to issues of marriage in chapter 7, and in chapters 8 and 10 he directs his attention to the problem of foods offered to idols. The issues of women wearing head covers and the common meals are the focus of chapter 11. In chapters 12–14, Paul expresses his unhappiness with "speaking in tongues" in the Corinthian gatherings, and in chapter 15 he weighs in on the issue of resurrection. Finally, in chapter 16 he talks about donations to the church in Jerusalem and about his travel plans. Most of these topics are introduced with the Greek expression *peri de*, which is often translated "now concerning" (7:1, 25; 8:1; 12:1; 16:1).

In short, 1 Corinthians tackles a wide range of topics and concerns. It is a rich letter that over the centuries has become a site of debate among exegetes. Unfortunately, we do not have anyone from first-century Corinth who can speak to us today. The only witness to those believers is Paul's letters to them. The focus of many scholarly works in the past two centuries has largely been on the search for Paul's opponents in Corinth.[1] Who were they? In answering this question, scholars speculate by making all kinds of textual and historical connections in order to fill the gaps that they see in the text. The following discussion will focus on scholarly works that blame the Jews for the problems in Corinth.

The book of Acts is the first to describe Paul's main opponents in Corinth as "the Jews." Throughout its episodes, Acts regularly depicts the Jews as the antagonists or the "bad guys" in the story. This tendency is not only seen in the book of Acts; the same narrative persists in modern biblical scholarship. Specifically relevant to us is that biblical scholars often blame the Jews for the divisions in Corinth. And one of the most vivid exegetical strategies used to vilify the Jews is to pose them as Paul's opponents there. In order to understand this trend in scholarship, we need to go back to the nineteenth-century German scholar, Ferdinand C. Baur, look closely at his works, and then see his influence on more recent biblical scholarship.

---

1. Jerry L. Sumney, *Identifying Paul's Opponents: The Question of Method in 2 Corinthians*, Journal for the Study of the New Testament Supplement Series 40 (Sheffield: JSOT Press, 1990).

Baur was the leading figure in the so-called Tübingen school, a group of Protestant scholars working in Tübingen, Germany, in the nineteenth century.[2] His operating metanarrative for the origins of Christianity is the tension between Jewish Christians (represented by Peter) and gentile Christians (represented by Paul).[3] Baur's reading of 1 Corinthians follows this grand narrative, and that letter also becomes one of the textual data points upon which he establishes his larger story of the early followers of Jesus.

In his landmark essay "Die Christuspartei in der korinthischen Gemeinde" ("The Christ Party in the Corinthian Community") published in 1831,[4] Baur attempts to reconstruct the history behind the schisms in Corinth by examining and pursuing the reference to the "Christ party" in 1:12. He argues that the community in Corinth—which was a Greek city—consists not only of gentile Christians, but also Christians with some kind of Jewish influence. One can see the hint of this Jewish presence in the names of the parties that Paul mentions in 1:12.[5] Many scholars, Baur included, assume that the names Peter, Apollos, and Paul are Jewish. But who are the "Christ party"? Baur rejects the ideas that (a) they are the followers of the apostle of James, the brother of Jesus, and that (b) this is a claim that they are the followers of Christ as opposed to Peter or Paul or Apollos.[6] Instead, Baur insists that there are only two parties in Corinth, one organized around Paul and one around Peter. It is thus a tension between a gentile Christian group and a Jewish Christian group.

Baur's explanation of the identity of the Christ party is based mainly on an interpretative strategy often called "mirror reading"—that is, reading Paul's rhetoric to reconstruct the identity of Paul's opponents.[7] Baur investigates Paul's statements that he has "the mind of Christ" (2:16), that he is a "servant of Christ" (4:1), that he is ready to be seen as a fool for the sake of Christ

---

2. For a more detailed discussion on this school of thought, see Horton Harris, *The Tübingen School: A Historical and Theological Investigation of the School of F. C. Baur* (Grand Rapids: Baker, 1990).

3. See Shawn Kelley, *Racializing Jesus: Race, Ideology, and the Formation of Modern Biblical Scholarship* (London: Routledge, 2005), chap. 3.

4. The English translation was published in 2021 by SBL Press. All the quotations in this chapter are based on this English translation: Ferdinand Christian Baur, *The Christ Party in the Corinthian Community*, ed. David Lincicum, trans. Wayne Coppins, Christoph Heilig, and Lucas Ogden (Atlanta: SBL Press, 2021).

5. Baur, *Christ Party*, 17.

6. Baur, *Christ Party*, 18–29.

7. John M. G. Barclay, "Mirror-Reading a Polemical Letter: Galatians as a Test Case," *Journal for the Study of the New Testament* 10 (1987): 73–93. Baur does not call this a "mirror reading." However, the strategy of interpretation he employs is in fact a rather typical mirror reading.

(4:10), and that he has seen Jesus Christ (9:1).[8] Baur claims that Paul makes all these apologetic statements because he wants to affirm his apostolic authority and to counter those who claim that they alone have a direct connection to Christ (i.e., the Christ party) because of their Jewishness. Based on his reading of 9:5, Baur argues that the Christ party refers to "all of the apostles who had enjoyed contact with Jesus, and . . . in an even narrower sense to [the brothers of the Lord], inasmuch as they, as relatives of the Lord, had an even closer relationship with him."[9] The Christ party, thus, are those who claim that they have an "external connection and kinship with Christ."[10] Much as Peter does, this group employs and appeals to the name of Christ to demonstrate that they are the true "Christ"-ians.[11] They regard themselves as superior to the gentile Christians because they were in a direct physical connection with Christ. Baur interprets Paul's words "we once considered Christ according to the flesh [Greek *kata sarka*]" in 2 Corinthians 5:16 as an indicator that his opponents think that they come from the same physical or bodily (Greek *sarx*) connection to Christ because they are Jewish.[12]

Reading Baur's works, one should notice that although Baur insists that Paul's opponents are "Jewish Christians,"[13] the problem with them is not necessarily their *Christianness* (thus, the *Christ* party), but their *Jewishness*. Therefore, when Paul speaks against his Jewish opponents, Baur says that he is "attack[ing] Judaism itself."[14] Unsurprisingly, he often calls them "Judaizing opponents" or "Judaizers" or "extreme Judaists." These are the same opponents, according to Baur's metanarrative, who are behind every letter that Paul has written. They may appear in different forms in each letter, but essentially they are the same group of people.[15] This is certainly a plausible scenario, at least in Corinth, because in the Roman period, there was a Jewish community in the city when Paul wrote this letter.[16] However, blaming the Jews for the problems in Corinth

---

8. Baur, *Christ Party*, 37.

9. Baur, *Christ Party*, 38.

10. Baur, *Christ Party*, 41.

11. Ferdinand Christian Baur, *Paul the Apostle of Jesus Christ: His Life and Works, His Epistles and Teachings* (Peabody, MA: Hendrickson, 2003), 276.

12. Baur, *Christ Party*, 47.

13. For a detailed discussion on the social and historical complexities of the Jewish-Christian identity constructions in the ancient world, see Annette Yoshiko Reed, *Jewish-Christianity and the History of Judaism* (Minneapolis: Fortress, 2022).

14. Ferdinand Christian Baur, *The Church History of the First Three Centuries*, trans. Allan Menzies (London: Williams & Norgate, 1878), 1:47.

15. Baur, *Christ Party*, 54–58.

16. See Jerome Murphy-O'Connor, "The Corinth That Saint Paul Saw," *Biblical Archaeologist* 47.3 (1984): 147–59.

and understanding the Christ party in Corinth to be a group of Judaizers are ideas rooted in a Judeophobic imagination of the history behind this text.[17]

One might ask: Isn't Paul Jewish too? Yes, but this is quite a complicated question for Baur, and his solution betrays Judeophobic logic. He believes that as an "absolute religion," Christianity was born "on Jewish soil."[18] So Paul *was* definitely a Jew. However, Baur argues that Paul was able to break "through the barriers of Judaism and rose out of the particularism of Judaism into the universal idea of Christianity."[19] (Note, already, for example, the negative description of Judaism as a "barrier" to Baur's "truth.") This radical change in Paul is nothing other than a "miracle"[20] or more precisely a miracle of "conversion."[21] Based on this notion of conversion and his reading of Galatians 1:17–24, Baur argues that Paul's visit to Jerusalem changed everything, because when he left Jerusalem "he seemed to turn his back on Judaism for ever."[22] Judaism in Baur's thought is marked primarily by a tribal particularity, which is to say that it is a religion tied to a particular ethnic group. And so, by embracing the universality of Christianity, Paul has (according to Baur) completely left Judaism. Every time Baur talks about the opposition between "Jewish Christians" and "gentile Christians," his assumption is that Paul is aligned with the gentile Christians.[23] Paul, in his view, moved beyond the particularity of Jewishness and embraced the absolute universal religion of Christianity. The underlying logic is that one cannot simultaneously be a Jew and a Christian. Being Jewish is in a direct opposition to being a Christian.[24] Baur's influence on the field of

17. See M. Adryael Tong's incisive analysis on the interconnectedness of Baur's thought to whiteness in "Banishing Baur: The Antisemitic Origins of White Supremacy in Biblical Studies," *Political Theology Network* (3 December 2020) (https://tinyurl.com/4sc3wdep).

18. Baur, *Church History*, 1:17.

19. Baur, *Church History*, 1:47.

20. Baur, *Church History*, 1:47.

21. Baur, *Church History*, 1:51. Cf. Christof Landmesser, "Ferdinand Christian Baur as Interpreter of Paul," in *Ferdinand Christian Baur and the History of Early Christianity*, ed. Martin Bauspiess, Christof Landmesser, and David Lincicum, trans. Peter C. Hodgson and Robert F. Brown (Oxford: Oxford University Press, 2017), 160.

22. Baur, *Church History*, 1:49.

23. In Peter C. Hodgson's apologetic defense of Baur, he argues that Baur thinks "Paul too could be regarded as a Jewish Christian." See Hodgson, "F. C. Baur's Interpretation of Christianity's Relationship to Judaism," in *Is There a Judeo-Christian Tradition? A European Perspective*, ed. Emmanuel Nathan and Anya Topolski, Perspectives on Jewish Texts and Contexts 4 (Berlin: de Gruyter, 2016), 34–35. Hodgson does not give any textual evidence to support this claim that Baur puts Paul under the umbrella of the Jewish Christian group.

24. Baur states (*Church History*, 1:57), for instance, "The Judaists [i.e., Paul's opponents] maintained it to be the absolute privilege of Judaism that only by the law and circumcision

New Testament studies cannot be understated, and the proliferation of these anti-Jewish readings of Paul persist in current scholarship.

What exactly is the relationship between Judaism and Christianity in Baur's system of thought? For Baur, their relationship can be seen as a

> progress[ion] from [the] minority and the restriction of boyhood to the majority and the maturity of manhood, from bondage to freedom, from the flesh to the spirit, so surely does Christianity stand high above Judaism; and it can only be regarded as an irrational inversion of the relation which God has ordained, to fall back from Christianity into Judaism. . . . [Paul] places Judaism and Christianity together under the light of a great religio-historical contemplation, and of a view of the course of the world before the universal idea of which the particularism of Judaism must disappear.[25]

This is a vivid articulation of a supersessionist theology and history, or, in the words of Margaret Y. MacDonald, a blunt "negative characterization of Judaism."[26] According to this line of argument, God ordained human history by *replacing* the particularity of Judaism with the universality of Christianity. It is therefore "irrational" to reverse such a progress of history. Christianity, according to Baur, stands at the apex of human history; it represents the maturity of religion. Judaism thus has to disappear. Connecting this metanarrative to the Corinthian conflict, Baur states: "In dealing with his opponents in Corinth, [Paul] takes up, as he did in the Epistle to the Galatians, the stand point of the higher religio-historical contemplation. Judaism and Christianity are related to each other as the old and the new [covenant]; the old one is antiquated and extinct, but the new one is bright and luminous."[27]

---

could any man be saved; while the apostle Paul set up the counter position, that whoever was circumcised, Christ would profit him nothing ([Gal 5] v. 2). According to the former it is in vain to be a Christian without being a Jew also. According to the latter it is in vain to be a Christian if, as a Christian, one chooses to be a Jew as well."

25. Baur, *Church History*, 1:59.

26. Margaret Y. MacDonald, "The Shifting Center: Ideology and Interpretation of 1 Corinthians," in *Christianity at Corinth: The Quest for the Pauline Church*, ed. Edward Adams and David G. Horrell (Louisville: Westminster John Knox, 2004), 279.

27. Baur, *Church History*, 1:65. In his exposition of Paul's Letter to the Galatians, Baur writes that this letter "places us in the midst of the great excitement of the critical struggle which had begun between Judaism and Christianity, in the decision of the momentous question whether there should be a Christianity free from Judaism and essentially different from it, or whether Christianity should only exist as a form of Judaism, that is to say, as nothing else than a modified and extended Judaism. But as everything which Christianity

For Baur, it is no coincidence that Christianity emerged during the universal rule of the Roman Empire: "The true point of contact . . . between Christianity and the Empire is the universal tendency which is common to both."[28] Just as the Roman Empire breaks all the ethnic and national barriers among people, so too Baur believes that Christianity works within the same universalizing force to overcome the particularistic religion of Judaism. Baur writes: "The universalism of Christianity necessarily presupposes the universalism of the Roman empire."[29] Baur's metanarrative, therefore, demonstrates an interconnectedness of imperialism and Judeophobia.

It is necessary to speak about Baur and Judeophobia because of the profound influence that his interpretation of 1 Corinthians had on modern biblical scholarship more broadly. Certainly, many scholars reject Baur's proposal.[30] However, many also adopt, revise, and expand it. Hans Lietzmann, for example, in his hugely popular three-volume church history (originally published between 1937 and 1944), echoes Baur's metanarrative when he declares that "wherever [Paul] went, the 'Judaizers' followed."[31] In his study of the conflict in 1 Corinthians, Michael Goulder openly states: "I am happy to have the ghost of Ferdinand Baur to preside over my studies. The criticism over his work can be answered, and the attack on his philosophical presuppositions was misguided. He was a master spirit."[32] Sure enough, Goulder's exegetical narrative explaining the story of the conflict in Corinth is simply an extension of Baur's meta-

---

possessed or was likely to attain in respect to its essential distinction from Judaism had been first brought to an historical reality by the Apostle Paul. And still entirely depended on his personal influence, the peculiar theme of the epistle [to the Galatians] is the vindication of Pauline Christianity, which at the same time must necessarily be also the personal vindication of the Apostle." Ferdinand Christian Baur, *Paul, the Apostle of Jesus Christ: His Life and Works, His Epistles and Doctrine*, 2nd ed., trans. Eduard Zeller, rev. Allan Menzies (London: Williams & Norgate, 1876), 1:253.

28. Baur, *Church History*, 1:2.

29. Baur, *Church History*, 1:4.

30. For example, see Johannes Munck, *Paul and the Salvation of Mankind* (Richmond: John Knox, 1959), chap. 4; Nils A. Dahl, "Paul and the Church at Corinth," in *Christian History and Interpretation: Studies Presented to John Knox*, ed. W. R. Farmer, C. F. D. Moule, and R. R. Niebuhr (Cambridge: Cambridge University Press, 2009), 313–35; L. L. Welborn, *Politics and Rhetoric in the Corinthian Epistles* (Macon, GA: Mercer University Press, 1997), chap. 1; MacDonald, "Shifting Center," 277–79.

31. Hans Lietzmann, *A History of the Early Church* (Cambridge: Clarke, 1993), 1:93. For a more detailed discussion on Baur's influence on Lietzmann, see Roy Bowen Ward, "The Opponents of Paul," *Restoration Quarterly* 10 (1972): 185–95.

32. Michael D. Goulder, *Paul and the Competing Mission in Corinth*, Library of Pauline Studies (Peabody, MA: Hendrickson, 1998), 15.

narrative of gentile Christians in fundamental conflict with Jewish Christians.[33] C. K. Barrett, while disagreeing with Baur's dating of the New Testament documents, states that "I too believe that Baur was right in principle."[34] Regarding the problem in Corinth, Barrett builds on Baur's work when he argues that Paul's opponents are "Jews, Jerusalem Jews, Judaizing Jews."[35] These are only three examples from a long list of scholars who built on Baur's historical reconstruction of the Corinthian conflict.[36] The legacy of Baur in biblical scholarship is not just "its disruption of the traditional image of a primitive church united and operating in complete apostolic harmony,"[37] but also a Judeophobic and imperialistic understanding of the history of religion.

Discussion Questions and Activity Suggestions

1. Read Ferdinand Baur's *The Christ Party in the Corinthian Community* and discuss this question: Why does Baur focus his attention only on the "Christ party" in 1 Corinthians 1 in order to reconstruct the history behind 1 Corinthians? What is he trying to achieve here?

2. What does Baur's reconstruction of the conflict in Corinth and its influence in the subsequent scholarly world tell us about the state of modern biblical scholarship?

3. Blaming "Judaizers" for the problem in Corinth is the legacy of this long history of Judeophobic interpretation in the New Testament scholarship. How can we combat this trend in scholarship?

4. Read 1 Corinthians 1–4 and pay close attention to Paul's discussion on the conflicts or divisions in Corinth. Do you agree with Baur that the problem here is a tension between Jewish (i.e., Peter) and gentile (i.e., Paul) Christians? Why?

33. Baur, *Christ Party*, 41.

34. C. K. Barrett, *On Paul: Essays on His Life, Work, and Influence in the Early Church* (London: T&T Clark, 2003), 221. Barrett basically expands Baur's narrative of the conflict between Peter and Paul by adding another group: "the Hebrews."

35. C. K. Barrett, "Paul's Opponents in II Corinthians," *New Testament Studies* 17.3 (April 1971): 251.

36. See also Jacob Jervell, *The Unknown Paul: Essays on Luke-Acts and Early Christian History* (Minneapolis: Augsburg, 1984); P. W. Barnett, "Opposition in Corinth," *Journal for the Study of the New Testament* 7.22 (1984): 3–17.

37. James D. G. Dunn, "Reconstruction of Corinthian Christianity and the Interpretation of 1 Corinthians," in *Christianity at Corinth: The Quest for the Pauline Church*, ed. Edward Adams and David G. Horrell (Louisville: Westminster John Knox, 2004), 298.

Further Reading

Baur, Ferdinand Christian. *The Christ Party in the Corinthian Community*. Edited by David Lincicum. Translated by Wayne Coppins, Christoph Heilig, and Lucas Ogden. Atlanta: SBL Press, 2021.

Fredriksen, Paula. *Paul: The Pagan's Apostle*. New Haven: Yale University Press, 2017.

Kelley, Shawn. *Racializing Jesus: Race, Ideology, and the Formation of Modern Biblical Scholarship*. London: Routledge, 2005.

Reed, Annette Yoshiko. *Jewish-Christianity and the History of Judaism*. Minneapolis: Fortress, 2022.

Tong, M. Adryael. "Banishing Baur: The Antisemitic Origins of White Supremacy in Biblical Studies." *Political Theology Network* (3 December 2020) (https://tinyurl.com/4sc3wdep).

17

2 Corinthians

TAYLOR M. WEAVER

Second Corinthians is one of the seven uncontested letters of Paul and displays part of the ongoing back-and-forth between Paul and a collection of Jesus-followers in Corinth. Despite being a genuine Pauline epistle that has not had any serious contestation in the history of biblical scholarship, it is relatively neglected when compared with the rest of Paul's body of writing. Part of this may be due to the letter's composite nature; most New Testament scholars believe it to be a collection of stitched-together letter portions, rather than a single letter written and sent at one time by Paul. The epistle doesn't really flow, and it appears to jump around, with drops in certain themes that may be picked back up later, as well as shifts in tone. Despite this pieced-together feel, the letter has long been a staple among Christians. It is clearly present in early Christian writings, with references by Marcion (as noted in Tertullian, *Against Marcion* 5.11–12), the author of the Epistle to Diognetus, and others in the second century and beyond.

The contents of 2 Corinthians were written sometime after 1 Corinthians, which was composed in the early to mid-50s. It was at least the third letter that Paul had written to the assemblies at Corinth, as evidenced in 1 Corinthians 5:9–13, where Paul refers to an earlier letter and expounds on his instructions (5:9 NRSV: "I wrote to you in my letter not to associate with sexually immoral persons"). Dating 2 Corinthians precisely is difficult because of differences in scholarly opinion about the number of fragments of which it is composed. If composed of several letters, 2 Corinthians would have multiple production dates, with fragments perhaps occurring years apart. The view that the letter is stitched together rather than being a solitary composition is nearly as old as historical-critical work on the New Testament, dating to at least the eighteenth century.[1]

Second Corinthians is an epistle that shows well Paul's personality, rhetorical techniques, and the ongoing contentious relationship between the *ekklēsiai* ("assemblies") in Corinth and Paul.[2] With regard to personality, 2 Corinthians displays the sometimes overwhelming parental attitude of Paul, mixed with assertions of authority, elements that are usually seen as characteristics of more widely read epistles, like 1 Corinthians and Galatians.[3] In those more well-known letters Paul uses authoritativeness as a rhetorical technique to undermine outsiders promoting theological ideas with which he disagrees. Second Corinthians reveals similar dynamics through Paul's sorrowful reflections, his pleas for assistance, authoritative posturing, and other rhetorical strategies.[4]

Besides displaying some useful information about the dynamics between Paul and congregations, portions of the language and rhetoric that Paul used to convince the Corinthian congregants has fueled Judeophobia, encouraging enduring stereotypes about Jewish people. Paul's framing of the differences between what he regards as proper theology on the one hand and improper on the other—often read as a dichotomy of Christian and Jewish—has lasted for millennia.

Many of the usual topics and themes found in Pauline epistles show up in 2 Corinthians. And some of these themes and topics acted as fuel for Judeopho-

---

1. In 1776 J. S. Semler published *Paraphrasis II: Epistolae ad Corinthos* wherein he put forth the thesis that 2 Corinthians was composed of at least two distinct letters (letter one is 2 Cor 1–9; 13:11–13; and Rom 16; letter two is 2 Cor 10:1–13:10). Other scholars propose different types of partition theories (some even seeing six distinct letters). For a good history of partition theories, see H. D. Betz, *2 Corinthians 8 and 9: A Commentary on Two Administrative Letters of the Apostle Paul*, Hermeneia (Minneapolis: Fortress, 1985), 3–36. Some scholars, though a minority, propose that 2 Corinthians is a single epistle. See the thorough lists in Christopher D. Land, *The Integrity of 2 Corinthians and Paul's Aggravating Absence* (Sheffield: Sheffield Phoenix, 2015), 2nn4–5; as well as Victor Paul Furnish's summation of reasons for supposing unity in *II Corinthians*, Anchor Bible 33A (Garden City, NY: Doubleday, 1986), 33–35.

2. Frederick Long, for instance, notes that "2 Corinthians may be the most complex of any book in the NT" and that Paul "brings out his full arsenal of rhetorical strategies"; *II Corinthians: A Handbook on the Greek Text* (Baylor: Baylor University Press, 2015), xvii.

3. See Elizabeth Castelli, *Imitating Paul: A Discourse of Power* (Louisville: Westminster/John Knox, 1991); and Antoinette Clark Wire, *The Corinthian Women Prophets: A Reconstruction through Paul's Rhetoric* (Minneapolis: Fortress, 1991).

4. See 2 Cor 3:7 and 5:16a for examples of arguments "from lesser to greater" or "from greater to lesser."

bia. For some readers, it may be difficult to detect anti-Jewish sentiments, especially if they are used to reading the epistle within a confessional environment. As with Galatians,[5] Paul is contending with another early faction in 2 Corinthians; many interpreters throughout history understood this alternative faction as being a "Judaizing" one. From early Christian commentary to the advent of modern biblical studies, readings persisted that named this alternative faction as the Judaizers, catalyzed by competing "Jewish" factions of the early Jesus movement (some even connected the faction to Peter), which was opposed to the Pauline "law-free, universalist gentile" Christianity.[6] While Paul may not have intended such a contrast, an author doesn't have final control over the reception of their text, and in some sense, then, intent is a side issue.

Another recurrent theme found in Paul's writings that shows up strongly in 2 Corinthians is replacement theology.[7] Replacement theology, while a mainstay in many corners of modern Christianity, easily leads down the road of Judeophobia. Replacement theology is the theological idea that Christianity "replaced" Judaism, that the God of Israel's chosen people shifted from Israel's descendants to Christians.[8] Some aspects of it even leak into political ideologies. Many scholars[9] view replacement theology, which Pauline literature inspired, as a precursor to antisemitism. Despite this, it shows up in readings of Romans 11:26, where Paul allegedly redefines "Israel" to mean followers of

---

5. Galatians (along with Romans) is especially well used in discussions regarding the anti-Jewishness of Pauline writing. In discussing 2 Corinthians, for instance, E. P. Sanders relies on a broader structure supplied by scholarship outlining those attitudes in Galatians and Romans; see "Paul on the Law, His Opponents, and the Jewish People in Philippians 3 and 2 Corinthians 11," in *Anti-Judaism in Early Christianity*, ed. Peter Richardson and David Granskou (Waterloo, Canada: Wilfred Laurier Press, 1986), 75–76.

6. Dieter Georgi sums this up well in his *The Opponents of Paul in Second Corinthians* (Philadelphia: Fortress, 1986), 1–9.

7. Michael G. Azar, "'Supersessionism': The Political Origin of a Theological Neologism," *Studies in Christian-Jewish Relations* 16.1 (2021): 1–25. A related term that one finds in these discussions is "supersessionism." However, one should be mindful of the history of this term, which emerged in the middle of the twentieth century "not in scholarly works of theological history or systematic theology, but in the hostile political environment of burgeoning American Christian support for the State of Israel's military superiority" (3).

8. Or, quoting Timothy P. Jackson: "The consuming error of Christian supersessionism is holding that to celebrate the son (Jesus) one must slay the father (Judaism), thus it falsely puts Gospel at odds with Torah"; *Mordecai Would Not Bow Down: Anti-Semitism, the Holocaust, and Christian Supersessionism* (Oxford: Oxford University Press, 2021), 121.

9. Some scholars disagree that there is a necessary connection between replacement theology and antisemitism. As an example, see Philip La Grange Du Toit, "Is Replacement Theology Anti-Semitic?," *In die Skriflig* 54.1: a2536.

Jesus.[10] While Romans is an easy place to see this, 2 Corinthians has been used for this theology as well, with passages like 3:6, where Paul designates himself a "minister of a new covenant" giving license for supersessionism, and 4:3–6, often read as a form of high Christology prooftexting the replacement of Israel with Christianity.[11]

History of Judeophobic Interpretation

In the rest of this essay, I want to look at several broad historical interpretations of 2 Corinthians that have played a part—whether large, small, overt, or implicit—in Judeophobia. I will examine portions of 2 Corinthians that fall into those historical interpretations. A text that has had a definite impact is 2 Corinthians 3:4–18 (which draws on Exod 34:29–30). Primarily, I will focus on readings by early Christian thinkers like Chrysostom and modern white supremacist interpretations. These interpretive communities/people are quite different, and yet they are premier examples of Judeophobic uses of 2 Corinthians. The influence of early Christian writers like Chrysostom persists because of their important place in the foundations of Christian thought, and contemporary supremacist movements represent readings that, while marginal, draw from a long interpretive history.[12] While the text itself may not be the catalyst for Judeophobic movements and ideas, we need to keep our eyes open as to how these texts can, and have, fueled and authorized such views.

As is the case with his other letters (e.g., Romans), Paul in 2 Corinthians can be read as expressing a peculiar relationship between Jews and the early (mostly?) gentile Christ groups. More specifically, here Paul talks about the nature of the law in ways that can appear provocative, to put it lightly (2 Cor 3:7–18). This particular section has been used in the support of supersessionist theologies because Paul appears to announce the "annulment of the old covenant."

The relationship between "law and grace" that Paul elaborates in 2 Corinthians (and many other places) is important because it is one of the reasons

---

10. N. T. Wright, *Paul and the Faithfulness of God* (Minneapolis: Fortress, 2013), 2:1242–58. See criticism by Joel Kaminsky and Mark Reasoner, "The Meaning and Telos of Israel's Election: An Interfaith Response to N. T. Wright's Reading of Paul," *Harvard Theological Review* 112.4 (2019): 421–46.

11. Wright, *Paul and the Faithfulness*, 681–82.

12. For an overview of broader interaction between early Christians like Chrysostom and Jews, see Marcel Simon, *Verus Israel: A Study of the Relations between Christians and Jews in the Roman Empire A. D. 135–425* (London: Littman Library of Jewish Civilization, 1996).

why some Jewish thinkers have been either skeptical of Paul or have spoken strongly and frankly against Paul, calling him "anti-Jewish," for instance.[13] Even some Jewish thinkers who generally like Paul understand him as setting up an identitarian binary that favors the Christian over the Jew, that "drives toward sameness."[14] Binaries may, as Jacques Derrida notes, auto-deconstruct (or, have built within them a necessarily destabilizing element) because they are unbalanced by nature. A binary is composed of opposing elements (e.g., Christian/Jew), with one being superior and one inferior. Paul often appears to set up a binary of law/grace, and that binary has historically been a foundational feature of many Christian readings of Paul, especially post-Reformation readings (though, certainly not exclusive to it). It is in these later Christian readings that this supersessionism is weaponized.

It is no secret that a common caricature of Judaism rests on a preoccupation with law at the expense of everything else. It is usual, for instance, for Christians to set up a binary of law/grace, with Judaism representing infatuation with a "dead law" completely devoid of grace, while Christianity represents a superseding revelation that is founded solely on grace; in these readings Christianity offers free salvation, while Judaism requires perfect obedience to the law. Scholarship has long recognized that such characterizations are false. E. P. Sanders, for instance, made a strong case in the late 1970s that the usual understanding of Judaism as being devoid of grace was patently false, being at the least highly reductive.[15] Summing up Sanders's early work, A. Andrew Das writes that "earnest striving to obey God's Law was a response to God's love rather than some legalistic means of earning it" and that within a "gracious framework with its provision for sin, no Jew would have to obey God's Law perfectly."[16] And plenty of other important works destabilized these outdated binary views, reminding readers well that Paul was, in fact, Jewish. Since the

---

13. Patrick Gray, *Paul as a Problem in History and Culture: The Apostle and His Critics through the Centuries* (Grand Rapids: Baker Academic, 2016), 122–23.

14. Daniel Boyarin, *A Radical Jew: Paul and the Politics of Identity* (Los Angeles: University of California Press, 1997), 208. Boyarin, agreeing with E. P. Sanders, writes that "Paul's main problem with Jews is that they are not Christians. . . . If the 'content' of Pauline Christianity is a drive toward sameness, the Jew is the very site of difference which both constitutes and threatens that sameness." He further notes that Paul's criticisms of particularisms fall into allegorizing the "Jew out of existence."

15. E. P. Sanders, *Paul and Palestinian Judaism: A Comparison of Patterns of Religion* (Minneapolis: Fortress, 1977). Despite being a major corrective within the recent history of scholarship, Sanders's work does have some significant flaws.

16. A. Andrew Das, "Paul and the Law: Pressure Points in the Debate," in *Paul Unbound: Other Perspectives on the Apostle*, ed. Mark D. Given (Atlanta: SBL Press, 2022), 134.

1990s, for instance, many writers (some characterize them as the Paul-within-Judaism perspective) emphasized that Paul was, indeed, Jewish, a fact that gets lost especially within Protestant New Testament scholarship. Pamela Eisenbaum, for instance, in her highly accessible book *Paul Was Not a Christian*, lays out the case nicely.[17] And, Matthew Thiessen makes an exhaustive case for such a Paul in his landmark volume *A Jewish Paul*.[18] Both make clear that Paul was not advocating for anti-Judaism, nor was he self-consciously creating the typical binary of law/grace that is so commonplace.

Christianity is often seen as "good" and "free," while Judaism is seen as "bad" or "outdated" and "false." Second Corinthians 3:7–18 is used as a prime example, showing up heavily in the receptions discussed below. Paul, here, is contrasting what he terms a "ministry of death" in 3:7 with the "ministry of the Spirit" in 3:8. While he admits that the "glory" being administered by the Spirit was present in that initial covenant, as seen on Moses's (veiled) face, he qualifies this in several ways. In 3:9 he emphasizes that his "ministry of justification" contains much more abundance of glory than what he calls a "ministry of condemnation." Second, he speaks of the "hardness of their minds," underscoring that his theological viewpoint paints those aligned with the "ministry of death" as being unable to comprehend "glory," which can only be understood "in Christ" (3:15–16). Such language suffuses 2 Corinthians. Whether there is a broader, architectural argument (because of the nature of the epistle, unlikely) or not, we can see this in 5:17, where Paul writes that "everything old has passed away; see, everything has become new" (NRSV). This is about, again, the "ministry of reconciliation" (5:18), mentioned in the earlier passage.

While some of this language may seem innocuous to confessional readers, it is also important to read it in light of the *history* of Judeophobia, which used the specific trope of "legalism versus grace" to inaccurately characterize both ancient and modern Judaism (and Christianity, for that matter) and the long-embedded understanding of Christianity as *superseding* Judaism.[19] Paul's language here, no matter the intent, is a fuel for these invasive tropes. And, to

17. Pamela Eisenbaum, *Paul Was Not a Christian: The Original Message of a Misunderstood Apostle* (New York: HarperCollins, 2009).

18. Matthew Thiessen, *A Jewish Paul: The Messiah's Herald to the Gentiles* (Grand Rapids: Baker Academic, 2023). See also his *Paul and the Gentile Problem* (Oxford: Oxford University Press, 2016), wherein he argues that Paul is targeting gentile circumcision in passages critical of "law."

19. Amy-Jill Levine, "When the Bible Becomes Weaponized: Detecting and Disarming Jew-Hatred," *Studia Theologica* 75.2 (2021): 182–204. Levine helpfully points out the em-

be clear, the intent is ambiguous, with scholars understanding Paul in diverse ways. Some, for instance, read Paul as saying (in a convoluted and abstruse way), merely, that the law given to Moses is not intended for his gentile audience.[20] Others read Paul as emphasizing a relationship to the "written covenant" that promotes nonliteralistic interpretations.[21] David Horrell suggests that Paul's contrast between covenants can be read as underscoring the primacy (or origination) of the "old," giving "Jerusalem a fundamental role in birthing the people whose identity takes its orientation from her."[22] Moreover, it is important to keep in mind that there is further ambiguity regarding Paul's *overall* view of the law, which destabilizes any neat, reductive binary between broad theological categories of law and grace (see, for instance, Rom 3:21–31).

Beyond those ambiguities in the text and within Paul's particular theological ideas (such as law or grace), other contextual matters can change the interpretation of, in particular, this conflict between differing covenants. Among many elements that shift interpretation we can note two important ones: demographics (or, rather, Paul's audience) and the already present conflicts with Corinth.[23] With regard to the latter, Margaret Thrall notes Paul's frequent attempts to legitimate his own authority. The discussion on the "glory" of his administration of the new covenant could *partially* be Paul's attempt at playing "apologetics" for himself (he is rather like Moses, but better, he may be saying, and therefore credible).[24] With regard to demographics, what was the composition of Paul's audience? Paul is often known as primarily ministering to the gentiles. While we cannot rule out any Jewish presence in a Pauline *ekklēsia*,

---

beddedness of these attitudes, which persist even among those who try to be sensitive to the topic.

20. See Paul B. Duff, *Moses in Corinth: The Apologetic Context of 2 Corinthians 3* (Leiden: Brill, 2015). Also see the novel argument by G. Anthony Keddie, which makes the case that Paul is actually critiquing Moses's mediation of the law, rather than the law itself; "Paul's Freedom and Moses' Veil: Moral Freedom and the Mosaic Law in 2 Corinthians 3.1–4.6 in Light of Philo," *Journal for the Study of the New Testament* 37.3 (2015): 267–89.

21. Guy Nave, "2 Corinthians," in *True to Our Native Land: An African American New Testament Commentary*, ed. Brian K. Blount et al. (Minneapolis: Fortress, 2007), 313–14.

22. David G. Horrell, *Ethnicity and Inclusion: Religion, Race, and Whiteness in the Constructions of Jewish and Christian Identities* (Grand Rapids: Eerdmans, 2020), 199–201.

23. Georgi, *Opponents of Paul in Second Corinthians*, 254. Georgi provides a pretty enduring reading of 3:7–18 that connects the language to Paul's opponents, who he contends are from a "'heretical' Moses-tradition."

24. M. E. Thrall, *2 Corinthians 1–7*, International Critical Commentary (London: T&T Clark, 1994), 237. This doesn't exhaust, of course, the various ways that the use of this rhetoric functions. Thrall notes that what Paul is doing is much more nuanced than simply that.

Corinth was most certainly gentile heavy.[25] This may raise questions as to what precisely the point of Paul's illustration is. But this brings up a larger question that is beyond the scope of this article: why does Paul allude and directly quote so many texts that his (mostly) gentile audience may not be as readily familiar with? What does this suggest about his audience?

John Chrysostom's Judeophobic Interpretation of 2 Corinthians

The danger of that popular legalism-versus-grace opposition is exemplified in the way John Chrysostom and many other early Christian authorities used 2 Corinthians in homilies. Several portions of 2 Corinthians were useful for making clear the contrast between the old and the new; speaking of the "Jews among them" he writes: "To enhance their own credit, these people made a pretense of receiving nothing, and because they had the gift of gab they were very arrogant. As it was likely that some people would be deceived by them, Paul rebuked them gently, though only after commending what was right in their behavior and attacking their silly pride in Judaism."[26] This, as well as other language and rhetoric employed by Chrysostom, should be read in light of his more overt, revealing writings. In his exceptionally vitriolic *Discourses against Judaizing Christians*, for example, Chrysostom refers to Judaism as a disease and to Jews as "pitiful and miserable" (1.5–6; similar comments in 2.5–6; 3.3).

Connected to this language, one sees in 2 Corinthians 5:17 some callbacks in Chrysostom's homilies on 2 Corinthians. In Homily 11, he notes that when Paul writes "the old things are passed away, behold, all things are become new," he is speaking not simply of "sins and impieties" that he mentions in the homily, but "Judaical observances" as well. While this can be seen as innocuous to Christians who are used to this language, it isn't; it matches well with broader themes of Judeophobia in Chrysostom, including the vitriolic language mentioned above and other portions of homilies on 2 Corinthians. Chrysostom is eager to make explicit a rejection of Judaism, even if that isn't in the scope of the passage.

In Homily 21 on 2 Corinthians, Chrysostom writes at length on an expository section following 2 Corinthians 10:6 ("and being in readiness to avenge [punish] all disobedience, when your obedience shall be fulfilled"). Here he

---

25. Benjamin Millis, "The Social and Ethnic Origin of the Colonists," in *Corinth in Context: Comparative Studies on Religion and Society*, ed. Steven J. Friesen, Daniel N. Schowalter, and James C. Walters (Leiden: Brill, 2010), 30.

26. John Chrysostom, *Homilies on the Epistles to the Corinthians* 1.1–2, as seen in Gerald Bray, *1–2 Corinthians*, Ancient Christian Commentary on Scripture (Downers Grove, IL: InterVarsity Press, 1999), 191–92.

references Marcion's use of Paul before briefly turning to the "blindness" of the Jews: "The Jews saw so many marvels happen before their eyes, yet straightway worshiped a calf. Again they saw Christ casting out demons, yet called him one that had a demon. But this was no imputation against him that cast them out, but an accusation of their understanding who were so blinded." Chrysostom further comments on the "arrogancy" of Jews in his discussion on the law in 2 Corinthians 3. As noted above, this section is easily used for Judeophobic purposes because Paul is dealing with the binary old/new, law/grace, letter/spirit. But it also connects well to Paul's many references to Moses's veil (which hides the glory from the ancient Israelites).

Second Corinthians 3:7–18 contrasts Moses's wearing the veil to cover the "glory" that affected him after his encounter with Yʜwʜ and Christ who removes that "veil." Paul, here, is referencing an important story from Exodus after Moses leads the Hebrews out of Egypt. He eventually encounters Yʜwʜ. He is told that he is allowed to see only the backside of Yʜwʜ as Yʜwʜ passes by where Moses is placed. Moses's seeing Yʜwʜ's backside imbues him with "glory," which manifests in his face glowing. He hides this glory behind a veil, though the reason for his "hiding" this glowing has been explained in multiple different ways in the interpretive history of Exodus.

This particular section of 2 Corinthians has a contested reception, and recent scholarship goes back and forth on what precisely Paul is trying to accomplish and what his actual point is. Nonetheless, a straightforward account is that Paul uses the figure of Moses and the glory that he is imbued with as a counterpoint to himself and the glory of his ministry of the Spirit. This opposition between the written law given to Moses (a so-called ministry of death; 3:7) and the ministry of the Spirit (3:8) is particularly ripe for critiquing Judaism.

With that in mind we can see first that Chrysostom picks back on what may be a reference to Marcion when he responds to portions of 2 Corinthians 3:

> Now by ministration of death he means the Law. And mark too how great the caution he uses in the comparison so as to give no handle to the heretics; for he said not, "which causes death," but, the ministration of death; for it ministers unto, but was not the parent of, death; for that which caused death was sin; but [the Law] brought in the punishment, and showed the sin, not caused it. For it more distinctly revealed the evil and punished it: it did not impel unto the evil: and it ministered not to the existence of sin or death, but to the suffering of retribution by the sinner.

He is careful to not throw out the "Old Testament." But, despite this he goes on to write an exceedingly critical evaluation of the "Jews":

See how he again cuts at the root of the Jewish arrogancy. For the Law was nothing else but letters: a certain succor was not found leaping forth from out the letters and inspiring them that combat, as is the case in Baptism; but pillars and writings bearing death to those who transgress the letters. Do you see how in correcting the Jewish contentiousness, by his very expressions even he lessens its authority, speaking of stone and letters and a ministration of death, and adding that it was engraven? Then even while seeming to praise the old things, he again mixes up accusation of the Jews. For having said, written and engraven in stones, came with glory, he added, so that the children of Israel could not look steadfastly upon the face of Moses; which was a mark of their great weakness and grovelling spirit.

A final example from Chrysostom on his homily on 2 Corinthians 3 is useful:

What is said, therefore, is no accusation of the Law, as neither is it of Moses that he then veiled himself, but only the senseless Jews. For the law has its proper glory, but they were unable to see it. "Why therefore are you perplexed," he says, "if they are unable to see this glory of the Grace, since they saw not that lesser one of Moses, nor were able to look steadfastly upon his countenance? And why are you troubled that the Jews believe not Christ, seeing at least that they believe not even the Law? For they were therefore ignorant of the Grace also, because they knew not even the Old Covenant nor the glory that was in it."

These examples reveal the ease with which 2 Corinthians can be used for Judeophobic purposes. Chrysostom is careful with his language. He doesn't blame the law. Those who deserve blame, in his mind, are the Jews who "believe not even the law."

While there are other examples of anti-Jewish sentiment in Chrysostom's reading of 2 Corinthians (and other glosses of Paul in his writings), the above points clearly to both subtle and overt Judeophobic sentiments in his use of Paul. Now, however, we turn to more contemporary readings.

Christian-Identity Judeophobic Interpretation of 2 Corinthians

While it may be a niche, and disturbing, contemporary example, some Christian Identity groups also understand the usefulness of 2 Corinthians for the purpose of advancing their ideological goals, including overt antisemitism.

The Southern Poverty Law Center notes that the foundational theological ideas undergirding Christian-Identity movements is that "white people, not Jews, are the true Israelites favored by God in the Bible."[27] The Anti-Defamation League expounds on this, writing that members "believe that whites of European descent can be traced back to the 'Lost Tribes of Israel.' Many consider Jews to be the Satanic offspring of Eve and the Serpent, while non-whites are 'mud peoples' created before Adam and Eve."[28] As could be expected, these movements do not mix well with other conservative Christian groups, such as evangelicals, due to many conservative Christian movements believing that Jewish people must return to "Israel" for apocalyptic fulfilment. If contemporary Jews aren't actually the true descendants of ancient Israel, and instead only Christian-Identity members are, then the complicated endgame that many conservative Christians are advocating is undermined. It throws their eschatological structure into crisis.[29]

Christian-Identity movements produce their own materials (including podcasts, books, online commentaries, etc.) that reveal a significant amount about how they regard traditional Christian texts. The passages below are easily accessible examples taken from a Christian-Identity website with some traction; the site's stated purpose is to "correct the record in regards to the history and origin of the peoples of Europe, and the reasons why they have adopted the Christian religion and must keep it, along with their ethnic identity and culture."[30]

A prime example of this is found in a commentary on 2 Corinthians 3–4, which was explored above. In a preface to the commentary, the author writes that Paul:

> is stating unequivocally that the Old Testament is for Christians, and that it is not at all for the so-called Jews. Paul says in 2 Corinthians 3:15 of those who rejected Christ that "until this day, whenever Moses is read a veil lies upon their hearts," and then he says of those who accepted Christ in verse

27. Southern Poverty Law Center, "Christian Identity" (https://tinyurl.com/bde43jvj).

28. ADL, "Christian Identity" (5 April 2017) (https://tinyurl.com/4drzed95). For a thorough source on the history, characteristics, and beliefs of the Christian Identity movement, see Michael Barkun, *Religion and the Racist Right: The Origins of the Christian Identity Movement* (Chapel Hill: University of North Carolina Press, 1997).

29. This disagreement isn't to say, of course, that antisemitism cannot also be present in conservative Christianity. Not all antisemitisms rely on the complete erasure of Jews or the subsumption of Judaism into Christian identity.

30. Christogenea.org (https://tinyurl.com/3y6xftxj). The main author of the materials on the site is William R. Finck Jr.

16 "But when perhaps you should turn to the Prince, the veil is taken away." So the Old Testament is not for the so-called Jews and the Jews are blinded as to its meaning. Rather, the Old Testament is only for Christians![31]

While "replacement theology" is problematic, this Christian-Identity author goes even further, in some sense, because those with Christian identity *always were* those for whom Moses's law was meant. This becomes a bit clearer in a commentary on 2 Corinthians 3:18:

As the children of Israel conform themselves to the law of God, they conform themselves to the image of Christ. Paul likens this to having "uncovered faces" which one may behold in a mirror, however that too is an analogy which must not be taken literally. Rather, the children of Israel become clearly manifest in the world as they conform themselves to Christ by keeping His law.[32]

Riffing off of 2 Corinthians 6, the author further makes explicit some of the foundational theological ideas of this white supremacist sect of Christianity. In 6:18 Paul quotes 2 Samuel, writing "and I will be your father, and you shall be my sons and daughters, says the Lord Almighty" (NRSV). In explicating this, the author of the Christian-Identity commentary presents a sort of diatribe:

If it were not for the systemization of deception, the term "Christian Identity" would not even exist. Paul of Tarsus was teaching Christian Identity: bringing the Gospel of God to the literal descendants of Israel who were the people of God even though they were alienated and dispersed into the nations of Europe. . . . White Europeans, becoming aware that they are actually ancient Israelites who are cleansed in Christ and beckoned to return to their God, must realize that in order to do so they must come out from among all of the jews [sic] and all of the races other than their own, for they are all unclean and rejected by God.[33]

The above examples are only a few of those found in the history of use of 2 Corinthians. In fact, they represent only a small amount of what is found

---

31. Christogenea.org, "The Epistles of Paul—2 Corinthians, Part 3: The Old Testament Is Only for Christians" (https://tinyurl.com/mrxj6ys2).

32. Christogenea.org, "The Epistles of Paul—2 Corinthians, Part 2: Comfort and Mercy" (https://tinyurl.com/4pwsahyd).

33. Christogenea.org, "The Epistles of Paul—2 Corinthians, Part 6: Come Out from among Them and Be Separate!" (https://tinyurl.com/mudc47k4).

even in the authors used. More Pauline portions of 2 Corinthians have been used for Judeophobic purposes and will likely continue to be used in this way. What should be studied about these examples are the interpretive communities and persons that are producing them.

Discussion Questions and Activity Suggestions

1. Scholarship is divided on who the "super-apostles" are that Paul mentions in 2 Corinthians 11:5. How does the identity of this group change the way that one reads Paul's comments surrounding his discussion on the group? If they were "Judaizers," does this make Paul's comments seem Judeophobic? Is the interpretation of this group as "Jews" or "Judaizers" supported by the text?

2. After reading Chrysostom and a commentary by a Christian-Identity author, what similarities and/or differences can you discern?

3. How does the dichotomy between covenants play out in 2 Corinthians 3? What does this dichotomy entail, and is it totalizing (i.e., how is it functioning in Paul's argument), or does reading the surrounding verses shift how it can be understood?

4. Does recognizing that Paul was Jewish change how you read those portions of Judeophobic commentary differently? How does it shift the interpretation of both the Pauline texts and the commentaries given by Chrysostom and the Christian-Identity author?

5. Read 2 Corinthians 3:7–18. Now reread the portion of Exodus that Paul is responding to (Exod 34:29–35). Note the similarities in the Exodus story and Paul's use of it. What significance do you detect in the differences, if any? Write these differences down and think back to some of the uses of this text that signal Judeophobia. Can you come up with different ways to read Paul's shifting of the text that aren't denigrating to Jewish people? Does reading Paul's augmentations of the text change if you understand Paul to be engaging with the text through what could be an allegorical reading? What about as midrash?

6. Recall the texts you just read. Imagine reading them to a small gathering of friends. Try performing it out loud. What do you think the effect of this text would be, if it was read aloud to a close-knit group, rather than read silently and individually?

7. Reread 2 Corinthians 3. Can you reimagine Paul's use of the text in a way that doesn't hint or gesture to Judeophobia? Experiment in rewriting, or even providing excurses or commentary on the text that clarifies it. Think

about how hard or easy it is. Also think about how communities and interpreters who were Judeophobic used the text. Would it be easy to slip into those types of readings today, especially after millennia of reading the text within traditions that have either overt or implicit Judeophobic readings at their foundation? Does the Judeophobic patina of the text seem to be essential to what Paul is communicating, or can it be sidestepped?

Further Reading

Duff, Paul B. *Moses in Corinth: The Apologetic Context of 2 Corinthians 3*. Leiden: Brill, 2015.

Garroway, Joshua. *Paul's Gentile-Jews: Neither Jew nor Gentile, but Both*. New York: Palgrave Macmillan, 2012.

Mason, Steve. "Paul without Judaism: Historical Method over Perspective." Pages 9–40 in *Paul and Matthew among Jews and Gentiles: Essays in Honour of Terence L. Donaldson*. Edited by Ronald Charles. London: T&T Clark, 2021.

Nave, Guy. "2 Corinthians." Pages 307–32 in *True to Our Native Land: An African American New Testament Commentary*. Edited by Brian K. Blount et al. Minneapolis: Fortress, 2007.

Sanders, E. P. "Paul on the Law, His Opponents, and the Jewish People in Philippians 3 and 2 Corinthians 11." Pages 75–90 in *Paul and the Gospels*. Edited by Peter Richardson and David Granskou. Anti-Judaism in Early Christianity 1. Waterloo, Canada: Wilfred Laurier Press, 1986.

Thrall, M. E. *2 Corinthians 1–7*. International Critical Commentary. London: T&T Clark, 2004.

Wire, Antoinette Clark. *2 Corinthians*. Wisdom Commentary 48. Collegeville, MN: Liturgical Press, 2019.

18

Galatians

ALANA M. VINCENT AND MARK A. GODIN

The epistle to the Galatians is one of the thirteen Pauline epistles in the New Testament. This relatively short text has had significant roles both in the development of Christian theology and in the church's understanding of the apostle Paul as a key figure in the history of Christian mission. For many Christians, the epistle provides motivation for championing equality, inclusion, freedom, and solidarity as values. At the same time, however, Galatians also contributes major scriptural foundations for Christian Judeophobia, including apparent warrants for supersessionism, presenting torah (referred to in the epistle, and subsequent Christian theology, as the law) as antithetical to the grace manifested in Jesus of Nazareth, construing Jewish religious practices as worthless and rendering Jewish particularism as divisive and antiegalitarian. Since the latter half of the twentieth century, various scholars have made diverse attempts to rescue the Paul of Galatians from anti-Jewish readings.

Galatians is one of the seven epistles whose Pauline authorship is generally accepted as genuine. Many of the other facts surrounding the letter remain less certain. The epistle is addressed to the Christ assemblies of Galatia, a region in central Anatolia (modern day Turkey) populated primarily by Celtic peoples (Gauls). There is no consensus on the exact Jesus-worshiping communities addressed by the epistle, or if "Galatia" refers to the Roman administrative province or the wider area.[1] Regardless of ongoing debate about their precise location, these were almost certainly communities of gentile followers

---

1. Hans Dieter Betz, "Galatians, Epistle to the," *Anchor Bible Dictionary*, ed. David Noel Freedman (New York: Doubleday, 1992), 2:872–75; Pheme Perkins, *Abraham's Divided Children: Galatians and the Politics of Faith* (Harrisburg, PA: Trinity Press, 2001), 1–3.

of Christ, rather than communities that consisted entirely or partly of Jewish Jesus-followers. The date of the epistle is also open to debate, although most scholars locate its composition somewhere between 40 and 60; while this means that the text represents the earliest strands of proto-Christian writing, it is not easy to ascertain exactly when in Paul's career the text comes, or where it fits in the canon of Pauline writings. Thus, there are still significant unanswered questions regarding the letter's history of transmission. Galatians was, however, firmly entrenched as a part of Christian scripture by the second century, when Marcion included it in his truncated collection of texts.

As typically read by scholars, the letter concerns a crisis occasioned by the Galatian community's contact with non-Pauline missionaries who promoted adherence to Jewish customs as a prerequisite for joining the Jesus movement, as shown by a number of direct attacks on Jewish practice and the efficacy of the law within the letter. Current scholars generally agree that these attacks should be understood as attacks specifically against gentile adoption of Jewish practices, rather than against either Jewish followers of Jesus or Jews who were not involved in the Jesus movement.[2]

The epistle opens with Paul accusing the Galatians of "turning to a different gospel" than what they had received (Gal 1:6–9). Paul argues in favor of the gospel that he had proclaimed, first by presenting his own credentials as an apostle of Christ among the gentiles (1:10–2:14) and then by contending that, because people become "children of God" and "Abraham's offspring" through faith in Jesus and what Jesus achieved, those not already under the law have no need to take the law and its markers (particularly circumcision) upon themselves (2:15–5:12). Some of the key points in Paul's argument include the following:

- The Galatians received the Holy Spirit not by "doing the works of the law" but by believing in the message of Christ (3:1–4).
- The covenant that God made with Abraham was extended to gentiles as God's promise embodied in Christ rather than through the law (3:16–18).
- The law taught what one should not do, acting as a guardian in one's youth,

---

2. See, for example, Krister Stendahl, *Paul among Jews and Gentiles* (Philadelphia: Fortress, 1976), 3; J. Louis Martyn, *Galatians: A New Translation with Introduction and Commentary*, Anchor Bible 33A (New York: Doubleday, 2004), 40; Perkins, *Abraham's Divided Children*, 12–16; Shaye J. D. Cohen, Introduction to "The Letter of Paul to the Galatians," in *The Jewish Annotated New Testament*, ed. Amy-Jill Levine and Marc Zvi Brettler, 2nd ed. (Oxford: Oxford University Press, 2017).

but once clothed with Christ, people from diverse origins are all adopted as God's children (3:21–4:7).

- The story of Abraham's wife Sarah and concubine Hagar can be read as an allegory in which those who follow Jesus are the sons of Sarah—and thus the true children of Abraham—while the people of Sinai are actually Hagar's children, born for slavery (4:22–31)

After this, Paul points to the ethical implications of faith (5:13–6:10) before concluding that, in the end, "neither circumcision nor uncircumcision is anything; but the new creation is everything!" (6:15).[3]

Throughout all of this, the epistle focuses on a few themes to which it returns continually. Paul points to the idea of being made "righteous" (also called justification) and how this is a gift from God through Christ. He writes about belonging, calling upon the members of the Galatian groups to reflect on how they had been adopted into God's family through the actions of Jesus that brought them into the covenant that God made with Abraham. The nature of this family is one of equality, Paul asserts, because Christ has nullified the force of standard divisions between people (3:28–29). Moreover, living in this new extended family community means being shaped to manifest in one's life the fruit of the Spirit: to love one's neighbors and bear the burdens of others.

Significantly, however, the letter is highly polemical in nature, presenting these themes in contrast with the ideals and understandings of unnamed opponents that Paul portrays as false or inadequate. Each theme has its antithesis: if righteousness is a gift from God, it cannot come from doing the works of the law; if those who believe in Christ are true children of Abraham, those who hold to Sinai are slaves; the "fruit of the Spirit" is proposed over and against the works of the flesh. While the ideas in Galatians have been important in themselves for Christians, the form of the argument has also been widely influential for Christian theological practice, building antagonism into the way that some theological thinkers construct doctrine. Following Paul's rhetorical style in Galatians requires not only setting up contraries but also opponents to be defeated or depicted as inferior. This need for antagonists greatly facilitated the urge in Christianity to make those who are different into enemies, with devastating consequences for non-Christians, Indigenous peoples, and more. In combination with the details of the argument of Galatians, Paul's rhetorical choices contributed to a tendency for Jews and Judaism in particular to be cast in the role of the opponents of Christianity.

---

3. All scripture quotations in this chapter are from the NRSV unless otherwise noted.

Anti-Jewish Interpretation of Galatians in Church Fathers and the Reformation

Galatians has a long history of anti-Jewish interpretation due not only to the overtly anti-Jewish rhetoric deployed by Paul but also due to its centrality in theological arguments concerning law and grace, as well as more subtle issues surrounding the interpretation of Galatians 3:28.

The main theme of Galatians, the distinction between grace and law, has been a major focus of commentary since the patristic era. Augustine's commentary introduces this focus in the preface, writing of the Galatians that "despite being called Christians, they still wanted to be under the burdens of the law—burdens that the Lord God had imposed not on those serving righteousness but on those serving sin. That is, he had given a righteous law to unrighteous people to point out their sins, not take them away. He takes away sins only by the grace of faith, which works through love (Gal 5:6)."[4]

The idea that the law was imposed "on those serving sin" creates an association between Jewishness and sinfulness (as well as unlovingness) that persists in the works of later commentators. Augustine further uses Galatians 3 as an occasion for proposing a distinction between ceremonial and moral aspects of the law, in which "the circumcision of the flesh, the weekly Sabbath, new moons, sacrifices and all the innumerable observances of this kind" are instances of the former, as opposed to torah prohibitions against murder, adultery, and false witness.[5] This division permitted Christians to understand the law as superseded without understanding that supersession involves a complete breakdown of the existing social order: the law is understood, in practice, as "the parts of the Torah that we don't like."

The theme of the law as burdensome and unnecessary in light of God's grace was especially attractive during the Reformation period, where Paul's "law" was read as a close analogy for "works." Martin Luther famously referred to Galatians as his "dear epistle," comparing it to his wife, Katharina von Bora—although it is unclear whether this statement was an indication of the level of affection in which he held both, or of the degree to which he depended on both for guidance.[6] Together with Romans, Galatians provided the

---

4. Augustine, *Augustine's Commentary on Galatians: Introduction, Text, Translation, and Notes*, ed. and trans. Eric Plumer (Oxford: Oxford University Press, 2003), 125.

5. Augustine, *Augustine's Commentary on Galatians*, 153.

6. Martin Luther, *Luther's Works*, vol. 54, *Table Talk*, ed. and trans. Theodore G. Tappert (Philadelphia: Fortress, 1967), 20.

underpinning to his doctrine of justification. Luther's primary concern in this development was a critique of the Roman Catholic Church and the importance of grace over works (by which he meant Catholic ritual and practices, such as indulgences, meant to "earn" salvation, rather than the Jewish practices such as *kashrut* and circumcision that were the focus of Paul in Galatians). However, in his critique of Catholicism, Luther relied on an understanding of Judaism (buttressed by Paul's oppositional rhetoric) as not merely superseded by but as actively opposed to the teachings of the gospels.

Similarly, John Calvin's commentary on Galatians employs anti-Judaism as the basis of its anti-Catholicism. In his commentary on 3:6, for example, he first rehearses a distinction between what he takes to be Paul's conception of righteousness, being founded on faith, and what he takes to be a Jewish understanding of the term: "Moses does not here treat of Christ, or of eternal life, but only mentions an earthly inheritance." This distinction, once established, enables him to make a comparative statement: "The Papists are not very different from the Jews; for, though they do not venture to inveigh against Paul, they entirely evade his meaning."[7] Catholics are equated to Jews in their failure to understand Paul, as well as their attachment to the earthly, rather than the eternal; they are both examples of religious error that was superseded by a new, better teaching. Calvin's rhetoric depends on his readers already understanding Galatians as a condemnation of Judaism and of Jews, in order to expand that understanding into a rationale for Calvin's rejection of Catholicism.

So while Reformation-era commentators such as Luther and Calvin were not deriving new Judeophobic ways of reading Galatians, they nevertheless ensured that Judeophobia remained central to the way that their followers continued to read the epistle.

Twentieth-Century Anti-Jewish Interpretation of Galatians

In the twentieth century, Christian commentators undertook a reevaluation of their interpretative traditions in light of the Holocaust, aimed at identifying and correcting anti-Jewish tendencies. This approach coalesced under the label "the New Perspective on Paul," which made a concerted effort to utilize historical scholarship in order to rescue the Pauline tradition from its Judeophobic

---

7. John Calvin, *Commentaries on the Epistles of Paul to the Galatians and Ephesians*, trans. William Pringle (Edinburgh: Calvin Translation Society, 1854), 86.

legacy.[8] The Lutheran theologian and bishop of Stockholm, Krister Stendahl (1921–2008), was one of the leading figures in this movement. He argued that Paul's original intent in Galatians was a far more narrowly targeted criticism of Judaizing Christians, rather than of Jewish practice in general. The "justification" in 2:16 was not, according to Stendahl, a synonym for "salvation" but rather "'justified' the status of Gentile Christians as honorary Jews," equal inheritors of the covenant with Abraham.[9] "Justification by faith," according to Stendahl, should therefore be understood narrowly as pertaining specifically to Paul's position on the circumcision controversy. Stendahl is at pains to highlight the distinction that Paul draws between the covenant with Abraham (originally marked by circumcision but replaced by faith) and the covenant with Moses (marked by torah), drawing attention to Paul's argument in 3:17–18 that "the law, which came four hundred thirty years later [than the covenant with Abraham], does not annul a covenant previously ratified by God . . . for if the inheritance comes from the law, it no longer comes from the promise." It is the noneternal, and therefore contingent, nature of the law that Stendahl argues Paul is emphasizing with his rhetorical invective against the law. He attempts to minimize the force of that invective in his summary of Paul's argument, writing that "the law came . . . as a harsh baby sitter to see to it that the children of Israel did not raid the refrigerator before the great party at which the Gentiles should also be present."[10] However, this depiction of the law does little to stem anti-Judaism in the present, as it leaves open questions about why Jews today would still be hanging out with their harsh babysitter instead of joining the party.

Similarly, J. Louis Martyn's Anchor Bible commentary argues that Galatians does not show Paul himself as anti-Jewish, because it presents the "promise" as occurring "prior to the distinction between sacred and profane" and Christ's fulfillment of the promise "involves the termination of the sacred/profane distinction that was introduced (by angels) at Sinai."[11] This is an attempt to frame Paul's rhetorical invective as opposed to all religion, rather than Judaism in particular; indeed, Martyn is at pains to argue that "no Jews are addressed in the Galatians letter, and no Jews are spoken about in the letter. Paul had, in fact, no reason to think that the members of his Galatian churches

---

8. The New Perspective on Paul was so named by James D. G. Dunn in a 1982 lecture of the same name, published in *Bulletin of the John Rylands Library* 65.2 (1983): 95–122; this was later expanded into a monograph: James D. G. Dunn, *The New Perspective on Paul*, rev. ed. (Grand Rapids: Eerdmans, 2008).

9. Stendahl, *Paul among Jews and Gentiles*, 5.

10. Stendahl, *Paul among Jews and Gentiles*, 19–20.

11. Martyn, *Galatians*, 39.

would come into contact with non-Christian Jews."[12] In Martyn's account, the transformation of Jews into symbols occurs in the epistle itself, rather than in later interpretations. However, the examples of religion that the new creation is meant to terminate are all drawn—in a move that follows Augustine's division between ceremonial and moral law—specifically from Judaism: "sacred rites such as circumcision . . . sacred times . . . special foods."[13] There is no suggestion, either in Galatians or in Martyn's commentary, that Christ came to terminate any practices specifically associated with, for example, the worship of Mercury. Here, again, the attempt to rescue Paul from accusations of anti-Judaism resulted in the commentary reinscribing Judeophobic tropes of unnecessary (or even ungodly) legalism.

To avoid overtly Judeophobic readings, modern commentators instrumentalize the Jewish religious practices described in Galatians, treating them as symbols of some other negative concept: human religion rather than apocalyptic faith, outward displays of piety rather than a relationship with God, flesh rather than spirit, markers of in-group identity, the desire for power, and cultural imperialism. Commentators who attempt to rescue Paul's text do so by claiming that Paul was not actually writing about Jews or Jewishness or Judaism, but about one of these other things, implying that the negative associations Paul's rhetoric depends on are acceptable as long as they are understood in a purely symbolic sense. The question about how these negative connotations impact understandings of actual Jewish religious practices since the time of Paul tends to go both unasked and unanswered.

For many Christians, however, the idea that Galatians fosters a spirit of antagonism and Judeophobia would likely seem shocking. Apart from the use of the epistle as a source for theological reflection on law and grace, Galatians has featured significantly in Christian formulations of personal and social virtues, from the fruit of the Spirit to understandings of belonging and unity, justice and equality. For many modern Christians, the end of the third chapter (3:23–29) provides a programmatic argument for inclusivity and solidarity as core values for church life. In particular, 3:28—"there is no longer Jew or Greek, there is no longer slave or free, there is no longer male and female; for all of you are one in Christ Jesus"—has become foundational for all manner of antiracist, antisexist, and antihomophobic work within churches and wider society.[14] This verse frequently appears as a point of reference in discussions of

---

12. Martyn, *Galatians*, 40.
13. Martyn, *Galatians*, 39.
14. The Presbyterian Church in Canada's *Social Action Handbook*, a compendium of

what the Christian community should look like and how churches should act to inspire and influence the political life of the world. For instance, Daniel L. Migliore's introductory text to Christian theology proclaims that the passage illuminates the Christian value of mutuality in interpersonal relationships, the true nature of the church, and baptism as being "the sacrament of *human solidarity in Christ with each other*, and especially with all those who are different, strange, and even frightening to us."[15] It is a text paired with the image of Christ as liberator of the oppressed.[16] Commentaries designed for Christian preachers most often focus on how the passage reveals that the new community created by Christ tears down harmful barriers between people—and that this work is not yet fully realized.[17]

But there is a darker side to these readings. Galatians' presentation of the church as a new community of equality and inclusivity positions it in contrast to the old community of the law. Commentaries that extol the benevolent inclusivity of 3:28 often do so by labeling the first-century Jewish community as holding to the law in an attempt "to maintain her privileged position as the chosen of God"[18] or underlining how the law constitutes a "temporary" or "incomplete" measure rendered no longer necessary by the advent of Christ and his new inclusive community.[19] Jewish religious practice remains the exemplum of the old community, and this leaves clear implications about the

---

excerpts of reports made by the denomination from 1948 to 2019, offers one good example of this, as it shows how one denomination appeals to Gal 3:28 concerning issues as varied as ethnic pluralism within the church (76), antiracism (83), pornography as a block to gender equality (127), the church's position on unity and equality in relation to Canada's constitution (135), and how nationalistic pride "must be subordinate to love of God and neighbour" (338). Available at "Justice Ministries Resources," *The Presbyterian Church in Canada* (https://tinyurl.com/3u6ex6wr).

15. Daniel L. Migliore, *Faith Seeking Understanding: An Introduction to Christian Theology*, rev. ed. (Grand Rapids: Eerdmans, 2004), 147, 161, 254, 294.

16. Jaroslav Pelikan, *Jesus through the Centuries: His Place in the History of Culture* (New York: Harper & Row, 1987), 209.

17. Charles B. Cousar, *Galatians*, Interpretation: A Bible Commentary for Teaching and Preaching (Louisville: John Knox, 1982), 10, 85–87; Fred B. Craddock et al., *Preaching through the Christian Year: Year C* (Harrisburg, PA: Trinity Press, 1994), 309–10; Jane Lancaster Patterson, "Commentary on Galatians 3:23–29," *Working Preacher* (23 June 2019) (https://tinyurl.com/y62bkret). Note that Gal 3:28 is in both the more established Revised Common Lectionary and the newer Narrative Lectionary, and so is read at regular intervals in churches that use either, which means that there are many resources dedicated to discussing the passage.

18. Cousar, *Galatians*, 89.

19. Craddock et al., *Preaching through the Christian Year*, 310; John Frederick, "Com-

people who continue to adhere to those practices. While commentaries might insist that 3:28 promotes unity-in-difference rather than an obliteration of human diversity, the text itself is not clear on that point. As Amy-Jill Levine notes: "To state that in the ideal world, or even in the purview of Christ, 'there is no longer Jew or Greek' sounds like the erasure of Jewish (and Greek) identity. Christian universalism thus entails the erasure of anything distinctly Jewish."[20] Positing equality founded in oneness, rather than pluralism or mutuality, creates conditions that justify religious coercion and Christian supremacy.

In the conclusion of the book *Abraham's Divided Children*, Pheme Perkins declares that "the Paul of Galatians cannot be enlisted in support of postmodern religious pluralism and toleration."[21] He is just too dualistic in the apocalypticism of his theological understanding, too much a thinker who divides people into those who are in and those who are out, both before and after his conversion. Perkins finally hints at a possible way forward, appealing to 6:2—"bear one another's burdens, and in this way you will fulfill the law of Christ"—and arguing that "in the twenty-first century those burdens must include the evils, suffering, and opprobrium heaped on nonbelievers in the centuries of Christian political and cultural domination."[22] But making that connection requires a choice about which ideas should take priority, and that choice depends on the interpreter's already existing values.

Contemplation of Galatians and the history of its interpretation reveals the epistle as a significant text in the consideration of major hermeneutical and theological questions: How much weight should the author's intentions (as much as one can discern them) carry in comparison to the use of a text by generations of religious adherents? Where does the responsibility for harmful readings of a text lie—and when you figure this out, what should you do about it?

Discussion Questions and Activity Suggestions

1. Paul's argument about adoption focuses on the Galatians (descendants of Celtic immigrants to Asia Minor from northern Europe) becoming children

---

mentary on Galatians 3:1–9, 23–29," *Working Preacher* (16 May 2021) (https://tinyurl.com/2x4jzv9r).

20. Amy-Jill Levine, *The Misunderstood Jesus: The Church and the Scandal of the Jewish Jesus* (New York: HarperCollins, 2006), 114.

21. Perkins, *Abraham's Divided Children*, 129.

22. Perkins, *Abraham's Divided Children*, 131.

of Abraham. Why do you think that Paul chose to emphasize the covenant with Abraham, rather than with Moses? What do you think the consequences of this choice are for Christian understandings of Jews and Judaism?

2. Commentators on Galatians tend to focus on Paul's intended meaning and the epistle's context in first-century life, without much discussion of the implications for present-day Christian life and ethics. What are the consequences of such an approach for modern readers of Galatians? What are the consequences of such an approach for relationships between Christians and Jews?

3. Contemporary exegetes argue that Paul's negative portrayal of Jewish practice applies only to Christians who adopt Jewish practices and shouldn't be understood as a negative portrayal of Judaism *in general*. Do you find this convincing? Why or why not?

4. Working either alone or with a partner, make a list of adjectives—as many as you can in five minutes.

- Now try to group those adjectives together—aim for two or three collections of attributes that look like they belong together (e.g., could be used to describe the same object). Is this a straightforward task? If you are working with a partner, do you agree on how to group things together? Why or why not? Do some of the words seem to fit together more naturally than others? Why or why not?

- Review the groups you have made. How do they relate to each other—can you identify one group as positive and another as negative? Can you identify pairs of opposites within those groups? Does placing the words in groups like this cause you to consider certain adjectives as more opposed to each other than you would if you encountered them separately?

- Now review the text of Galatians and make lists of the attributes Paul applies to Jewish and to Christian religious practices. Do these lists align with the groups you've already made? Are there words on these lists that seem more opposed to each other because of the way they're grouped than you would think of them being if you encountered them in another context?

- Choose one of these key passages from Galatians—2:15–16; 3:23–29; 4:21–31; or 6:12–16—and, in the light of what you have just done, consider how the passage functions in Paul's argument. What associations are created by Paul's choice of language? How do these associations contribute to the overall argument of Galatians? What do you think Paul is trying to achieve through the form and style of this argument? What effect might Paul's rhetorical choices produce in readers, both in Paul's time and afterward?

Further Reading

Johnson Hodge, Caroline. "The Question of Identity: Gentiles as Gentiles—but also Not—in Pauline Communities." Pages 153–74 in *Paul within Judaism: Restoring the First-Century Context to the Apostle*. Edited by Mark D. Nanos and Magnus Zetterholm. Minneapolis: Fortress, 2015.

Kahl, Brigitte. *Galatians Re-Imagined: Reading with the Eyes of the Vanquished*. Minneapolis: Fortress, 2010.

Levine, Amy-Jill. *The Misunderstood Jew: The Church and the Scandal of the Jewish Jesus* (pages 78–82 and 114–17). New York: HarperCollins, 2006.

Nanos, Mark D. *The Irony of Galatians: Paul's Letter in First-Century Context*. Minneapolis: Fortress, 2002.

Perkins, Pheme. *Abraham's Divided Children: Galatians and the Politics of Faith*. Harrisburg, PA: Trinity Press, 2001.

Sanders, E. P. "Did Paul Break with Judaism?" Pages 231–40 in Sanders's *Comparing Judaism and Christianity: Common Judaism, Paul, and the Inner and the Outer in Ancient Religion*. Minneapolis: Fortress, 2016.

Stendahl, Krister. *Paul among Jews and Gentiles* (pages 7–40). Philadelphia: Fortress, 1976.

19

Ephesians

EMILY J. GATHERGOOD

The Epistle to the Ephesians belongs to the thirteen-letter Pauline corpus of the New Testament, in accordance with its self-presentation as correspondence from Paul, the Jewish apostle to the nations (1:1; 3:1–13). Ephesians offers instruction in the core tenets of Paul's gospel, and its practical significance for life in the ethnically diverse community of Christ-followers. Ephesians is thus an important source for understanding the construction of Jewish and gentile (non-Jewish) identities in the early Jesus movement, and beyond. The letter's uncontested early reception as an authoritative apostolic writing and its subsequent canonization as Christian scripture secured its historic and ongoing influence in shaping Christian views of Jews and Judaism.

The theology of Ephesians is recognizably Pauline in its twin emphases on divine grace and the inclusion of gentiles in the people of God. The divine Father's grace—that is, his "gift" or "benefaction"—is fundamental to Ephesians' notion of salvation. Grace is the basis on which believers are blessed, predestined, chosen, adopted, redeemed, forgiven, theologically educated, marked with the Holy Spirit, and promised a glorious inheritance (1:3–14). Grace, rather than "good works" (moral achievement), is the means by which people transition from death to eternal life (2:1–10). Grace has relational implications, reconciling Jews and gentiles to God and to each other, as siblings in one holy family (2:11–22). Grace is the foundation of Paul's teaching ministry and the premise of his message that "the gentiles are co-heirs, co-members of the body, and co-owners of the promise in Christ Jesus" (3:1–13). Grace is given for the flourishing of the whole community (4:1–16). And grace is the ethical basis for discipleship, the reason to live sinless lives worthy of the gifts of God that have already been received (4:17–6:20).

The key concept of belonging in the divine community is further articulated through the distinctively Pauline idiom of being "in Christ" (1:1, 3, 11, etc.). The Pauline metaphors for the church as the "body" of Christ and the "wife" of Christ accentuate the interdependent and loving nature of the union (5:21–33). There is also a hierarchical dynamic in play: as the head controls the body, and (in ancient patriarchal societies) the husband rules the wife, so Christ is understood to be sovereign in the church. God's endgame in the cosmic battle with the supernatural forces of evil is to extend the scope of that which is "in Christ" until all things in the heavens and on earth are united under his benevolent lordship (1:15–23). To that end, those who are "in Christ" are equipped and empowered to participate in his ascendency (6:10–20). In sum, Ephesians' construal of salvation in terms of divine grace, gentile inclusion, and union with Christ broadly aligns with the theology of other undisputedly Pauline letters.

The occasion of Ephesians is difficult to determine since its message is more general than particular to a community. Contextual details are sparse, though the location of Paul in prison (3:1; 4:1) and the anticipation of the letter's delivery via Paul's coworker Tychicus (6:21–22) give a sense of historical verisimilitude. The Ephesian address ("in Ephesus"; 1:3) is dubious, being absent from several important early manuscript witnesses to the text. Some scholars posit an original address to the Laodicean church, given the letter's early reception as such by the mid-second-century Paulinist, Marcion of Sinope.[1] The letter presupposes a certain familiarity between the apostle and the addressees in its opening gambit, which responds to news of their faith and love with prayers of thanksgiving and intercession (1:15–23). Given its generic feel, the letter may well have been designed like Colossians and 1 Peter to circulate translocally among multiple churches throughout Asia Minor (cf. Col 4:15–16; 1 Pet 1:1).

Ephesians' claim to Pauline authorship has been a matter of contention in modern critical scholarship since its deposition by Edward Evanson (1792) and the Tübingen school.[2] Various features of the letter are interpreted as indications of its inauthenticity. The principal literary issue is the substantial overlap with material in Colossians (roughly one quarter), which raises the question of Ephesians' derivative origin. Did Paul repeat himself? Did a Pauline imita-

---

1. For discussion of the textual variants of address and the case for Laodicea, see Douglas A. Campbell, *Framing Paul: An Epistolary Biography* (Grand Rapids: Eerdmans, 2014), 308–12.

2. The history of scholarly opinion on the question is charted by Harold W. Hoehner, *Ephesians: An Exegetical Commentary* (Grand Rapids: Baker, 2002), 6–20.

tor draw inspiration from Colossians? Further linguistic peculiarities include the quantity of special vocabulary and the notably verbose style. Can these inconsistencies be adequately explained by Ephesians' own subject matter? The most substantive issue is whether certain theological emphases constitute developments of thought that reflect the vantage point of a later, postapostolic era. For instance, is Ephesians' vision of the Christ-worshiping community as a single universal organism an expression of second-generation ecclesiology, over against Paul's tendency to delineate individual local assemblies? For many scholars, Ephesians' subtle differences from the undisputed letters amount to a cumulative case against its authenticity. The letter therefore tends to be approached as a pseudonymous fan fiction that draws on the genius and authority of the apostle, sometime in the late first century.

Judeophobic Interpretation of Ephesians

Ephesians conveys a largely positive perspective on Jews, as well as a positive reception and retransmission of Jewish convictions and practices. The author's doctrines of God and humanity are profoundly shaped by Jewish traditions. The central affirmation of God's singularity in the Shema (Deut 6:4–5) is the cornerstone of an appeal for unity in the community (Eph 4:3–6). Jewish eschatological apocalypticism provides the framework for the mystery motif (1:9; 3:1–13; 5:32; 6:19), the cosmological dualism of heaven-and-earth (1:3; 2:6; 3:10; 6:12), and the division of salvation history into "ages" (1:10, 21; 2:7; 3:9). Jewish messianism is fundamental to the relational idea of being "in Christ" (1:3–14). Jesus's death is explained in terms of the Jewish sacrificial cult, as a fragrant offering that solicits the forgiveness of sins (1:7; 5:2). The presupposition that all people are categorized into two ethnic groups, Jew and gentile, reflects a Jewish-centered perspective on social identity (2:11–22). The othering of gentiles as "being aliens from the commonwealth of Israel and strangers to the covenants of promise, having no hope and without God in the world" (2:12 NRSVue) assumes Jewish preeminence in divine-human relations. Jewish moral superiority is implied by the unfavorable stereotyping of gentiles as ignorant, hardhearted, corrupt, and impure—a rhetorical strategy that reinforces in-group and out-group identities and serves as a foil for the overcoming of differences in Christ (4:17–22).[3] Ethical living is defined in relation to the cre-

---

3. On the author's negative construction of gentile identity, see Matthew Thiessen, "The Construction of Gentiles in the Letter to the Ephesians," in *The Early Reception of Paul the*

ation mandate in Genesis 1:28 and covenantal concepts of holiness, righteousness, and obedience to the ten commandments (Eph 4:23–29; 5:28–31; 6:1–3). Ephesians' connection with Jewishness is evidently strong, and particularly in light of the author's negative presentation of gentiles it seems likely that the author was Jewish, whether Paul or a Jewish Christ-follower drawing on the literary heritage of Paul. Even so, the letter has a checkered heritage; anti-Jewish readings have proliferated throughout its history of reception, from the patristic era (beginning with Marcion in the mid-second century) to the present day.[4] Reading Ephesians responsibly in the post-Holocaust world involves facing up to its role in the construction of a dark theological matrix in which hatred of Jews has gestated.

Ephesians 2:11–22

The remainder of this chapter will focus on Judeophobic interpretation of Ephesians 2:11–22, a contentious passage that theologically repositions Jewish and gentile ethnic identities. In these verses, Christ is said to bring about a profound reconfiguration of the hostile relationship between citizens of Israel ("the circumcision") and foreign nationals ("the foreskin"):

> For [Christ Jesus] himself is our peace, who has made both groups one and has broken down the barrier of the dividing wall, the hostility, in his flesh, having abolished the law of commandments in regulations, that he might create in himself one new humanity from the two, thus making peace, and might reconcile both to God in one body through the cross, by which he killed the hostility. (Eph 2:14–16 [my translation])

The "barrier of the dividing wall" alludes to the architecture of the Jerusalem temple complex, that is, the stone balustrade that marked off the inner courtyard and sanctuary as sacred space forbidden to gentiles. The basic idea here is that Christ overcame the ethnic estrangement between Jews and gentiles by reimagining the role of the Law (torah) that demarcated the ethnic

---

Second Temple Jew: Text, Narrative, and Reception History, ed. Isaac W. Oliver and Gabriele Boccaccini with Joshua Scott, Library of Second Temple Studies 92 (London: T&T Clark, 2019), 13–25 at 16–20.

4. On Marcion's anti-Jewish reading of Eph 2:15, see M. David Litwa, *The Evil Creator: Origins of an Early Christian Idea* (Oxford: Oxford University Press, 2021), 109–22.

boundary between them. The argument problematizes the hostility arising from observance of the laws, ordinances, and rituals that were central to ancient Israel's covenantal identity as a Yahweh-worshiping nation and that set them apart from other nations (who worshiped other gods and observed other ancestral customs)—particularly male circumcision, dietary regulations, and Sabbath rest.[5] As we shall see, the blunt statement that Christ "abolished the law" in order to make peace through the creation of "one new humanity" has long been misunderstood as a flat denial of the ongoing positive value of Jewish distinctiveness in the divine economy.[6]

In the patristic era, a decidedly anti-Jewish reading was pitched by the illustrious bishop of Antioch, John Chrysostom (circa 347–407), whose veneration as a saint and theologian of the church secured an enduring legacy for his teaching. According to Chrysostom, Christ united Jews and gentiles by abolishing the "dividing wall" of the law, since law observance was an insurmountable obstacle to peaceful Jew-gentile relations: "For so long as they continued still Jews and gentiles, they could not possibly have been reconciled. And had they not been delivered each from his own peculiar condition, how had they ever arrived at another and higher one? For the Jew is then and not till then united to the gentile when he becomes a believer."[7]

As Chrysostom saw it, the reconciliation of Christ-believing Jews and gentiles entailed the Jews' relinquishing of the law that had sustained interethnic enmity. His conviction that Christ "has destroyed the very law itself" led him to the hegemonizing and exclusivist conclusion that there was no place in the church or in the world for the continuation of Jewish particularity. For Chrysostom, the birth of Christianity was effectively the death of Judaism.

Chrysostom developed this insidious line of reasoning in a series of polemical sermons against Judaizing Christians (386–87), which railed against the participation of Antiochene Christ-believers in Jewish customs, rituals,

---

5. Circumcision is prescribed in the Abrahamic covenant (Gen 17). On the eighth day after birth, infant boys undergo the surgical removal of the foreskin from the penis. Dietary regulations prescribe permitted foods, forbidden foods, and guidelines for food preparation (Lev 11 and Deut 14). Sabbath is a weekly day of rest from work (Exod 20, 31, 35). On the contested question of what exactly constituted law observance in the first century, see Karin Hedner Zetterholm, "The Question of Assumptions: Torah Observance in the First Century," in *Paul within Judaism: Restoring the First-Century Context to the Apostle*, ed. Mark D. Nanos and Magnus Zetterholm (Minneapolis: Fortress, 2015), 79–103.

6. For another Pauline discussion of the enduring value of the law, see Rom 3:21–31.

7. John Chrysostom, "Homily 5," in *A Commentary on the Epistle to the Galatians and Homilies on the Epistle to the Ephesians,* trans. William John Copeland (Oxford: Parker, 1840), (Eph 2:11–16), 151–52.

and festivals.[8] With rhetorical flair, Chrysostom deployed an array of hateful, dehumanizing tropes to denounce Jews for their rejection of Christ. He condemned Jews collectively as bloodguilty Christ-killers who have "no chance for atonement, excuse, or defense" for this ultimate transgression.[9] He typecast Jews as morally degenerate, demon-possessed, and accursed enemies of God. And he took this train of thought to its (inevitable?) conclusion, declaring Jews to be legitimate subjects of marginalization, punishment, and violence, as beasts "fit for slaughter."[10] Ironically, Chrysostom's reading of the vision of ethnic rapprochement in Ephesians 2:11–22 served his separatist ideology and opened up conceptual space in which the persecution of Jews could be rationalized as prosocial.

Judeophobic readings of Ephesians 2:11–22 were popular throughout late antiquity and into the medieval era, particularly in the writings of the Protestant Reformers. The leading French theologian John Calvin (1509–1564) was unequivocal in his commentary about Christ's cancellation of the Jewish laws that marked ethnic difference:

> The ceremonies, by which the distinction [between Jews and gentiles] was declared, have been abolished through Christ. What were circumcision, sacrifices, washings, and abstaining from certain kinds of food, but symbols of sanctification, reminding the Jews that their lot was different from that of other nations . . . ? Paul declares not only that the gentiles are equally with the Jews admitted to the fellowship of grace, so that they no longer differ from each other, but that the mark of difference has been taken away.[11]

For Calvin, as for Chrysostom, Christ's unification of Jews and gentiles involved the destruction of the badges that had previously distinguished them, which constituted an insurmountable wall of partition. Peaceful relations could be achieved only through Jews repudiating Jewish ways of life and acquiescing to Christ as the mediator between God and all people. As Calvin took it, God's new creation of one social "body" in Christ was a universalizing

---

8. John Chrysostom, *Discourses against Judaizing Christians*, trans. Paul W. Harkins, Fathers of the Church 68 (Washington, DC: Catholic University of America Press, 1979).

9. John Chrysostom, *Discourses against Judaizing Christians* 6.1.7.

10. John Chrysostom, *Discourses against Judaizing Christians* 1.2.6.

11. John Calvin, *Commentaries on the Epistle of Paul to the Galatians and the Ephesians*, ed. and trans. William Pringle, Calvin's Commentaries 21 (Edinburgh: Calvin Translation Society, 1854; repr. Grand Rapids: Baker, 1979), 191–203 at 196.

and exclusionary move: the integration of all nations into God's household required the elimination of Jewish uniqueness.

In modern critical scholarship, under the influence of Enlightenment ideology of race as a prime marker of human difference, anti-Jewish readings of Ephesians 2:11–22 continued to dominate the interpretive landscape. The German Lutheran historical theologian Adolf von Harnack (1851–1930) is representative in drawing from the Hegelian and Darwinian notion of *Entwicklung* (development) to give an evolutionary interpretation of the "one new humanity from the two": the people of Christ "represent the new grade on which human history reaches its consummation, a grade which is to supersede the previous grade of bisection [into Jew and gentile], cancelling or annulling . . . national distinctions."[12] According to Harnack, the church was a new sociopolitical entity that transcended the ethnoracial distinctions between Israel and the nations to the point of their cancellation. The text depicts the church as nullifying and replacing the Jew-gentile paradigm with "a higher unity." For Harnack, Ephesians' negative framing of the ethnic particularity of Judaism over against the universality of Christianity undermined the ongoing validity of Israel as a people. Christians were "the people of the future," "the *true* Israel" to whom "all the prerogatives and claims of the Jewish people" were transferred. Harnack's reading of the church as supranational in contradistinction to the Jew-gentile binary paved the way for explicitly racialized readings of Christians as the superior "third race" (*tertium genus*), which were popular throughout the twentieth century.[13]

In the wake of the Holocaust, reflection on the contribution of Christian replacement theology to the antisemitic ideology of the Nazi regime prompted reconsideration of the exegetical plausibility of traditional supersessionist readings of Ephesians 2:11–22 that diminished the value of Jewish distinctiveness in and beyond the church. The Swiss Reformed theologian Markus Barth (1915–1994) championed a revisionist interpretation that emphasized the unity-in-diversity of Jews and gentiles.[14] Barth argued that the main theme of

12. Adolf von Harnack, *The Mission and Expansion of Christianity in the First Three Centuries*, 2 vols., trans. James Moffatt (London: Williams & Norgate, 1904 [German original 1902]), 1:243, 240–41.

13. For example, Andrew T. Lincoln, *Ephesians*, Word Biblical Commentary 42 (Dallas: Word, 1990), 122–66; Ernest Best, *A Critical and Exegetical Commentary on Ephesians*, International Critical Commentary (Edinburgh: T&T Clark, 1998), 233–90.

14. Markus Barth, *Israel und die Kirche im Brief des Paulus an die Epheser*, Theologische Existenz Heute 75 (Munich: Kaiser, 1959); Barth, *The Broken Wall: A Study in the Epistle to the Ephesians* (Valley Forge, PA: Judson, 1959), 115–27; Barth, *Ephesians 1–3: A New Translation with Introduction and Commentary*, Anchor Bible 34 (Garden City, NY: Doubleday,

the passage is Christ's "naturalization" of gentiles into the nation of Israel. For Barth, the point is not that baptized gentiles are successors of Israel, but joint citizens. The "dividing wall of hostility" that Christ broke down is not the law as such but the divisive function of the law: "The apostle intends to say that there no longer need be enmity between Jews and Gentiles because of the mark [of circumcision] distinguishing both."[15] According to Barth, Israel retains covenantal primacy, and gentile proselytes are incorporated *as gentiles*, without the requirement to assimilate through "Judaizing" (adopting Jewish customs). The "one new humanity" is a unity of ethnic difference, of Jew and gentile, circumcised and foreskinned. Furthermore, for Barth, although Ephesians' vision of Jew-gentile reconciliation has a christological locus, it nevertheless "embraced *all* Jews, not merely the 'remnant' that believes in the Messiah already come."[16] Israel's divine election is not portrayed as conditional upon allegiance to Christ, since (in contrast to Rom 9–11) there is "no hardening of the Jews, no throwing away 'vessels of wrath,' no cut-off branches or thrown-out slaves mentioned."[17] Thus for Barth, Ephesians reserves theological space for the legitimacy of Jews outside the church, as people ever in possession of their birthright, the irrevocable covenants of promise.

Recent scholarship has begun to push back against the deeply embedded tradition of agonistic, contemptuous, and triumphalist readings that have dominated Ephesians' reception and to move in a less incendiary, less dangerous direction.[18] These newer perspectives contest the conventional "supersessionist" understandings of Israel's obsolescence and replacement by the church, foregrounding the Jewishness of Ephesians' message and acknowledging the enduring religious significance of Jewish identity. The impetus for reevaluating previous approaches is not simply exegetical and theological, but existential. Interpreting Ephesians responsibly in the post-Holocaust world involves reckoning with its troubling history of complicity in fostering Christian Judeophobia.

1974), 253–325; Barth, *The People of God*, Journal for the Study of the New Testament Supplement 5 (Sheffield: JSOT Press, 1977), 29–49.

15. Barth, *Ephesians 1–3*, 280.

16. Barth, *People of God*, 49.

17. Barth, *People of God*, 46.

18. E.g., Tet-Lim N. Yee, *Jews, Gentiles, and Ethnic Reconciliation: Paul's Jewish Identity and Ephesians*, Society for New Testament Study Monograph 130 (Cambridge: Cambridge University Press, 2005); Elisabeth Schüssler Fiorenza, *Ephesians*, Wisdom Commentary 50 (Collegeville, MN: Liturgical Press, 2017), 23–31; Andrew Rillera, "Tertium Genus or Dyadic Unity? Investigating Sociopolitical Salvation in Ephesians," *Biblical Research* 66 (2021): 31–51.

Discussion Questions and Activity Suggestions

1. How would you characterize Ephesians' depiction of Jews and their ancestral customs? Give examples.

2. Paula Fredriksen argues that in the ancient world "the gods run in the blood"; gods and humans formed kinship groups, such that cult and ethnicity were intertwined. How might this illuminate our understanding of the relations between Israel, the gentile nations, and Christ's "one new humanity" in Ephesians 2:11–22?

3. In Andrew Rillera's "nonsupersessionist" reading of Ephesians, the church is not a homogenized ethnic singularity but a "dyadic unity" of Jews and gentiles, in which the ethnic distinctions of both groups are preserved rather than obliterated. How might this approach challenge contemporary Christian Judeophobia?

4. Read Ephesians 2:11–22 alongside Paul's discussion of Israel and the nations in Romans 9–11, paying particular attention to how these two texts construct the Jew-gentile relationship with respect to Christ. How do their stories of salvation compare? What are the key points of agreement and difference? For each text, draw a concept map to illustrate their portraits of salvation for Israel and the gentile nations.

Further Reading

Dunning, Benjamin H. "Strangers and Aliens No Longer: Negotiating Identity and Difference in Ephesians 2." *Harvard Theological Review* 99 (2006): 1–16.

Fredriksen, Paula. "How Jewish Is God? Divine Ethnicity in Paul's Theology." *Journal of Biblical Literature* 137 (2018): 193–212.

Harrill, J. Albert. "Ethnic Fluidity in Ephesians." *New Testament Studies* 60 (2014): 379–402.

MacDonald, Margaret Y. "The Politics of Identity in Ephesians." *Journal for the Study of the New Testament* 26 (2004): 419–44.

Ophir, Adi, and Ishay Rosen-Zvi. *Goy: Israel's Multiple Others and the Birth of the Gentile*. Oxford Studies in the Abrahamic Religions. Oxford: Oxford University Press, 2018.

Rillera, Andrew R. "Tertium Genus or Dyadic Unity? Investigating Sociopolitical Salvation in Ephesians." *Biblical Research* 66 (2021): 31–51.

Schüssler Fiorenza, Elisabeth. *Ephesians* (pages 23–31). Wisdom Commentary 50. Collegeville, MN: Liturgical Press, 2017.

Thiessen, Matthew. "The Construction of Gentiles in the Letter to the Ephesians." Pages 13–25 in *The Early Reception of Paul the Second Temple Jew: Text, Narrative, and Reception History*. Edited by Isaac W. Oliver and Gabriele Boccaccini with Joshua Scott. Library of Second Temple Studies 92. London: T&T Clark, 2019.

20

Philippians

MARK D. NANOS

Philippians 3 plays an important role in the legacy of Christian Judeophobia. The received readings present an interesting, arguably insightful case for discussing the longstanding tradition of portraying the apostle Paul as the quintessential convert, a Jew who not only turned away from Judaism, but, and most relevant for this volume, one who thereafter opposed the continued value and practice of being a Jew or beholden to observing torah, which is devalued as obsolete and antithetical to Christian identification and ideals.[1] For example, Christian theology highlights 3:8 to warrant understanding Paul to denounce his prior Jewish identification and behavior as merely "crap"[2] compared to his new "Christian"[3] identification and behavior. Paul's invectives

---

1. In traditional Christian theological imagination and discourse, the use of "law" for torah carries the implied judgment that the Mosaic covenantal obligations, especially ritual ones, are inherently the opposite of the ideals at the heart of the new Christian covenant of love and freedom. On the contrary, even when "law" is used in traditional Jewish discourse, the ideal at the heart of the concept remains linked to the Hebrew meaning of torah, namely, God-given "guidance/instruction" for Israel's covenant relationship, in which Israel's (response, i.e., grateful) fidelity (faithfulness) to God's guidance corresponds to God's (initiating, i.e., grace-based) fidelity (faithfulness) to Israel.

2. Or "shit" (3:8; *skybala*), often euphemistically translated "rubbish," presumably to avoid use of crass language; nevertheless, the idea of total renunciation remains clear.

3. Except when I am trying to articulate the traditional viewpoints in traditional terms, I will use the less anachronistic "Christ-followers." Based on the extant evidence, not least Paul's own letters, "Christian" and "Christianity" were not yet used to describe these people or their groups. More importantly, the usage of these terms to discuss Paul's messages can obscure that, for him and this movement, there were Jews and non-Jews, some of whom were followers of Jesus as Messiah (Christ), but none of whom had either collapsed those

in 3:2 (supplemented by those in 3:18–19) are even more influential for this theological meaning-making in highly contrastive Jew/Christian terms. For Paul is understood to denounce those who advocated the ritual practice of circumcision and other "behavior" enjoined in torah as the "mutilation," "evil workers," and, most graphically telling for this legacy, as "dogs."

I expect that many if not most contemporary Christians, even if aware of this legacy in general terms, will be surprised, even shocked, to learn that by the Middle Ages Christian clergy no less than laity commonly referred to Jews as dogs and treated them accordingly—in Paul's name, by appeal to this text, which they combined with a pronouncement made by Jesus in the gospels. This invective became a popular way for Christians to refer to Jews and weaponize it theologically to, for example, justify ghettoization of Jews in order to protect "the church," that is, "the body of Christ," from the defilement of "the Host" by caricaturing Jews as hungry dogs who want to take bread from the table of the children (Matt 15:26–27).[4] We will review the extant origins of the interpretive decisions that gave birth to this Judeophobic legacy,[5] which

---

identifications into a new categorical one (Christian) yet, or begun to think of their movement as something other than a (subgroup) form of Judaism (that is, Jewish ways of thinking and living embodied in Jewish subgroups). I also avoid the use of "gentile," opting for "non-Jew" because it can obscure that, in Paul's worldview, they were simply not Jews, which is relevant for evaluating his arguments contextually, and because "gentile" has become conflated with "Christian" since his time. For clarity when discussing Paul's messages, it is important (although admittedly cumbersome) to describe the figures discussed in specific terms, as "Christ-following Jews" (e.g., Paul), "Christ-following non-Jews" (e.g., most if not all of his target addressees), or "Jews" and "non-Jews" (e.g., also often identified as "pagans" or "idolaters") who are not Christ-followers. See my "Paul and Judaism: Why Not Paul's Judaism?," in *Reading Paul within Judaism*, vol. 1 of *Collected Essays of Mark D. Nanos* (Eugene, OR: Cascade, 2017), 3–59 (originally 2010).

4. See Kenneth Stow, *Jewish Dogs: An Image and Its Interpreters: Continuity in the Catholic-Jewish Encounter*, Stanford Studies in Jewish History and Culture (Stanford: Stanford University Press, 2006), 6–8, 13–36. The legacy included a number of stunning elements, for example, denouncing synagogue prayers as "barking." Stow assumes the accuracy of the prevailing interpretations of the texts of Paul and the gospels in his analysis of the ways that they were put to use in Christian history, which bears witness to the probability that this interpretive legacy is simply repeated rather than examined in the sources he reviewed, and thus assumed to accurately reflect the aims of both the historical Paul and gospel writers.

5. For more detailed examination of the evidence than can be undertaken herein, upon which this essay depends, see my "Paul's Reversal of Jews Calling Gentiles 'Dogs' (Philippians 3:2): 1600 Years of an Ideological Tale Wagging an Exegetical Dog?," *Biblical Interpretation* 17 (2009): 448–82; for additional examination of the received readings and the alternatives I propose instead, see my "Paul's Polemic in Philippians 3 as Jewish-Subgroup Vilification of Local Non-Jewish Cultic and Philosophical Alternatives," *Journal for the Study*

remain especially relevant because they are repeated to this day in contemporary commentary discussions of Philippians 3 and thus continue to shape the way Christians interpret Paul and use his polemic to think and talk about Jews and Judaism, usually without expressing any distance or disclaimer on either historical or moral grounds. We also will explore why the interpretive decisions from which these legacies emerged involve highly questionable and unnecessary translations and interpretations of the texts, and thus should not continue to be repeated without qualification as if self-evidently true or morally benign. Just as importantly, we will explore why Paul's original usage probably had nothing to do with opposing Jewish people or the advocacy of Jewish practices. Rather, and ironically, in view of the certainty of this legacy, we will see that the most likely targets of Paul's invective were non-Jewish people and influences in Philippi.

The Received Reading of Philippians 3

In Philippians 3, Paul abruptly introduces two sets of warnings. A reader of the NRSV will encounter Paul warning against "dogs," "evil workers," and "those who mutilate the flesh" in 3:2.[6] Although the targets of these invectives—at least one of which (dogs) is always (and almost certainly correctly) assumed to be metaphorical—are not explicitly named Jews or accused of advocating the circumcision (understood to signify becoming Jews and practicing Judaism) of "Christians," there has been no uncertainty of this interpretive conclusion since at least the fourth century. The supposed advocates of Judaism for Christ-following non-Jews whom Paul denounces in this polemic are traditionally named "Judaizers," and their activity "Judaizing" (even though grammatically inaccurate).[7] They are most often identified as Christian Jews representing the

---

of Paul and His Letters 3.1 (2013): 47–92; and my "Out-Howling the Cynics: Reconceptualizing the Concerns of Paul's Audience from His Polemics in Philippians 3," in *The People beside Paul: The Philippian Assembly and History from Below*, ed. Joseph A. Marchal, Early Christianity and Its Literature (Atlanta: SBL Press, 2015), 183–221.

6. NRSV annotation adds: "G[ree]k the mutilation."

7. Lexically (in Greek equivalents as well as in English), "Judaizing/Judaizers" refers to those adopting Jewish identity or behavioral norms (e.g., proselytes judaize), not to those promoting them; moreover, the -izing/-izers ending supplies a negative (prejudicial) valence, unlike, for example, the decision to characterize those who advocate becoming Christians not as Christian*izers* or mission*izers* but positively as Christian mission*aries*. The accusation of "Judaizing" or being "Judaizers" became and lives on in inter-Christian rhetoric, where no Jews or Judaism are at issue, serving as a way to polemicize the motives,

commonly supposed opposition to Paul's mission, or to Pauline Christianity, by the Jerusalem-based Jewish Christians under the leadership of the original apostles. Naturally, this identification of the conflict in terms of advocacy of torah versus Paul's supposed denunciation of it can and logically does often bleed over into the implied (when not overtly stated) judgment that Paul's opposition is to any Jews or even non-Jews (Christ-followers or not) who advocate the practices of Judaism for Christ-followers.[8]

Philippians 3:18–19, wherein Paul differentiates his addressees from some people or groups as "enemies of the cross of Christ," whose "god is the belly," whose "glory is in their shame," and whose "minds are set on earthly things," is usually enlisted as an additional indicator that Paul has in his sights those who advocate Jewish practices. Interpretations typically reflect premises that live in traditional Christian anti-Jewish stereotypes. In order, these include viewing these "others" attacking the value of Jesus's crucifixion and faith alone apart from "Judaizing" (if not also being Christ-killers); being shameless mutilators of foreskin ("Judaizers"); refusing to eat with non-Jews (misanthropic); and being outward-ritual oriented, carnal, proclaiming works-righteousness, and advocating legalism and ethnocentrism.

The traditional interpretation can be traced back at least to the church father John Chrysostom, who claimed that Paul's warning to beware of "the dogs" represented a reversal of an ostensibly common Jewish (arrogant, stand-offish, mean-spirited) prejudicial habit of calling non-Jews (usually termed

---

teachings, or behavior of rival Christians or Christian groups. Tellingly, this polemical slam is able to accomplish its exclusion of the Christian other's aims as if self-evidently Jewish (or too Jewish) for Christians even though not related to Jews or the practice of Judaism in any way, and without the need to explain why a Christian or Christian group being Jewish or behaving in some Jewish ways by definition represents a negative trait. In other words, it has taken on a life after Paul's time that makes it not only anachronistic but counterproductive for historical discussion of Paul and his texts and communities, and in general, misleadingly introduces Jews and Judaism as a negative foil in Christian discourse; continued usage should be avoided. See Shaye J. D. Cohen, *The Beginnings of Jewishness: Boundaries, Varieties, Uncertainties*, Hellenistic Culture and Society 31 (Berkeley: University of California Press, 1999), 175–97.

8. I discussed this dynamic and its apparently largely unrecognized problematic implications toward non-Christ-following Jews and their practices. When the rivalries are framed as inter-/intra-Christian, the "problem" is often interpreted to be that the "other" Christians are doing something (too) Jewish, regularly reflected in the (damning but apparently not necessary to explain) declamation that they are guilty of "Judaizing"; see my "How Inter-Christian Approaches to Paul's Rhetoric Can Perpetuate Negative Valuations of Jewishness—Although Proposing to Avoid That Outcome," in *Reading Paul within Judaism*, 63–76; originally *Biblical Interpretation* 13.3 (2005): 255–69.

"gentiles") "dogs," which Paul thus simply reversed toward the Jews ("Judaizers"). Commentaries to this day reflect Chrysostom's reasoning, implicitly
when not also explicitly. They assert not only that Jews called non-Jews dogs
but that, in dog-eat-dog fashion, Paul was thereby justified to express such
prejudice in this degrading way. One might expect to find discussions that
Paul, by doing so, is guilty of producing the same kind of invective toward
Jews (or whoever was targeted) that they posit for Jews toward themselves
and apparently (and reasonably) find so offensive, or call for their audiences
to eschew repeating this unkind turn of phrase; but the commentaries reveal
no such concern.[9] Instead, and in spite of Paul's own proscription elsewhere
of such behavior as fleshly and antithetical to walking in spirit (Gal 5:13–21),
Paul's interpreters traditionally not only justify his behavior, but repeat it as
if both accurate and commendable to proceed to talk about Jews this way to
interpret this text, if not also Paul's view of Jews and Judaism more broadly.

Chrysostom's proof, which remains the proof most often encountered to
this day if one examines the commentaries on Philippians, is based on com-
bining Philippians 3:2 with Matthew 15:26–27.[10] Therein Jesus dismisses the
Canaanite woman seeking his help, declaring "It is not fair to take the children's food and throw it to the dogs" (NRSV). She replies: "Yes, Lord, yet
even the dogs eat the crumbs that fall from their masters' table." The same
incident is reported, with some differences, in Mark 7:24–30, where she is
identified as "a Gentile [literally Greek], of Syrophoenician origin" (NRSV).
From this, Chrysostom and those he influenced created "an image of Christian
children hungering for the Eucharist, which 'Jewish dogs' incessantly plot to
steal, consume, savage, or pollute."[11] In Chrysostom's homilies on Philippians,
Jews are presented as "greedy of vile lucre and fond of power" who "corrupt

9. Comments on 3:2 in Homily 10 of Chrysostom, *Homilies on the Epistle of St. Paul to
the Philippians*.

10. E.g., widely popular among evangelical pastors, Gerald F. Hawthorne, *Philippians*,
Word Biblical Commentary 43 (Waco, TX: Word, 1983), 125, refers the reader to Matt 15:21–
28; Otto Michel, "κύων, κυνάριον," *Theological Dictionary of the New Testament* (Grand
Rapids: Eerdmans, 1965), 3:1101–4; Hermann Leberecht Strack and Paul Billerbeck, *Kommentar zum Neuen Testament aus Talmud und Midrasch*, 6 vols. (Munich: Beck, 1922–1961),
1:724–25; 3:62–22, as the basis for stating baldly: "The Jews were in the habit of referring
contemptuously to Gentiles as dogs—unclean animals with whom they would not associate
if such association could be avoided. . . . Paul now hurls this term of contempt back 'on the
heads of its authors.' . . . To Paul the Jews were the real pariahs that defile the holy community, the Christian church, with their erroneous teaching."

11. Stow, *Jewish Dogs*, xiv–xv; Stow's ideological-critical discussion of the Christian tradition's development of the notion of "Jewish dogs" starts from the consensus view that Paul

the gospel" and seek "to draw aside the faithful" by preaching "both Christianity and Judaism at the same time."[12] Although Chrysostom was referring to Christ-following Jews (as "Judaizers"), he logically extended this vitriol to all Jews, because returning from participation with non-Christian Jews in the synagogues and festivals brings the polluting influence into the church and the eucharistic meal.[13]

We can only briefly discuss some of the many problematic elements in the legacy interpretive decisions.[14] As for the gospel evidence, one might expect Jesus to declaim that the woman should analogize herself to a dog, but he is not presented to do so. The legacy interpreters do not seem particularly concerned with what this suggests about Jesus's moral leadership, but rather, with alerting their reader that this as prototypical *Jewish* behavior. Even if this was true, shouldn't a Jewish *Jesus* rise above that? Regardless, there are several exegetical matters to note: (a) the woman, responding to Jesus's metaphorical use of dogs, does not call herself a dog but analogizes her situation to that of dogs who are valued positively; (b) she does not say Jews, or Jesus, called her or her children dogs, but rather responds based on Jesus analogizing her situation to that of family dogs who do not expect to be fed as equals to the children; and (c) she is identified and responds in ambiguous terms that connote that she may be a descendant of the northern Israelite tribes who suffered forced intermarriage under the Assyrians (Syrophoenician/Canaanite). In other words, she indirectly identifies herself as in some way potentially a

---

in Phil 3:2 was referring to "Judaizing" Christian-Jews as dogs; in other words, he accepted the traditional Christian interpretation rather than investigating its bases.

12. John Chrysostom, "Homily 10," in *Chrysostom: Homilies on Galatians, Ephesians, Philippians, Colossians, Thessalonians, Timothy, Titus, and Philemon*, A Select Library of the Nicene and Post-Nicene Fathers of the Christian Church 13, First Series, ed. Philip Schaff (Grand Rapids: Eerdmans, 1979), 230. Chrysostom goes on to ensure that his reader knows that the Jews are not to even have the "advantage" the Canaanite woman's appeal affords to the dogs. Citing Matt 15:27, he writes: "But that they might not have this advantage, since even dogs are at the table, he adds that, whereby he makes them aliens also, saying, 'Beware of the evil workers'; he admirably expressed himself, 'beware of the evil workers.'" See also Chrysostom, "Introductory Discourse 3"; Chrysostom, *Eight Homilies against the Jews* 1.11.1–2. Over the centuries, Christians added other texts that supposedly strengthened the claim; see Strack and Billerbeck, *Kommentar zum Neuen Testament*, 1:722–24; 3:621–22; and Michel, "κύων, κυνάριον." I explain in my "Paul's Reversal" why each of these examples also involves misreading the evidence.

13. Chrysostom, *Eight Homilies against the Jews* 2.3.5. The link between the Eucharist and the saying of Matt 7:6 to keep what is holy from the dogs is made as early as Didache 9.5, to articulate an injunction that prohibits the unbaptized from participation.

14. See my "Paul's Reversal," 22–27.

fellow Israelite if not a Judean (and thus, perhaps, entitled to be included in Jesus's mission "to the lost house of Israel"). Therefore, she is not identified in this gospel passage as a prototypical non-Jew or called a dog for being a non-Jew, and this is pronounced by none other than Jesus (on behalf of his followers), undermining the supposed, even if flawed, basis for the legacy interpretation's justification.

It also bears noting that this story appears in the gospels, which postdate Paul's letter. For the Philippians to decode that Paul's reference to dogs is a reversal based upon the gospel evidence, which as noted is the most common cross-reference provided to warrant this connection, requires not only that they know Paul to be hostile toward the promotion of Jewish practices so that he could be expected to reverse this invective toward Jews, but also that he and they knew that Jews called non-Jews "dogs" simply for being non-Jews (which is highly doubtful, see below). But more than that, this requires Paul to both know and expect the Philippians to know this Jesus story, even though there is no evidence that such gospels already existed or were known to Paul or in Philippi by this probable date.[15] In short, the usual justification for appeal to this gospel evidence to warrant not only the exegetical traditions for Philippians 3 but all the more the reasoning for the Christian legacy fear of Jews as dogs who seek to defile the bread of Christ requires reasoning from highly improbable, not to mention hostile, premises.

The evidence for the reversal on which the legacy exegesis of 3:2 (and concomitantly 3:18–19) depends is even more problematic, as surprising as that might seem. Why? Well, in short, there is simply *no* evidence, literary or material, that Jews ever called non-Jews "dogs" for being non-Jews; *none*.[16]

Chrysostom refers only to the gospel accounts, which we have discussed and which, ironically, for him, requires reasoning that Jesus is evidence of such Jewish behavior rather than the denunciation thereof. He names no other Jewish evidence. Some later and especially twentieth-century New Testament

---

15. Philippians is usually dated to the late 50s or early 60s, and Paul's death to the mid-60s, while these gospels are dated to several years or decades after the Roman destruction of Jerusalem in 70.

16. All of the supposed evidence is examined and dismissed in my "Paul's Reversal," 10–22. I am pleased to report that this research has been well received and even altered some investigations, although, to my knowledge, most of these have continued to work from the premise that Paul's invectives target advocates of circumcision. See, e.g., Christopher Zoccali, *Reading Philippians after Supersessionism: Jews, Gentiles, and Covenant Identity*, New Testament after Supersessionism (Eugene, OR: Cascade, 2017); Ryan D. Collman, "Beware the Dogs! The Phallic Epithet in Phil 3.2," *New Testament Studies* 67 (2021): 105–20.

specialists refer to some biblical texts (usually Psalms) and much later rabbinic texts as evidence, but I demonstrated that none of these provide such evidence, even anachronistically, even after hundreds of years of suffering being called dogs by Christians and treated as if dogs.[17] In some cases the targets are non-Jews, in most cases fellow Jews or Israelites; the vitriol is based on their role as rivals that threaten the writer's interests, not their ethnicity per se. Just like in many other discourses, metaphorical use of "dog" can be used both positively (e.g., tenacity, loyalty) and negatively (compare "bitch"), and the reason for the choice of terms can be determined only by context. Like many swear words, dog-related invectives may be used without conscious choice and make little sense literally; such words are often used, to this day, to express negative sentiment that makes little sense of the choice (think about the many, often incoherent ways that "shit" or "son of a bitch" or "bastard" are used today, with no literal-based intention). After we discuss the other epithets, we will return to discuss more probable targets for Paul's invectives.

Paul's second epithet in 3:2, "evil workers," is simply too vague to offer the support normally derived from it in the legacy readings. They proceed from the a priori premise that Paul is targeting Jews advocating Jewish practices for Christ-followers and then, by circular reasoning, conclude that by "works" Paul means "works-righteousness," which fits the foil that Christian theologians created as the problem with Judaism to which Paul objects. We do not have space to discuss the many weaknesses in this conclusion, but it is sufficiently challenged in recent New Testament scholarship to leave this aside.[18] What remains, however, is the concomitant responsibility to challenge the way that legacy foil remains active for exegesis of this passage. We will return to the topic with several more likely alternatives from non-Jewish actors/forces.

The interpretation, including translation, of the invective "mutilation" in 3:2 is inextricably tied to the premise that Paul has in view "Judaizers," by which is meant, wrongly, as already noted, those who promote Judaism, especially signified in this view by the rite of circumcision. This tradition is so deeply engrained that, as noted above, even when Bibles translate the Greek properly as "mutilation," they might add an annotation to clarify how the reader should understand it, that is, as "mutilators" or, as in the case of the NRSV, vice versa. Greeks and Romans who were not Jews regularly expressed repulsion at Jewish circumcision as "mutilation," representing a shameful disfiguring of the body.

---

17. See my "Paul's Reversal."

18. E.g., E. P. Sanders, *Paul and Palestinian Judaism: A Comparison of Patterns of Religion* (Philadelphia: Fortress, 1977).

But the legacy view requires that this was now Paul the convert's valuation of this rite and that of his ideal (Christ-following convert) reader.

The received view reasons from the premise that the "Judaizers" are on a mission to advocate circumcision in opposition to Paul's gospel, which supposedly omitted this rite. This identification, although circular, governs the unanimous conclusion that Paul is here expressing his opposition to their particular (usually: alternative gospel) aims. In addition, they are usually identified as missionaries of the Christian Judaism led by the Jerusalem-based original apostles, a decision that plays an important role in the way that Christian origins are constructed around rivalry between Pauline and Jerusalem/Jewish factions of Christianity, the latter guilty of retaining the value of torah when ideally, in traditional Pauline terms, they should not. However, nowhere in this letter does Paul indicate the arrival of any such people or efforts or that he is opposed to Jewish identity or practices. We will discuss below how the adversaries he names are non-Jews proceeding from agendas that have nothing to do with advocating that the addressees become circumcised (Jews).

There are more threads around which these judgments are made than we can examine here, but challenging the prevailing thinking requires discussing some of them. For example, the consensus reasoning posits that when Paul follows these warnings with the assertion that "we are the circumcision" in 3:3, he is thus claiming that "Christians" have, in a spiritual instead of a crass fleshly way, replaced Jews as the rightful claimants to the divine promises made to "the circumcision," since the way Paul addresses his recipients indicates they probably consist of mostly if not entirely non-Jews (males having foreskins). I also suspect that they are mostly if not entirely non-Jews; however, Paul did not write "we are the *spiritual* [or *true*] circumcision" or, even more clearly, that "we are not the circumcision," although some translations and many interpretive comments do so.[19] The ideological bias is betrayed by this: if the

---

19. Note that the NRSV indicates that Paul is announcing that they have "replaced" the targets of his invectives, assumed to be advocating circumcision: "For *it is* we *who* are the circumcision" (emphasis added; "it is" and "who" are not in the Greek: *hēmeis gar esmen hē peritomē*). Literally, the contrast is being made with those who represent "mutilation," as if the opposite of "circumcision," even though the addressees presumably are not circumcised (just as Jewish women were not, but would be included in this synecdoche). That is, circumcision here functions as a synecdoche for Jewish communal identification (think "red/blue" states in US political rhetoric, even though not everyone in any state is a member of the majority party in a given state). In other words, they have joined Jewish groups, not groups of idolaters who practice mutilation, and should thus now take their cues from Jewish cultural norms, like the rest of those Paul names in this verse—which are all Jewish values!

proper translation of 3:2 was "mutilators [of the flesh]" (NRSV), then Paul's assertion in 3:3 should be translated correspondingly, "we are the mutilators [of the flesh]."

In addition to the puzzling choice to assert "we are the *circumcision*" if Paul regarded circumcision equivalent to mutilation, it is illogical for him to include in his list of (superior) Jewish credentials in 3:5 that he was "*circumcised* on the eighth day." If he now (de)valued this rite from a Greco-Roman elite perspective—or wanted his addressees to do so—we should expect him to write that he was (shamefully) "*mutilated* on the eighth day," by no choice of his own. However, Paul's turn of phrase makes sense if he saw his assembly members, foreskinned non-Jews no less than circumcised Jews, now united together in a Jewish movement, which, like Jewish movements in general, probably struggled to keep the value of this signifying rite salient in the face of prejudicial degradation as mutilation by Greek and Roman neighbors and rulers. In other words, this language instead betrays that Paul was engaged in highlighting the contrast between *his addressees' Jewishness* (the practices of Jewish cultural norms in their assemblies), whether they were Jews (circumcised males, or women, who were not circumcised in Jewish cultures) or not, and their *neighbors'* (and for the non-Jews addressed, their own former) *cultural norms*, which Paul polemicizes in the synecdoches mutilation, evil workers, and dogs.

When we recognize that Paul lists these elements not to conflate but to contrast them with Jewish cultural norms, it is clear that non-Jewish Christ-worshipers (who might hold themselves to Jewish standards of behavior, and even suffer for doing so) would immediately interpret Paul's polemic to apply to pagan norms, not to Jewish ones. These norms more likely indicate negative valuation of cults and their gods/goddesses, philosophical groups, or other competing and perhaps attractive ways that Paul may fear his target non-Jews might try to negotiate the Jewishness of their identity in order to escape or at least minimize negative, marginalizing consequences. In the case of non-Jews, they might be quite unfamiliar with the marginalization that Jewish minority community members had learned to overcome and seek either to retain certain non-Jewish cultural practices or else be suffering from their families and neighbors precisely for completely breaking away from these.

Although the legacy readings interpret the language in 3:18–19—which includes mention of opposition to the cross, concern about the belly, this-worldly orientation, and glorying in shame—to indicate "Judaizers," once we recognize the slim basis for introducing Jews or Jewish practices to interpret the language in 3:2–3, we can readily recognize how ill-suited each of these are for signifying Jews or Judaism in 3:18–19. After all, the dietary customs require that the faithful are not to be controlled by their appetite desires, unlike, say, the Epicureans. The only accusation that might be applied to Jews, but not to Christ-following ones (which, strangely, are the usual suspects in the legacy reading), is of being "enemies of the cross of Christ." But the accusation of being "enemies" applies all the more naturally, at this early date, to those who have imprisoned Paul for his claims about Jesus (1:7, 12–30; cf. 2:14–15), that is, the Romans and other non-Jewish elites, for proclaiming someone they executed as a possible terrorist. Interestingly, unlike the referents in 3:2, even legacy interpreters note that these vague charges could make sense of concern about various cults and philosophical groups, and I demonstrated in detail why that is more likely (see below).[20]

The final argument for the legacy interpretation revolves around reading Paul's negative valuation of his appeal to the Jewish credentials of which he can boast to support his right to contest the influence of those he opposes in Philippi as "crap" (*skybala*) in 3:8. That Paul refers to this among the honors that still define his status, combined with the rhetorical purpose for invoking them to support the identification in Messiah (a Jewish identifier) that he shares with the non-Jews he addresses, who (not being born or raised Jews) cannot boast similarly, betrays the consensus deduction that he is renouncing his Jewish identity or the value of Jewish practices. That deduction depends on misreading the comparative, prescriptive purpose of this declamation, which Paul extends to "everything" (*panta*), not just his Jewish credentials, as if this was a statement describing Paul's present (converted) state from the perspective of a former Jew who no longer subscribed to this identity or its behavioral norms (i.e., Judaism). However, Paul's authority to instruct them to resist who and what he targets in this passage is predicated upon his still enjoying the Jewish credentials to do so—and that they know he does. This approach has little chance of being persuasive if he does not still have the right to make this boast-based case. Paul is making a comparative point: they share a superordinate identity in Messiah, regardless of perhaps suffering as non-Jews in some ways that Paul, as a Jew, does not. This rhetoric requires that his readers know the enormous, continued value of his Jewish credentials, but he wants them to understand that, if put in theoretical this-or-that terms, they share the same highest value, identification together with Paul in Messiah. Read apart from

---

20. For details, see esp. my "Paul's Polemic in Philippians 3"; and my "Out-Howling the Cynics."

context, the purpose of Paul's declamation is—and in my view has been—entirely misconstrued.

Toward Reversal of This Judeophobic Tale

If not Jews (or non-Jews) promoting Judaism, not least circumcision for the Christ-following non-Jews, who and what did Paul probably target with the invectives in 3:2? The most probable sources are local non-Jews. Paul's non-Jews, being in the early stages of Jewish (subgroup) communal enculturation, are vulnerable to such influencers and influences from their native culture. On the one hand, they may be attracted to retain or incorporate certain non-Jewish norms and affiliations; on the other hand, they may be suffering loss of face or goods for failure to do so. For example, as in Corinth apparently (1 Cor 8–10), they might reason that withdrawing from eating cult-offered food and drink creates a (too) hard price to pay, and thus consider ways to negotiate the problems posed: "Why not assert that it is no longer sacred for 'us' as Christ-followers so we do not have to withdraw so completely from normal family, local, and imperial events because these involve food and drink and activities dedicated to gods and heroes/rulers we no longer respect?" Whether one or the other or some of both, Paul's rhetorical approach betrays a calculated effort to "other" certain local non-Jewish influences (that he presumes are or could) negatively impact his addressees' commitment to Christ.

There are many indicators in the letter that Paul and his addressees in Philippi are primarily concerned about non-Jewish pressure. Throughout Philippians, apart from chapter 3, commentators recognize that Paul focuses on the Roman contextual conflicts he and they face—and for good reason. Philippi was not just another Roman city, but a Roman colony. Colonies were highly stratified according to Roman status-based standards; thus, even Greeks, Macedonians, and Thracians who populated the city competed for honor and access to goods by way of Romanization. Roman religious practice incorporated the local gods and cults. Inscriptions indicate that even foreign cults such as the Egyptian gods and Cybele were linked to the practice of imperial cult. In addition, the extant literary evidence besides Philippians indicates that the tensions in Philippi were with non-Jews over issues related to the way Paul's influence threatened normative idolatrous practices.

In the first case, in 1 Thessalonians 2:1–2, Paul recounts that in Philippi he was insulted insolently (with *hubris*) because his confession of a Jewish figure (Christ/Messiah) ran afoul of the idolatrous cultural orientation of the

Philippian cults toward many gods, including the Romans' celebrated lord and savior of humankind, Caesar. In the second case, in Acts 16:16–21, although a later account and not written by Paul, the author expects his audience to find believable that Paul casts a spirit out of a slave woman tasked with the evil work of selling prophecy/divination (*manteuomenē*),[21] a kind of "belly talking"/ventriloquism especially associated with the cult of Apollo, also with the goddess Cybele (cf. Phil 3:19). Her owners purportedly drag Paul and Silas before the local magistrates and accuse them of engaging in *Jewish* activities that are unlawful according to *Roman* customs.

In addition, 1 Kings 18:1–22:4 offers a graphic example that could inspire a scriptural-based reason to select each of these three epithets to express opposition toward non-Jewish cultural threats. Therein Elijah (to whom Paul explicitly compares himself in Rom 11:1–5) refers to "evil working false prophets" (1 Kgs 18:19–19:1) who "mutilate themselves" in order to "persuade" the gods (18:28, with a verbal form of the same word Paul uses), and the house of Ahab and Jezebel is condemned to be eaten by *dogs* (21:22–29; cf. 2 Kgs 9:33–37; 10:11, 17). Paul's choice of language could simply reflect stereotypical polemics toward idolatrous challengers, or, if his addressees are facing conflicts arising from idolatrous cults or rival philosophical groups, then be quite directly related to their own situation without ever supposing they represent Paul's concerns about Jews or the promotion of Judaism. For example, in the context of the city of Philippi, one might expect (from the point of view of a Jewish writer) that mutilation would be a term of reference to signify those castrated, such as the *galli* of the Cybele cult, or some other kind of mutilation associated with similar religious observances (cf. 1 Kgs 18:28). Self-mutilation is widely associated with "pagan" groups and the way that they seek to provoke God to action (to persuade by or trust in flesh), including by those who employ magic. A Jew such as Paul might also associate such behavior with Cynics.

If Paul's recipients knew that the issues Paul addressed arose from non-Jewish sources, then they would likely regard Paul to be punning on similar sounds (paronomasia) and lexical elements (i.e., cutting). Rather than *conflate* them as synonymous, they would instead recognize they played to a Jewish-oriented cultural *contrast* between them as entirely incompatible with the values and behavior to which his addressees should be beholden. "Mutilation" (*katatomē*, "cutting *into*") is antithetical to their new Jewish-ish cultural identity in Messiah/Christ, signified instead by the Jewish rite of "circumcision"

---

21. The Septuagint uses *manteuomai* to proscribe the practices of non-Israelites: Deut 18:10 (cited in Acts 3:22 and 7:37); 1 Sam 28:8; 2 Kgs 17:17; Jer 27:9 (= LXX 34:9); Ezek 12:24; 13:6, 23; 21:21, 23, 29; 22:28; Mic 3:11.

(*peritomē*, "to cut *around*"). Although they are not to undertake the latter because they are not Jews or born to Jews, circumcision (neither circumcised people nor advocates thereof) is not the "cut" about which he is warning them. When his rhetoric is approached this way, we can interpret his inclusive assertion that "*we* are the circumcision" to exemplify a positive synecdoche. In Philippians 3:3 Paul seeks to shape the self-identification of his addressees in Jewish group-identification terms, albeit with a Jesus-as-Messiah-subgroup orientation shared neither by their non-Jewish families and neighbors nor by most of the Jews in Philippi they interact with, assuming there are any Jews. And if there are, they would presumably agree that, besides the claims for Jesus and thus the warrant for these non-Jews resisting circumcision, the other ideals represent their own Jewish norms: "For we are the circumcision, who serve God in/by spirit [*or* who serve (enabled) by God's Spirit] and boast [revel/glory] in Christ [Messiah] Jesus and do not trust in [*or* do not persuade (gods, events, or people) by] flesh [i.e., mutilation])."[22]

Turning to the invectives themselves, the vagueness of the language used and the many potential targets for the time and place make identification problematic, and, as noted, it could be echoing elements from 1 Kings. Obviously, Paul could target several different people and behaviors simultaneously with each of these invectives. Since the commentary tradition has never seriously investigated alternatives, one must proceed basically from scratch. But the evidence from Paul's time as well as the language choices and arguments he makes in Philippians 3 and throughout the letter lead me to propose that the most obvious targets for the epithets in Philippians 3 include cult figures such as Silvanus, Diana, Cerberus, Hekate, and Cybele; philosophical groups such as Cynics; or some combination of figures such as these.

The first group of options includes gods and goddesses associated with dogs, who can also be signified by the invectives "evil workers" and "mutilation."[23] Silvanus and Diana are portrayed with their dogs in the simple reliefs carved into the hills overlooking Philippi. Not only are such "inscribed images" representative of the normal usage of *katatomē*, namely, "to cut into/inscribe/incise," for example, rocks and coins, rather than to signify "mutilation," these ancient cult sites remain visible in Philippi to this day. Hekate was a goddess involved in conducting the dead to Hades, associated with childbearing and childrearing, and often invoked in the "evil work" of magic. She was often pictured not only

---

22. See my "Paul's Non-Jews Do Not Become 'Jews,' But Do They Become 'Jewish'? Reading Romans 2:25–29 within Judaism, alongside Josephus," in *Reading Paul within Judaism*, 127–54.

23. See esp. my "Paul's Polemics in Philippians 3," 66–71.

accompanied by dogs but also with a dog's face, and dogmeat was used in the "suppers" offered at the crossroads where her sculptures stood. The orgiastic rituals of the cult of Cybele involved the mutilation of its initiates; they castrated themselves. From Paul's cultural point of view, it might seem salient to disparage any one or all these as practicing evil, and like dogs, acting shamefully.

The second group of options are philosophical groups, which often called rival philosophers "dogs," most notable and literally the Cynics.[24] When we refer to the Cynics, we are actually using a Latinized form of the Greek word for "dogs"; namely, they called themselves and were called *kyōn* and *ho kynikos*, for whom behaving "doggishly" was a badge of honor.[25] Paul uses Cynic-like phrases such as "boldness of speech [*parrēsia*]" (Phil 1:14, 20; cf. Diogenes Laertius, *Lives* 6.69) and "our citizenship is in heaven" (Phil 3:19–20; cf. Diogenes Laertius, *Lives* 6.63). Paul's harsh approach and use of crass language (e.g., "crap") reflects Cynic norms; he may be engaged in trying to out-cynic the Cynics through a Jewish-based countercultural tune. His use of athletic imagery in Philippians 3:12–16 and his focus on self-denial throughout Philippians 3 and 4:5–13 parallel common Cynic tropes and emphases on the need for disciplined persistence in the face of resistance (*askēsis*) in order to avoid succumbing to the conventional measures of success, which corresponds also to Paul's appeal to and yet relativization of his own Jewish measures of success (cf. Diogenes Laertius, *Lives* 6.27–30, 45, 49, 70–71; Epictetus, *Discourses* 3.22.51–52). The purposefully wretched state Cynics chose, unbathed with long unkept hair, torn and dirty cloaks, defecating in public, cannibalism, living in an urn at the Cybele shrine with its practice of mutilation, eating the meal offerings left at crossroads for the dog-faced goddess Hekate, as well as their defacing (*katatomē*) of currency, could certainly be polemicized as mutilation associated with evil workers according to Jewish norms. Any and all of these could also be indicated in the dissociating portrayals of the "other" Paul decries in Philippians 3:18–19.

Conclusion

Who and what Paul targeted with his invectives in Philippians 3 are clearly unclear. But clearly not unclear is that most, if not all, of the bases for the

---

24. See esp. my "Paul's Polemics in Philippians 3," 71–88; and my "Out-Howling the Cynics."

25. Cf. Philo, *Planter* 151; Diogenes Laertius, *Lives* 6; Lucian, *Demonax* 21; Athenaeus, *Deipnosophistae* 3.96–99; Clement, *Miscellanies* 8.12.4–7.

familiar legacy Judeophobic interpretations are without merit. There is no logical reason to deduce that Paul or his addressees knew a stereotype of non-Jews as dogs when there is no extant literature to warrant it; or that he was a (Christian) convert (from Judaism) who had come to regard circumcision as "mutilation"; or that he made the morally compromising decision to reverse this unattested invective to target Jews for advocating Jewish practices including circumcision by deriding them as "dogs," "mutilators," or "evil workers" in 3:2; or to describe them by any of the polemics listed in 3:18–19. It becomes readily apparent that there are a number of alternatives to explore that could make better sense of Paul and that he likely opposed when we approach this rhetoric from the perspective that he remained a Jew who practiced and promoted a Jewish way of life in his assemblies, including for non-Jews, and that his addressees knew this about Paul, including that he expected them to become more, not less, Jewish culturally.

As a result of allegiance to the gospel-based way of life that Paul advocated, the Philippian non-Jews would likely suffer status degradation and concomitant deprivation. They would have to abandon certain native non-Jewish norms such as family, local, and imperial cult and associated ways of life, thereby becoming (too) culturally Jewish yet at the same time not choosing the familiar course of completing proselyte transformation to legitimate this behavior and associated expectations of their Jewish neighbors no less than their non-Jewish ones—since the gospel denied that option to them.[26]

Paul's polemical approach could suggest, in one direction, that he supposed they were tempted to retain some non-Jewish cultural practices in order to minimize the negative consequences of their new level of Jewishness, or, in the other direction, that they needed some encouragement in the face of suffering from those who advocated the necessity of continuing to practice native non-Jewish cultural practices since they had not become proselyte Jews. Their choice not to comply with normal expectations of them as non-Jews would be understood to pose a threat of retaliation from the neglected gods and the rulers to whom they had to answer, not only for themselves but for their families and neighbors. In either case, or even both, Paul's invectives were not designed to degrade the value and attraction to Jewish cultural norms, but quite the opposite: to highlight a sharp contrast between their new identity among the circumcision (Jews and Jewish cultural norms) and the non-Jewish

---

26. See my "Re-Framing Paul's Opposition to *Erga Nomou* as 'Rites of a Custom' for Proselyte Conversion Completed by the Synecdoche 'Circumcision,'" *Journal of the Jesus Movement in Its Jewish Setting* 8 (2021): 75–115.

people and norms from which they came and to which they remained in some way beholden, or, at least, to whom they were responsible to answer (i.e., "justify" this deviance).

If one should nevertheless conclude that, historically, Paul's invectives targeted Jews and the advocacy of Jewish norms, hopefully sufficient reasons have been given, historical and moral, to provoke reconsideration of repeating these demeaning invectives as if either self-evidently true or appropriate ways to talk about Jews and Judaism today. The same moral imperative applies to whomever and whatever one decides that Paul sought to demonize with this polemic, or whomever and whatever one considers the threatening "other" of their own time. For those for whom Paul is an inspired guide, there is certainly good reason to consider how to qualify his rhetorical behavior contextually and to embrace instead the ideal that was arguably of the highest order for him; that is, to serve the best interests of one's neighbor; put differently, to generously love one's neighbor as one wants to be generously loved.

Discussion Questions and Activity Suggestions

1. Why was the traditional line of interpretation likely developed and attractive in the early development of gentile Christianity? Relatedly: Why has it remained attractive in Christianity? What role might circular reasoning and confirmation bias play in the legacy interpretation?

2. In light of this chapter's arguments, if someone remains convinced that this text expresses negative views toward Jews promoting Judaism, whether a form of Christianity or not, how would you advise them to qualify the way in which they make a historical case for their interpretation with respect to how it should be, for example, applied or preached today?

3. Read through Philippians in one pass looking for clues to the focus of Paul's concerns, and those he projects onto his addressees. Make a list of the features you discover with these questions in mind: Are they primarily from non-Jews and non-Jewish forces, such as (a) Roman rulers, norms, and those charged with policing them or (b) local rulers, norms, and those charged with policing them? Or are they primarily from Jews and advocacy of Jewish practices as threats? Does Philippians 3 appear to correspond with the rest of your findings, or represent a change of focus? If the latter, do you see a way to reconcile this anomaly?

Further Reading

Nanos, Mark D. "Out-Howling the Cynics: Reconceptualizing the Concerns of Paul's Audience from His Polemics in Philippians 3." Pages 183–221 in *The People beside Paul: The Philippian Assembly and History from Below*. Edited by Joseph A. Marchal. Early Christianity and Its Literature. Atlanta: SBL Press, 2015.

———. "Paul's Polemic in Philippians 3 as Jewish-Subgroup Vilification of Local Non-Jewish Cultic and Philosophical Alternatives." Pages 142–91 in *Reading Corinthians and Philippians within Judaism*. Vol. 4 of *The Collected Essays of Mark D. Nanos*. Eugene, OR: Cascade, 2017. Originally published in *Journal for the Study of Paul and His Letters* 3 (2013): 47–92.

———. "Paul's Reversal of Jews Calling Gentiles 'Dogs' (Philippians 3:2): 1600 Years of an Ideological Tale Wagging an Exegetical Dog?" Pages 111–41 in *Reading Corinthians and Philippians within Judaism*. Vol. 4 of *The Collected Essays of Mark D. Nanos*. Eugene, OR: Cascade, 2017. Originally published in *Biblical Interpretation* 17 (2009): 448–82.

Stow, Kenneth. *Jewish Dogs: An Image and Its Interpreters*. Stanford Studies in Jewish History and Culture. Stanford: Stanford University Press, 2006.

Zoccali, Christopher. *Reading Philippians after Supersessionism: Jews, Gentiles, and Covenant Identity*. New Testament after Supersessionism. Eugene, OR: Cascade, 2017.

21

Colossians

HARRY O. MAIER

The Epistle to the Colossians is one of the thirteen New Testament letters attributed to Paul. Since the nineteenth century there has been debate over its authorship. Many, including this author, argue it is an example of a letter written in the name of but not by Paul.[1] The debate over composition centers on the letter's distinctive vocabulary and syntax, its cosmic affirmations about Jesus, its statements about the Christ assembly (church), its view toward the second coming of Jesus, and its ethics, especially as they relate to women and slaves. The letter presupposes that Paul has not met his audience (2:1) and that he has heard about them from his coworker, Epaphras, who was the one who taught Paul's gospel (1:7–8; also 4:12–13). Some scholars argue that Epaphras was the author.

The part of the letter that chiefly concerns us here is 2:8–23. In this polemical section, the author warns against those who "prey" on the audience "by philosophy and empty deceit" (2:8 NRSV). He admonishes that no one pass judgment on the Colossians on account of "food and drink or of observing festivals, new moons, or Sabbaths" (2:16 NRSVue). Further, he states that nobody should "disqualify" members, "insisting on self-abasement and worship of angels, taking their stand on visions, puffed up without reason by their sensuous mind" (2:18 [my translation]). He criticizes those who "submit to regulations," which he quotes: "Do not handle! Do not taste! Do not touch!" (2:21 NRSVue). These rules, he says, are all perishable and have "an appearance of wisdom in promoting rigor and devotion and self-abasement and severity

---

1. Defenders of Pauline authorship argue that it is one of his last letters, written in the 60s. Scholars who contend that he did not write it propose a wide range of dates, from a time when Paul was still alive in the 60s through to the 80s.

to the body, but they are of no value in checking the indulgence of the flesh" (2:23 [my translation]). These statements are framed by the author's affirmation of the audience as having "a circumcision made without hands" (2:11 ESV). In 3:11 he states that in the Colossian assembly "there cannot be Greek and Jew, circumcised and uncircumcised, barbarian, Scythian, slave, free, but Christ is all in all." Taken together, these passages are used to advance the belief that Paul taught Christianity as a replacement for Judaism.

The first thing to notice about Paul's list of objections is that they are couched in rhetorical speech. It is unlikely that the people Paul portrays would have described themselves as promoting "empty deceit," having a "sensuous mind," or championing "self-abasement," even though scholars use these descriptions as empirical statements of fact to construct a profile of opponents. Additionally, it is not clear whether the author is talking about a single phenomenon, several of them, or even empirical realities. Further, while the author is opposed to such things, it is not obvious the Colossians are, otherwise rhetorically weighted injunctions against them would be unnecessary. Finally, while the author polemicizes against actions and ideas associated with Judaism, it is does not follow, despite what many commentators argue, that the letter is criticizing Jews. It is as possible that he is critiquing non-Jews who adopted Jewish practices for ends the author opposes.

Anti-Jewish Interpretation of Colossians

From the early church onward, commentators assumed that Paul's opponents were Jewish. "Festival or a new moon or a Sabbath" together with "regulations" and "human precepts and doctrines," as the affirmation of a circumcision made without hands, may have been the launchpad for reconstructing a polemic against Jews. They served to bolster many interpreters' stereotypical view of Jews and Judaism as a ritually bound, legalistic religion of works righteousness. And since the author contends that the opponents are "puffed up," the text helped to promote a view of Jewish tradition promoting arrogance and self-dependence rather than Christian humility and trust in God. The image of Jews alleged to be "preying" on people similarly contributes to the idea of a sinister religion out to get unsuspecting Christians. The writer of Colossians could not have had any of these ideas in mind because he was writing at a time when there was no such thing as a Christian religion separate from Judaism. Nevertheless, this is how the text is sometimes operationalized in debunking Judaism. It to these appropriations that we now turn.

Before considering anti-Judaism in the history of interpretation, I want to make a disclaimer and to offer a brief note about my sources. First, the disclaimer: the points of view presented are dark and sinister interpretations that have resulted in violence against and the murder of millions of Jews, most tragically in the Shoah, but also from late antiquity onward. Second, the sources: I elected to draw citations for the next two sections of this essay from two volumes in series published by an evangelical press (Ancient Christian Commentary on Scripture and Reformation Commentary on Scripture), to foreground the way there are certain cultural default mechanisms that shape the way modern Christians approach the Bible.[2]

In the introduction to the commentary on Colossians, Thomas Oden, the general editor of the series, writes: "The Ancient Commentary on Scripture has three goals: the renewal of Christian *preaching* based on classical Christian exegesis, the intensified study of Scripture by *lay* persons who wish to think with the early church about the canonical text, and the stimulation of Christian historical, biblical, theological and pastoral *scholarship* toward further inquiry into the scriptural interpretation of the ancient Christian writers."[3] The commentary series was produced, the editor continues, because "recent biblical scholarship has so focused attention on post-Enlightenment historical and literary methods that it has left this longing largely unattended and unserviced."

These are laudable aims and one can only welcome attention to the broad range of the history of interpretation of texts such as Colossians to help nurture thoughtful study. Yet, when one turns to both the selection of texts (of which a representative selection is quoted below) and the introduction to them by the editors, the problem of anti-Judaism appears. For example, in the introduction to Colossians 2:6–15, where Paul polemicizes against angel worship

---

2. Peter J. Gorday, ed., *Colossians, 1–2 Thessalonians, 1–2 Timothy, Titus, Philemon,* Ancient Christian Commentary on Scripture, New Testament 9 (Downers Grove, IL: IVP Academic, 2014); Graham Tomlin, *Philippians, Colossians,* Reformation Commentary on Scripture, New Testament 11 (Downers Grove, IL: IVP Academic, 2013). An advantage of this decision is that these texts can be found in one place and that students can use the series to see the ways early Christian and Reformation thinkers constructed Judaism in their interpretation of other New Testament writings.

3. Thomas Oden as cited in Gorday, *Colossians,* xi (emphasis original). The introduction to the Reformation Commentary shares a similar orientation: like the Ancient Christian Commentary Series, it is committed "to the renewal of the church through careful study and meditative reflection on the Old and New Testaments, the charter documents of Christianity, read in the context of the worshiping, believing community of faith across the centuries" (Tomlin, *Philippians, Colossians,* xv).

and adherence to certain rituals, the volume editor offers a summative sketch of contents of the documents he cites:

> In living the Christian life one must not be deceived by false and outward appearances, being led to embrace these, either in understanding or in behavior, rather than the true reality of Christ. . . . Indeed, Christians are bound, in practicing the disciples and observances of their religion, to be sure that these are understood only from the perspective of Christ, so that they may be pursued in the right spirit and with right determination. . . . The temptation to become absorbed in the worship of angels is a lure to superstition and bondage to the law once again . . . , while it also raises the question of false claims and a prideful spirituality.[4]

After each phrase, he cites the names of early Christian authors who represent these views. Since the series set a threefold task of stimulating "Christian historical, biblical and pastoral *scholarship*," the views Peter Gorday catalogues from the ancient sources harmonize with the theological desiderata of the editors. Since the goal is to remediate the errors of post-Enlightenment biblical scholarship, one is left with the conclusion that however anti-Jewish these voices may be, they are nevertheless ones that can stimulate, presumably positively, Christian scholarship. Moreover, because there is no contextualization of the citations, presented as they are one after another without discussion, one has the impression that they transcend time and space and were generated through prayer and spiritual devotion, rather than arising from the culturally bound and often politically fraught life situations that shaped them.

The general editor of this series is aware that early Christian authors inveighed against Judaism. He argues, however, that they were not antisemitic. He states that they were not disparaging Jews as belonging to an inferior race. This is true; indeed, they could not have done so, since the racial theory that is foundational to antisemitism was invented in the nineteenth century. But this argument does not absolve early Christian authors from supersessionism or its later Judeophobic results. The editor argues: "The patristic texts that appear to modern readers to be anti-Semitic in most cases have a typological reference and are based on a specific approach to the interpretation of Scripture—the analogy of faith—which assesses each particular text in relation to the whole trend of the history of revelation and which views the difference between Jew and Gentile under christological assumptions and not merely a matter of ge-

---

4. Gorday, *Colossians*, 37.

netics or race."[5] Typology (using events or figures from the past as analogous anticipations of future realities) is indeed one of the chief ways that Christians use the Hebrew Bible to draw connections between the two Testaments. But this does not sidestep the challenge of supersessionism, namely replacement of a Jewish phenomenon with a Christian one that renders the former defunct or deficient apart from reference to Jesus.

Early Christianity

In Colossians 2:14 Paul states that the death of Christ "canceled the bond that stood against us with its legal demands . . . , nailing it on the cross" (my translation). For early commentators this prompted a comparison between a life based on obedience to the law and one centered in a resurrected life free from sin. Representative of this view is Theodore of Mopsuestia (circa 350–428), who claimed that the law demanded that we "fulfill all of its provisions" and since this meant that it was impossible not to sin, the law did not "allow us to pursue righteousness because of its legal demands" (*Commentary on Colossians*).[6] Only Christ frees from sin, and in doing so "the law becomes superfluous." Similarly, Severian of Gabala (circa 355–425) describes Israel as "crying aloud" because of the law that "was given as a curse on transgressors" (*Pauline Commentary from the Greek Church*).[7] Eusebius of Caesarea (circa 260–circa 340) interprets the warning not to allow anyone to pass judgment over consumption of foods as resting on the replacement of Hebrew Bible regulations as a shadow of things to come, which, once realized, have no more binding effect (*Proof of the Gospel* 4.16–17).[8] Severian of Gabala argues that Christians should "reject Jews who would urge us to keep the law" (*Pauline Commentary from the Greek Church*).[9] Likewise, Augustine (354–430) states that since "Judaism . . . is justly repudiated and condemned," a Christian "must first consider as alien to himself those ancient observances which have clearly ceased to be necessary" (*Letters* 196.2.8).[10]

Next, the worship of angels that Paul opposes in 2:18, Origen (circa 184–circa 253) observes, was informed by the apostle's "education in Jewish doc-

---

5. Oden, as cited in Gorday, *Colossians*, xxvii.
6. Gorday, *Colossians*, 33; the editor furnishes precise citations and modern editions.
7. Gorday, *Colossians*, 33.
8. Gorday, *Colossians*, 38.
9. Gorday, *Colossians*, 38.
10. Gorday, *Colossians*, 39.

trines" (*Against Celsus* 5.8).[11] Blending 2:18 with the reference to the law given through angels in Galatians 3:19, Theodore of Mopsuestia argues that Paul is here rejecting the Jewish idea of angels as ministers of the law, and that those who adhered to angel worship were Jews who were warning Christians to avoid the anger of angels for not keeping the law (*Commentary on Colossians*).[12] Those who promote rules for not handling, touching, and tasting (Col 2:21) according to John Chrysostom (347–407) demonstrate "a Jewish weakness" (*On Virginity* 77.2–78.3).[13]

To summarize, these points of view, presented in a variety of literary forms (sermons, moral treatises, apologetic and polemical literature, commentary), generalize Jewish identity and religion as retrograde, obsolete, ritual bound, and slavishly legalistic phenomena that Christianity replaced with liberating religion. As such there is little or no interest in an accurate depiction of what they reject, only to create profiles that serve the rhetorical aims of the authors.

The Reformation

Moving to the Reformation, the supersessionist treatment of Judaism is shriller. Thus, The Geneva Bible (1560) invokes Jewish circumcision as "a public profession and handwriting of the miserable state of humankind: for circumcisions did declare our natural pollution; the purifyings and washing signified the filth of sin; the sacrifices testified that we were guilty of death, which were all taken away by Christ's death (*On Colossians* 2:14).[14] Commenting on the death of Jesus as canceling a legal bond, Jacobus Arminius (1560–1609) states that "the ceremonial law was abrogated by the cross"; the law's "abolition as ejected in part by the power of God, in the destruction of all obligation of observance was taken away with the destruction of Jerusalem and of the temple, in which was the seat of religion, and the place appointed for those religious observances, against the contumacy of the unbelieving Jews. From this period the legal ceremonies began to be mortiferous" (Disputation 12: *On the Law of God*).[15] John Calvin (1509–1564) argues that Jewish ceremonies did nothing but point people

11. Gorday, *Colossians*, 39.

12. Gorday, *Colossians*, 39.

13. Gorday, *Colossians*, 42.

14. Tomlin, *Philippians, Colossians*, 194; the editor furnishes sources of citations from modern critical editions.

15. Tomlin, *Philippians, Colossians*, 194–95.

to obligation: "Grace was in a manner suspended until the advent of Christ." Without the knowledge of the Christian revelation that Jewish rituals pointed toward, "the ceremonies themselves sealed the condemnation." The Jewish law functions only to testify to guilt before the judgment of God (*Commentary on Colossians* 2:14).[16] Martin Luther (1483–1546) interprets Colossians' critique of Sabbath observance as the sign that "Paul and the New Testament abolish the Sabbath, to show us that the Sabbath was given to the Jews alone, for whom it is a stern commandment." In the New Testament, he argues, "the Sabbath is annihilated as regards the crude external observance, for every day is a holy day" (*How Christians Should Regard Moses*).[17]

Where Paul describes food, drink, and festivals as "shadows of things to come" (2:17), Philip Melanchthon (1497–1560) explains that he means "to show that God gave the law for these two purposes: to control the flesh and to fill with fear, or make humble" (*Notes on Paul's Letter to the Colossians* 2:17; *Colossians*, 65–66).[18] Warning against worshiping angels in 2:18, John Davenant (1572–1641) explains that Jews "under the pretext of humility, . . . introduced that worship. For they were unworthy to approach God directly, so the intercession of angels was to be solicited." This was not true humility, he argues, "but a preposterous and superstitious humility forced on the minds of Christians by those seducers" (*Exposition of Colossians* 2:18).[19] Jews who through their rituals insist on self-abasement, Johannes Bugenhagen (1485–1558) contends, "commit a fraud. . . . It is out of self-interest that they teach another righteousness other than Christ's. . . . Most of all, they are doing the works of feigning humility and modesty. With superstitious fictitious visions, they speak of the life of angels, seducing and deluding nearly the whole world. With a haughty sanctimony, they dogmatically assert the hypocrisy and yeast of the Pharisees to the unintelligent who fail to cling to the head" (*Annotations on Colossians* 2:18–19).[20]

The early Christian views presented in the first section are more remote from modern ones, but since much of contemporary Western Christianity is founded on Reformation views, the genealogical connections are much more immediate and formative for how Christians deploy the Bible to advance mistaken views about Jews and ancient (not to mention modern) Judaism. In the

---

16. Tomlin, *Philippians, Colossians*, 195.
17. Tomlin, *Philippians, Colossians*, 199.
18. Tomlin, *Philippians, Colossians*, 200.
19. Tomlin, *Philippians, Colossians*, 201.
20. Tomlin, *Philippians, Colossians*, 203.

Reformation view, the law serves to identify a human plight whose solution is faith in Jesus. But Jews are more than a foil for Christian religion. They are seductive, avaricious, arrogant, bound to ceremonial religion, and superstitious. Anti-Jewish hysteria and virulent waves of persecution across western and eastern Europe in the Middle Ages funded such views in the Reformation, and many reformers perpetuated them. Martin Luther was among the harshest proponents. His treatise attacking Jews was republished by German Lutherans in the 1930s to support Nazi ideology.[21]

Modern Interpretation

For the past 150 years scholars have tried to reconstruct a profile of opponents described in Colossians 2:8–23. Many of the proposals endorse the polemical language of Colossians to describe what the author rejects and link it to ancient Judaism. The "Colossian error" is a typical phrase modern scholars use to portray the ideas Paul polemicizes against. Other terms and phrases include (to list only a few): heresy, heretical teaching/doctrine, radical legalism, Jewish-pagan syncretism, Judaizing, a Jewish condition, a step backward into Judaism from Paul's gospel, the taint of Judaism, Jewish magical practices that lured Colossians from Paul's gospel, heretical Jewish propaganda, and typically Jewish problems. Lionel Windsor uses the phrase "supersessionist over-readings" of Colossians to describe these exegetical moves.[22] Such over-readings occur when scholars draw inferences from texts that exceed the bounds of the evidence or when they stitch together passages from other parts of the Bible to create a portrait the data under consideration does not warrant. Moreover, when modern interpreters either adopt the author's polemical language or build on it with their own descriptions, they participate in what Elisabeth Schüssler Fiorenza names the dynamics of "othering." They advance the author's negative constructions of what they reject.[23]

I turn now to a representative example of a "supersessionist over-reading" of Colossians in which several negative terms and phrases used to criticize

---

21. Martin Luther, "On the Jews and Their Lies," *Luther's Works*, vol. 47, *The Christian in Society IV*, trans. Martin H. Bertram (Philadelphia: Fortress, 1971), 268–93.

22. Lionel J. Windsor, *Reading Ephesians and Colossians after Supersessionism: Christ's Mission through Israel to the Nations* (Eugene, OR: Cascade, 2017), 12.

23. Elisabeth Schüssler Fiorenza, *Rhetoric and Ethic: The Politics of Biblical Studies* (Minneapolis: Fortress, 1999), 180–82.

Judaism appear.[24] I do not intend to pillory the commentator but rather to illustrate the way modern exegesis often creates caricatures of first-century Judaism. This example could be multiplied many times over as Windsor's overview of Colossian scholarship indicates.[25] The writer uses a variety of negative descriptions to portray the issues Paul opposes as "stemming from the heart of Jewish life." He argues that when Paul speaks of "philosophy" he is referring to first-century Judaism, which he argues was a defined religious system. The "Jewish heretics" Colossians opposes replaced Paul's gospel with adherence to commandments. The apostle "addressed a religious community endangered by mere human [i.e., Jewish] tradition."[26] "After liberation from a legal system, obeying such a system again was a step backward" for these Christians.[27] Colossians opposes legalism, which is "any philosophy or movement that assumes God's blessing comes from keeping the law, whether Jewish law or human law," namely the assumption that through "a contractual relationship . . . God can be bought by human effort."[28] Drawing on Paul's language of 2:16–17, that festival, new moon, or Sabbath are "only a shadow of what is to come," the commentator argues that Paul is rejecting Judaism: "The terminology reinforced the interpretation that these were aspects and outworkings of the Jewish law. The Jewish system can easily be understood as 'vaguely resembling' the truths of the New Testament." He continues: "A shadow is inferior in that it imperfectly resembles the object. No one prefers the shadow to the substance. Thus the reality is of more significance and value than the shadow. The shadow is anticipatory. In historical sequence, 'the old covenant' shadow came first and provided a representation of the 'new covenant' object."[29] The error of the Jews that Colossians rejects is the idea that there is any continuing validity to Jewish observances and hence Judaism.

There are multiple problems with this line of reasoning. Most importantly, first-century Jews as well as modern ones did/do not understand their relationship with God as based on a contractual system of winning God's blessing through keeping the law. This is a traditional Christian misrepresentation of Jewish teaching about obedience to the torah. Ancient and modern Jews kept/ keep the commandments to celebrate their relationship with God, not to earn

24. Richard R. Melick Jr., *Philippians, Colossians, Philemon: An Exegetical and Theological Exposition of Holy Scripture*, New American Commentary 32 (Nashville: B&H, 1991).

25. Windsor, *Reading Ephesians and Colossians*, 28–77.

26. Windsor, *Reading Ephesians and Colossians*, 180–81.

27. Windsor, *Reading Ephesians and Colossians*, 182.

28. Windsor, *Reading Ephesians and Colossians*, 263.

29. Windsor, *Reading Ephesians and Colossians*, 268.

it. Further, when Colossians was written, there was no systemized Judaism that could function as the philosophy the commentator ascribes to the letter's opponents. First-century Judaism was diverse, indeed diverse enough to include the Christ religion of Colossians. Next, the author assumes that the Colossians left a former life of Greek religion for the worship of Christ, not that they migrated from Judaism to Christianity. Thus, they could not have taken a "step backward" into Jewish legalism. Finally, there is no reason to suppose that when the author advances abstinence from certain kinds of food and drink and criticizes "festival, or new moon, or Sabbath" that he is rejecting Hebrew Bible observances or demoting Judaism as a shadow of Christianity. The interpretation requires a series of equivocal treatments of the evidence that rest on a long tradition of anti-Jewish exegesis. It cherry-picks texts from Paul's other letters (often from passages that are sites of considerable exegetical debate) to turn Colossians into a letter of Christian supersessionism. Finally, the point made above deserves repeating, that while Colossians polemicizes against practices that relate to Jews, it cannot be concluded that the author opposes Judaism, only the use of Jewish customs by gentiles for ends he rejects.

Discussion Questions and Activity Suggestions

1. How does awareness of the diversity of first-century Judaism and Christianity invite us to appraise language of orthodoxy and heresy in the description of opponents biblical writers address?

2. Read Cynthia Briggs Kittridge and Claire Miller Colombo's comments on Colossians 2:6–23, pages 172–78 in their Wisdom Commentary. What is an alternative to using "othering" language when describing the positions that Colossians rejects?

3. How have the descriptions recorded in the Ancient Christian Commentary on Scripture and Reformation Commentary on Scripture helped to create an academic culture that might promote "supersessionist over-reading" in contemporary study of Colossians?

4. Read chapter 1 of Lionel J. Windsor's *Reading Ephesians and Colossians after Supersessionism*, entitled "Prior Readings of Ephesians and Colossians," and compare this with his chapter 7, entitled "Jews, Gentiles, and the Apostolic Mission in Colossians."

5. Read the introduction to Colossians 2:8–23 in either the Ancient Christian Commentary on Scripture or Reformation Commentary on Scripture. Rewrite an introduction in the light of the discussion in this essay. What

would you want a modern reader coming to this material for the first time to know?

6. Read Robert Royalty's account of the argument Colossians is addressing as an intrareligious debate among Christ-followers rather than an interreligious argument between Jews and Christians. How does Royalty invite us to rethink the letter's polemic?

Further Reading

Francis, Fred O., and Wayne A. Meeks, eds. *Conflict at Colossae: A Problem in the Interpretation of Early Christianity Illustrated by Selected Modern Studies.* Rev. ed. Missoula: Scholars Press, 1975.

Kittridge, Cynthia Briggs, and Claire Miller Colombo. "Colossians." Pages 123–200 in *Philippians, Colossians, Philemon.* Wisdom Commentary 51. Collegeville, MN: Liturgical Press, 2002.

Royalty, Robert, Jr. "Dwelling on Visions: On the Nature of the So-Called 'Colossians Heresy.'" *Biblica* 83.3 (2002): 329–57.

Tinsley, Annie. *A Postcolonial African American Re-Reading of Colossians: Identity, Reception, and Interpretation under the Gaze of Empire.* New York: Palgrave Macmillan, 2013.

Windsor, Lionel J. *Reading Ephesians and Colossians after Supersessionism: Christ's Mission through Israel to the Nations.* Eugene, OR: Cascade, 2017.

22

1 Thessalonians

JILL HICKS-KEETON

Before it became anyone's scripture, 1 Thessalonians was just a letter to a group of Jesus-followers in Thessalonica. It is addressed from Paul, Silvanus, and Timothy, though Paul typically gets the most credit for authorship. First Thessalonians is widely thought to be one of the earliest available letters of Paul, which also makes it one of the earliest pieces of writing in the New Testament and, therefore, one of the earliest extant pieces of literature from the Jesus movement. Many scholars date the letter to the early 50s.

Clues in 1 Thessalonians help us historicize Paul as an apocalyptic Jewish Jesus-follower working to bring gentiles—"pagans"—to venerate Israel's deity, as believed to be revealed in Jesus. Take 1 Thessalonians 1:9–10, for example, a passage that may reproduce content of Paul's preaching: "For they report about us what kind of welcome we had among you and how you turned to God from idols to serve a living and true God and to wait for his Son from heaven, whom he raised from the dead—Jesus, who rescues us from the coming wrath" (NRSVue). Paul believes the pagan recipients to have forsaken the veneration of their own deities for that of his God, the best God, the God who lives. Now, he says, they all await the return of this God's resurrected son. There is a "coming wrath" from which Paul and his audience wish to be delivered. Paul anticipates that both Jesus and judgment will come swiftly and will surprise outsiders, "like a thief in the night" (5:2). But Paul and his converts, who belong to the day, not the night, will be saved (5:9).

First Thessalonians represents Paul's coaching of these Jesus-followers on how to behave and what to think in the interim, right now. Indeed, the letter is part of Paul's wider regime of surveilling and attempting to direct his communities of converts. First Thessalonians is thus a disciplinary letter. Many readers understand Paul's tone as affectionate, as he frames himself as a wet nurse caring for new Christ worshipers (2:7) and as a father guiding them (2:12). But ultimately his purpose is not to express affection but to convince the Thessalonian Jesus-followers to do as he says and, often, to do as he does. "Imitation" is a frequent Pauline theme, including in 1 Thessalonians (e.g., 1:6; 2:14).[1] While they have been waiting for Jesus to come back, the Thessalonian Jesus-followers have apparently encountered unspecified "afflictions" (3:3–7), most likely social ostracism for having withdrawn from normal public cultic activities. Paul advises them to live "to please God" (4:1), which includes controlling their sexuality and minding their own business (4:2–12).[2] They are to live "quietly" so as to be respectable (as defined by elite Roman men).

First Thessalonians is in some ways an experimental letter. In 4:13–18, Paul appears to theologize on the fly. The Thessalonians had apparently encountered a new problem and written to Paul about it: *What is going to happen to the Thessalonian Jesus-followers among us who have died before Jesus got back?* It is a reasonable question, one that also stands potentially to challenge Paul's authority or the truthfulness of the revelation he preaches that he received. The question gets a grand answer, one that not only imparts new, helpful information but also functions to defend Paul from potential critique. *Do not worry about them*, Paul says. *When Jesus returns, they will rise first!* The dead-in-Christ are not forgotten or even disadvantaged, he assures them. Jesus will come in the air, spectacularly. The dead will rise and meet him there. Only then will those who are still alive be taken up to meet Jesus as well. Paul appears to include himself in the ones who will be alive when it happens. (He got that wrong.)

The letter ends with rapid-fire instructions, including to respect authority within the Jesus movement and to abstain from every evil, followed by a request for prayer, greetings, and a directive to read the letter aloud to the community.

The question of anti-Judaism and 1 Thessalonians revolves around a single passage. We read this in 2:13–16:

---

1. See esp. Elizabeth A. Castelli, *Imitating Paul: A Discourse of Power* (Louisville: Westminster John Knox, 1991).

2. See James N. Hoke, "Be Even Better Subjects, Worthy of Rehabilitation: Homonationalism and 1 Thessalonians 4–5," in *Bodies on the Verge: Queering Pauline Epistles*, ed. Joseph A. Marchal (Atlanta: SBL Press, 2019), 83–114. For critical imaginative work on how women and oppressed men might have heard and negotiated Paul's advice, see Melanie Johnson-DeBaufre, "'Gazing upon the Invisible': Archaeology, Historiography, and the Elusive Wo/men of 1 Thessalonians," in *From Roman to Early Christian Thessalonikē*, ed. Laura Nasrallah, Charalambos Bakirtzis, and Steven J. Friesen (Cambridge: Harvard University Press, 2010), 73–108.

We also constantly give thanks to God for this, that when you received the word of God that you heard from us you accepted it not as a human word but as what it really is, God's word, which is also at work in you believers. For you, brothers and sisters, became imitators of the churches of God in Christ Jesus that are in Judea, for you suffered the same things from your own compatriots as they did from the Jews who killed both the Lord Jesus and the prophets and drove us out; they displease God and oppose everyone by hindering us from speaking to the gentiles so that they may be saved. Thus they have constantly been filling up the measure of their sins, but wrath has overtaken them at last. (NRSVue)

There are some serious interpretive problems here that are not apparent from reading just one English translation (see the suggested activity below). The "wrath," for example, is attached to a verb whose tense is actually ambiguous. The wrath could be a singular event in the author's past, or it could refer to an envisioned future event that has already been determined but not yet executed. Further, the Greek underlying "at last" could alternately be translated with something like "completely," which further complicates whether the wrath is believed to be past, present, or future since the phrase could indicate degree rather than duration. Ambiguous, too, is whom the author envisions as being targets of the wrath, having killed Jesus and the prophets, whether "the Jews" or some Jews or some Judeans.

Resolutions to these interpretive problems frequently hinge on post-Holocaust Christian readers' discomfort with the notion that Paul would say such things about Jews. Would Paul really have joined other ancient accusers who represented Jews as haters of humanity? Would Paul really have said that Jews killed Jesus? Not only is such a claim historically inaccurate, since crucifixion is a distinctively Roman punishment, but it is also an odd thing for a Jewish person, as Paul was, to say. It is especially off, some Pauline interpreters think, given Paul's positive statements about Jews and Israel in his Letter to the Romans (esp. Rom 9–11).

A major reason this passage has become such a problem for many modern readers is because of the enduring history of anti-Jewish and antisemitic violence attached to the accusation of Jews as Christ-killers. Blaming Jews for the death of Jesus has been a longstanding wellspring of Christian anti-Judaism, one that is entangled with similarly ahistorical and yet powerful accusations, including deicide, ritual murder of Christian children, and ritual cannibalism (often called the blood libel).[3] Framing Jews as "Christ-killers" became a popu-

---

3. Jeremy Cohen, *Christ Killers: The Jews and the Passion from the Bible to the Big Screen* (Oxford: Oxford University Press, 2007), 93.

lar way for elite Christian men in the four centuries following the advent of the Jesus movement to work out their own theologies, identities, and anxieties.[4] They were invested in arguing for the superiority of Christianity over Judaism even as they were working to disentangle them from one another.

Early Christian writers needed to explain, in part, why their God had apparently rejected Jews in favor of Christians, whom they believed to have superseded them in God's revelatory economy. Justin Martyr, to take but one example, writing in the first half of the second century, says that the reason Jews suffered the loss of the Jerusalem temple, among other tragedies, is divine judgment on them, which was justly deserved for having killed Jesus. (Incidentally, the fall of the Jerusalem temple in 70 is an easy historical event to attach to the enigmatic wrath of 1 Thess 2:16.) In *Dialogue with Trypho* 16, Justin writes to his imaginary Jewish interlocutor: "Accordingly, these things have happened to you in fairness and justice, for you have slain the Just One, and His prophets before Him; and now you reject those who hope in Him, and in Him who sent Him—God the Almighty and Maker of all things—cursing in your synagogues those that believe on Christ."[5] The mention of prophets here suggests that Justin might have 1 Thessalonians in mind.

The enduring nature of the deicide myth is apparent in polls conducted in the United States in recent decades. A 2013 Anti-Defamation League survey, for example, showed that over a quarter of respondents believed Jews killed Jesus.[6] As biblical scholar Candida Moss quipped at the time, they're wrong—"but they do read their Bible."[7] Because of the long history of anti-Jewish violence directly connected to the deicide charge, many Bible readers, especially Christians, are now embarrassed by this passage in 1 Thessalonians. The embarrassment itself is worth interrogating.

Scholars and other Bible readers often engage in rehabilitation projects to neutralize 1 Thessalonians 2:13–16, to take the teeth out of a passage that truly bites. One popular strategy is to claim that Paul did not write these sentences. They were interpolated into a manuscript of 1 Thessalonians after the fact, or so the hypothesis goes. This theory has the benefit of absolving Paul of

4. See Cohen, *Christ Killers*, for further examples.

5. Saint Justin Martyr (110–165), *Dialogue with Trypho*, trans. Alexander Roberts and James Donaldson (https://tinyurl.com/2h7m66hj).

6. Anti-Defamation League, "Antisemitic Attitudes in the U.S.: A Guide to ADL's Latest Poll" (27 January 2020) (https://tinyurl.com/47pxam6e).

7. Candida Moss, "Sorry, America, You're Wrong, the Jews Did Not Kill Jesus" (5 November 2013) (https://tinyurl.com/bp9636jr).

an ahistorical claim that many believe a first-century Jewish man could not have thought, much less mobilized. While it is true that the passage could be removed and the letter retain a natural flow, there is no material evidence to support the interpolation theory. All extant manuscripts of 1 Thessalonians include the passage, and all in the same place.

Another strategy is to say that Paul wrote it but he was exaggerating for rhetorical effect. This reading affirms that 1 Thessalonians does not give us access to what actually happened. It does not even give us access to what Paul actually thought.[8] It gives us instead a persona created to persuade. It gives us access to rhetorical moves. Perhaps, then, Paul was deploying "polemical hyperbole" to get something he wanted: in this case, to convince his converts that those who persecute them will get what's coming to them.[9] This theory enjoys the benefit of appreciating that Paul's authority was precarious, his writing aspirational. It avoids lionizing Paul, even as it participates in an apologetic project to absolve him. This tactic for dealing with the problem passage shifts focus away from historical questions—Did Jews kill Jesus? Did Paul think Jews killed Jesus?—and rightly wonders why Paul might have told his Thessalonian converts that Jews killed Jesus.

Yet saying Paul didn't write it or didn't really mean it doesn't make the problem passage disappear from the New Testament. No matter whose ancient hand it came from or what Paul was trying to do with it if he did write it, it is in modern Bibles. It is scripture for many Bible readers. When 1 Thessalonians is encountered in its canonical place, these Paul-rehabilitation arguments matter little. Even though 1 Thessalonians was written earlier than the New Testament gospels by two to four decades (or more), readers today typically do not encounter 1 Thessalonians apart from the narratives of Jesus's life and death memorialized in Matthew and John or apart from the dramatization of Paul's missionary activity found in the book of Acts. This means that 1 Thessalonians is often read within a web of interpretive practice that includes Matthew's "may his blood be on us and our children" (Matt 27:25) and John's "children of the devil" (John 8:44) and Acts' narrative depiction of Paul charging Jews with Christ killing (Acts 13:27–29). Isolating 1 Thessalonians from other New Testament passages requires a leap of historical imagination for readers today

---

8. See the excellent discussion in Sarah Rollens, "Inventing Tradition in Thessalonica: The Appropriation of the Past in 1 Thessalonians 2:14–16," *Biblical Theology Bulletin* 46.3 (2016): 123–32.

9. Carol J. Schlueter, *Filling up the Measure: Polemical Hyperbole in 1 Thessalonians 2:14–16*, Journal for the Study of the New Testament Supplement 98 (Sheffield: JSOT Press, 1994).

accustomed to the canon. This means that historicizing 1 Thessalonians cannot completely deal with the anti-Jewish potential of this passage.

Discussion Questions and Activity Suggestions

1. If your Bible has 1 Thessalonians in it, your Bible says that Jews killed Jesus. How might varieties of biblicism approach such an ahistorical claim? In your judgment, does the historical fact that Romans killed Jesus mitigate the anti-Jewish potential of this text? What possibilities and pitfalls can you see in attempts to neutralize this text that depend on historical accuracy? Is history helpful? Is it enough?

2. One major reason that interpreters puzzle over this passage is because of outsized interest in *what Paul thought*. Melanie Johnson-DeBaufre shows that 1 Thessalonians 2:14–16 can be read as a "site of collective Christian memory" rather than an access point to the thought or theology of Paul. If we understand interpretations of the problem passage as doing ethical work for the interpreter rather than engaging in historical reconstruction, how might we assess our own reactions to the passage or proposed solutions to it?

3. In commentary that speculates on how 1 Thessalonians can best be made meaningful by Chinese Christians, Yeo Khiok-khng claims that "Pauline eschatology constantly nurtures imaginative hope." His commentary ignores the so-called problem passage and focuses instead on how this letter can be leveraged for communal ethical goods if one prioritizes Paul's statement in 1 Thessalonians 5:15: "See that none of you repays evil for evil, but always seek to do good to one another and to all" (NRSVue). What do you make of Yeo's spotlight on this ethical imperative? Can materials in 1 Thessalonians be marshaled to counterbalance the apparent anti-Judaism? Is imagination useful? Is hope?

4. A close investigation of English translations of 1 Thessalonians 2:13–16 can help modern readers appreciate more deeply the instability of this text, along with the wide range of meanings that can attach to it. Compare and contrast this passage as it appears in the NRSVue, NIV, and ESV. (These translations are available for free online from a number of sources.) Don't forget the footnotes! What differences do you notice? Does the text as rendered in the NRSVue, NIV, and ESV actually say the same thing? Or are they fundamentally different? Who is fashioned as killers? Whom are they envisioned to have killed? What kind of punishment are they imagined to

endure? When, and for how long, and to what degree? Make a list before proceeding to the two case studies below.

- *Disparity-in-focus #1: Punctuation matters*—Did you notice a seemingly small appearing and disappearing comma? Since the Greek texts of 1 Thessalonians do not contain our English equivalent of punctuation, the editors and translators of these English versions had to make judgments about where punctuation should appear in an English translation. What difference does this comma, or its absence, make in each of these translations? (Hint: it affects *who* or who is *not* in view as those "who killed.") Does the presence or absence of this comma affect, mitigate, or resolve the potential anti-Judaism of the passage? How does this appearing and disappearing comma help us think about this text's resistance to easy answers or even stable meaning?

- *Disparity-in-focus #2: Footnotes do heavy lifting*—Take a closer look at footnotes in the NRSVue that are not in the NIV or ESV. Two of them offer readers what "other ancient authorities" contain for certain words or phrases. That means that with its footnotes, the NRSVue gives readers choices for how to read certain words in this passage (even if one choice is prioritized over the other by relegating one to a footnote). These footnotes reveal to us that the text is not only unstable in English but is also unstable *in our available Greek manuscripts* of the letter. Some say "wrath"; others say "God's wrath." Some say "the prophets"; others say "their own prophets." What are the semantic differences here? What do you make of this text's fundamental instability?

  What do you make of the decision of the NIV and ESV editors to resolve this textual instability for their readers?

  The ESV contains one distinctive footnote, though. Notice that this version uses a footnote to clarify that rendering the word underlying "Jews" (*Ioudaioi*) as merely "Jews" is insufficient. How does the footnote interpret "Jews" for the reader? What interpretive, or ethical, work does this move do? How does it compare to the work done by the appearing and disappearing comma?

Further Reading

Cohen, Jeremy. *Christ Killers: The Jews and the Passion from the Bible to the Big Screen*. Oxford: Oxford University Press, 2007.

Johnson-DeBaufre, Melanie. "'Gazing upon the Invisible': Archaeology, Historiography, and the Elusive Wo/men of 1 Thessalonians." Pages 73–108 in

From Roman to Early Christian Thessalonikē. Edited by Laura Nasrallah, Charalambos Bakirtzis, and Steven J. Friesen. Cambridge: Harvard University Press, 2010.

———. "A Monument to Suffering: 1 Thessalonians 2:14–6, Dangerous Memory, and Christian Identity." *Journal of Early Christian History* 1.2 (2001): 91–118.

Levine, Amy-Jill. *The Misunderstood Jew: The Church and the Scandal of the Jewish Jesus* (pages 87–117). San Francisco: HarperCollins, 2006.

Rollens, Sarah. "Inventing Tradition in Thessalonica: The Appropriation of the Past in 1 Thessalonians 2:14–16." *Biblical Theology Bulletin* 46.3 (2016): 123–32.

Schlueter, Carol J. *Filling up the Measure: Polemical Hyperbole in 1 Thessalonians 2:14–16*. Journal for the Study of the New Testament Supplement 90. Sheffield: JSOT Press, 1994.

Smith, Abraham. "The First and Second Letters to the Thessalonians." Pages 304–22 in *A Postcolonial Commentary on the New Testament Writings*. Edited by Fernando F. Segovia and R. S. Sugirtharajah. London: T&T Clark, 2009.

Yeo Khiok-khng. "1 Thessalonians." Pages 500–503 in *Global Bible Commentary*. Edited by Daniel Patte. Nashville: Abingdon, 2004.

23

2 Thessalonians

CAVAN CONCANNON

The Second Letter to the Thessalonians is one of the thirteen letters in the New Testament that name Paul as their author. Most modern scholars argue that as many as six of the letters associated with Paul in the New Testament are pseudepigraphic, meaning that they were written by someone other than the historical Paul. Second Thessalonians is one of these disputed Pauline letters, with biblical scholars largely split as to whether it was written by Paul or not.[1]

The letter opens with Paul's greetings to the *ekklēsia* in Thessaloniki and names Paul, Silvanus, and Timothy as coauthors (1:1), mirroring the same greetings found in 1 Thessalonians 1:1. After a brief thanksgiving extolling the faith of the Thessalonians (2 Thess 1:3–4), the authors discuss the divine judgment that they expect to accompany the second coming of Jesus (1:5–12). Noting that the Thessalonians have experienced some sort of social affliction from outsiders, again mirroring a theme in 1 Thessalonians (2:2, 14–16; 3:3–4; 4:11), the authors promise that God will mete out vengeance "against those who do not know God and on those who are not obedient to the good news of our Lord Jesus" (2 Thess 1:8).[2] Those who believe in Jesus are urged to endure their current afflictions, relying on the promise that God will inflict the punishment of "eternal destruction" upon the unbelievers who trouble the Thessalonians (1:9).

---

1. Beverly Roberts Gaventa, *First and Second Thessalonians*, Interpretation (Louisville: Westminster John Knox, 1998), 94; Maarten J. J. Menken, *2 Thessalonians* (New York: Routledge, 1994), 27–44; Abraham J. Malherbe, *The Letters to the Thessalonians*, Anchor Bible 32B (New Haven: Yale University Press, 2000), 349–76.

2. All scripture quotations in this chapter are my own unless otherwise noted.

As to when the coming of Jesus and the divine judgment will occur, the authors suggest an elaborate timeline of obscure eschatological events (2:1–12). The authors register concern that the Thessalonians may have been persuaded, "either by spirit or by word or by letter, as though from us, that the day of the lord has arrived" (2:2). In order to combat what they see as an incorrect understanding, the authors lay out a timetable based on the activities of a number of metaphysical agents: the lawless one, the restraining force, the mystery of lawlessness, and Satan. It is only when the drama surrounding these agents is completed that the Thessalonians should expect the return of Jesus. Until then, they should wait patiently, holding fast to the traditions that have been passed on to them by the authors (2:15).

The authors then move to admonitions against those who have become idle and have stopped working (3:6–14). It is possible that expectations of the coming end of the world led some in the Thessalonian group to stop working, but this is not stated in the text. It is also not clear why the authors are concerned about this behavior. Perhaps it placed an undue burden on other members of the group to provide for those who had ceased to work. A more likely concern is that such members threatened the respectability of the Thessalonians group in the eyes of outsiders.

The letter concludes with a benediction and Paul's signature: "This greeting is in my hand, Paul's. It is a sign in every letter. I write this way" (3:17). This closing line is interesting for a number of reasons. First, it erases Silvanus and Timothy as coauthors, focusing solely on Paul. Second, it is not accurate. Of the letters in the Pauline archive, only 1 Corinthians and Colossians end with Paul appending his own handwriting at the end (1 Cor 16:21; Col 4:18).[3] This strange claim, given what we know about other letters associated with Paul, has been one of the reasons why modern biblical scholars question the authenticity of the letter.

Earlier biblical scholars argued that 2 Thessalonians was pseudepigraphical because its elaborate eschatological scenario, in which the lawless one had to contend with the restraining force before Jesus could come back (2:1–12), contradicted the more imminent eschatology of 1 Thessalonians 5:1–11.[4] The most compelling recent theory for why 2 Thessalonians was not written by

---

3. Paul also directs the reader to his handwriting toward the end of Galatians (6:11) and Philemon (19), though these are not final greetings, as the authors of 2 Thessalonians claim is always Paul's sign.

4. William Wrede, *The Authenticity of the Second Letter to the Thessalonians*, trans. Robert Rhea (Cambridge: Clarke, 2017).

Paul comes from Steven Friesen.[5] Friesen argues that 2 Thessalonians seems to be in competition with 1 Thessalonians over which is more authentically Pauline. Second Thessalonians claims Paul's own handwriting and also frets over other letters that might have been written in Paul's name advocating a more imminent eschatology (2:2). From these observations, in addition to 2 Thessalonians largely copying material from 1 Thessalonians, Friesen concludes that 2 Thessalonians is a pseudepigraphical Pauline letter, written at a later time in which the legacy of Paul was in dispute. The evolving archive of Pauline literature among early Christians, of which 2 Thessalonians was a part, shows that the memory of Paul was hotly contested. New letters of Paul were written to help shape the answer to the question, What would Paul and his theology look like? Whether or not the letter stems from Paul, it will still be important to see how its history of interpretation involved Judeophobic interpretations.

In contrast to other New Testament texts, including 1 Thessalonians, 2 Thessalonians does not include any explicit criticism of Jews or Judaism. Second Thessalonians also does not include any of the touchstones of later Pauline anti-Judaism, such as a polemic against the law or the invocation of prophetic scriptural citations from the Hebrew Bible. To see the ways in which 2 Thessalonians has been used to do harm to Jews and Jewish communities, we have to look to the complicated history of how 2 Thessalonians' eschatological timeline has been used by Christian readers. This takes us back to the enigmatic passage in 2:1–12, in which the authors lay out the timeline that must take place before Jesus's final return:

> We ask you, siblings, concerning the presence of our Lord Jesus Christ and our being gathered together with him, that you not quickly be made unstable of mind or scared, either through spirit or a word or a letter, as though from us, that the day of the lord has come. Let no one deceive you at all. That day will not come unless the falling away comes first and the man of lawlessness is revealed, the son of destruction, who opposes and exalts himself above every so-called god or cult object, so that he takes his seat in the temple of god, declaring himself that he is god. Do you not remember that when I was yet with you I said these things to you? And now you know

5. Steven J. Friesen, "Second Thessalonians, the Ideology of Epistles, and the Construction of Authority: Our Debt to the Forger," in *From Roman to Christian Thessalonike: Studies in Religion and Archaeology*, ed. Laura Nasrallah, Charalambos Bakirtzis, and Steven J. Friesen (Cambridge: Harvard University Press, 2010), 189–210.

about the restraining force, that will reveal him in his own time. For the mystery of lawlessness is already at work, only until the one who restrains [*katechon*] is out of the way. And then the lawless one will be revealed, whom the Lord Jesus will destroy with the spirit of his mouth and deactivate by the manifestation of his presence. The presence [of the lawless one] is according to the work of Satan in all power and signs and false marvels and every unjust trick for those who are perishing. These did not accept the love of truth so that they be saved. For this reason God sends to them an energetic delusion, so that they believe what is false, in order that all who have not believed in the truth but consented to injustice will be judged.

As noted above, this timeline of eschatological events has been used as evidence that 2 Thessalonians was not written by Paul, since it is not clear that it coheres with what Paul, Silvanus, and Timothy wrote in 1 Thessalonians 5:1–11. But most Christian readers of the text have not focused on the similarities or differences with 1 Thessalonians, but with the identities of the obscure mythological agents that are mentioned.[6] As we will see, through some interpretative maneuvers, it becomes increasingly common to posit Jewish figures in this apocalyptic scenario.

The central drama of the eschatological timeline revolves around the "man of lawlessness," an agent of Satan, who works behind the scenes in the present. After a falling away, a restrainer, which has heretofore kept the man of lawlessness from being known, will be removed. At this point the lawless one will exalt himself as god before the world, and then presently will be destroyed by Jesus at the parousia (that is, the return of Jesus). While the denouement of this cosmic struggle is foreordained, the tension in the story revolves around the restrainer. What is he or it (the Greek word is used twice, in both the masculine and neuter)? What role does this restraining force play? When will it be removed?

Ancient Christian interpreters, beginning in the second century, recognized that the passage's enigmatic narrative complicated their interpretive efforts, especially since the authors make it clear that the details behind the story had already been delivered to the Thessalonians in person (2:5).[7] Augustine,

6. See, for example, Anthony C. Thiselton, *1 and 2 Thessalonians through the Centuries* (Malden, MA: Wiley-Blackwell, 2011), 211–44.

7. For a catalogue of premodern Christian interpretations of 2 Thess 2, see Massimo Cacciari, *The Withholding Power: An Essay on Political Theology* (New York: Bloomsbury Academic, 2018), appendix 1. Several other important medieval commentaries on 2 Thessalonians by Ham of Auxerre and Thietland of Einsiedeln can be found in Steven R. Cartwright

for example, notes that only the original audience of the letter would have the context to understand what was being described specifically: "Thus we who have not their knowledge wish and are not able even with pains to understand what the apostle referred to, especially as his meaning is made still more obscure by what he adds. For what does he mean by 'For the mystery of iniquity does already work: only he who now holds, let him hold until he be taken out of the way: and then shall the wicked be revealed'? I frankly confess I do not know what he means" (*City of God* 20.19).

Few ancient readers recognized such limits on their interpretive imaginations. Most found that they could clarify the ambiguities of the passage by putting it into conversation with other biblical texts, notably Revelation, Daniel, and the letters of John. The key intertextual link that opened up new avenues for interpreters was the association of the man of lawlessness with the antichrist, a figure that appears in the New Testament only in the Johannine letters (1 John 2:18, 22; 4:3; 2 John 7). Once forged, these intertextual connections shaped most later interpretations of the passage, including those of modern political philosophers.[8] The first extant Christian interpreter to make this connection was Irenaeus (*Against Heresies* 5.25). These intertextual connections formed a larger tapestry of cryptic details, stretching from the various beasts of Daniel's prophecies and Revelation's visions to the eschatological expectations of Jesus and Paul. Such connections also led to figurations of the eschaton that identified Jews as partisans on the side of the antichrist. For example, Hippolytus merges the figure of the restrainer as antichrist with prophecies from the book of Daniel to argue that the antichrist will rebuild Jerusalem and the temple and align himself with the Jews as their king (*Commentary on Daniel* 49–50; see also his *Demonstratio de Christo et Antichristo* 5–6). For later interpreters, like Haimo of Auxerre (ninth century), the antichrist will circumcise himself in Jerusalem and the Jews will then flock to him as the true Messiah (*Exposition of the Second Letter to the Thessalonians* 2.4).

If the man of lawlessness becomes firmly marked as a figure for the antichrist, the identity of the restrainer or the restraining force is more malleable. Tertullian identifies the Roman Empire with the restraining force (*Apology* 32; so also Jerome, *Epistle* 71). So long as the empire remains in place, the evils associated with the coming of the eschaton are kept in abeyance. For Tertul-

---

and Kevin L. Hughes, *Second Thessalonians: Two Early Medieval Apocalyptic Commentaries* (Kalamazoo, MI: Medieval Institute, 2001).

8. See, for example, Giorgio Agamben, *The Time That Remains: A Commentary on the Letter to the Romans* (Palo Alto: Stanford University Press, 2005), 109.

lian, writing in defense of Christians to the emperor, Christians perform an important role by praying to their God for the health of the empire, helping to ensure that the restrainer of the eschaton remains in place.[9] If the restrainer of 2 Thessalonians 2 is the Roman Empire, then the eschatological drama will only really start when the empire has fallen, creating a chaos in which the true workings of Satan and the man of lawlessness can be revealed.[10] Medieval Christian interpreters in the West would struggle with this identification of the restrainer with the Roman Empire, since the empire in the West had fallen. Adso of Montier, writing in the tenth century, would stretch the notion of what counted as the Roman Empire, arguing that the Frankish kingdom functioned still as an extension of the empire's role as restrainer (*Treatise on the Antichrist*).[11] As Arthur Bradley notes, what started as a stopgap theory of the state is transformed "into a permanent fixture in an interregnum that now seemingly stretches outward toward infinity."[12]

John Chrysostom, writing in the fourth century, agreed with Tertullian that the restraining force was the Roman Empire, arguing that once the empire was out of the way the antichrist would come in the anarchy that followed (*Homily Four on the Second Epistle to Thessalonians*).[13] But Chrysostom also knows of other Christian interpreters who think that the restraining force is the "grace of the Holy Spirit." Chrysostom does not say what these interpreters mean by this phrase. Theodore of Mopsuestia, joining Chrysostom in rejecting the identification of the restrainer as the Holy Spirit, implies that the blessings that come from the Holy Spirit, such as the miracles that were wrought by the apostles, were what some Christians thought acted as a restraining force.[14] Writing a generation later, Theodoret of Cyrrhus critiques those who think that the Holy Spirit is that which restrains, since the third member of the trinity could not

9. Though he does not cite 2 Thessalonians, Melito of Sardis associates the flourishing of Christian groups with the divine blessing of the Roman Empire (Eusebius, *Ecclesiastical History* 4.26.5–11).

10. Ambrosiaster thus connects the "falling away" of 2:3 with the "fall" of Rome, which will initiate the coming of the antichrist and then the return of the Lord (*Commentary on Paul's Second Epistle to Thessalonians* 2.6–7).

11. Cited in Cacciari, *Withholding Power*, 160.

12. Arthur Bradley, *Unbearable Life: A Genealogy of Political Erasure* (New York: Columbia University Press, 2019), 145–46.

13. Chrysostom thinks that Paul does not come out and say that the empire was the restrainer for fear of being thought seditious rather than eschatologically descriptive.

14. H. B. Swete, *Theodori episcopi Mopsuesteni*, vol. 2, *Thessalonians–Philemon, Appendices, Indices* (Cambridge: Cambridge University Press, 1882).

be "wholly consumed" (*Commentary on the Second Epistle to Thessalonians*).[15] However, he is also not persuaded that the Roman Empire is the restrainer. Theodoret argues that it is God's will that withholds the antichrist's appearance, which allows for the gospel to be proclaimed to the nations before the end comes. Much later, the Protestant reformer John Calvin would take a similar position, arguing that God withheld the full coming of the antichrist until the gospel had been spread to the whole world.[16] For Calvin, the restraint was part of God's plan for salvation.

One can see in this brief foray into the history of premodern Christian interpretation the outlines of how Christian reflection on the restrainer can feed into anti-Judaism. As early Christian competition with other forms of Judaism morphed over time into associations of Jews with the antichrist or Satan, Jews came to be seen as one aspect of the evil forces that had to be held back by state power or as a group that needed to be evangelized out of existence to bring about the return of Christ. Thinking on the restrainer thus folded into broader Christian patterns of anti-Judaism.

In the twentieth century, the concept of the restrainer took a further turn in being weaponized for both anti-Judaism and Christian nationalism, two concepts that are often intertwined.[17] One of the legal architects of the Nazi regime, Carl Schmitt, reconfigured the restrainer, using the Greek term *katechon*, as a key element of his political theology. For Schmitt, the *katechon* is the key concept in Christian political thought, bridging eschatological expectation with Christian imperial power.[18] If early Christians theorized that their God used the Roman Empire for good, Schmitt takes this notion further. The *katechon* is what allows Christians to exercise political power in the interval between now and the eschaton. Without this concept, according to Schmitt, Christians would be paralyzed by waiting for the eschatological return of Jesus. With it, Christian empire can organize itself and exert itself as a historical power that plays the role of restraining the antichrist. Thus, for Schmitt, the *katechon* is the mechanism by which Christians enter into political life in the

---

15. Quoted in Cacciari, *Withholding Power*, 151–52.

16. John Calvin, *Commentary on 2 Thessalonians*, 2:6, in *Commentaries on the Epistles of Paul the Apostle to the Philippians, Colossians, and Thessalonians*, trans. John Pringle (Grand Rapids: Eerdmans, 1948).

17. Paul A. Djupe and Jacob Dennen, "Christian Nationalists and QAnon Followers Tend to Be Anti-Semitic. That Was Seen in the Capitol Attack," *Washington Post* (26 January 2021) (https://tinyurl.com/2wj7eyw8).

18. Carl Schmitt, *The Nomos of the Earth in the International Law of the Jus Publicum Europaeum*, trans. G. L. Ulmen (New York: Telos, 2006), 60.

shadow of the eschaton as those who are able to exercise imperial power, and by which one can justify the wielding of that power as a fight to restrain the forces of the antichrist.[19] In such a framework, there seem to be no limits on how the state can act in service of its Christianized mission. Such thinking anchored the legal regime that Schmitt helped design under the Nazis, but has also returned in the dominionist theologies of contemporary American Christians, most famously in those associated with the New Apostolic Reformation.[20]

In the wake of Schmitt's work on the *katechon*, a number of political philosophers attempted to rethink how the restraining force might anchor a different political order than that envisioned by Schmitt. The Italian philosopher (and, more recently, COVID skeptic) Giorgio Agamben argued that the *katechon* is the force, represented by any state or political order, that holds back the mystery of messianic time, which is characterized by lawlessness (*anomos*) or law rendered inactive.[21] In other words, the *katechon* might not anchor Christian political power at all, but gesture toward the undoing of the law of the state itself.[22] The restrainer of 2 Thessalonians 2 thus traverses the realm of the political, from the conservative and radical forces of law and empire to the liberating energies of messianic anarchy. For thinkers like Schmitt, who was himself a Nazi partisan, the *katechon* remains an appealing figure for grounding both imperialist Christian nationalism and the antisemitism that comes with such orientations.

Discussion Questions and Activity Suggestions

1. Compare 1 Thessalonians 4–5 and 2 Thessalonians 2:1–12. What are the main events that these texts connect with the eschaton? Who are the main

19. Schmitt's reading of the *katechon* aligns itself uncomfortably with his broader work on political theology, which relies on the concept of the "state of exception" that sees political life as a site of conflict between friend and enemy in which the sovereign is the one who decides outside of the law where the line between friend and enemy is drawn. See Carl Schmitt, *Political Theology: Four Chapters on the Concept of Sovereignty*, trans. George Schwab (Chicago: Chicago University Press, 2005).

20. Brad Christerson and Richard Flory, *The Rise of Network Christianity: How Independent Leaders Are Changing the Religious Landscape* (Oxford: Oxford University Press, 2017).

21. Agamben, *Time That Remains*, 108–11.

22. Cacciari, *Withholding Power*; and Roberto Esposito, *Immunitas: The Protection and Negation of Life* (Cambridge: Polity Press, 2011), 57–66, make similar attempts to revitalize the *katechon* outside of Schmitt's characterization.

figures? What timelines do these texts suggest for who and what will happen in the lead-up to the end?

2. Having thought through the details of these two accounts of the end, how might you make them into one story? What gaps would you need to fill in? What information would you need to add? Now try it another way: how might you make these into two different stories? How does the story change if you add in the polemics against the enemies of followers of Jesus in 2 Thessalonians 1?

3. Read through the appendices of Massimo Cacciari's *The Withholding Power*, in which the author catalogues the different interpretations of the *katechon* in premodern Christian authors. What details do these authors emphasize, add, or ignore in order to make sense of this ambiguous figure? What other biblical texts are used to help flesh out the story? Finally, if you were to try and make this figure make sense to a modern context, what details would you add?

Further Reading

Bradley, Arthur. "Unleashed: Schmitt and the Katechon." Pages 141–62 in Bradley's *Unbearable Life: A Genealogy of Political Erasure*. New York: Columbia University Press, 2019.

Cacciari, Massimo. *The Withholding Power: An Essay on Political Theology*. New York: Bloomsbury Academic, 2018.

Gaventa, Beverly Roberts. *First and Second Thessalonians*. Interpretation. Louisville: Westminster John Knox, 1998.

Gillman, Florence, Mary Ann Beavis, and HyeRan Kimm-Cragg. *1–2 Thessalonians*. Wisdom Commentary 52. Collegeville, MN: Liturgical Press, 2016.

Thiselton, Anthony C. *1 and 2 Thessalonians through the Centuries*. Malden, MA: Wiley-Blackwell, 2011.

24

1, 2 *Timothy and Titus*

MICHAEL SCOTT ROBERTSON

T he Pastoral Epistles—1 Timothy, 2 Timothy, and Titus—are a group of
documents within the New Testament that were written likely in the early
second century.[1] These writings do not discuss Jews or Jewish practices frequently, but in the few instances that they do, the reception of these verses has
been decidedly anti-Jewish. In this chapter, I discuss the verses in the Pastoral
Epistles that lend themselves to anti-Jewish bias, and I contend that they do
not, in their original context, malign Jews writ large. I then examine ancient
reception of some of these verses in Jerome's *Commentary on Titus*, showing
that he interprets the Pastoral Epistles in an anti-Jewish sense. I finish by discussing two modern groups—the Aryan Nations and QAnon—and show that
they too interpret the Pastoral Epistles in an anti-Jewish sense.

Notable Passages

Within the Pastoral Epistles, the most notable passages that can be construed
as anti-Jewish are in Titus. The first is 1:10–11: "There are many who are insubordinate, empty talkers, and deceivers, especially those of the circumcision,
whom it is necessary to silence."[2] This statement is the beginning of a discussion of the out-group, that is, those whom the author considers not to be in
his group, in 1:10–14. By naming "those of the circumcision," this places Jews,
or at least a group of Jews, within the out-group.

---

1. Douglas Campbell, *Framing Paul: An Epistolary Biography* (Grand Rapids: Eerdmans,
2014), 339–403.
2. Unless otherwise noted, all translations in this chapter are my own.

Some scholars argue that the entire out-group is made of Jews.[3] They argue that the phrase "especially those of the circumcision" (*malista hoi ek tēs peritomēs*) should be translated "that is, those of the circumcision." Under this translation, the "many who are insubordinate" are defined as Jews and the derogatory comments are applied only to Jews. This translation, however, is not the most natural way to understand the phrase.[4] The term under question, *malista*, is usually translated "especially,"[5] which indicates that "those of the circumcision" are a subset of the oppositional group under discussion.

What then does the phrase "especially of the circumcision" describe? Within the larger unit, there is a second ethnographic label: Cretan.[6] Titus 1:12 indicates that the main ethnographic label for the group is Cretan, by saying, "One of their own prophets says, 'Cretans are always liars, evil beasts, lazy gluttons.'" This quote is not found in any Jewish prophet, but instead, it comes from a Cretan "divine man," Epimenides. Through the way this passage discusses Cretans and Jews, it is evident that the two ethnic identities rhetorically intersect.[7] The term discussed above, *malista*, preceding the description of the Jews subordinates that ethnographic label to the Cretan label. Thus, the rhetoric of the passage has Cretan Jews within its purview rather than Jews writ large.

In the same section of Titus is the second mention of Judaism. In 1:14, the letter says: "Do not pay attention to Jewish myths." Scholars debate what these "Jewish myths" are, with some suggesting that it refers to Jubilees, the Ascension of Isaiah, or the Testaments of the Twelve Patriarchs.[8] Others suggest that these myths are somehow related to the Old Testament.[9] The letter, however,

---

3. T. C. Skeat, "'Especially the Parchments': A Note on 2 Tim 4:13," *Journal of Theological Studies* 30 (1979): 173–77.

4. Vern Sheridan Poythress, "The Meaning of μάλιστα in 2 Timothy 4:13 and Related Verses," *Journal of Theological Studies* 53.2 (2002): 523–32.

5. W. Bauer, F. W. Danker, W. F. Arndt, and F. W. Gingrich, *A Greek–English Lexicon of the New Testament and Other Early Christian Literature*, 3rd ed. (Chicago: University of Chicago Press, 2000), s.v. μάλιστα; H. G. Liddell, R. Scott, H. S. Jones, and R. McKenzie, *A Greek-English Lexicon*, 9th ed. (Oxford: Clarendon, 1996), s.v. μάλα; J. P. Louw and E. A. Nida, *Greek-English Lexicon of the New Testament: Based on Semantic Domains*, 2nd ed. (New York: United Bible Societies, 1989), s.v. μάλιστα.

6. See Manuel Vogel, "Die Kreterpolemik des Titusbriefes und die antike Ethnographie," *Zeitschrift für die neutestamentliche Wissenschaft* 101 (2010): 252–66.

7. Marianne B. Kartzow, "An Intersectional Approach to Early Christian Memory: The Case of the Pastoral Epistles," *Journal of Early Christian History* 1.2 (2011): 125.

8. Jerome D. Quinn, *The Letter to Titus: A New Translation with Notes and Commentary and an Introduction to Titus, I and II Timothy, the Pastoral Epistles*, Anchor Bible 35 (New York: Doubleday, 1990), 110.

9. I. Howard Marshall, *The Pastoral Epistles*, International Critical Commentary (London: T&T Clark, 1999), 207.

is not clear as to the exact referent of these myths. Although the term "myth" (*mythos*) could have a neutral meaning,[10] the placement within a polemical section against an out-group indicates that it has a negative function. This places, in some way, Jewish thought (the extent of which is unknown) definitively within the sphere of those outside the group.

Some scholars hold other portions of 1:14–15 to be referencing Jewish practices. In 1:14, the letter tells its readers not to pay attention to "commands of people, which turn away from the truth," which is often interpreted as a polemic against the Jewish law.[11] Further, in 1:15, the letter reads: "All things are clean to those who are clean, but to those who are defiled and unbelieving, nothing is clean." Scholars often comment that this last verse references Jewish purity laws or customs.[12] While it remains a possibility that these verses do discourage certain Jewish practices, the double ethnographic label in 1:10–16 makes it difficult to establish such an interpretation with any certainty. Because the out-group is also labeled Cretan, 1:14–15 could have Cretan practices in view. Indeed, Cretans were famous in antiquity for their laws (Plato, *Minos* 321). Thus, while 1:10–16 does marginalize certain Jews and Jewish myths, it is not clear if it seeks to malign any other aspects of Jews or Judaism.

These two portions of Titus that discuss Judaism inhabit an important place within the rhetoric of Titus. The letter begins with a typical epistolary introduction in 1:1–4, and then it discusses categories of leaders with the titles *episkopoi/presbyteroi* ("community overseers" and "elders") in 1:5–9.[13] The pericope concerning *episkopoi/presbyteroi* defines the in-group the letter constructs. The *episkopoi/presbyteroi* are the leaders of the group as they are the ones doing the teaching and rebuking those who oppose the group (1:9). These verses give a long list of qualities that these leaders are to embody, such as blamelessness (1:6–7), holiness (1:8), and self-control (1:8). Through this description of the leaders of the group, the letter portrays a prototype,

---

10. For example, Menander Rhetor (Διαίρεσις τῶν ἐπιδεικτικῶν 338.6), writing in about the third century CE and quoting the fifth-century BCE Acusilaus, notes that some do not consider myths and genealogies to differ. F. Jacoby, *Die Fragmente der griechischen Historiker (FGrH)* (Leiden: Brill, 1923), 1:47–48.

11. Quinn, *Titus*, 112–14; Norbert Brox, *Die Pastoralbriefe*, 5th ed., Regensburger Neues Testament 7 (Regensburg: Pustet, 1989), 289.

12. Quinn, *Titus*, 112–14.

13. The relationship between the *episkopoi* and *presbyteroi* in Titus is not clear. See Michael Theobald, "Von den Presbytern zum Episkopos (Tit 1,5–9): Vom Umgang mit Spannungen und Widersprüchen im Corpus Pastorale," *Zeitschrift für die neutestamentliche Wissenschaft* 104.2 (2013): 221–22.

which encapsulates the ideal group member[14] and thus paints the picture of in-group membership.

Titus 1:10–16 describes the opposite of 1:5–9. Members of the out-group are labeled with direct contrasts to the *episkopoi/presbyteroi*, such as they are unruly (1:10), unfaithful (1:14), and abominable (1:16). Describing the out-group functions to draw boundaries for the in-group by describing what the members of the group should not be.[15] Within this context, the letter gives far more weight to Jews and Jewish myths than the low number of occurrences would suggest. It vilifies them as part of the opposition or out-group. Although, as seen above, this section discusses only a group within Judaism, it nevertheless sets the stage for later use of this passage as anti-Jewish, and antisemitic, polemic.

First Timothy contains a verse that is similar to Titus 1:14 and is often interpreted in a like manner. First Timothy 1:4 says: "Do not pay attention to myths and endless genealogies, which cause useless speculation rather than godly training which is in faith." Myths and genealogies are discussions that readers are admonished to avoid since they are antithetical to godly training. Thus, they are presented as contrary the life of faith. The mention of myths and genealogies in this verse is often interpreted to mean Jewish speculations on the Old Testament.[16] However, unlike in Titus 1:14, neither the myths nor the genealogies are specifically labeled "Jewish." Further, other than two vague mentions of the "law" in 1 Timothy 1:7–8, there is nothing in the context that would suggest that the myths and genealogies are Jewish. Instead, the connection between 1 Timothy 1:4 and Judaism is often made through importing to this passage the context of Titus 1:14.[17] Without imposing Titus on 1 Timothy, this verse does not necessarily imply any anti-Jewish sentiments.[18]

---

14. Michael A. Hogg et al., "Why Do People Join Groups? Three Motivational Accounts from Social Psychology," *Social and Personality Psychology Compass* 2/3 (2008): 1273–74.

15. Michael Hogg and Scott Reid, "Social Identity, Self-Categorization, and the Communication of Group Norms," *Communication Theory* 16.1 (2006): 10–20.

16. Marshall, *Pastoral Epistles*, 365; William D. Mounce, *Pastoral Epistles*, Word Biblical Commentary 46 (Nashville: Nelson, 2000), 20. Raymond F. Collins, *I & II Timothy and Titus: A Commentary*, New Testament Library (Louisville: Westminster John Knox, 2002), 27, does not specifically mention the "Old Testament," but he does say that these myths are Jewish.

17. See, e.g., Lyn M. Kindson, *Persuading Shipwrecked Men: The Rhetorical Strategies of 1 Timothy 1*, Wissenschaftliche Untersuchungen zum Neuen Testament 2/526 (Tübingen: Mohr Siebeck, 2020), 126–27.

18. For other issues of anti-Jewish interpretations of 1 Timothy, see Benjamin J. Lappenga, "'Formerly a Blasphemer and a Man of Violence': First Timothy and the Othering of Jews," *Journal of Religion and Violence* 5.3 (2017): 232–52.

Second Timothy also contains the term "myth," and scholars frequently bring it into similar discussions.[19] Second Timothy 4:4 says: "And they will turn the ears away from the truth and turn to myths." The term for "myths," here, is used in a negative sense as it is contrasted with "the truth." Similar to 1 Timothy 1:4, this verse does not label the myths Jewish, nor does the context suggest that these myths would necessarily be Jewish. Instead, because scholars often assume 2 Timothy has the same context as 1 Timothy, and 1 Timothy 1:4 has already been conflated with Titus 1:14, the myths of 2 Timothy are often interpreted as speculations on the Old Testament. By labeling these myths in 1 Timothy and 2 Timothy as speculations on the Old Testament, scholars set uses of the Hebrew Bible into conflict with the practices these texts promote. These vague descriptions are elastic enough to encompass a broad range of readings of the Hebrew Bible. In turn, this explanation of the passages mentioned above become anti-Jewish. As can be seen, conflating the three Pastoral Epistles into, essentially, one document leads to anti-Jewish uses of all three texts. Since the problematic interpretations of each Pastoral Epistle is similar, I focus in the following only on the Titus passages to demonstrate the anti-Jewish and antisemitic trend throughout the history of their interpretation.

Ancient Reception

A well-known issue in studying the Pastoral Epistles is the lack of extant, early receptions of these documents.[20] Although earlier authors, such as Clement of Alexandria, cite Titus, Jerome's fourth-century *Commentary on Titus* provides one of the earliest extant commentaries on Titus. His comments on both verses identified above as potentially anti-Jewish betray interpretations that move in a decisively anti-Jewish direction. In discussing 1:10, Jerome says: "They are Jews of the circumcision who at that time endeavored to destroy the nascent church of Christ and to introduce the precepts of the law."[21] Jerome generalizes the phrase "those of the circumcision," which was shown above to be restricted to Cretan Jews, such that it now refers to Jews at large. Jerome places on the Jews their attempts to "destroy the nascent church" and "introduce the precepts of

---

19. See Mounce, *Pastoral Epistles*, 576.

20. See Carsten Looks, *Das Anvertraute bewahren: Die Rezeption der Pastoralbriefe im 2. Jahrhundert* (Munich: Herbert Utz, 1999).

21. All translations of Jerome's *Commentary on Titus* are from Thomas P. Scheck, trans., *St. Jerome's Commentaries on Galatians, Titus, and Philemon* (Notre Dame: University of Notre Dame Press, 2010).

the law." Both of these phrases marginalize and demonize the Jews. The first does so by painting the Jews as the one (and apparently only ones!) who attempted to end the movement of which Jerome and his intended readers were a part. They are thus the archenemies of the faith. Introducing "precepts of the law" then makes them enemies of the Pauline gospel, as Jerome comments that this idea was developed further in Galatians and Romans.

Jerome's commentary on 1:14, however, contains much more anti-Jewish sentiment. He says: "Let us 'be content' with the Jews for a little while, and let us patiently listen to the nonsense of those who are called wise among them; and then we will understand what are the 'Jewish myths' without the authority of Scripture, without any claim on reason, of those who fabricate certain fabulous things. . . . If, after the coming of Christ, someone is 'mutilated,' and not circumcised, he serves 'Judaic myths' and the commands of men who turn away the truth." Jerome provides incendiary statements about the wise men of the Jews. He calls their wisdom "nonsense" and adjures his readers to tolerate them "for a little while." He accuses the Jews of fabricating "certain fabulous things,"[22] and he demeans their rite of circumcision as mutilation.

In these sections of Jerome's commentary, he uses the two mentions of Jews and Judaism in Titus to launch an assault on Jews. The Jews are consistently marginalized, maligned, demonized, and demeaned. Just the mention of Jews in the discussion of the out-group gave Jerome license to attack the Jews of his day.

Modern Reception

The anti-Jewish use of the Pastoral Epistles did not stop in late antiquity. Modern groups also use Titus as warrant for anti-Jewish and antisemitic stances, two of which will be examined here: the Aryan Nations and QAnon.

The Aryan Nations is a white supremacist group in the United States that fits within the Christian-Identity movement.[23] It was established in the 1970s by Richard Butler, who remained the group's leader until his death in 2004.[24] The group peaked in the 1980s and went bankrupt following a 1999 lawsuit

---

22. See John Chrysostom, *Homilies on 1 Timothy*, Homily 13, for similar statements using 1 Timothy.

23. Bill J. Leonard and Jill Y. Crainshaw, *Encyclopedia of Religious Controversies in the United States*, 2nd ed., 2 vols. (Santa Barbara, CA: ABC-CLIO, 2013), 45.

24. Leonard and Crainshaw, *Encyclopedia of Religious Controversies*, 45.

brought against it by the Southern Poverty Law Center.[25] Like other Christian-Identity groups, the Aryan Nations holds to a "two-seedline" or "Serpent seed" doctrine wherein the Jews are Satan's offspring through Eve and the Anglo-Saxons descend from Adam.[26] Through this teaching, they believe that all other races are subordinate to the Anglo-Saxons.[27]

In the 1990s, this group published a pamphlet entitled "Where to Look in the Bible: Jews."[28] This pamphlet begins with the phrase "where to look in the Bible" followed by a series of questions followed by a command to read a particular verse or passage of the Bible. For example, the first question is "who was the Bible written for?" This question is followed by the command: "Read Genesis 5:1," where the reader is supposed to find the answer to the aforementioned question. One of the questions in this pamphlet is "should we give heed to Jewish fables?" The answer to this question is "Read Titus 1:14." The beginning of this verse reads, as mentioned above: "Pay no attention to Jewish myths." Although the question seemingly restates the relevant portion of 1:14 in the form of a question, the context shows that it is coopted for a highly antisemitic polemic. A few more questions from the pamphlet show the antisemitic context of the pamphlet more clearly. One reads: "Are we to 'hate' the Jews since they are God's enemies? Read Psalms [*sic*] 139:19–22." Another reads: "Are the Jews anti-Christ? Read 1 John 2:22." Through these rhetorical maneuvers, the Aryan Nations intends the reader to understand that the Bible is intrinsically hostile to Jews. Thus, similar to readers in antiquity, the Aryan Nations read Titus 1:14 as implying antisemitism and anti-Judaism.

QAnon is a "conspiracy theory that claims there is a secret cabal of devil-worshiping Democrats and elites that feed off the blood of children."[29] According to this conspiracy theory, former US president Donald Trump is the only one who can save the country from this cabal, and he is actively working behind the scenes to bring about its demise.[30] QAnon began in 2017 with an anonymous author (Q) claiming online that he possessed high-level (level Q) security clearance in an intelligence agency of the United States.[31] Since its foundation, the canon of Q posts has grown exponentially.

---

25. Leonard and Crainshaw, *Encyclopedia of Religious Controversies*, 45.

26. Leonard and Crainshaw, *Encyclopedia of Religious Controversies*, 46.

27. Leonard and Crainshaw, *Encyclopedia of Religious Controversies*, 46.

28. Emily Suzanne Clark and Brad Stoddard, eds., *Race and New Religious Movements in the USA: A Documentary Reader* (London: Bloomsbury Academic, 2019), 147–58.

29. Mia Bloom and Sophia Moskalenko, *Pastels and Pedophiles: Inside the Mind of QAnon* (Redwood City: Stanford University Press, 2021), 4.

30. Bloom and Moskalenko, *Pastels and Pedophiles*, 4.

31. Bloom and Moskalenko, *Pastels and Pedophiles*, 5.

In a QAnon discussion board, an author labeled "Anonymous" posted a series of Bible verses "proving" that "Jesus was not a Pharisee/Talmudic Jew; He damned them . . . repeatedly!"[32] This was in reply to a chain of antisemitic posts, and it answered a challenge to "Read a Bible."[33] Anonymous uses Titus four times to say that Jesus was not a Jew. He notes 1:13–14 commenting that Jews are "purveyors of fables." At three separate points, he turns to 1:10, saying that the Jews are "disobedient," "seducers," and "vain talkers."[34] Through these references to Titus, the author hopes to prove that the Jews are "damned" and that Jesus, therefore, could not have been a Jew himself. This use of Titus is in line with that of Jerome and the Aryan Nations seen above. These verses provide fodder for those looking to malign Jews and spread antisemitic prejudice.

Conclusion

Within the Pastoral Epistles, two verses stand out as having potential for use in anti-Jewish and antisemitic rhetoric—Titus 1:10 and 1:14. In the context of Titus, these verses have a more limited rhetorical function, referring to a group of Cretan Jews. However, interpreters often read the connection between Jews and myths in Titus into 1 Timothy and 2 Timothy, producing anti-Jewish and antisemitic interpretations of these texts. From the earliest receptions in Jerome to modern times with the Aryan Nations and QAnon, the Pastorals have frequently been deployed for maligning Jews and Jewish practices. Thus, even though the Pastorals do not contain polemics against Jews qua Jews, the reception of the Pastorals shows that they can be used in ways that are both anti-Jewish and antisemitic.

Discussion Questions and Activity Suggestions

1. In light of the way the phrase "those of the circumcision" in Titus 1:10 has been understood, how important is the language we use in regard to groups of people?

32. Anonymous (10 May 2021) (16:39:42) (7) no. 13873401, */qresearch/-QResearch: Research and Discussion about Q's Crumbs* (10 June 2021) (16:39:42) (https://tinyurl.com /mryzfn3u).
33. Anonymous no. 13873363, */qresearch/-QResearch* (10 June 2021) (16:35:18) (https:// tinyurl.com/mryzfn3u).
34. Anonymous no. 13873363, */qresearch/-QResearch* (10 June 2021) (16:35:18) (https:// tinyurl.com/mryzfn3u).

2. The two modern groups discussed in this chapter pick verses out of context to underpin their antisemitism. How does context help us understand the original meaning of a particular verse or passage?
3. Some scholars argue that the opponents in Titus 1:10–16 are primarily Jewish. What is another way to read the ethnicity of the opponents?
4. How can the phrase "Jewish myths" in Titus 1:14 be used in anti-Jewish polemic?
5. How does placing elements of Jewish identity in the discussion of the out-group contribute to anti-Jewish readings of Titus?
6. Read Titus 1:10–16 and Galatians 2:11–21. Examine the ways in which each passage treats the opposition. Discuss how they compare and contrast. What kind of aspects of the other do these passages focus on. Why?

Further Reading

Huizenga, Annette. *Moral Education for Women in the Pastoral and Pythagorean Letters: Philosophers of the Household.* Leiden: Brill, 2013.

Kartzow, Marianne B. "An Intersectional Approach to Early Christian Memory: The Case of the Pastoral Epistles." *Journal of Early Christian History* 1.2 (2011): 119–34.

Lappenga, Benjamin J. "'Formerly a Blasphemer and a Man of Violence': First Timothy and the Othering of Jews." *Journal of Religion and Violence* 5.3 (2017): 232–52.

Scheck, Thomas P., trans. *St. Jerome's Commentaries on Galatians, Titus, and Philemon.* Notre Dame: University of Notre Dame Press, 2010.

Stegemann, Wolfgang. "Anti-Semitic and Racist Prejudices in Titus 1:10–16." Pages 217–94 in *Ethnicity and the Bible.* Edited by Mark G. Brett. Leiden: Brill, 1996.

25

Philemon

MARY ANN BEAVIS

Philemon is Paul's shortest letter, made up of a mere twenty-five verses. It is usually classified as a personal letter from Paul to the householder Philemon, to two other individuals, Apphia and Archippus, and to the church (*ekklēsia*) to which they belonged (Phlm 1–2). Throughout the letter, Paul repeatedly mentions that he is imprisoned (Phlm 1, 9, 10, 13, 23). Traditional interpretation places Paul's incarceration in Rome, but a more likely location is Ephesus, which was much closer to Colossae, a city associated with Onesimus (cf. Col 4:9). The heart of the letter is Paul's request concerning a man called Onesimus (Phlm 10), whose name ("Useful") and explicit references (Phlm 16) indicate that he was a slave who had embraced the gospel due to Paul's influence.

Although it's clear that Paul was asking for a favor relating to Onesimus (Phlm 13), it's notoriously difficult to discern what he actually wanted. Since the fourth century, the dominant interpretation is that Onesimus had run away from Philemon's household, somehow met up with Paul in prison, and that Paul wanted Philemon to receive the errant slave back without punishment as a brother in Christ. It is more likely, however, that Onesimus had actually been sent by Philemon to look after Paul during his imprisonment, and that Paul wanted Philemon to let Onesimus remain with Paul so that he could continue to assist him in service of the gospel. If so, Paul might simply have been asking for a loan or transfer of ownership—or he might have been hinting that Philemon should free Onesimus.

In the nineteenth century, these competing interpretations of Philemon were used by both pro-slavery advocates and anti-slavery activists to support their positions. The former frequently cited the many passages in both Testaments, including Philemon, that take slavery for granted as "a necessary social institution like the family or the school."[1] After all, "Abraham owned slaves and the Mosaic Law encouraged Israelites to make slaves from the nations around them. Jesus praised the faith of the Roman centurion without suggesting he free his slave, Paul did not demand that Philemon free his slave, and Paul provided moral instruction for both masters and slaves that included instructions to slaves to obey their masters, even cruel ones, with utter fidelity."[2] In contrast, the anti-slavery pastor Albert Barnes argued that the God of the New Testament established principles that would ultimately result in the abolition of slavery[3]—an implicitly supersessionist contrast with the Old Testament God, who, by implication, condoned slavery. More recently, attention has turned to the figure of Onesimus—was he a passive pawn in a negotiation between two "free" men (remember, Paul was a prisoner at the time), or did he have an active role in seeking Paul's intervention? Early Christian tradition suggests the latter, remembering Onesimus as a revered bishop, missionary, and martyr.

Jews and Judaism

There is no overt reference to Jews or Judaism in Philemon, or even to the Jewish scriptures. This may be because the members of Philemon's house-church were gentile, or simply because the letter is so short. Perhaps the lack of explicitly Jewish content is why the letter is sometimes seen as an early example of "Christian" brotherly love of the apostle for a believing slave.[4] This led to the obfuscation of the profoundly Jewish character of the letter, since it was written at a time when there was no such thing as "Christianity"; irrespective of the identity of the recipients, the letter was written in the context of sectarian Judaism. Moreover, it is likely that Paul's Jewishness figured significantly in his treatment of Onesimus, since Torah teaches that fugitive slaves should be given refuge (Deut 23:15–16); the refrain "remember that you were slaves in Egypt" (15:15; 24:18; cf. 6:21) would have tempered Paul's attitudes to the enslaved. For Paul, the yearly celebration of Passover, with its repeated recollection of Israel's slavery in Egypt, would have been part of his spiritual DNA. Another relevant story from Torah is the

---

1. Molly Oshatz, "No Ordinary Sin: Antislavery Protestants and the Discovery of the Social Nature of Morality," *Church History* 79.2 (2010): 334.

2. Oshatz, "No Ordinary Sin," 336.

3. Albert Barnes, *The Church and Slavery* (Philadelphia: Parry & McMillan, 1857), 42.

4. See, e.g., Murray J. Harris, *Slave of Christ: A New Testament Metaphor for Total Devotion to Christ* (Downers Grove, IL: InterVarsity, 1999), 58–59.

restoration of Joseph, sold into slavery by his jealous brothers, but restored to his family many years later (Gen 37:12–36; 45:1–15). Barbara Geller notes that "rabbinic law, like earlier biblical law, had greater restraints on the power of the slave-owner over the slave than did Roman law."[5]

Paul's intercession on behalf of Onesimus doesn't mean that the baptismal formula proclaiming that men and women, Jews and Greeks, slaves and free, were all one in Christ Jesus (Gal 3:28) resulted in the freeing of baptized slaves on a widespread basis (1 Cor 7:21; cf. Col 3:18–4:1; Eph 5:22–33). In Galatians, Paul affirmed the solidarity of slaves and free (Gal 3:28) but a few paragraphs later contrasted the son of the slave Hagar with the freeborn Isaac (4:21–31). As Geller puts it: "Paul envisioned slaves as free and equal in the church while not seeking the abolition of slavery."[6] Believing slaves likely wished for something more.

In antiquity, slavery was an accepted social institution, and few ancient thinkers ever questioned it, let alone contemplated its abolition. A few Greek utopian writers imagined societies without slaves,[7] but the only real-life utopian communities, the Essenes and the Therapeutae, were Jewish, and both are said to have eschewed slavery (Josephus, *Antiquities* 18.1.5 §21; Philo, *On the Contemplative Life* 70; *Every Good Man Is Free* 79); "Josephus says that the Essenes believe the ownership of slaves contributes to injustice, and Philo states that the Essenes view slave ownership as unjust and as destroying nature's ordinances of equality."[8] It was many centuries before slavery was legally abolished on a widespread basis. However, forms of slavery continue to exist today, affecting many millions of people.

Some Key Passages

As suggested above, the letter contains some hints that Onesimus was behind Paul's request to Philemon. That is, Paul was writing "on behalf of" (Phlm 10), rather than "for" or "concerning" Onesimus (as most translations render *peri tou*). It is important to remember that at time of writing, Onesimus was attend-

5. Barbara Geller, "The Epistle of Paul to Philemon," in *The Jewish Annotated New Testament*, ed. Amy-Jill Levine and Marc Zvi Brettler (Oxford: Oxford University Press, 2011), 404.

6. Geller, "Philemon," 404.

7. See Emily Fairey, "Slavery in the Classical Utopia: A Comparative Study," PhD diss., City University of New York, 2006.

8. Geller, "Philemon," 404.

ing to the prisoner Paul's physical and psychological needs by providing him with food, water, and companionship. Paul, in return, would have been grateful to Onesimus and, of course, to Philemon who had sent him (Phlm 4–7). An illustration of the gratitude of a prisoner for a slave's services is found in the Jewish historian Josephus. He tells the story of Herod Agrippa, who, when he was imprisoned by the emperor Tiberius (*Antiquities* 18.6.6 §§192–94), was offered a drink of water by a slave named Thaumastus when he was baking in the sun. Agrippa was so grateful that when he was freed and became king of Judea, he bought Thaumastus, freed him, and made him steward over his estate. Perhaps Onesimus asked Paul, or at least hinted to him, to show his gratitude by asking Philemon to release him for service to the gospel. As a slave in Philemon's household, Onesimus would have known how best for Paul to write on his behalf.

Another expression that takes on a deeper meaning in this context is Paul's reference to Onesimus as his child (*teknon*): "whose father I have become during my imprisonment" (Phlm 10 NRSV). The Greek text says nothing about fatherhood, but uses the verb *egennēsa* to refer to the new relationship between the two men. The verb *gennaō* can be translated either "to beget" (i.e., impregnate) or "to give birth to." Although most translations choose the former, thus portraying Paul as Onesimus's spiritual father, there are many ancient accounts of women giving birth in prison, most famously the martyr Felicity, a slave who was arrested along with her mistress Perpetua, herself the mother of an infant. Thus, the verse would be better interpreted: "Onesimus, whom I gave birth to in chains" (cf. LXX Isa 66:9; 4 Maccabees 10:2), an image of Paul "giving birth" in adverse circumstances.

The phrase "that he might be of service" (Phlm 13 NRSV) is another expression that is often underappreciated. The word translated here "be of service" (*diakonē*) is related to the nouns *diakonia* and *diakonos*, which in early Christianity referred to the ministry of a deacon. The duties of early Christian deacons included visiting and attending to the needs of prisoners, exactly the kinds of service or ministry that Onesimus would have offered Paul (cf. Col 1:7; 4:7; Eph 6:21).

Discussion Questions and Activity Suggestions

1. Can you think of any other ways that Paul's Jewishness might have influenced his relationship with Onesimus?

2. Do you think it's significant that the only ancient communities (the Essenes and the Therapeutae) said not to have kept slaves were Jewish?

3. Bibliodrama is a form of imaginative, unrehearsed role playing where participants explore biblical stories and characters aided by a facilitator. It is a kind of midrash (a Jewish form of biblical storytelling) pioneered at the Jewish Theological Seminary in New York that has spread to a variety of settings, both Jewish and Christian. The activity suggested here is a simple Bibliodrama exercise. First, read the letter to Philemon aloud in class (each student can read a verse or two). Divide the class into two groups. One group is "Paul," the second is "Onesimus." In character (i.e., in the first person), ask each group to discuss their personal thoughts and feelings on their situations. What are their hopes and fears for the future? How does Paul as a free Jewish man feel about Onesimus, an enslaved gentile? What does he want from him? From Philemon? How does Onesimus feel about his relationship with Paul? What does he want to come out of the letter to Philemon? When the two groups have had a chance to explore their characters, bring them into dialogue with each other. What would Paul like to say to Onesimus? What would Onesimus like Paul to know?

4. Have students read the letter aloud, a few verses at a time. In small groups, ask students to identify prescript, body, and conclusion of the letter. Why does the body of the letter have such a long thanksgiving? Where is Paul, who is Philemon, and what situation is he addressing? Who is the bearer of the letter? What does Colossians 4:12 imply about the location of Philemon? How does Paul's Jewish identity bear on his request to Philemon?

Further Reading

Beavis, Mary Ann. *The First Christian Slave: Onesimus in Context.* Eugene, OR: Wipf & Stock, 2021.

Geller, Barbara. "The Letter of Paul to Philemon." Pages 402–5 in *The Jewish Annotated New Testament.* Edited by Amy-Jill Levine and Marc Zvi Brettler. Oxford: Oxford University Press, 2011.

Glancy, Jennifer. *Slavery in Early Christianity.* Minneapolis: Fortress, 2006.

Harrill, J. Albert. *Slaves in the New Testament: Literary, Social, and Moral Dimensions.* Minneapolis: Fortress, 2006.

Hezser, Catherine. *Jewish Slavery in Antiquity.* Oxford: Oxford University Press, 2010.

26

Hebrews

KYU SEOP KIM

As one scholar notes: "It seems that few biblical texts have influenced Christians' understanding of the relation between Jews and Christians more than has Hebrews."[1] Hebrews is also "more responsible than any other New Testament writer for our expression 'Old Testament.'"[2] In this vein, Hebrews deserves closer attention with regard to the issue of Judeophobia.

Hebrews was circulated as a part of early collections of Paul's letters (e.g., P[13], P[46]) possibly from the early-mid-second century, and several early interpreters including Origen of Alexandria and John Chrysostom attributed its authorship to Paul. But Hebrews was anonymously composed,[3] and the title "To Hebrews" was superscribed by a later editor. Hebrews was likely included into the Pauline letter collection only in the final stage of the formation of the Pauline corpus. So, the identity of the author and the specific provenance remain unknown.[4] Yet, the understanding of Hebrews as a Pauline letter was one of the factors that influenced its early interpreters to view it as a document that contrasts the "inferior old covenant" to the "superior new covenant."

---

1. Jesper Svartvik, "Reading the Epistle to the Hebrews without Presupposing Supersessionism," in *Christ Jesus and the Jewish People Today: New Explorations of Theological Interrelationships*, ed. Philip A. Cunningham et al. Grand Rapids: Eerdmans, 2011), 79.

2. Daniel J. Harrington, *What Are They Saying about Hebrews?* (New York: Paulist, 2005), 4.

3. Pace Clare Rothschild, who concludes that Hebrews was composed as a Pauline pseudepigraphon and an amplification of the existing Pauline corpus. See *Hebrews as Pseudepigraphon: The History and Significance of the Pauline Attribution of Hebrews*, Wissenschaftliche Untersuchungen zum Neuen Testament 235 (Tübingen: Mohr Siebeck, 2009), 215–16.

4. On the reception history of Hebrews, see Craig Koester, *Hebrews: A New Translation with Introduction and Commentary*, Anchor Bible 36 (New York: Doubleday, 2001), 19–63.

It is likely that Hebrews was written in the late first century. The author refers to the temple practices using the present tense, but not to describe the state of the Jerusalem temple. Instead, the present tense is used to describe the cultic activities that happened in the wilderness sanctuary after the exodus out of Egypt. Other documents written after 70 also mention the temple cult using the present tense (e.g., Josephus, *Against Apion* 2.77; Epistle to Diognetus 3:2–5).[5] Therefore, the use of present tense in Hebrews does not necessarily show that it was written before the destruction of the Jerusalem temple in 70. Based on how Hebrews is used in 1 Clement, it seems like Hebrews was written before 95–97. Most scholars think that Hebrews was written after the First Jewish War (66–73).[6]

In this period, it seems obvious that certain social pressures put the faith of the recipients in jeopardy (e.g., Heb 10:32–36). For this reason, some interpreters believe that Hebrews was written to prevent its recipients from reverting to Judaism (the so-called relapse theory)[7] and that the author relegates the Levitical cultic system as obsolete for this purpose. It is often argued that the Levitical code is dismantled in Hebrews, and therefore that Hebrews was written in a polemical context against Judaism. In this context, earlier exegetes were influenced by the tradition of reading Hebrews like Galatians (e.g., Gal 4:9: "how can you turn back again?"). However, we should notice that there is no explicit mention in Hebrews that Jesus worshipers attempted to return to Judaism, or that they were in specific conflict with Judaism or Jewish synagogues.

Moreover, the phrase "not to fall away from the living God" in Hebrews 3:12 is an expression that suggests a non-Jewish audience: "Take care, brothers, lest there be in any of you an evil, unbelieving heart, leading you to fall away from the living God" (ESV). This expression appears to be closely related to the notion of reverting back to idol worship (apostasy), and it would not make sense that Jews in the first century would deny any association with the "living God" while the parting of the ways had not been completed.[8] Therefore, it is likely that Hebrews was written for gentile Jesus worshipers who may have been at

---

5. Koester, *Hebrews*, 53.

6. On the date, see Alan C. Mitchell, *Hebrews*, Sacra Pagina 13 (Collegeville, MN: Liturgical Press, 2006), 7–11.

7. So, Graham Hughes, *Hebrews and Hermeneutics: The Epistle to the Hebrews as a New Testament Example of Biblical Interpretation*, Society for New Testament Study Monograph 36 (Cambridge: Cambridge University Press, 1979), 55.

8. "The parting of the ways" refers to ancient schism between Judaism and Christianity and was a multifaceted process that continued until mid-second century. See Paula Fredriksen, "What 'Parting of the Ways'? Jews, Gentiles, and the Ancient Mediterranean City," in *The Ways That Never Parted: Jews and Christians in Late Antiquity and the Early Middle Ages*, ed. Adam H. Becker and Annette Yoshiko Reed (Tübingen: Mohr Siebeck, 2003), 35–63.

risk of returning to their previous pagan practices, rather than primarily for Jewish Jesus worshipers.

Recently, some scholars such as David M. Moffitt observed that the heavenly sacrifice of Christ is not merely figurative, but was in fact offered physically,[9] and other interpreters highlight that Hebrews reflects "intra-Jewish debates."[10] As such, the book should be understood from "within Judaism," not "against Judaism." This debate is crucial to understanding whether Hebrews intrinsically conveys Judeophobia or not.

Contrary to previous interpretations, it is highly unlikely that the author of Hebrews considered the law to have been abolished since the cultic regulations were observed *through* Christ's heavenly cult in Hebrews. Christ's heavenly sacrifice in Hebrews is not simply symbolic, but is presented as a physical offering performed in accordance with the covenant-renewal rite and the Day of Atonement in Hebrews 9. Therefore, the Sinai ritual and Levitical code were not "abolished," but rather "observed" in the heavenly temple.

In my opinion, "the old covenant" indicates certain continuity with "the new covenant" in Hebrews (as shown in the following section). The Levitical code—including sacrifice, sanctuary, and high priesthood—is still valid in the priestly discussions that describe the new covenant cult of Christ, which is informed and shaped by "the old covenant" cult. So, the cult of Christ does not replace the old Jewish cult. Instead, "Zion rerepresents Sinai"[11] and "becomes a 'new Sinai'" in Hebrews 12:22–29.[12]

Anti-Jewish Interpretation of Hebrews by the Church Fathers and the Reformation

Hebrews does not contain any explicit accusations against Jews. Yet, anti-Jewish interpretations of Hebrews are usually linked with "supersessionism"

---

9. For this view, see David M. Moffitt, *Atonement and the Logic of Resurrection in the Epistle to the Hebrews* (Leiden: Brill, 2011).

10. This can be referred to as the in-house theory. E.g., Richard B. Hays, "'Here We Have No Lasting City': New Covenantalism in Hebrews," in *The Epistle to the Hebrews and Christian Theology*, ed. Richard Bauckham et al. (Grand Rapids: Eerdmans, 2009), 151–73. See also Morna D. Hooker, "Christ, the 'End' of the Cult," in *The Epistle to the Hebrews and Christian Theology*, ed. Richard Bauckham et al. (Grand Rapids: Eerdmans, 2009), 189–212.

11. Kyu Seop Kim, *The Firstborn Son in Ancient Judaism and Early Christianity: A Study of Primogeniture and Christology* (Leiden: Brill, 2019), 220.

12. David M. Allen, *Deuteronomy and Exhortation in Hebrews: A Study in Narrative Re-presentation* (Tübingen: Mohr Siebeck, 2008), 216.

(or replacement theology), since Hebrews is often viewed by exegetes as a prooftext that the new covenant through Jesus Christ "replaced" the old covenant made with Jews. As R. Kendall Soulen comments: "According to this teaching [i.e., supersessionism], God chose the Jewish people after the fall of Adam in order to prepare the world for the coming of Jesus Christ, the Savior. After Christ came, however, the special role of the Jewish people came to an end and its place was taken by the church, the new Israel."[13]

Thus, the replacement theology sets forth the exclusion of Jews and the election of Christians and can be regarded as a kind of Judeophobic phenomenon in terms of its origin and developments. Christian theological repudiation of the Jewish law and practices is traditionally traced to Hebrews,[14] and this interpretation was appropriated for a theology in which Christians "replaced Jews" in the early church. The first example of this interpretive framework comes from Origen (circa 184–circa 253), who alludes to Hebrews 7:14 ("for it is evident that our Lord was descended from Judah"; NRSV) and infers that the real Jews are Christians (*Homilies on Jeremiah* 9.1).

One of the most important interpreters of Hebrews in late antiquity, however, is John Chrysostom (circa 347–407). During the medieval era, Chrysostom's *Homilies on Hebrews*, which were translated into Latin, had significant impact and were extensively read and quoted by many Hebrews exegetes. Furthermore, it serves as an important source in Martin Luther's *Lectures on Hebrews* and influenced the interpretation of Hebrews by the later Protestant reformers.[15] Chrysostom accentuates the superiority of the new covenant over the old covenant and the antithesis between the two covenants. This view heavily influenced the medieval and modern interpretation of Hebrews. Chrysostom criticizes the Sabbath observance by Jews and their adherence to the temple rituals in his *Homilies on Hebrews*. Because the authorship of Hebrews was ascribed to Paul by most church fathers, Chrysostom often interpreted this text through a Pauline lens (e.g., *De laudibus sancti Pauli* 4.12); Chrysostom's Judeophobic interpretation of Paul's letters therefore applies also to Hebrews. While the author of Hebrews does not deal with the issue of circumcision and the Sabbath, Chrysostom comments that circumcision, sacrifice, and Sabbath observance are "shadows" in *Homilies on Hebrews* 13.3. He also reads "fleshly" (*sarkinēs*;

---

13. R. Kendall Soulen, "Karl Barth and the Future of the God of Israel," *Pro Ecclesia* 6 (1997): 413–28 (esp. 413–18).

14. In this chapter, the cult or the cultic practices refer to the rites performed in the temple within Judaism. These practices generally entail the offering of sacrifices designated by the Torah.

15. Kenneth Hagen, "The Problem of Testament in Luther's 'Lectures on Hebrews,'" *Harvard Theological Review* 63 (1970): 64.

Heb 7:16) in a negative sense as Paul often uses it (e.g., Gal 3:3; 4:23)[16] and notes that the law "was in many respects unlawful [*anomos*]."[17] While the author of Hebrews mentions that the priesthood of Christ is not to be designated according to the order of Aaron (Heb 7:11), Chrysostom states that "[Christ] *excluded* [*exebalen*] the order of Aaron" in *Homilies* 13.2.[18] Moreover, although Chrysostom writes that "the law itself . . . is not weak, but we" (*Homilies* 13.4), he interprets "abrogation" in Hebrews 7:18 as "substitution" and "abandonment." So, Chrysostom conveys through his *Homilies on Hebrews* that the Jewish law was substituted and even forsaken by God.

Exegetes in the medieval and early modern era also tended to highlight a discontinuity between the old (deemed earthly) and new (heavenly) covenants following Chrysostom.[19] For example, Johannes Bugenhagen (1485–1558) concludes that Hebrews was addressed to Jewish converts and explicates the purpose of Hebrews as follows: "He [Paul] feared for them lest they be overcome with temptations and afflictions or slide back into infidelity in time of scarcity."[20] Thus, Bugenhagen regards "returning to Judaism" as backsliding and asserts that "defecting" from Christ to Moses is "notorious blasphemy against God."

In contrast to Chrysostom, John Calvin (1509–1564) does not regard Hebrews as Pauline and does not single out its specific author. In his *Commentary on Hebrews*, Calvin explicates Hebrews 2:13, saying that Jews "in rejecting Christ . . . in turn were rejected by God and perished." In this vein, Calvin conveys "punitive supersessionism"[21] by describing the exclusion of Jews as a punishment on the ground that they rejected Christ. Furthermore, as shown below, Calvin states that Jews have been "replaced" due to their unbelief: "This being so God addresses not only Isaiah whom He orders to seal the law and the testimony, but in his person all his ministers who in time to come will battle with people's unbelief, and above all Christ whom the Jews were to treat with

16. Cf. a positive use of "flesh" in Heb 2:14: "Since, therefore, the children share flesh [*sarkos*] and blood, he himself likewise shared the same things" (NRSV).

17. Translation from Philip Schaff, ed., *Saint Chrysostom: Homilies on the Gospel of St. John and the Epistle to the Hebrews*, Select Library of the Nicene and Post-Nicene Fathers of the Christian Church 14 (Edinburgh: T&T Clark, 1989), 428.

18. Schaff, *Saint Chrysostom*, 427.

19. Kenneth G. Hagen, *A Theology of Testament in the Young Luther: The Lectures on Hebrews*, Studies in Medieval and Reformation Thought 12 (Leiden: Brill, 1974), 54.

20. Translation adapted from Kenneth Hagen, *Hebrews Commenting from Erasmus to Bèze, 1516–1598* (Tübingen: Mohr Siebeck, 1981), 10.

21. Punitive supersessionism refers to an idea that Jews were rejected by God since God abrogated the covenant with them for their sins.

greater insolence than all the prophets before Him. Now we see that those who are substituted in the place of Israel not only reject His Gospel, but attack Him Himself with fury."[22] Here, Calvin notes that "the Jews" who were substituted in the place of Israel repudiated the gospel and furiously assailed Christ.

Anti-Jewish Interpretation of Hebrews in the Modern Era

Some modern interpretations of Hebrews also insinuate Judeophobia or supersessionism, in part because of the significant influence of these earlier interpretive traditions. We can categorize the four Judeophobic tendencies in the interpretation of Hebrews since the twentieth century as follows. First, some exegetes write that the Mosaic law was superseded by Christ (e.g., Lane). Second, some scholars interpret Judaism in Hebrews as a "religion of righteousness by works" (e.g., Bultmann). Third, Judaism in Hebrews is interpreted as a religion belonging to the earth, contrasted to the heavenly realm (e.g., Käsemann). Fourth, it is believed that the author of Hebrews identifies the church as a kind of "true Israel" (e.g., Moule).

William Lane represents a supersessionist interpretation in its classical sense when he explicates Hebrews 8:13: "The principle that a new act of God makes the old obsolete (cf. 7:11–12) reflects an eschatological outlook that perceives the Mosaic and Levitical institutions as fulfilled and superseded by Christ."[23] Lane understands the relationship between the new covenant and the old covenant in a replacement-theological way as above. Although no term equivalent to the verb "supersede" is used in the whole of Hebrews, Lane writes that Christ "superseded" the Mosaic and Levitical institutions.

On the other hand, Rudolf Bultmann interprets Hebrews in light of the antithesis he constructs between the grace of Christianity and the merits of Judaism in Paul's letters. Bultmann understands Hebrews in terms of the dichotomy between "divine grace and human action." In this vein, Judaism in Hebrews is viewed as a kind of merit-based religion by Bultmann: in Hebrews, "the idea is given up that God's grace must or can be won by human offered sacrifice; and that led by implication to the insight that the church does not need persons of special quality (i.e., priests) to mediate between it and God. Christ's sacrifice

22. John Calvin, *Calvin's Commentaries on the Epistle of Paul the Apostle to the Hebrews and the First and Second Epistles of St. Peter*. trans. William B. Johnston (Grand Rapids: Eerdmans, 1963), 29.

23. William Lane, *Hebrews 1–8*, Word Biblical Commentary 47 (Dallas: Word, 1991), 210.

made God's grace operative once and for all, and he is the high priest of the Congregation."[24] Thus, Bultmann applies his perspective that Judaism is an inferior "religion of righteousness by works" to his understanding of Hebrews.

By contrast, some scholars consider the situation of the recipients of Hebrews to be unrelated to Judaism. Ernst Käsemann, for example, argues that the author of Hebrews was not interested in distinguishing the identity of Christ worshipers from Jews.[25] Käsemann argues that interpreting Hebrews as an attempt to separate Christianity from Judaism is "a product of fantasy."[26] However, he also writes that "in 3:5ff, it is already made clear that the first [covenant] was voided through Israel's unbelief . . . the great diastasis of Hebrews is between 'the heavenly and the earthly,' in which the Jewish cult is seen as a specific representative of what is earthly."[27] So, similarly to Bultmann, Käsemann contends that in Hebrews a contrast is placed between inferior and superior[28] and that Judaism is an earthly and inferior entity. He ultimately concludes that Jewish identity is not the main concern of Hebrews since it was already abandoned by the recipients: "Since even the sacral institutions are still of an earthly nature, the new people of God . . . must forsake them, must always and everywhere abandon what is earthly."[29] On the one hand, Käsemann attempts to avoid anti-Jewish interpretations by observing that Hebrews is not in conflict with Judaism, but on the other hand, he falls into a supersessionist trap, considering Judaism as an inferior and earthly entity in contrast to Christianity as a superior and heavenly one.

The so-called relapse theory also leads to supersessionism, a clear example of which is found in the scholarship of C. F. D. Moule: "To go back into Judaism . . . is to desert the Crucified and to join the ranks of the crucifiers. The only way to life is the way forward, not back. . . . We [Christians] alone are citizens of that true Jerusalem. . . . Thus there emerges in succession to the primitive, unexamined assumption, 'of course we Christians are Jews,' a polemical and carefully reasoned apologetic for the Church of Christ as alone the real Church of Israel."[30] Moule writes that the author of Hebrews had the idea that "return-

---

24. Rudolf Bultmann, *Theology of the New Testament*, trans. Kendrick Grobel (New York: Scribner's Sons, 1951), 115.

25. Ernst Käsemann, *The Wandering People of God: An Investigation of the Letter to the Hebrews*, trans. Roy. A. Harrisville and Irving L. Sandberg (Philadelphia: Augsburg, 1984), 24–25.

26. Käsemann, *Wandering People of God*, 24.

27. Käsemann, *Wandering People of God*, 57, 59.

28. Käsemann, *Wandering People of God*, 59.

29. Käsemann, *Wandering People of God*, 58.

30. C. F. D. Moule, *The Birth of the New Testament*, 3rd ed. (San Francisco: Harper & Row, 1982), 60.

ing" to Judaism is a betrayal of Christ and that only Christians are "citizens of true Jerusalem" and that the church of Christ is "the real church of Israel" in Hebrews. This view clearly falls on a supersessionist reading of Hebrews.

Apart from the anti-Jewish interpretations of Hebrews, current scholars sharply diverge on whether Hebrews is innately Judeophobic or not. We can organize the Jewish or anti-Jewish nature of Hebrews as follows. First of all, it should be pondered whether anti-Jewish patterns emerge in Hebrews. We must take into account that, in contrast to a text like Melito of Sardis's *On Pascha* (especially 45, 73, 92–93; circa 160–70), there is no negative portrayal of Jews or a denial of their status in Hebrews. Nor does Hebrews allude to rivalry or actual conflict with Judaism or substitution of Jews by the church.

By the same token, we should also consider the following elements: (1) the denial of the Jerusalem temple offering; (2) the denial of the current priesthood; and (3) the existence of a messiah. All three elements are also found in the Qumran texts. Messianism per se does not necessarily have antisemitic implications (contra Rosemary R. Ruether)[31] since the concept of a "Christ" (i.e., a messiah) originated from Judaism and the portrayal of Christ as a priestly and royal messiah in Hebrews is clearly Jewish.[32] The concept of a priestly messiah appears also in the Qumran texts (e.g., 1QS 9:11; CD A 14:19; 4Q174). As such, the description of a particular messianic figure does not necessarily lead to Judeophobia. In the Dead Sea Scrolls and Jewish literature, we trace the critiques on the contemporaneous Jerusalem temple and the ideas of the alternative (heavenly) temple and high priesthood, which are analogous to Hebrews. Thus, Hebrews can be exactly understood within the Jewish ritual worldview.

Therefore, Hebrews is deeply rooted in Judaism, and the author of Hebrews does not explicitly repudiate the old covenant and its cultic system.[33] Rather, Hebrews exhibits continuity as well as discontinuity between the new and the old covenant. It should be considered that, in Hebrews, Christ's heavenly sacrifice is not merely figuratively performed but is physically offered according to the covenant-renewal rite (e.g., 9:15–23) and the Day of Atonement (e.g., 9:7). In this context, therefore, the Sinai ritual and the Levitical code are not "abol-

---

31. Cf. Rosemary R. Ruether, *Faith and Fratricide: The Theological Roots of Anti-Semitism* (New York: Seabury, 1974).

32. See Eric F. Mason, *"You Are a Priest Forever": Second Temple Jewish Messianism and the Priestly Christology of the Epistle to the Hebrews* (Leiden: Brill, 2008).

33. For the concept of the covenant in Hebrews, see Susanne Lehne, *The New Covenant in Hebrews*, Journal for the Study of the New Testament Supplement 44 (Sheffield: Sheffield Academic, 1990).

ished" but rather "observed" in the heavenly temple. As Eyal Regev notes: "Hebrews embraces traditional Jewish cultic ideas," and the author of Hebrews "acknowledges the efficacy of the high priest and sacrifices for contending with sin."[34] In addition, if the recipients of Hebrews are a community that includes gentile worshipers, that circumcision is not mentioned in Hebrews suggests that the Jewish attributes related to circumcision were no issue in Hebrews.

The author of Hebrews makes use of a rhetorical construction known as syncrisis (or "comparison"). In classical rhetoric, syncrisis often made comparisons with objects considered noble.[35] There are five comparisons in Hebrews: (1) the angels and Jesus (1:5–14); (2) Moses and Jesus (3:1–6); (3) the Aaronic high priests and Jesus (5:1–10); (4) the Levitical priesthood and the Melchizedekian priesthood (7:1–10:18); and (5) Sinai and Zion (12:18–24). The purpose of syncrisis was not to demean the object of comparison but to help to shift one's gaze from an object to another more suitable object by the comparison. If so, the adjective "better" in the "better hope" (7:19) and "better covenant" (7:22) does not presuppose that the old covenant and ceremonial rules are inherently inferior, but rather to capitalize on the (ongoing) value and authority of that covenant in order to reinforce the author's view of the "new" covenant.

The argumentation framework by syncrisis in Hebrews, however, can be understood as "the lesser to greater" argumentation (*a minore ad maius*). As such, the old covenant is not a symbol of deficient Judaism, but represents a previous way of relating to God that serves as an example for the present generation. This is emphasized by the *a minore ad maius* argumentation. The old covenant encourages people to be faithful to their promises to God and reject the worship of other gods associated with imperialism.[36] In this context, what the author was concerned with in Hebrews was not "reverting to Judaism" but "apostasy" from it. Thus, the core message of Hebrews by "the lesser to greater" argumentation can be summarized as follows: If "apostasy is punished under the lesser covenant mediated by angels, how much more will it be punished in the case of 'so great a salvation' announced by the Lord himself."[37] In this

---

34. Eyal Regev, "Hebrews' High Priestly Christology: Models, Method and Aim," *Religions* 12 (2021): 1.

35. Michael Wade Martin and Jason A. Whitlark, "The Encomiastic Topics of Syncrisis as the Key to the Structure and Argument of Hebrews," *New Testament Studies* 57 (2011): 415–39.

36. Michael Wade Martin and Jason A. Whitlark, *Inventing Hebrews: Design and Purpose in Ancient Rhetoric*, Society for New Testament Studies Monograph 171 (Cambridge: Cambridge University Press, 2018), 270.

37. Martin and Whitlark, *Inventing Hebrews*, 267.

respect, the argumentation by syncrisis in Hebrews does not disparage Judaism, but rather relies on its authority and truth.

Hebrews 7:18 and Judeophobia

Hebrews 7:18 is one of the most problematic verses in Hebrews: "There is, on the one hand, the abrogation of an earlier commandment because it was weak and ineffectual" (NRSV). Ostensibly, this verse indicates that the whole Mosaic law is useless and inefficacious and thus was finally abolished. Interpreters often assume that the "legal requirement" in 7:16 refers to the earthly realm (*sarkinēs*) of the law in imagined opposition to some "better," heavenly realm. However, "flesh" in 7:16 does not seem to mean "earthly" or "carnal" but is closer to the sense of "concerning physical descent" (NRSV). So, the phrase "a legal requirement concerning physical descent" in 7:16 does not refer to the entire Mosaic law, but rather to "the regulations requiring the birth from the tribe of Levi" based on 7:11–12. Therefore, a better way of understanding 7:16 is to read it as referring only to amendments to the regulations concerning the priesthood, rather than the entire covenant. As discussed above, Christ's heavenly sacrifice in Hebrews was offered according to the Levitical regulations (e.g., 12:24). Again, then, what is delineated in 7:18–19 is not the repudiation or the abolition of the whole ritual law, but the declaration of the new priestly genealogy that is designated according to the order of Melchizedek (cf. Ps 110:4), which is also found in ancient Jewish literature (e.g., Jubilees 13:25–27; Genesis Apocryphon 22:15; Josephus, *Antiquities* 1.10.2 §181; cf. 11Q13). Therefore, Hebrews 7:18–19 is not essentially Judeophobic or supersessionist, but it should be read as an intramural discussion from "within Judaism."

Conclusion

In short, Hebrews was compiled by early editors into the Pauline corpus along with Paul's letters regardless of its authentic origin, and thus later interpreters understood it in accordance with their (often Judeophobic) interpretation of Pauline letters. The church fathers, including John Chrysostom, found themes in Hebrews such as the abolition of the law, the superiority of the new covenant over the old, and the discrepancy between the two covenants, and these views had a great influence on later interpreters. However, I argue that Hebrews should be understood in the first-century context, especially "within Judaism," and must be interpreted from a standpoint distinct from that of Paul, which enables the readers to interpret Hebrews from a nonsupersessionist perspective. The orientation for a new reading of Hebrews can be formulated as follows:

1. Hebrews does not reflect an actual conflict with Jews and was probably not written to Jewish Christians attending synagogues. What the author warns of in Hebrews is not returning to Judaism, but apostasy. So, the recipients of Hebrews were not required to distinguish their identity from Jewish identity. Hebrews must be understood from "within Judaism."

2. In Hebrews, the sacrifice of Christ is not figurative, but actual, and it is offered according to the Jewish law. Hebrews is not to be understood through the lens of Paul's letters in which it is traditionally believed that an all-out critique of the law exists (although this is also problematic). Therefore, the Jewish law in Hebrews is not repudiated, and any change (7:12, 18) in the law is limited to the regulation of the priestly genealogical origin.

3. Hebrews puts forward continuity as well as discontinuity between the new and the old covenants, and thus the new covenant is presented as a renewed covenant.

Discussion Questions and Activity Suggestions

1. Discuss how Hebrews 8:13 can be read in a nonsupersessionist view.
2. Read Hebrews 10:28–29 as a from "the lesser to the greater" argument and discuss the results from the reading and the differences from our earlier understanding of these verses.
3. Read Hebrews 12:25–26 as a from "the lesser to the greater" argument and discuss how such a perspective might help us to gain a fresh understanding of the contrast between Sinai and Zion in 12:18–29.
4. Read *On Pascha* by Melito of Sardis. Compare how Melito's views—on the Jews, the law, the temple, and the sacrifice—differ from those of Hebrews.
5. In small groups, discuss how portions of Hebrews not covered in this chapter might be better understood from within a Jewish ritual worldview.

Further Reading

Eisenbaum, Pamela. "Religion and Ritual, Sacrifice and Supersession: A Utopian Reading of Hebrews." Pages 343–56 in *Hebrews in Context*. Edited by Gabriella Gelardini and Harold W. Attridge. Leiden: Brill, 2016.

Gelardini, Gabriella. "Hebrews, an Ancient Synagogue Homily for Tisha be-Av: Its Function, Its Basis, Its Theological Interpretation." Pages 107–28 in *Hebrews: Contemporary Methods—New Insights*. Edited by Gabriella Gelardini. Leiden: Brill, 2005.

Hays, Richard B. "'Here We Have No Lasting City': New Covenantalism in Hebrews." Pages 151–73 in *The Epistle to the Hebrews and Christian Theology*. Edited by Richard Bauckham et al. Grand Rapids: Eerdmans, 2009.

Levine, Amy-Jill. "Supersessionism: Admit and Address Rather Than Debate or Deny." *Religions* 13.2 (2022): 155 (https://tinyurl.com/3fw4tsfj).

Regev, Eyal. "Hebrews' High Priestly Christology: Models, Method, and Aim." *Religions* 12.11 (2021): 971 (https://tinyurl.com/5x5xmc5p).

Svartvik, Jesper. "Reading the Epistle to the Hebrews without Presupposing Supersessionism." Pages 77–91 in *Christ Jesus and the Jewish People Today: New Explorations of Theological Interrelationships*. Edited by Philip A. Cunningham et al. Grand Rapids: Eerdmans, 2011.

27

James

CHANCE E. BONAR

The Epistle of James is one of the seven catholic epistles in the New Testament. While often overlooked in favor of the gospels or Pauline epistles, James provides us with an important window into the diversity of Jesus-adherents in the first century.

James claims to be written by "James, an enslaved person of God and of the Lord Jesus Christ" (1:1).[1] Most scholars agree that the author of James is meant to refer to the brother of Jesus. It is unlikely that James himself wrote this letter before his death in the 60s CE, but rather that the text is attributed to him in the late first century.[2] James is addressed to the "twelve tribes of the diaspora" (1:1), alluding to the twelve tribes of Israel that were scattered throughout the Mediterranean and Near East. While many scholars presume that James is referring to torah-observant Jesus-adherents outside of Palestine, some argue that James is in fact addressing Jews.[3] The writer famously refers to Jesus only twice (at most, in 1:1 and 2:1) and does little to depict his recipients as fellow Jesus-adherents.

James pulls heavily from material also present in Jesus's Sermon on the Mount (Matt 5–7) and interacts with Paul's teachings on the law, faith, and Abraham (Jas 2:18–24; cf. Gal 2:11–3:24; Rom 3:19–5:1). Scholars debate whether James is critiquing Paul's understanding of the relevance of Jewish customs

---

1. All scripture quotations in this chapter are my own unless otherwise noted.

2. On the authorship, date, and geographical origin of James, see Dale C. Allison Jr., *A Critical and Exegetical Commentary on the Epistle of James*, International Critical Commentary (New York: Bloomsbury, 2013), 3–32, 94–98.

3. Dale C. Allison Jr., "The Jewish Setting of the Epistle of James," *In die skriflig* 49.1 (2015): 3–4.

for non-Jewish Jesus-adherents (e.g., circumcision, Sabbath observance, food laws), or if James is correcting a misinterpretation of Paul's argument by those who think that "having faith" means they no longer need to care about socioeconomic disparities nor are obliged to materially support others in their community.[4] This debate about the relationship between James and Paul is key to understanding the relationship between the reception of James, antisemitism, and Judeophobia.

James was not as quickly and universally accepted as authoritative compared to, for example, many of the gospels or Pauline epistles. Origen of Alexandria is the first to cite James, in the third century, claiming that it was written by the brother of Jesus (*Commentary on Romans* 4.8.2). In the fourth century, church historian Eusebius labeled James as "disputed," since not many earlier Christian writers mentioned it and not every church that Eusebius knew of used it (*Ecclesiastical History* 2.23.25; 3.25.3). Fourth-century Christians didn't agree on whether James had the same authority as other early Christian literature, with Athanasius of Alexandria favoring it, but the writer of the Muratorian Fragment not mentioning it. This early hesitancy around James is important for how later Christians use James to anti-Jewish ends, since it was often read as straying from Paul's treatment of Jews and Judaism.

James presents us with a different vantage point to apprehend what Jesus-adherents were doing or were anxious about. The author doesn't focus on ecclesiastical ranks (e.g., bishops or elders) or particular concerns over food laws, Sabbath observance, idolatry, or sexual immorality—topics common among Pauline letters like 1 Corinthians and other catholic epistles like 1 Peter. James, instead, has a different focus: the construction of a shared, practical ethical paradigm.

James itself does not contain vitriolic accusations against Jews or Jewish practices like circumcision or Sabbath observance. On the contrary, James is often read as a document written by a torah-observant Jesus-adherent—as a Jewish Jesus-believer. Its Jewish origin and affiliation, however, are exactly what led some Christians to interpret James as "too Jewish" and, thus, not a fully "Christian" text. Anti-Jewish interpretation and use of James—especially James 1–2—stems from its reception among early Christians and its relation to Pauline texts and arguments. Here, I provide two related examples of Christian anti-Jewish interpretations of James that imagine the text as "too Jewish."

---

4. Margaret M. Mitchell, "The Letter of James as a Document of Paulinism?," in *Reading James with New Eyes: Methodological Reassessments of the Letter of James*, ed. Robert L. Webb and John S. Kloppenborg (London: T&T Clark, 2007), 75–98.

James as Interpreted by Martin Luther

The first example comes from Martin Luther (1483–1546), the German Reformation theologian. Luther famously took a strong stance against considering James as comparable to most New Testament literature. He first commented on James in 1522 in his preface to his German translation of the New Testament, the Lutherbibel. Luther suggested that, although James contains some edifying sayings, he did not consider it to be written by one of Jesus's apostles or to be one of the chief books of the New Testament because "it is flatly against St. Paul and all the rest of Scripture in ascribing justification to works."[5] Alluding to James 2:14–17, Luther believed that James contradicted Paul's teaching that there is no need for Torah observance for those who have faith, instead suggesting that one needs both faith and works (= torah observance) to be saved. Similarly, he criticized James because "its purpose is to teach Christians, but in all this long teaching it does not once mention the Passion, the resurrection, or the Spirit of Christ."[6] Luther presumed that all New Testament texts written by apostles should contain the same message about Jesus. So a text like James, which doesn't focus on Jesus's life or death, could not be apostolic. In a later-redacted statement, Luther famously accused James of being an "epistle of straw" because of its lack of the gospel message.[7]

Luther famously became more openly anti-Jewish in his biblical interpretation later in life, culminating in his publication of *On the Jews and Their Lies* (1543).[8] Just a year earlier, Luther again criticized James and his statement was recorded by his students:

> We should throw the Epistle of James out of this school, for it doesn't amount to much. It contains not a syllable about Christ. Not once does it mention Christ, except at the beginning [Jas 1:1; 2:1]. I maintain that some Jew wrote it who probably heard about Christian people but never encountered any. Since he heard that Christians place great weight on faith in Christ, he thought, "Wait a moment! I'll oppose them and urge works alone." Thus he did. He wrote not a word about the suffering and resurrec-

---

5. Martin Luther, *Luther's Works*, vol. 35, *Word and Sacrament I*, ed. and trans. E. Theodore Bachmann (Philadelphia: Muhlenberg, 1960), 395–97 at 396.

6. Luther, *Luther's Works*, 35:396.

7. Luther, *Luther's Works*, 35:362.

8. On Luther's developing hostility toward Jews, see Isaac Kalimi, "Martin Luther, the Jews, and Esther: Biblical Interpretation in the Shadow of Judeophobia," *Journal of Religion* 100.1 (2020): 42–74, esp. 54–58.

tion of Christ, although this is what all the apostles preached about. . . . The ancients recognized this, too, and therefore they didn't acknowledge this letter as one of the catholic epistles.[9]

While still condemning James as a text not written by an apostle, lacking an interest in Jesus's life and death, and not being acknowledged by some early Christians, Luther took another step: He claimed that a Jew had forged James in order to attack Christians and, purportedly, infiltrated the New Testament under the name of Jesus's brother. Luther saw himself as a defender of Paul's message that Jesus-adherents should simply have faith in Christ and shouldn't need to observe torah or—by extension—need to do any types of works to be saved. In doing so, Luther read James as a threat to the gospel preached through Paul and the other apostles, and thus that James was "too Jewish" to be held in high esteem or trusted as apostolic.

James Interpreted in the Modern Era

The second example of anti-Jewish interpretations of James comes from European and American scholars and preachers from the eighteenth through the twentieth centuries.[10] In many instances, preachers and academic commentators brought their own anti-Jewish sentiments to their reading of James by presuming that any negative attribute James argues against must have been a common vice of Jewish people. For example, in Siegmund Jakob Baumgarten's 1750 writing on 1:19–20, in which James calls for the reader to be quick to listen and slow to anger, he argues that it was "the evil habit of Jews of that time to dispute about everything, to speak against all things which they did not understand, and even to dispose of a teacher of unknown things."[11] Likewise, Arthur Carr's 1896 commentary on James suggested that the rich oppressors described in 4:13–5:6 must have been Jews because of a natural affinity of "Semitic" people for trade and commerce.[12] Although just a few examples among

9. Martin Luther, *Luther's Works*, vol. 54, *Table Talk*, ed. and trans. Theodore G. Tappert (Philadelphia: Fortress, 1967), 424–25.

10. Many of these examples are indebted to the encyclopedic work in Allison, *James*, 107, 291, 513, 592, 642–43; and Allison, "Jewish Setting," 2.

11. Siegmund Jacob Baumgarten, *Auslegung des Briefes Jacobi* (Halle: Joh. Justinus Gebauers, 1750), 63. English translation from Allison, *James*, 291.

12. Arthur Carr, *The General Epistles of St. James* (Cambridge: Cambridge University, 1896), 56–57; see Allison, *James*, 642–43.

many, various readers of James—especially before World War II—understood James to be exhorting Christians away from more worldly and sinful "Jewish" practices, even though James does not explicitly mark his moral exhortations in reference to Judaism or Jewish people.

Beyond associating James's moralizing polemic with stereotyped Jewish characteristics, some readers also follow Luther in claiming that James is basically a Jewish text with some Christianity sprinkled on top. Adam Clarke, for example, argued in the mid-nineteenth century that its "style and manner are more that of a Jewish prophet than a Christian apostle,"[13] and well-known New Testament scholars like Rudolf Bultmann and Adolf von Harnack remarked that James lacks explicitly Christian material that one might expect from it.[14] While perhaps more subtle than explicitly anti-Jewish readings of James, such interpretations still imagine James in the middle of a zero-sum game between Judaism and Christianity, in which it can only be characterized as Jewish *or* Christian. In such readings, James is critiqued for not saying enough about Jesus and for being more Jewish than Christian. But we might ask: by whose standard is James not saying enough about Jesus, and by whose standard is James not Christian enough?

Recent scholarship has begun to rehabilitate James's reputation after centuries of being in the shadow of Lutheran interpretation, has decoupled it from the Pauline legacy, and has read James in light of the concerns and experiences of minoritized communities. There is still much work to be done by readers of the New Testament to view James not as an excessively Jewish anomaly, but as a window into a different set of concerns that a torah-observant Jesus-adherent tried to address.

Discussion Questions and Activity Suggestions

1. What does the expectation for James to be more explicitly Christian, or the claim that James is more Jewish than Christian, tell us about modern readers of the text? What might it tell us about the first recipients of James?

13. Adam Clarke, *The New Testament of Our Lord and Saviour Jesus Christ* (London: Lane & Tippett, 1856), 2:1824.

14. Adolf von Harnack, *Geschichte der altchristlichen Literautur bis Eusebius*, vol. 2, *Die Chronologie*, 2nd ed. (Leipzig: Hinrichs, 1958), 1:490; Rudolf Bultmann, *Theology of the New Testament* (New York: Scribner's Sons, 1955), 2:143.

2. Dale Allison suggests that James isn't written by a Jewish Jesus-adherent to fellow Christians, but to fellow Jews. How might our reading of James change if the target audience is Jews rather than Christians?

3. In Elsa Támez's reading of James from a Latin American perspective, she argues that typical Protestant and Western academic readings of James that assert that it lacks Christ don't make sense, because James makes heavy use of Jesus's Sermon on the Mount (Matt 5–7) to produce its moral exhortations. What do you think it means that Western scholars often read James looking for stories of Jesus's life, death, and resurrection, but have not considered James's moral teachings to be clearly Christian?

4. Read the first two chapters of James alongside two of Paul's arguments—Galatians 2:11–3:26 and Romans 3:19–5:11. Pay attention to how Paul is characterizing law and faith, as well as how Paul uses the example of Abraham from Genesis 15:6 to argue that Abraham was deemed righteous by God *before* circumcision or the reception of Jewish laws. Note that Paul explicitly refers to how his argument applies to Jews and gentiles. Now, pay attention to how James characterizes faith and works, as well as how James uses Abraham to argue that Abraham's faith in God was only completed through his work—namely, his willingness to sacrifice his son Isaac (Gen 22:1–19). Note that James is *not* explicitly referring to how this argument applies to Jews and gentiles. Is Paul's argument about faith and law the same argument that James provides about faith and works, or are they different? How are these two authors using words like law, faith, and works? Are both authors using Abraham's story in similar or different ways to prove their point? Some scholars argue that James is written to combat Paul, others argue that it is written without Paul in mind, and still others argue that James is correcting a misunderstanding of Paul's message. Do you find any of these explanations convincing? Why or why not?

Further Reading

Allison, Dale C., Jr. "The Jewish Setting of the Epistle of James." *In die skriflig* 49.1 (2015): 1–9.

Batten, Alicia. "Ideological Strategies in the Letter of James." Pages 6–26 in *Reading James with New Eyes: Methodological Assessments of the Letter of James*. Edited by Robert L. Webb and John S. Kloppenborg. London: T&T Clark, 2007.

Byron, Gay L. "James." Pages 461–75 in *True to Our Native Land: An African Amer-*

ican New Testament Commentary. Edited by Brian K. Blount. Minneapolis: Fortress, 2007.

Lane, Jason D. *Luther's Epistle of Straw: The Voice of St. James in Reformation Preaching*. Historia Hermeneutica Series Studia 16. Berlin: de Gruyter, 2018.

Támez, Elsa. *The Scandalous Message of James: Faith without Works Is Dead*. New York: Crossroad, 1990.

28

1 and 2 Peter

SCOTT S. ELLIOTT

Although the writers of 1 Peter and 2 Peter both identify themselves as "Peter" (1 Pet 1:1; 5:1; 2 Pet 1:1; 3:1), they were written by different authors, neither of whom was the disciple of Jesus depicted in the gospels and Acts.

Addressed to non-Jewish recipients, 1 Peter was written to console and encourage readers experiencing various sorts of localized societal harassment for their beliefs and practices, and to advise them on how to navigate the experiences and feelings associated with becoming increasingly marginalized from conventional society. Thus, the letter is focused on issues of identity carved out and defined in relation to others, both Jews and gentiles. On the one hand, the writer addresses the problem by pointing out that their suffering is temporary and unjust, likening it to Jesus's suffering. However, he also attempts to mitigate it by urging his readers to play nice and forgo resisting, and by insisting that they see and regard their suffering as validation and as a source of blessing. According to Janette H. Ok, the writer of 1 Peter transforms Christian social identity into an ethnic identity by way of using "ethnic reasoning" that recasts Christ-followers in the guise of Jewish traditions in which they are portrayed as sharing.[1] While this may serve to provide group cohesion and solidarity, it also reflects a sort of cultural appropriation. The letter was most likely composed sometime in the late first century, but there is little evidence to indicate whence it was written.

Second Peter may well be the latest of the writings that make up the New Testament, perhaps dating to the early or even mid-second century. This is supported most notably by the author's effort to address the delay of Jesus's

---

1. Janette H. Ok, *Constructing Ethnic Identity in 1 Peter: Who You Are No Longer* (London: Bloomsbury/T&T Clark, 2021).

return (2 Pet 3:3–10), which he does by arguing that God has a different view of time and that the delay is effectively an act of mercy in that it affords opportunity for more people to repent. Second Peter focuses pointedly on apostolic tradition and authority while also drawing on Stoicism, and it shares an intimate literary relationship with the letter of Jude, from which the writer borrows heavily in his efforts to portray the character of his opponents. The material from Jude is well suited to the purposes of 2 Peter because it is generic in nature and functions to vilify rather than to identify and accurately describe those in view.

Anti-Jewish Interpretation and Use of 1 Peter

First Peter is rife with material reflecting a Judeophobic sentiment. Much like Hebrews, it presents a supersessionist perspective in which the church is perceived as having replaced or supplanted ancient Israel. While there may be some problems with labeling Hebrews as supersessionist, those problems are not present in 1 Peter, which "systematically transfers to [its gentile audience] many of the key terms associated with God's covenant with Israel."[2] As Stephen D. Moore explains it, "historical Israel is erased in 1 Peter as this covenant terminology is applied without remainder to the letter's Gentile audience."[3] First Peter 1:18, which reads "you were ransomed from the futile ways inherited from your ancestors,"[4] is therefore somewhat ironic. Given that the recipients are gentiles, "ancestors" likely refers to the pagan religions of Greeks and Romans. However, that the writer refers to them as "exiles of the Dispersion" (1:1) and then proceeds over the course of the letter to describe them in terms used throughout the Hebrew Bible for the ancient Israelites suggests a supersessionist perspective in which they have become the protagonists in Israel's narratives but are free of all the practices that constitute that role. Indeed, works like 1 Peter lay the foundation for and affirm the anti-Jewish biases held by many modern readers.

The writer performs this transference in a variety of ways. For example, he suggests that Israelite seers were searching for that which has been revealed to Christians, stating:

2. Stephen D. Moore, *Revealing the New Testament* (West Stockbridge, MA: Thinking Strings, 2017), 530.
3. Moore, *Revealing the New Testament*, 530.
4. All scripture quotations in this chapter are from the NRSV unless otherwise noted.

This salvation, [that] the prophets who prophesied of the grace that was to be yours made careful search and inquiry, inquiring about the person or time that the Spirit of Christ within them indicated when it testified in advance to the sufferings destined for Christ and the subsequent glory. It was revealed to them that they were serving not themselves but you, in regard to the things that have now been announced to you through those who brought you good news by the Holy Spirit sent from heaven—things into which angels long to look! (1 Pet 1:10–12)

In 1 Peter 2:4–10, the author treats select Hebrew Bible passages as metaphors in a manner that at best incorporates gentile Christ-followers into Israelite narrative and tradition, and at worst replaces Jews/Israel altogether, thereby appropriating Jewish identity. He identifies Christ-followers as "living stones" and "a chosen race, a royal priesthood, a holy nation, God's own people." In other words, he views Jesus-followers as alive and vibrant, part of a new and improved people of God. Therefore, he instructs them to "let [themselves] be built into a spiritual house, to be a holy priesthood, to offer spiritual sacrifices acceptable to God through Jesus Christ." And he portrays Jesus as the one who was rejected by Jews and as the one who now causes Jews to stumble and fall because they disobeyed, just as they were always destined to do.

In the following chapter, the writer addresses wives and says they have become daughters of Sarah, and he imagines the survival of Noah's family in the ark amid the flood (Gen 6–9) as a prefigurement of baptism whereby Christians are now saved, "not as a removal of dirt from the body, but as an appeal to God for a good conscience, through the resurrection of Jesus Christ" (1 Pet 3:18–22). Paula Fredriksen and Oded Irshai identify the strategy of allegorical interpretation as a fundamental and fecund arrow in the quiver of Christians who rejected Jewish practices but wanted to maintain a positive connection between Christ and the God of the Hebrew Bible.[5] They write: "An interpretive style of thinking which aimed to discern what a text truly meant as opposed to what it merely said, allegory provided early Christians with a means of altering the frame of reference for the ancient Jewish scriptures."[6] Hence, by way of such maneuvers, Christians could contend that a "full," "correct," "spiritual" understanding of the Hebrew scriptures was one

---

5. Paula Fredriksen and Oded Irshai, "Christian Anti-Judaism: Polemics and Policies," in *The Cambridge History of Judaism*, vol. 4, *The Late Roman-Rabbinic Period*, ed. Steven T. Katz (Cambridge: Cambridge University Press, 1984), 977–1034.

6. Fredriksen and Irshai, "Christian Anti-Judaism," 980.

that recognized such writings as pointing beyond themselves and that led to revelations regarding Christ and the church.[7]

While some contemporary anti-Jewish readings of 1 Peter simply follow the lead of its author and pick up where he left off,[8] a rather ironic alternative approach has been to propose that the audience of 1 Peter is Jewish. With the underlying premise that the letter was written by the historical Peter, himself a Jew, Jim R. Sibley assembles and enlists a long list of interpretive history, textual evidence, and topical matters in support of his position and then turns his attention to the implications.[9] The most significant of those implications for the purposes of this chapter is that, according to him, the contrast in 1 Peter 2:4–10 "is not between Jews and Gentiles nor Christians and pagans, but it is between Jews who believe in Jesus and Jews who do not."[10] Paradoxically, Sibley purports to be combating supersessionist readings, yet everything about it is focused on Jews (both ancient and modern) who have accepted Jesus. However, as Michael Cook points out, "since, in Jewish theology, a Jew who professes belief in Jesus as the Messiah has thereby, by definition, become a Christian—and is no longer a Jew—in effect the only persons mentioned . . . with whom modern Jews can readily identify is with [*sic*] those not accepting Jesus, and the New Testament *is* hostile toward these Jews. It *is* therefore anti-Jewish."[11] It is telling that an abridged version of Sibley's article is available on the "One for Israel" website, an organization that describes itself as "an initiative of native-born Israelis on the forefront of high-tech media evangelism, proclaiming salvation to Israel, raising up spiritual leaders . . . and equipping them with the tools they need to transform our communities." To wit, the im-

---

7. Fredriksen and Irshai, "Christian Anti-Judaism," 980–81.

8. See, e.g., Brent E. Parker, "The Church as the Renewed Israel in Christ: A Study of 1 Peter 2:4–10," *Southern Baptist Journal of Theology* 21 (2017): 41–52. Parker concludes: "For Peter, the church is the eschatological people of God that is inextricably linked to the promises and heritage of OT Israel" (46), and goes on to say: "National Israel is a typological pattern not unlike other OT persons, events, and institutions, but Israel is a type of the church in only a secondary fashion because it is Jesus Christ who is the chief antitype and true Israel. It is because of Jesus Christ, the living stone and chosen cornerstone, and the wonderous work he has achieved on the cross that the eschatological people of God, the church, is indeed the new temple, the royal priesthood, the chosen race, God's possession and holy nation, and recipients of mercy" (48–49).

9. Jim. R. Sibley, "You Talkin' to Me? 1 Peter 2:4–10 and a Theology of Israel," *Southwestern Journal of Theology* 59 (2016): 59–75.

10. Sibley, "You Talkin' to Me?," 73.

11. Michael Cook, "The New Testament: Confronting Its Impact on Jewish-Christian Relations," in *Biblical Studies Alternatively: An Introductory Reader*, ed. Susanne Scholz (Upper Saddle River, NJ: Prentice Hall, 2002), 291–307 at 296 (emphasis original).

plicit claim that the best Jews themselves are advocating for Jewish acceptance of Christian perspectives disguises a supersessionist ideology.

Anti-Jewish Interpretation and Use of 2 Peter

With regard to anti-Jewish sentiment, 2 Peter is nothing like 1 Peter. In fact, it is quite lacking in anything of that nature. The writer alludes several times to stories and teachings from the Hebrew Bible. But virtually all of those allusions are used in the writer's polemical attack on his opponents, who do not appear to be Jewish, and most of that material was purloined from Jude. In other words, material from the Hebrew Bible is presented as object lessons and as illustrations of the manner in which God thinks and acts. As noted above, it is virtually impossible to pinpoint precisely who the perceived opponents of 2 Peter were, but the substance of their contention is clear: namely, that despite all the promises that Jesus would return, the long passage of time in which nothing has changed suggests that he will not (see 2 Pet 3:3–4). After lambasting those who would dare propound such a thing, he makes his case in defense of the belief that Jesus will return and responds to the challenges prompted by the lateness thereof.

If there is anything in 2 Peter that perhaps gestures toward anti-Judaism (i.e., other than the ambiguous and generic character of the writer's polemic that allows for it if a reader is already predisposed), it may be the statement found in 3:15b–16: "So also our beloved brother Paul wrote to you according to the wisdom given him, speaking of this as he does in all his letters. There are some things in them hard to understand, which the ignorant and unstable twist to their own destruction, as they do the other scriptures." Whether the writer is equating Paul's letters with scripture or affirming their already existing status as such, he elevates them and places them on par with the Hebrew Bible, thereby indicating that he regards certain early Christian writings to command the same regard as the Law and the Prophets. It should be noted, however, that the focus is primarily on apostolic authority, which the writer presumes he and Paul share in common.

Discussion Questions and Activity Suggestions

1. The *Oxford English Dictionary* defines "identity politics" as "the adherence by a group of people of a particular religion, race, social background, etc., to political beliefs or goals specific to the group concerned, as opposed to conforming to traditional broad-based party politics." Do you think 1 Peter reflects this

sort of rhetorical work? Why or why not? Can you find any popular instances of readers appealing to 1 Peter in the midst of engaging in identity politics?

2. The *Oxford English Dictionary* defines "cultural appropriation" as "the unacknowledged or inappropriate adoption of the practices, customs, or esthetics of one social or ethnic group by members of another (typically dominant) community or society." Does 1 Peter reflect cultural appropriation? What contemporary examples of Christians appropriating Jewish culture can you identify?

3. Prooftexting entails appealing to biblical material in order to support a claim without regard for the context of the material being cited. Would you label the writer's use of the Hebrew Bible in 2 Peter an example of prooftexting? Why or why not? Does so much of it being taken from Jude factor into your assessment?

4. Evaluate and debate the evidence and arguments concerning the authorship and/or audience of 1 Peter. Which are the strongest, and which are the weakest? Identify two or three key implications and consequences of deciding one way or the other on each issue.

5. The character and characterization of Peter in Matthew, Mark, and Acts varies considerably. Compare each to the implied authors of 1 Peter and 2 Peter. Which one(s) do you see most reflected and how? Discuss the implications of this for Petrine traditions and the authority or canonicity of early Christian writings associated with Peter.

6. Jude and 2 Peter clearly share a literary relationship. Compare and contrast Jude 4–18 and 2 Peter 2:1–3:3. Do both writers have the same individuals in view, or are their representations so generic that they can be applied to any perceived opponent?

Further Reading

Aichele, George. *The Letters of Jude and Second Peter: Paranoia and the Slaves of Christ.* Sheffield: Sheffield Phoenix, 2012.

Ok, Janette H. *Constructing Ethnic Identity in 1 Peter: Who You Are No Longer.* London: Bloomsbury/T&T Clark, 2021.

Perkins, Pheme, Eloise Rosenblatt, and Patricia McDonald. *1–2 Peter and Jude.* Wisdom Commentary 56. Collegeville, MN: Liturgical Press, 2022.

Schüssler Fiorenza, Elisabeth. *1 Peter: An Introduction and Study Guide: Reading against the Grain.* London: Routledge, 2017.

29

1, 2, and 3 John

HUGO MÉNDEZ

Nestled near the end of the Christian Bible are three of the shortest and most enigmatic texts in the New Testament: the letters of 1, 2, and 3 John. The three texts bear an obvious resemblance to the Gospel of John, taking up many of its distinctive ideas and idioms, including such unusual expressions as "abide in God," "walk in the light," and "do the truth." But the three have their own distinct profiles. The longest, 1 John, is an anonymous exhortation directed to an unspecified and probably general readership, which provides theological and moral instruction. By contrast, 2 and 3 John assume the style and conventions of personal letters, offering more specific instructions to individual parties. At less than 250 words apiece, they are also the two shortest texts in the New Testament, containing no more text than could fit on a single papyrus sheet.

We know nothing of the author(s) of these works—neither their number nor their individual identities—since all three are technically anonymous. Ancient Christians attributed all three to the same author as the Gospel of John,and indeed, the real authors of these texts seem to inhabit the voice of the narrator of John. Like the gospel's narrator, for instance, the narrator of 1 John positions himself as an eyewitness who can speak for those who "have heard . . . seen . . . looked upon and touched" Jesus (1 John 1:1; cf. John 1:14). He also uses all the distinctive expressions typical of the gospel's narrator. In turn, 2 and 3 John present themselves as works by a nameless, enigmatic "elder" (2 John 1; 3 John 1), but each closely mirrors the voice of the narrators of John and 1 John. Despite these similarities, however, contemporary scholars believe the texts were probably written by different hands than the gospel, noting subtle but appreciable differences in the ideas and language of all these texts.[1]

---

1. Consider, for example, Raymond E. Brown, *Epistles of John*, Anchor Bible 30 (Garden

Although most scholars assume that the three letters date to around the time the Gospel of John was written (circa 100), the reception history of these texts suggests that at least 2 and 3 John may date to a much later time.[2] The earliest text to mention or quote 2 John is Irenaeus's late-second-century work, the *Refutation of All Heresies*, while our earliest mention of 3 John is contained in a third-century work known only through a fourth-century source—that is, a fragment of Origen's *Hypotyposes* (circa 240) preserved in Eusebius's *Ecclesiastical History*.[3] No less problematically, the earliest mentions of these texts also indicate widespread doubts about the authenticity of the two shorter letters, suggesting that they may be literary fakes. In the third century, Origen reports that "not all [Christians] think [2 and 3 John] are genuine," and in the fourth century, Eusebius ranks the two among the texts "disputed" by Christians.[4] This skepticism was especially strong among Syriac-speaking Christians, who did not incorporate these texts into their Bibles until the sixth century.

Despite this opposition, however, the three texts gradually cemented a place in all Christian Bibles. From that privileged position, they influenced the direction of Christian ideas, attitudes, and practice with some negative consequences on Jewish-Christian relations.

Judeophobia in the Johannine Letters

Unlike the Gospel of John, which includes several especially negative portrayals of Jews, the letters of 1, 2, and 3 John lack any mentions of Jews, Judaism, and Jewish practices. There is good reason to think, then, that the three epistles emerged in temporal, geographic, or literary contexts in which Christians saw

---

City, NY: Doubleday, 1982), 19–35; Raimo Hakola, "The Reception and Development of the Johannine Tradition in 1, 2, and 3 John," in *The Legacy of John: Second-Century Reception of the Fourth Gospel*, ed. Tuomas Rasimus (Leiden: Brill, 2010), 24–35.

2. Excellent surveys of the early circulation of 2 and 3 John appear in Judith Lieu, *The Second and Third Epistles of John* (Edinburgh: T&T Clark, 1986), 5–36; and James Barker, "The Acts of John within the Johannine Corpus," in *Studies on the Intersection of Text, Paratext, and Reception: A Festschrift in Honor of Charles E. Hill*, Texts and Editions for New Testament Study 15 (Leiden: Brill, 2021), 342–52, 355–57.

3. Irenaeus cites 2 John in *Refutation of All Heresies* 3.16.8, albeit confusing or conflating the source with 1 John (cf. *Refutation of All Heresies* 3.16.5). In turn, Origen's mention of 2 John appears in Eusebius, *Ecclesiastical History* 6.25.10. Barker, however, is skeptical that Origen knew 3 John, proposing that Eusebius might have inserted the reference to the letter here; "Acts of John," 346–48.

4. Origen's comment is reproduced by Eusebius in *Ecclesiastical History* 6.25.10. Eusebius's own comments on 2–3 John appear in *Ecclesiastical History* 3.24.17; 3.25.3.

the task of self-definition over and against Jews as less of a priority. That being said, it would be a mistake to distance these texts entirely from anti-Jewish attitudes or rhetoric. The first two subtly support the gospel's anti-Jewish presentation, and each served as a resource for Christian anti-Judaism and Judeophobia in later generations.

The most problematic feature of these texts is the extent to which they extend and even elaborate the sharp dualistic worldview of the Gospel of John—a worldview that associates "the Jews" with the devil and the demonic. In the gospel, Jesus tells "the Jews," "you are of your father, the devil" (8:44).[5] Consistent with this messaging, the narrator of 1 John claims that "everyone who believes that Jesus is the Messiah is a child of God" (5:1; cf. 5:5) while casting all others—including, undoubtedly, Jews—as the "children of the devil," who form a "world" that is plunged "in death" (3:10, 14). Several verses go so far as to suggest that all those in "the world" are possessed by the devil. In one, the author claims: "The one who is in you is greater than the one who is in the world" (4:4). In another, he writes: "We know that we are of God, and the whole world is in the power of the evil one" (5:19).

This dualism leads 1 John to rhetorically construct a hostility between "the world" and those who believe in Jesus. "The world hates you," the narrator of 1 John tells his readers, also indicating that those in "the world" are intrinsically "murderers" (3:11–15). In turn, the narrator calls believers to a similarly adversarial posture, urging them: "Do not love the world or the things in the world. If anyone loves the world, love for the Father is not in them" (2:15).

Antichrist in the Johannine Letters

Another source for anti-Jewish attitudes in later generations is the vocabulary of "antichrist" sprinkled across the epistles (1 John 2:18–23; 4:1–6; 2 John 7–9). Although other early Christian texts anticipate the rise of evil powers at the end of time (e.g., 2 Thess 2:1–12; Rev 13, 17), the letters of 1 John and 2 John are the first known texts to specifically speak of a coming antichrist, introducing the term into Christian discourse. The letters offer scant and, frankly, ambiguous information regarding this entity or figure.[6] Some verses associate antichrist with those "who deny that Jesus is the Christ"—a description evocative of Jewish views of Jesus (1 John 2:22; perhaps also 4:3). Other verses,

---

5. All scripture quotations in this chapter are my own unless otherwise noted.

6. The question of who the "antichrists" represent is a complex one. See Ruth B. Edwards, *The Johannine Epistles* (Sheffield: Sheffield Academic, 1996), 57–68.

however, associate antichrist with those "who do not confess that Jesus Christ has come in the flesh" (2 John 7; cf. 1 John 4:1–6)—a description possibly targeting second-century teachers who questioned whether Jesus had come in a material body (i.e., so-called docetists).[7]

Over the next several centuries, these brief, ambiguous, and relatively opaque references to antichrist became sites of intense speculation for Christians—much of it inflected in anti-Jewish and Judeophobic directions. Coordinating a number of disparate texts and traditions, including 1 John and 2 John, a wide segment of early Christian writers identified the coming antichrist as the messiah for which Jews still hope, and thus also, a person of Jewish descent. The late second-century writer Irenaeus, for one, claims that the future antichrist comes from the Israelite "tribe of Dan" (*Refutation of All Heresies* 5.30.1–2). Likewise, Cyril, the fourth-century bishop of the church of Jerusalem, relates that the antichrist will present himself as "the man of the race of David, who shall build up the temple that was erected by Solomon" and that "he will be worshiped by the Jews" (*Catechetical Lectures* 15.15). And in his *Commentary on Daniel*, the fifth-century Latin writer Jerome describes the antichrist as "he who is destined to arise from a small nation, that is from the Jewish people" and who "by means of intrigue and deception . . . shall secure the government" (*Commentary on Daniel* on Dan 11:24).

The notion that the antichrist would be ethnically Jewish was more than a speculative point about a single individual. In the hands of Christian writers and preachers, it was the ultimate discredit to the Jewish people and a badge of their supposed spiritual darkness. According to Pope Gregory the Great (sixth century), the Jews "are preordained to be under [antichrist's] rule" because of their "sins" and even now "reverence even him by their evil lives" (*Moralia* 19.34; cf. 29.75). Likewise, in a section in which Peter the Venerable (twelfth century) calls Jews the "excrement of the human race" and compares them to "apes," "beasts," and "dogs," he writes: "These are your mysteries, O Jews. . . . The eggs that you incubate . . . are the eggs of asps . . . after you had wickedly incubated them for a long time, they will produce the one who is to come at the end of the world, the antichrist, the king of all the ungodly. . . . You have incubated the deadly egg for such a fruit for a long time" (*Against the Jews* 3, 5).

The notion of Jews as progenitors and future allies of the antichrist was a pervasive topos of Christian ritual and art in the medieval and early modern periods. In medieval Constantinople, professions of faith required converts

---

7. On the parameters and problems of "docetism" as a scholarly category, see T. Christopher Hoklotubbe, "What Is Docetism?," in *Re-Making the World: Christianity and Categories; Essays in Honor of Karen L. King*, ed. Taylor G. Petrey et al. (Tübingen: Mohr Siebeck, 2019), 49–71.

from Judaism to recite the words: "Above all, I renounce antichrist, whom all the Jews await in the figure and dress of Christ."[8] Meanwhile, in the medieval West, the same system of ideas was widely represented in religious painting, passion plays, and antichrist plays. These popularized what had by then become an established legendarium of the antichrist's future career, encompassing his circumcision, his rebuilding of the temple of Jerusalem, his conquests, and his violent persecutions of Christians. In these depictions, Jews were represented as the foremost agents of, and most sinister coconspirators with, this coming evil power. Public performances of these dramas were especially incendiary, fueling outbursts of violence as well as economic boycotts and lasting ethnic suspicion.[9]

Detail from the Ebstorf World Map. American Geographical Society Library, University of Wisconsin-Milwaukee Libraries. https://collections.lib .uwm.edu/digital/iiif/agdm /16400/full/full/0/default.jpg

Unsurprisingly, the same expectations became interwoven with other antisemitic canards reverberating into the modern period. In the Middle Ages, the idea was juxtaposed with blood libel, as seen in the Ebstorf World Map (thirteenth century), which depicts Jews as "unclean people . . . who will accompany the antichrist," and "who eat human flesh and drink human blood."[10]

But perhaps the most damaging legacy of the notion of a Jewish antichrist is its role in seeding modern conspiracy theories positing Jewish quests for world domination. This idea is the natural end of the idea that Jews will conspire with a future antichrist. It has also proven to be the inspiration for an astonishing scope of violence and mass murder. Beneath the *Protocols of the Elders of Zion*, pogroms, Nazi propaganda, the Holocaust, and modern forms of antisemitic, white supremacist, Christian nationalist, and ultranationalist thought lies a deeper interpretive history springing from a few brief letters near the end of the New Testament.

8. Joseph Aloysius Assemanus, *Codex Liturgicus Ecclesiae Universae*, 15 vols. (Rome, 1749), 1:105.

9. On these plays and the legendarium they depicted through performance, see Andrew Gow, "The Jewish Antichrist in Medieval and Early Modern Germany," in *Medieval Encounters: Jewish, Christian, and Muslim Culture in Confluence and Dialogue* (Leiden: Brill, 1996), 249–85.

10. Ebstorf World Map: "Hic inclusit Alexander duas gentes immundas Gog et Magog, quas comites habebit Antichristus. Hii humanis carnibus vescuntur et sanguinem bibunt"; *Die Ebstorfer Weltkarte: Kommentierte Neuausgabe in zwei Bänden*, ed. Hartmut Kugler, 2 vols. (Berlin: Akademie Verlag, 2007), 1: no. 8/7, no. 15/A2.

Discussion Questions and Activity Suggestions

1. This chapter situates 1, 2, and 3 John within the history of anti-Jewish or Judeophobic attitudes even though none of the three expressly mentions Jews or Judaism. Is it always necessary for a text to directly name a target to disparage a particular group or inspire attitudes of hate? How could a text, work of art, or speech be harmful to a group even if it does not directly attack such a group? Can you think of examples from more recent decades?
2. In the first two centuries, a significant number of Christians were ethnically Jewish. Some scholars—for example, Raymond Brown—assume that the initial audience(s) of 1, 2, and 3 John included many persons of Jewish descent. Others—for example, Adele Reinhartz—believe the texts may have been addressed primarily to non-Jewish audiences. How would these possibilities impact our reading of the letters as effectively anti-Jewish or predisposed to an anti-Jewish interpretation? Should the author's identity make any difference at all?
3. The Johannine letters are framed by a sharp dualism that sets insiders ("us/ we") over and against outsiders ("the world"). Take a sheet of paper and divide it into columns, one side labeled "Us" and the other "The World." Now read through 1 John 2–5 and keep track of the attributes characteristic of each side, filing them under the appropriate columns. Reflect on your list. What sorts of attitudes might such a dualistic worldview engender? How do these compare to those projected toward Jews through the centuries?

Further Reading

Frey, Jörg. "Dualism and the World in the Gospel and Letters of John." Pages 274–91 in *The Oxford Handbook of Johannine Studies*. Edited by Judith M. Lieu and Martinus C. de Boer. Oxford: Oxford University Press, 2018.

Hill, C. E. "Antichrist from the Tribe of Dan." *Journal of Theological Studies* 46 (1995): 99–117.

Lieu, Judith M. *The Theology of the Johannine Epistles*. Cambridge: Cambridge University Press, 1991.

Michael, Robert. *A History of Catholic Antisemitism*. New York: Palgrave Macmillan, 2008.

30

Jude

SCOTT S. ELLIOTT

In contrast to what one finds when considering the gospels or the letters of Paul, little attention is given to Jude in either sermons or scholarship.[1] Uncertainties abound regarding virtually every aspect of the letter. Yet, the message of Jude seems straightforward: as the writer sees it, bad people have infiltrated the ranks of the writer's imagined community, and dire warnings are warranted. The letter is rife with vitriol, chock full of prooftexts, and replete with ominous admonitions. The vagueness and generality concerning who the writer's perceived opponents were leave even trained biblical scholars with little more than best guesses. Nevertheless, it seems clear that the writer had in view some other early group of Jesus-followers. To be sure, vague ambiguity can have its own persuasive effect. Indeed, the fuzziness of the writer's image allows for virtually any "other" to match the description when readers employ Jude to cast aspersions on those with whom they disagree in order to shore up the boundaries of their own group.

The author of the letter identifies himself as the brother of James and thus, by extension, the brother of Jesus. If true, then the letter would have been written rather early. It is more likely, however, that the letter is pseudonymous (i.e., written by someone else in Jude's name) and probably written in the late first or early second century. A later date is supported by the writer's references to "the faith" (i.e., in the sense of a shared tradition; cf. Eph 4:4–5)

---

1. This introduction is adapted from Scott S. Elliott, "Resonance, Repetition, and Re-Remembrance: Re-Translation as Perpetual Pre-writing," in *[Re]Gained in Translation I: Bibles, Theologies, and the Politics of Empowerment*, ed. Sabine Dievenkorn and Shaul Levin (Berlin: Frank & Timme, 2022), 25–45.

and to "the apostles." The letter's place of origin is really anyone's guess. Some argue for Jerusalem because it suits the family connection if one imagines the writer to be the brother of Jesus. Others argue somewhat more broadly that it was written from a Palestinian Jewish context and that it reflects an early form of Jewish Christianity evidenced most of all by the writer's high regard for 1 Enoch. Whatever one concludes, the author and his general context are almost certainly Jewish as evidenced by his intimate familiarity with, and extensive use of, the Hebrew scriptures and other extracanonical texts (e.g., 1 Enoch, Assumption of Moses). In the end, however, the letter's geographical context has little if any bearing on its interpretation.

Jude is occasioned by a perceived threat. The writer indicates that despite his intention to write a letter "about the salvation we share," he instead found it "necessary" (a word indicating an intense need dictated by either external exigency or internal impulse) to appeal to his readers "to contend for the faith that was once for all entrusted to the saints. For certain intruders have stolen in among you, people who long ago were designated for this condemnation as ungodly, who pervert the grace of our God into licentiousness and deny our only Master and Lord, Jesus Christ" (Jude 3–4 NRSV). Proposals regarding the specific identity of the opponents run the full gamut. After cataloging and glossing everything the writer of Jude has to say about them, Michael F. Bird concludes that "if these intruders are real, we are probably to imagine something like a cross between the pseudo-apostles and false-prophets mentioned in the Didache and the lurid descriptions of the love feasts held by the Carpocratians described by Clement of Alexandria."[2] Be that as it may, George Aichele's juxtaposition of Jude and 2 Peter to the mid-twentieth century sci-fi classic *Invasion of the Body Snatchers* perhaps provides a better alternative for how to think about the rhetoric and tenor of the letter in relation to who the supposed bad people were and why they were bad in the mind of the writer. Aichele notes that "pastoral power stands always in reciprocal relation to its own resistance or refusal. . . . Orthodoxy cannot exist until it defines itself by contrast to heresy."[3] Noting in particular the reference to setting up divisions in Jude 19 and its use by scholars to identify the opponents as Gnostics, Aichele rightly points out "it is the letter of Jude, not the opponents, that makes this claim and sets up these divisions."[4] He notes that what the reader presumes

2. Michael F. Bird, "Who Are the Opponents in the Epistle of Jude?," *Patheos* (1 September 2017) (https://tinyurl.com/3mbtu7pn).
3. George Aichele, *The Letters of Jude and Second Peter: Paranoia and the Slaves of Christ* (Sheffield: Sheffield Phoenix, 2012), 17.
4. Aichele, *Jude and Second Peter*, 18.

to know regarding the audiences and opponents of Jude is largely a function of its place in the New Testament canon and Christian tradition, which leads him to conclude that "by omitting this information, each letter opens ways for generalized readings by any group of Christians against any others."[5]

Peter S. Perry states that "Jude is written to a Jewish believing community in order to persuade them to reject antinomian (i.e., 'against law') teachers and to encourage one another to live out the moral implications of faith in Jesus Christ as Master and Lord. For Jude, the Jewish law as mediated by angels (the 'glorious ones') describes how a Christian should behave, especially sexual behavior."[6] Perry goes on to explain that the writer of Jude reads the Jewish scriptures through a typological lens, which means that he understands certain characters and events to prefigure, betoken, or epitomize people and situations in his own context and thus to evoke connotations that lend a certain sort of meaning to contemporary circumstances.

Despite the wide-ranging suggestions regarding who the writer of Jude has in view as the target of his vitriolic ravings, few explicitly suggest Jews, Jewish leaders, or so-called Judaizers (that is, Jewish and gentile Jesus-followers who insisted that new gentile adherents must observe Jewish practices such as circumcision). In fact, whoever the writer is targeting acts, in his estimation, based on what he perceives to be an antinomian attitude. In other words, he understands his opponents to represent a form of Christianity that believed the Jewish law had no claim on them because they believed their worship of Jesus freed them of any responsibility to its moral and ethical demands. The impetus for the writer's judgment appears to be what he regarded as sexual licentiousness on their part. Nevertheless, owing to the vagueness of its criticism and the pliability of any accusation of antinomianism, the history of interpretation and reception of Jude is littered with debates in which parties identify those on the other side with Jude's opponents.

Tertullian (circa 160–circa 220), Origen (185–253), and Clement of Alexandria (died circa 215) all recognized Jude as scripture. However, the incorporation of 1 Enoch was a problem for some, and the way they handled it is a problem from the perspective of this volume. For instance, arguing for acceptance of 1 Enoch over against "the Jews" who rejected it, Tertullian concludes: "Nor, of course, is this fact wonderful, that they did not receive some Scriptures which spake of Him whom even in person, speaking in their presence, they were not to receive" (*The Apparel of Women* 1.3; trans. Sydney Thelwall). Meanwhile, commenting on the reference to "people who long ago

---

5. Aichele, *Jude and Second Peter*, 19.
6. Peter S. Perry, "Jude," *Oxford Biblical Studies Online* (https://tinyurl.com/52ua6nht).

were designated for this condemnation as ungodly" (NRSV) in Jude 4, Clement of Alexandria explains: "Not that they might become impious, but that, being now impious, they were ordained to judgment. 'For the Lord God,' he says, 'who once delivered a people out of Egypt, afterward destroyed them that believed not'; that is, that He might train them through punishment. For they were indeed punished, and they perished on account of those that are saved, until they turn to the Lord" (fragment 2).

Regarding the reference to "the Lord" saving the people out of Egypt, ancient manuscripts reflect a variety of possibilities. For example, some have "Jesus" or "the Lord Jesus" in place of "the Lord."[7] Most translators opt for "the Lord." However, translators of the increasingly popular (in some circles) English Standard Version followed the variants and translated the verse: "Jesus, who saved a people out of the land of Egypt, afterward destroyed those who did not believe." Here, two possibilities emerge, either of which reflects and promotes an anti-Jewish, supersessionist posture. First, the writer of Jude himself or someone in the earliest stages of the text's transmission equated Jesus with the God of the Israelites and placed him at the center of the exodus narrative. Alternatively, those responsible for the ESV were influenced by a Judeophobic bias. Either way, one example of how evangelicals have defended this decision is provided by James Midwinter, who concludes by saying that Jude reflects a high Christology and a "unique redemptive-historical perspective . . . on the pre-incarnate salvific ministry of our Lord and Savior, Jesus Christ," and that it enables readers to better understand and appreciate "our Savior's trans-testamental work of redemption."[8]

It is clearly the ambiguity of the writer's target that makes Jude susceptible to Judeophobic readings. Hence, for example, despite nothing in his own analysis requiring it, Phillip J. Long concludes his blog post on the opponents in Jude by making an unnecessary passing reference to Jews when he states: "If this is the background for the opponents in Jude, then once again we have evidence for an earlier date to the book, and perhaps another indication that the problems were caused by people, *perhaps Jews*, failing to challenge their pagan world with their new faith."[9] In the end, Jude functions like a mirror that, when held up, all too often reveals a reader's own Judeophobia.

---

7. The 27th edition of Nestle-Aland *Novum Testamentum Graece* (1993) had *kyrios*, but the 28th edition (2012) has *Iēsous*.

8. James Midwinter, "Who Led the Israelites Out of Egypt? An Examination of Jude 5," *Foundations* 75 (2018): 21–33 at 22 and 32.

9. Phillip J. Long, "Who Were Jude's Opponents?" (29 March 2018) (https://tinyurl.com/2wedbck4) (emphasis added).

Discussion Questions and Activity Suggestions

1. The rhetoric of Jude relies on vilification (Jude 4, 8, 12–13, 16). This was a common practice in Hellenistic rhetoric, and it persists in contemporary social media and politics. The goal of vilification is not description but evaluation. It does not aim to ensure understanding of those described but rather to affect the reader's judgment of them. It depends on types and stereotypes rather than concrete details. What might lead or even force a writer to use generic terms and trite rhetorical tropes when describing perceived opponents?

2. Why are groups so intent on identifying opponents? When are they most inclined to do so? What is the source of such identifications if not the text itself, if the descriptions in the text are vague and ambiguous? What accounts for how readers fill these gaps?

3. List the characteristics the writer uses in the picture he paints of the intruders (Jude 4, 6, 7, 8, 10, 12, 16, 19). What sort of image materializes? What reaction does such an image provoke? Next, read the stories of those groups and individuals to which the writer compares the intruders (Gen 4:1–16; 6:1–6; 18–19; Num 14:1–24; 16; 22–24; 1 Enoch 6–12). Discuss whether or to what extent the writer fairly represented those groups and individuals. What would be necessary for the writer's opponents to fit these profiles?

4. Find a politician's stump speech or a political debate online. Compare and contrast it with Jude. Are similar characterizations employed? By what standard or authority are the speaker's opponents judged? To what tropes and/or examples does the speaker appeal? What are the implications and ramifications of the speaker's rhetoric?

Further Reading

Aichele, George. *The Letters of Jude and Second Peter: Paranoia and the Slaves of Christ*. Sheffield: Sheffield Phoenix, 2012.

Bauckham, Richard J. *Jude, 2 Peter*. Word Biblical Commentary 50. Waco, TX: Word, 1983.

Jacobs, Andrew S. "The Letter of Jude." In *The Jewish Annotated New Testament*. Edited by Amy-Jill Levine and Marc Zvi Brettler. Oxford: Oxford University Press, 2011.

Reese, Ruth Anne. *Writing Jude: The Reader, the Text, and the Author in Constructs of Power and Desire*. Leiden: Brill, 1995.

31

Revelation

JUSTIN P. JEFFCOAT SCHEDTLER

F ew biblical books inspire the imagination like the book of Revelation. Despite its humble beginnings as a text purportedly authored by an imprisoned follower of Jesus near the end of the first century, on a remote island off
the coast of modern-day Turkey, for an audience that likely consisted of those
among the lower rungs of the socioeconomic and political order, the text has
wielded enormous influence.

Much of Revelation's enthralling power resides in its mythic, monstrous,
and allusive creatures: the woman clothed with the sun, the four horsemen,
a beast from the sea with many heads, angels who wreak havoc upon the earth,
and so on. Such creatures certainly evoke the imagination, but who do they
represent, if anyone or anything in particular? Discerning the identities of
these elusive figures seems to be the key to unlocking Revelation's mysteries,
but the task is complicated by their never being identified explicitly, rather
only suggestively and obliquely.

Some figures are recognizable through only thinly veiled allusions. For
example, the heavenly "Lamb standing as if it had been slaughtered" (Rev
5:6, 9, 12) clearly evokes the crucified Jesus, but a reader might be forgiven for
wondering why the author didn't instead introduce the glorified Jesus a bit
more candidly, for example: "You know, Jesus, the Messiah who was crucified
in Jerusalem under Pontius Pilate a few years ago?" Other creatures are less
easily identifiable, including many of the objects of Revelation's wrath. The
beast is well known by its (now ghastly) number 666, but identifying the figure
lying behind the symbolic number has proven frustratingly difficult. Many
who claim special knowledge and/or interpretive abilities seek to identify the
beast, but the almost innumerable suggestions (a quick Google search reveals

proposals ranging from Pope Leo X to Adolf Hitler, from the General Secretary of the United Nations to QR codes, from Donald Trump to Elon Musk) testify to the inherent difficulty—and ambiguity—in the task.[1]

The challenge, then, appears to consist of acquiring the proper lenses to see through these veiled allusions and ultimately to make meaning of the text. However, finding these lenses isn't as easy as one might think. Many interpreters suggest a strategy in which the text is read in light of the historical (which is to say, the social, cultural, political, economic, and religious) environment(s) in which it was produced. With such a lens, Revelation's elusive imagery becomes much less ambiguous. The accoutrements of Roman imperial authority (e.g., its military apparatus, religious practices, social customs, economy, and even the emperor himself) can be detected conspicuously and consistently under attack throughout the Apocalypse: the harlot of Babylon comes into view as a representation of some facet of imperial life, perhaps the city of Rome or the cult of the Mother Goddess, Cybele, one of Rome's important politico-religious institutions; those who mourn her destruction in Revelation 18 appear as those who participated—and benefitted—from this very institution. And so on with the host of terrific creatures who haunt the pages of the book of Revelation.

Within this oppressive landscape, Revelation presents an optimistic claim: God provided a Messiah who will bring about the end of Roman imperial reign and initiate a glorious eschatological age in which God and God's Messiah will reign over God's people forever. The vivid imagery of eschatological battles throughout Revelation depicts symbolically how this will unfold.

How many in the original audience would have recognized these allusions, and would have recognized the connotations and implications intended by the original author(s), is unclear—some clearly did. Much more certain is that those *not* familiar with the historical milieu in which the text was written are much, much less likely to do so. Instead, they are prone to substitute historical lenses with lenses of their own making, lenses through which Revelation's beasts do not appear as Roman imperial monsters from the text's own time and place but instead the monsters from the interpreter's own time and place. This (mis)interpretive flexibility is part of what has given the book of Revelation its immense power throughout history, as it has been (mis)used as a roadmap for identifying good and bad throughout history.

---

1. Alas, many scholars believe that 666 refers specifically to Nero for a number of reasons. See Hans-Josef Klauck, "Do They Never Come Back? Nero Redivivus and the Apocalypse of John," *Catholic Biblical Quarterly* 63 (2001): 683–98.

Within this general history of (mis)interpretation, those readings in which Revelation's horrid creatures are identified as historical Jewish figures are conspicuous and widespread. In fact, Revelation has long functioned as a vehicle for Judeophobia and antisemitism in Christian (and even non-Christian) circles. In what follows, we consider two symbolic tropes that have been particularly susceptible to anti-Jewish interpretation: (1) the "synagogue of Satan" in Revelation 2:9 and 3:9 and (2) the beast from the sea in Revelation 13:1–10.

Synagogue of Satan

Twice in Revelation an entity is identified as the "synagogue of Satan":[2]

> I know about the slander of those who say they are Jews and are not, but are a synagogue of Satan. Do not be afraid of what you are about to suffer. Beware, the devil is about to throw some of you into prison so that you may be tested, and for ten days you will have affliction. Be faithful until death, and I will give you the crown of life. (Rev 2:9–10)

> I know that you have but little power, and yet you have kept my word and have not denied my name. I will make those of the synagogue of Satan, who claim to be Jews though they are not, but are liars—I will make them come and fall down at your feet and acknowledge that I have loved you. (Rev 3:8–9)

These references come from the first three chapters of Revelation, which are made up of letters to different communities in Asia Minor. In the first letter, those who "say they are Jews and are not" are accused of slandering the Christ worshipers in Smyrna, which results in their suffering (2:9–10). For this reason, the slanderers are characterized as evil in no uncertain terms—that is, as a part of a "synagogue of Satan"—and condemned to suffer as a result. In order to understand this accusation, it is necessary to explore further the parties involved and the nature of the slander itself.

Although it is not explicit in the letter, it is likely that the group who believe they are being slandered in Smyrna understood themselves to be Jewish, which is to say, Jewish Christ-believers. In other words, the Christ-worshiping community in Smyrna, and likely in the other cities singled out in Revelation,

---

2. All scripture quotations in this chapter are my own translation unless otherwise noted.

for example, Pergamum, Ephesus, and so on, had not abandoned their Jewish identity, beliefs, or practices when they began to follow Jesus. On the contrary, they understood Jesus in many ways that make sense only when viewed through Jewish lenses, for example, Jesus was the Jewish Messiah (e.g., 1:1, 2, 5, 9; 11:15; 12:10; 20:4, 6; cf. 22:21) whom the God of Israel had sent to establish a "new Jerusalem" (3:12; 21:2).

The identification of those who "say they are Jews but are not" presents greater difficulties. Some argue that this group referred to *non*-Christ-worshiping Jews in Asia Minor, which is to say, Jewish people who shared similar theological convictions as the Jewish Christ worshipers—for example, the belief in the one true God of Israel—but who did *not* follow Jesus.[3] Others maintain that those who "say they are Jews but are not" instead refers to a group of Jesus-followers with whom John of Patmos had significant ideological disagreements.[4]

At any rate, it seems probable that the slander consisted of this group, whether it was *non*-Christ-worshiping Jews or non-Christ-worshiping gentiles, castigating the Jesus-following Jews in Smyrna for not participating in cultic honors for the Roman emperor, that is, offering sacrifices, prayers, hymns, and so on, to the emperor and his family.[5] The refusal of Christ-worshiping Jews to take part in such conduct was a consequence of their belief that such cultic honors were tantamount to worship for a god and as such inappropriate for anyone who believed that such worship should be reserved for God and Christ alone (e.g., 4:11; 5:11–13). Indeed, the issue of whether to offer worship to the emperor was one with which Christ-following and non-Christ-following Jews often wrestled. At stake was one's sociopolitical standing vis-à-vis the Roman authorities. Participation in worship of the emperor signaled a person's acceptance and even promotion of the ruling imperial authorities and fostered social, political, and even economic opportunities as a result. Failure to participate signaled not only a reluctance to promote imperial political systems, but a likelihood of reduced sociopolitical-economic standing as a result. So, there was often disagreement about whether—and to what degree—a religious group ought to participate given the potential benefits and pitfalls.

---

3. Adela Yarbro Collins, "Vilification and Self-Definition in the Book of Revelation," *Harvard Theological Review* 79 (1986): 308–20.

4. David Frankfurter, "Jews or Not? Reconstructing the 'Other' in Rev 2:9 and 3:9," *Harvard Theological Review* 94 (2001): 403–25.

5. Others suggest an analogous problem whereby Christians refused to pay a special tax imposed by the Romans on Jews to allow them freedom in religious practice. See Mark R. J. Bredin, "The Synagogue of Satan Accusation in Revelation 2:9," *Biblical Theology Bulletin* 28.4 (1998): 160–64.

When communities (including it seems those addressed by John of Patmos) refused to offer these imperial honors, they were oftentimes persecuted and even imprisoned by the Roman authorities, which may be alluded to in 2:10 (i.e., "the devil is about to throw some of you into prison").[6] During their imprisonment, community members would be "tested" by the Roman authorities (cf. "so that you may be tested" in 2:10) for their loyalties to the emperor by requiring them to publicly honor the emperor. Members would then be faced with a dreadful dilemma: remain faithful to God but lose their life or demonstrate loyalty to the emperor and save their life.

The letters to the church in Smyrna and Philadelphia encourage those in John's communities to remain faithful to God and the Lamb in this predicament by rejecting public honors for the emperor:

Be faithful until death! (Rev 2:10)

Yet you have kept my word and have not denied my name. (Rev 3:8)

Though they may lose their life at the hands of the Roman authorities, Revelation promises that they will receive something far greater as a result, namely, the "crown of life" (2:10; cf. 3:12; Heb 2:9; Martyrdom of Polycarp 17:1), which symbolizes eventual power over their accusers ("I will make them come and fall down at your feet" in Rev 3:9) and perhaps eternal life. At the same time, the letter denounces in no uncertain terms those "who say they are Jews and are not" who had imperiled the community in the first place by alerting Roman authorities to their failure to worship the emperor. The charge that they are a part of the "synagogue of Satan" reveals the depth of animosity toward those who would bring accusations of this sort.

It is reasonable to ask whether the attitudes directed toward the accusers in Revelation 2 and 3 reflect anti-Jewish sentiments on the part of the author of Revelation and/or those in the communities to whom the letters were addressed. Indeed, those who "say they are Jews but are not" *were* likely to be Jewish people whose actions were condemned and whose Jewish identity itself was questioned on the basis of their purported actions against Jesus-followers in Smyrna. However, the question of the anti-Jewish tenor of these texts is complicated by the fact that the author of Revelation was also likely Jewish,

---

6. Similar claims are made in Acts 17:5–8 and 18:12–17 and variously in Pauline literature. See Jan Lambrecht, "Jewish Slander: A Note on Revelation 2,9–10," *Ephemerides Theologicae Lovanienses* 75 (1999): 421–29.

as were the majority of the communities in Asia Minor to whom Revelation was addressed. Thus, while the rhetoric is clearly anti-Jewish, it can be distinguished functionally—if not formally—from similar rhetoric from *non*-Jewish sectors, for example, Romans, gentile Christians, as well as subsequent anti-Jewish rhetoric from Christians when the demarcations between Jews and Christians became more entrenched, conspicuous, and widespread. Those characterized as members of the "synagogue of Satan" were not so named *because* they were Jewish, or because their actions were somehow inherently Jewish and thereby considered evil. On the contrary, they were characterized so negatively precisely because they failed to live up to the Jewish ideals established by the Jewish author of Revelation. In other words, Revelation claims that they were not Jewish enough! Thus, the attacks in Revelation 2 and 3 cannot be considered a Christian attack upon Jews, or upon Judaism, in terms recognizable from late antique, medieval, and contemporary discourse, but instead early, intra-Jewish discourse about what it meant to be truly Jewish. For this reason, some question the whether the term "anti-Jewish" or "antisemitic" is appropriate at all when characterizing these texts.

This has not prevented subsequent Christian "interpreters" (I use this term very loosely) from ignoring this historical reality altogether and employing the term "synagogue of Satan" as a means of characterizing Jewish people in the worst possible terms. In his famous study of antisemitism, Joshua Trachtenberg cites this phrase as among the most important and prevalent in the early church for promoting anti-Jewish attitudes among early gentile Christians. Indeed, the history of early Christian appropriation of the "synagogue of Satan" was part and parcel of an even larger rhetorical trajectory in which gentile Christians characterized Jewish people as demonic. Gregory of Nyssa claimed they were "advocates of the devil . . . a Sanhedrin of demons" (*Homilies on the Resurrection* 5). John Chrysostom regularly launched attacks of these sorts, claiming that demons dwelt in Jewish synagogues and that Jewish people themselves were demonic (e.g., *Discourses against Judaizing Christians* 1–8). So widespread were these associations by the end of the fourth century that noted Catholic scholar of antisemitism Edward Flannery claimed that mainstream Christians had by then come to think of Jewish people generally as "semi-satanic" figures.[7]

The association of Jewish people and Judaism itself with the devil only intensified in subsequent Christian thought. Building on Trachtenberg's work, Richard Emmerson, Moshe Lazar, and many others demonstrated the preva-

---

7. Edward Flannery, *The Anguish of the Jews* (New York: Macmillan, 1964), 47–65.

lence of such associations in literature, theater, art, and official declarations in Catholic, and then Protestant, traditions. Indeed, Revelation's "synagogue of Satan" was instrumental in setting this trajectory, and it continues to demonstrate a currency in contemporary Christian rhetoric today. For example, the American evangelist Billy Graham used the phrase in a pejorative sense during a private conversation with then-President Richard Nixon in 1973. In recently released White House audio recordings, Nixon can be heard criticizing the "stupid" decision of the Israeli government to shoot down a civilian Libyan airliner and lamenting the possibility that such an act would aggravate already prevalent antisemitic ideologies.[8] In this milieu, Graham claims that the Bible "talks about two kinds of Jews" and then uses the term "synagogue of Satan" to allude to Jewish media executives whom he believed to be responsible for distributing inappropriate media: "They're the ones putting out the pornographic literature. They're the ones putting out these obscene films."

This was not the first conversation with the President in which Graham revealed anti-Jewish sentiments (e.g., in a 1972 conversation with President Nixon, Graham stated his belief that there were a cadre of American Jews who had a "stranglehold" on the United States, and who would take "this country down the drain" unless the stranglehold were "broken"), though this instance is remarkable in that he employed Revelation's "synagogue of Satan" to do so. The conversation thus reveals that Graham and Nixon were engaging in a long-standing Christian interpretive tradition in which the "synagogue of Satan" is employed as a shorthand way of associating Jewish people with demonic forces. In other words, certain behaviors are not only identified as depraved but they are identified as intrinsically *Jewish*; in so doing, Judaism itself is demonized. Moreover, when certain "bad" behaviors are imagined to be intrinsically Jewish, Jewish people themselves tend to be dehumanized. In fact, this very thing happens later in the conversation, when Nixon claims that such (Jewish media executives) "don't deserve to live," and after which Graham wonders aloud whether their "Jewish friends" have a "death wish." In the aftermath of the release of these audio recordings in 2009, Graham was rightly accused of demonstrating precisely the kinds of antisemitic attitudes to which Nixon had previously alluded during their conversation.

The phrase has attained such a currency that it has been appropriated by non-Christians to similar ends. For example, Louis Farrakhan, the national

---

8. Richard M. Nixon (President) and William F. ("Billy") Graham, "Conversation 662–004," 21 February 1973, White House, Washington, DC, audio recording (https://tinyurl.com/umwjudvj).

representative of the Nation of Islam, regularly employs the term to denote Jewish people whom he understands to be responsible for all sorts of the world's problems. In May 2013, Farrakhan told a congregation in Detroit that the "synagogue of Satan" had "mastered civilization now, but they've mastered it in evil."[9] Because Farrakhan appropriated Revelation's "synagogue of Satan" as a shorthand way of associating Jewish people—and their successes, real or imagined—with Satanic forces in the world on his personal Twitter account, Twitter removed his status as a verified user in June 2018.

These examples demonstrate that the "synagogue of Satan" trope served as a vehicle for some Christians and Muslims to demonize Jews and Judaism as terrifying and dangerous. Indeed, through its continued (mis)appropriation, the myth of the demonic Jew persists. It is for this reason that certain translations modified the wording of the text in order to eliminate perceived anti-Jewish connotations. For example, Revelation 2:9 (cf. 3:9) in the American Family Bible, the phrase "those who say they are Jews but are not" is replaced with "them which say they are religious, and are not," with the presumed intent of preventing Christians from demonizing and dehumanizing Jewish people through a misinterpretation of these verses.

A Jewish Antichrist

The demonization of the Jewish people and Judaism itself has also taken shape through the (mis)identification of Revelation's beast from the sea (13:1–10). Characterized as working under the influence of Satan to deceive people to worship itself rather than God and the heavenly Lamb, this creature is identified by his symbolic number 666 (13:18). Many scholars believe they identified a historical figure behind the depiction of the beast through the use of gematria, an ancient system whereby letters in ancient alphabets were assigned numerical values (e.g., the first letter in the alphabet equals 1, the second letter equals 2, and so on) so that people, places, and things could be identified in a veiled way through numerological codes.

When scholars assign numerical values to letters in the Aramaic alphabet (which would have been used by the earliest Christians) according to known gematria systems from the ancient world and then transliterate these letters into Greek (the language of the New Testament), they arrive at the figure of Caesar (emperor) Nero, the letters in whose name adds up precisely to 666.

9. ADL, "Farrakhan: In His Own Words" (20 March 2015) (https://tinyurl.com/3tkx8es4).

The identification and negative characterization of the emperor as a beastly creature under the power of Satan makes sense in light of the general outlook of Revelation as a whole, in which Roman imperial power is deemed responsible for persecuting and even killing Christians.

At any rate, subsequent Christian interpreters associate this figure with a host of characters far removed from the one who was originally intended. Common in early Christian speculation was the blending of this beastly character with the figure of the antichrist, a demonic figure imagined to represent an unholy mirror-image of Christ who would come during a period of tribulation to deceive and assault the people of God. Though the term "antichrist" is never mentioned in Revelation (the *only* uses of "antichrist" in the New Testament are 1 John 2:18, 22; 4:3; 2 John 7), the groundwork for the eventual consolidation between Revelation's beast and the antichrist is evident—for example, like the antichrist, the beast is imagined to appear at the dawn of an eschatological age under the control of Satan.

By the Middle Ages, a fully developed and composite mythology of the antichrist was evident, having incorporated aspects of apocalyptic villains from Daniel, 1–2 John, 2 Thessalonians, and Revelation (not only the beast[s] in Rev 13 but also the "synagogue of Satan" trope discussed above). Consequently, at least in some Christian circles, Revelation's beast and the antichrist had become one and the same. By the medieval period, commentaries on the Apocalypse regularly identify Revelation's beast as the antichrist. If you've heard that the antichrist bears the number 666, then you're a witness to the reality that the amalgamation of Revelation's beast with the antichrist remains prevalent in popular culture today!

Despite clear indications in Revelation that the antichrist would be non-Jewish, Christian commentators nevertheless often and variously insinuate that the antichrist figure is somehow associated with the Jewish people. One longstanding trope claims that the antichrist would be born of Jewish parents, either through natural human intercourse or by means of satanic insemination of a human woman (and thus a parodical inversion of the story of Christ's conception). Inasmuch as certain Jewish circles envisioned the Messiah to arise from the tribe of Dan, so Christian interpreters suggest the genealogy of the antichrist from this tribe. So, too, Christian interpreters presume that the antichrist would hail from a symbolic center of evil, for example, Babylon or Chorazin (cf. "woe to you, Chorazin" in Luke 10:13). In this vein, medieval French and German antichrist plays would depict Jewish prostitutes seducing satanic suitors for the purpose of producing the antichrist.

Coinciding with the Jewish lineage of the antichrist was the notion that he would attain wide support among Jews in order to attain power, a notion substantiated by the presumption that the Jewish people who had rejected the *true* Christ would be most susceptible to follow a false one. Such claims were widely disseminated via dramatizations and artistic visualizations in which Jewish people and institutions were characterized in no uncertain terms as under the influence of the devil. Dramatic and artistic tropes that pitted Christian against Jew are broadly attested, including the widely attested figure *Ecclesia* (the church) and her foil *Synagoga* (the synagogue), through which Jews and Judaism were associated with the devil and demonic forces and adversaries of the church. The ubiquity of these dramatic characterizations of the Jewish antichrist led naturally to the conclusion that Jewish people themselves were satanic and antithetical to Christianity. Consequently, they generated anti-Jewish fervor, as indicated when European cities were forced to take measures to protect Jewish citizens in the aftermath of such performances.

Similarly, visual representations of *Synagoga* were permeated with satanic allusions, for example, accompanied by a goat, her eyes covered by the devil's hand—or the devil's arrow piercing her eyes—and so on. When *Synagoga* is presented in these ways confronting images of Christ, for example, piercing the Lamb or holding a Christian chalice upside-down, the image of *anti*-Christ is unequivocal. Some of the first printed books in German consist of tales of the Jewish antichrist (e.g., the anonymous *Antichrist (Endkrist-)Bildertext*), while German songs were composed as musical adaptations of these narratives (e.g., Michel Beheim's *Von des endicristes Leben*).

While the origins of a Jewish antichrist can be traced to the early church and its flourishing evident in the medieval Christian church, the rhetoric remains evident in various contemporary Christian spheres. For example, the presumption that the antichrist must be Jewish as a corollary of Jesus's Jewish ancestry remains prevalent. Christian evangelist Jerry Falwell was long a proponent of such a notion. Speaking to a large audience of Christians in January 1999 on the topic of the coming millennium, Falwell reiterated his view that the antichrist would be Jewish: "He will be a full-grown counterfeit of Christ. Of course he'll be Jewish. Of course he'll pretend to be Christ." When asked about the anti-Jewish tenor of these comments, Falwell insisted that they were not intended to be (nor were they actually) anti-Jewish but rather a consequence of Jesus's own Jewish identity: "If he [the antichrist]'s going to be the counterfeit of Christ, he has to be Jewish."[10]

Such notions are hardly new but rather part and parcel of a long history of Christian speculation that relies on suspicions about the antichrist rather than

---

10. Associated Press, "Antichrist Is Alive, and a Male Jew, Falwell Contends" (16 January 1999) (https://tinyurl.com/ymvdfke6).

on biblical texts (including those in Revelation) in which the antichrist seems almost certainly *not* to be Jewish. Insofar as the figure of the antichrist tends to reflect society's greatest fears, it should come as no surprise that anti-Jewish sentiments in contemporary society continue to fuel speculation that the antichrist will be Jewish. One sees this not only insofar as the antichrist is imagined to be Jewish but also characterized in terms that reflect other contemporary haunts and fears. For example, in a sermon delivered from the pulpit of his church on the eve of the American invasion of Iraq in 2003, prominent evangelist John Hagee not only claimed that the antichrist would be Jewish on the basis of his (mis)reading of biblical texts but also a "homosexual" with "fierce features" who would make Adolf Hitler "look like a choirboy."[11] Christian broadcaster Rick Wiles makes similar claims, identifying the antichrist as a "homosexual Jew" who will use artificial intelligence and the mechanisms of a "surveillance society" to take over the world.[12] As in earlier Christian speculation on the nature of the antichrist, such speculation moves effortlessly and dangerously from speculation on the Jewish ancestry and/or identity of the antichrist to an association of Judaism itself with demonic forces. Thus, Wiles says of the modern state of Israel: "They will rule the world. The antichrist system will be Israel. That's it. That's what we're up against. That is who is going to come against the body of Christ. That is the seat of Satan."[13]

Monsters in Our Midst

The foregoing discussion reveals that two literary tropes in the book of Revelation—the "synagogue of Satan" and the "beast[-as-antichrist]"—have long been loci of anti-Jewish speculation. But why is this so?—especially when the preponderance of historical evidence suggests that the original (Jewish Christian) author(s) of Revelation did not employ these tropes in order to launch an attack against Jews or Judaism.

In what follows, I propose that anti-Jewish interpretations of these texts are not simply misguided or misinformed approaches to the book of Revelation (though they are indeed both) that are easily remedied with readily available

11. Max Blumenthal, "Pastor Hagee: The Antichrist Is Gay, 'Partially Jewish, As Was Adolph Hitler' (Paging Joe Lieberman!)" (6 December 2017) (https://tinyurl.com/38xjdbw7).

12. Nick Duffy, "Evangelical TV Host Claims the Antichrist Will Be a 'Homosexual Jew'" (29 May 2018) (https://tinyurl.com/26f8thpc).

13. ADL, "TruNews and Rick Wiles: 'End Times' Anti-Semitism and Anti-Zionism" (8 May 2019) (https://tinyurl.com/2s3br38v).

historical-critical antidotes. Rather, these readings reveal more insidious impulses funded by deeply embedded prejudices that cannot easily be overcome. Monster theory provides a framework for investigating how literary motifs like the "beast" and the "synagogue of Satan" function insidiously to incite fear in an audience and how the association of these monstrous characters with historical Jewish figures can be explained—and remedied—as a projection of entrenched anti-Jewish sentiments.

Across cultures, monsters are recognizable by their bizarre and fantastical features. They are often *hybrid* creatures, incorporating disparate characteristics into a single entity, for example, Frankenstein's monster who is a composite being made up of disparate body parts, a Gorgon (like Medusa) who has the body of a woman but snakes for hair, or the computer as in the movie *2001: A Space Odyssey* who takes on (devious) human traits. They are also typically *liminal* creatures insofar as they inhabit spaces simultaneously that are not otherwise accessible to humans, for example, zombies, who inhabit both the world of the dead and that of the living. In each of these ways, monsters break the rules. Because of this, monsters appear unfamiliar and out of place and thus inherently grotesque and terrifying.

Because monsters break the norms and rules of society, they perform a valuable sociological function, providing a roadmap of these societal cultural norms and rules: of what is considered acceptable and what is not, who is deemed in and out, and the precise boundaries thereof. In other words, by illuminating the contours and the limits of a culture and then transgressing these limits, monsters become indicators of what a society deems comfortable as well as society's collective cultural fears and anxieties.

Revelation is replete with monsters who appear and function precisely this way, that is, entities whose hybrid and liminal characteristics render them bizarre and grotesque, terrifying and dangerous.[14] In fact, many figures that are not typically identified as monsters nevertheless fit the definition, for example, angels who travel effortlessly between heaven and earth, locusts who are "invested with strategic abilities, virtual invulnerability, a hankering for human flesh" (9:3–11),[15] and even the representation of the glorified Jesus, who is characterized as a lion (5:5) and a lamb (5:6–14), and the "rider called Faithful and True" (19:11–21) whose earthly death prompted his journey to heavenly enthronement.

---

14. Heather Macumber, *Recovering the Monstrous in Revelation* (New York: Lexington/Fortress, 2021).

15. Sara Ahmed, *Cultural Politics of Emotions* (New York: Routledge, 2004), 50–51.

Likewise, Revelation's monsters function to demonstrate the cultural boundaries of the author(s) who imagined them. For example, the dreadful harlot in Revelation 17 makes drunk and fornicates with those who venture into her sphere, thus highlighting the dangers of cultural accommodation with Rome. Likewise, the destructive beast in Revelation 13 reveals the belief that Rome's political and military apparatus was ruinous to Jewish Christians in Asia Minor in the first century and thus antithetical to the powers of God.

These facets of "monsterification" can help to explain why in many Christian contexts Jewish figures are associated with the monsters in Revelation. Inasmuch as monsters delineate the normative boundaries of a culture, pointing out who fits in and out of a society, the association of Jewish figures with the monsters in Revelation reveals how they are perceived in cultural contexts in which they appear as the monster. Put another way, when Jews are identified as the monsters in Revelation it is because they are identified as outsiders who do not fit normative cultural (religious, political, economic, etc.) standards of the societies who deem them so. Consequently, they are regarded as terrifying, dangerous, and evil. Thus, the process of monsterification reveals as much about the cultures in which such interpretations fester as it does about the objects of monsterification. However, those who become monsters tend to suffer real consequences inasmuch as the vitriol and punishment meted out upon Revelation's literary monsters is transferred to their real human counterparts.

To the extent that interpreters associate Revelation's frightening, unnatural, and ultimately evil monsters with Jewish figures, they participate in a long trajectory of anti-Jewish (mis)interpretation of Revelation with deep roots in certain modes of Christian (and non-Christian) thought. The antidote to this misinterpretation of Revelation may consist of a greater understanding of the historical realities that provided the impetus for Revelation's (non-Jewish) monsters, and of active resistance to the tendency to make monsters out of marginalized members of society—Jewish or otherwise.

Discussion Questions and Activity Suggestions

1. What elements of the Apocalypse appear to be Christian? What elements of the Apocalypse appear to be Jewish? Do any of the Christian and Jewish elements overlap?

2. Why might contemporary Christians fail to recognize the Jewish elements in the Apocalypse? What do contemporary Christians lose with respect

to their understanding of the Apocalypse when they fail to recognize the Jewish elements in the text?

3. How does an understanding and appreciation of the Jewish elements of the Apocalypse challenge presumptions and/or notions of the anti-Jewish character of the text?

4. One of the premises of the preceding discussion is that the Apocalypse was written by a Jewish follower of Jesus to an audience of Jewish followers of Jesus, such that the criticism of "those who say they are Jews but are not" and those in the "synagogue of Satan" cannot simply be understood as a Christian attack upon Judaism but as an intra-Jewish critique of the ways some (non-Christian) Jews were acting toward other (Christian) Jews. One of the ways to appreciate this is by exploring the Jewish dimensions of the Apocalypse:

    a. Read the heavenly throne-room scene in Revelation 4, paying attention to the description of God, the divine throne, those surrounding the throne, and the other accoutrements in the throne room. Compare this scene with those in Isaiah 6, Ezekiel 1, and Daniel 7. Which elements of the heavenly throne room in Revelation 4 appear to draw from these antecedent visions? In what ways does Revelation 4 modify them?

    b. The Songs of the Sabbath Sacrifice are Jewish hymnic fragments found at Qumran.[16] In what ways does the angelic liturgy in Revelation (i.e., 4:8–11; 5:9–13; 7:10–12; 11:15–18; 12:10–12; 15:3–4; 16:5–7; 19:1–8) resemble the angelic liturgy in the Songs of the Sabbath Sacrifice?

5. Write a response to one of the figures identified above (Billy Graham, Richard Nixon, Jerry Falwell, Louis Farrakhan, John Hagee), addressing the anti-Jewish tenor of their comments in light of the ideas presented in the preceding discussion.

Further Reading

Ahmed, Sara. *Cultural Politics of Emotions.* New York: Routledge, 2004.

Carey, Frances, ed. *The Apocalypse and the Shape of Things to Come.* Toronto: University of Toronto Press, 1999.

Carroll, Noel. *The Philosophy of Horror; or, Paradoxes of the Heart.* New York: Routledge, 2003.

16. Carol Newsom, *Songs of the Sabbath Sacrifice: A Critical Edition,* Harvard Semitic Studies 27 (Atlanta: Scholars Press, 1985) (https://tinyurl.com/a565jrc6).

Duff, Paul. "The 'Synagogue of Satan': Crisis Mongering and the Apocalypse of John." Pages 147–68 in *The Reality of Apocalypse: Rhetoric and Politics in the Book of Revelation*. Edited by David L. Barr. Atlanta: SBL Press, 2006.

Emmerson, Richard Kenneth. *Antichrist in the Middle Ages: A Study of Medieval Apocalypticism, Art, and Literature*. Seattle: University of Washington Press, 1981.

Gow, Andrew. "The Antichrist in Medieval and Early Modern Germany." *Medieval Encounters* 2.3 (1996): 249–85.

Hill, C. E. "Antichrist from the Tribe of Dan." *Journal of Theological Studies* 46 (1995): 99–117.

Lambrecht, Jan. "'Synagogues of Satan' (Rev. 2:9 and 3:9): Anti-Judaism in the Book of Revelation." Pages 279–92 in *Anti-Judaism and the Fourth Gospel*. Edited by Reimund Bieringer et al. Louisville: Westminster John Knox, 2001.

Lazar, Moshe. "The Lamb and the Scapegoat: The Dehumanization of Jews in Medieval Propaganda." Pages 38–79 in *Anti-Semitism in Times of Crisis*. Edited by Sander L. Gilman and Steven T. Katz. New York: New York University Press, 1991.

Macumber, Heather. *Recovering the Monstrous in Revelation*. Lanham, MD: Lexington, 2021.

McDonald, William C. "Red Jews and the Antichrist as the Jewish Messiah: Michel Beheim's Endicrist (c. 1455), with a Translation." *Mediaevistik* 28 (2015): 195–215.

O'Hear, Natasha, and Anthony O'Hear. *Picturing the Apocalypse: The Book of Revelation in the Arts over Two Millennia*. Oxford: Oxford University Press, 2015.

Trachtenberg, Joshua. *The Devil and the Jews*. New Haven: Yale University Press, 1943.

32

Epistle of Barnabas

JEREMIAH N. BAILEY

The Epistle of Barnabas is an early Christian theological treatise presented in the form of a letter. While the text itself is anonymous, both manuscript titles and early citations of the text attribute it to Barnabas, a coworker of Paul. According to Acts, Barnabas was a Levite (Acts 4:36) and an instrumental figure in Paul's transition from opposing to supporting the Jesus-followers (9:21–30; 11:22–30). Traditions about Barnabas are comparatively scarce in early Christianity, though some early church figures believed Barnabas was the author of Hebrews (Tertullian, *Modesty* 20.1–5).[1] Clement of Alexandria not only cites the work but cites it as scripture (*Miscellanies* 2.6, 7, 18, 20), and it appears alongside the Shepherd of Hermas at the end of the New Testament in the important fourth-century Bible manuscript Codex Sinaiticus, indicating that for some Christians it remained authoritative for a time.

Since the letter mentions the destruction of the Second Temple by the Romans in the Jewish-Roman War (Barnabas 16:4), an event that occurred in 70, the Epistle of Barnabas must have been composed after this date. This passage also discusses the possible future rebuilding of a temple on the grounds that would not have been possible after Emperor Hadrian banned Jews from Jerusalem and built a temple to Jupiter there in 135.[2] The work, therefore, must have

---

1. See the interesting discussion in Erik A. Boer, "Tertullian on 'Barnabas' Letter to the Hebrews' in *De Pudicitia* 20.1–5," *Vigiliae Christianae* 68 (2014): 243–63.

2. On the debate over which temple is meant and the relevance of that question for the dating of the text, see Anthony Sheppard, "The Letter of Barnabas and the Jerusalem Temple," *Journal for the Study of Judaism* 48 (2017): 531–50; James Carleton Paget, *The Epistle of Barnabas: Outlook and Background*, Wissenschaftliche Untersuchungen zum Neuen Testament 2/64 (Tübingen: Mohr Siebeck, 1994), 9–30, 66–68.

been composed between 70 and 135. Within this range, there are several strong proposals for a more definite date, including potential allusions to events under Emperor Nerva in the late 90s or Emperor Hadrian in the early 130s.

The author offers virtually no clues about their identity in the introduction of the letter, claiming a desire only to share what they have received from the Lord with others upon whom the Spirit has been poured out (1:3). Traditional elements of a letter opening—like a greeting and expression of thanksgiving—are offered, but only in the vaguest of terms. The recipients, for example, are merely described as "sons and daughters," and the author alludes in a general manner to a visit among them and subsequent travel (1:3–4). The letter opening and closing, thus, are thought by many scholars to be artificial elements used as a framing device for a theological treatise. The author downplays overt appeals to authority by claiming that they are writing to this community "not as a teacher but as one of you" (1:8), but also suggests that they are in possession of knowledge about "things present or things to come" that must be spoken in parables (17:2).[3]

The material in Barnabas 18–20 is distinct from what precedes, being an extended discussion on the "way of light" and the "way of darkness." The awkward transition in 17:2–18:1—"So much, then, for these things. But let us move on to another lesson and teaching"—makes clear that the author made somewhat clumsy use of another document. Adaptations of this document, known as the Two Ways, are preserved in both (pre-Christian) Jewish and early Christian texts. The Two Ways offers instruction on the paths of light and darkness and how to know which path one is walking. The argument presented in the first part of Barnabas (2–17) does not flow logically, instead jumping from subject to subject with minimal attempts to connect what comes next to the preceding material.[4] This loose structure and adaptation of previously existing material could indicate that Barnabas is a sort of evolved literature that represents the accumulation of teachings over time that were gathered together and given the form of a letter.[5] Given that the text is first attested in Alexandria and that it consistently makes use of allegorical interpretation that is strongly associated with that city, it is highly likely that the Epistle of Barnabas origi-

---

3. All quotations of Barnabas are from Michael W. Holmes, *The Apostolic Fathers: Greek Texts and English Translations*, 3rd ed. (Grand Rapids: Baker Academic, 2007).

4. An observation shared by many readers of Barnabas. See, for example, Paget, *Barnabas*, 99.

5. Robert A. Kraft, *Barnabas and the Didache*, Apostolic Fathers: A New Translation and Commentary 3 (New York: Nelson, 1965), 1–3.

nated there.[6] It must be concluded, then, that despite the consistency of the attribution of the text to Barnabas in tradition and the authority it retained for several centuries in early Christianity, the association with the Barnabas who worked alongside Paul is clearly fraudulent.

Barnabas as a Student of Jews and Anti-Jewish Polemicist

The Epistle of Barnabas's harsh criticism of Jews is, perhaps, its most famous and defining feature. This is made all the more strange by the virtual absence of appeals to explicitly Christian sources. Barnabas not only adapts the pre-Christian teaching on the Two Ways, but the author shows broad overlap with Jewish reading practices in Alexandria, relies on late Jewish apocalyptic texts, and even shows familiarity with traditions that survive only in rabbinic Jewish texts.[7] Unlike many other Christian authors writing in the late first or early second century, Barnabas shows an almost complete dependence on Jewish material, barely appealing to the sayings of Jesus and making no clear reference to the texts that came to form the New Testament.[8] Since the texts of the Hebrew Bible (in Greek translation) and later Jewish literature form the totality of Barnabas's authoritative material, Barnabas's use of them to paint Christians as the true people of God requires a complex reading strategy.

The most obvious part of this reading strategy is the author's commitment to allegorical interpretation. This method of reading presupposes that the literal elements of a text have an additional nonliteral meaning, one that is often portrayed as more deeply spiritual than the literal one or only accessible to the right kind of readers. So, for example, Barnabas argues that the prohibition against eating pork is really an allegorical instruction not to associate with people who are like pigs, meaning those who live in greed or luxury (10:3).[9]

6. See the discussion in Paget, *Barnabas*, 30–42; Reidar Hvalvik, "The Epistle of Barnabas," in *The Cambridge Companion to the Apostolic Fathers*, ed. Michael F. Bird and Scott D. Harrower (Cambridge: Cambridge University Press, 2021), 270–72; Ferdinand R. Prostmeier, "The Epistle of Barnabas," in *The Apostolic Fathers: An Introduction*, ed. Wilhelm Pratscher, trans. Elizabeth G. Wolfe (Waco, TX: Baylor University Press, 2010), 33.

7. Paget, *Barnabas*, 101–85.

8. Although Barnabas shows some interesting similarities to letters of Paul, establishing a direct link is quite difficult. See, for example, the careful treatment in James Carleton Paget, "Paul and the Epistle of Barnabas," *Novum Testamentum* 38 (1996): 359–81.

9. For a complex and interesting example of this phenomenon related to the hare, see Clare K. Rothschild, "Down the Rabbit Hole with Barnabas: Rewriting Moses in Barnabas 10," *New Testament Studies* 64 (2018): 410–34.

This style of interpretation was common in the ancient world but was notably present in the Jewish community in Alexandria. The Alexandrian Jewish scholar Philo often interpreted texts from the Mosaic law in a similar manner, but what differentiates Barnabas is the rejection of the literal meaning altogether. Thus, while Philo and Barnabas both offer allegorical interpretations of God's command to circumcise male descendants of Abraham, Philo maintains the validity and necessity of the literal practice of circumcision by seeing two valid levels of meaning (*On the Migration of Abraham* 89–93), while Barnabas views Jewish literal interpretation as misunderstanding the divine commands altogether.

In addition to thoroughly allegorizing the Jewish sources he utilizes, Barnabas also presents a highly unusual literal reading of the story of the exodus. Barnabas argues that God really did lead the Israelites out of Egypt and to Mount Sinai where he made a covenant with them, but they lost that covenant almost immediately through their unrighteousness. The book of Exodus describes an incident where Moses is up on the mountain encountering God but is instructed to go down because the people made an image of God in the form of a golden calf. When Moses comes down from the mountain, he smashes the tablets that had been inscribed by God (Exod 32). Barnabas sees this not simply as divine anger but as the exact moment when Israel lost the covenant (Barnabas 4:8). Even before Barnabas, some Jewish writers seem to be aware of the way gentiles might misinterpret this story. For example, the Jewish historian Josephus, writing to an audience he knew would include Romans, omits the story in his retelling of the exodus (*Antiquities* 3.5.7 §§95–99). If this concern was present among Alexandrian Jews in Barnabas's time as well, the choice to focus the attack on this passage of Exodus may be a deliberate attempt to hit his opponents in a sensitive spot.

In any case, Barnabas's interpretation of the Jewish scriptures is atypical in this regard. Most early Christian sources, including those that are overtly anti-Jewish, tend to see the Jewish covenant as valid and complete, but also superseded by the new covenant offered by Jesus. This allows Barnabas to view all the instruction in the Jewish scriptures as directed at the followers of Jesus rather than the ancient Jews who received it, because they had already been rejected by God. Israelite failure to understand the proper allegorical nature of the laws is simply more proof from Barnabas's perspective that they were inappropriately fixated on matters of fleshly existence that overshadowed the true spiritual meaning (10:9). On the other hand, Barnabas's assertion that the Jews lost the covenant at Sinai forces Barnabas into unusual arguments like the absolute denial of Jesus's descent from David (12:8–11).

Although Barnabas only rarely mentions the Holy Spirit directly (1:3), the discourse around true and proper knowledge offered by God to his chosen people permeates the entirety of the letter. True knowledge is required to properly understand the sacred texts, but this true knowledge can come only from God. At the same time, it is Barnabas's allegorical interpretation that proves that it is Christ-followers and not Jews who have the covenant and that makes clear "whether this people or the former people is the heir, and whether the covenant is for us or for them" (13:1). The argument, then, is essentially circular: only we know the right meaning of the text because only we have the covenant, but also anyone who cannot see this is the case from the scriptures must not have proper understanding.

This dynamic is particularly clear in Barnabas's interpretation of circumcision. True circumcision cannot be a matter of something so simple and meaningless as the foreskin, the removal of which is practiced by Syrians, Arabs, and Egyptians as well (9:6). Rather, true circumcision is a circumcision of the ears: "He circumcised our ears in order that when we hear the word we might believe" (9:4). Circumcision of the ears is the result of the transformation achieved when one joins the Christ community, and true wisdom and understanding becomes attainable.[10] This understanding available only to the chosen community is a repeated theme, particularly in places where Jews and Christ-followers are being contrasted (e.g., 2:9; 6:10; 8:7; 10:9).

With competing Jewish readings undermined by the uncircumcised ears of his opponents, Barnabas attacks some of the most common elements of Jewish belief. Not only have the Jews misunderstood circumcision as about flesh, but, indeed, they believe that only because they were fooled by an evil angel (9:4).[11] They cannot understand the sacrifices ordained by Moses, because "they did not listen to the voice of the Lord" (8:7). They misunderstand the dietary restrictions of Moses, because "their fleshly desires" caused them to perceive them as if "they referred to actual food" (10:9). The Sabbath teaching, when properly cross-referenced to the six-day creation event and the observation of Psalm 90:4 that a day is like a thousand years to the Lord, must be understood as an allegorical prediction of Christ's second coming when the earth

---

10. On the interplay between group membership and proper interpretation, see Jason N. Yuh, "Do as I Say, Not as They Do: Social Construction in the Epistle of Barnabas through Canonical Interpretation and Ritual," *Harvard Theological Review* 112 (2019): 273–95; Katja Kujanpää, "Salvaging the Scriptures for Us: The Authoritative Scriptures and Social Identity in the Epistle of Barnabas," *Early Christianity* 11 (2020): 475–95.

11. Probably a reference to the devil. See Isaac T. Soon, "Satan and Circumcision: The Devil as the ἄγγελος πονηρός in Barn 9:4," *Vigiliae Christianae* 76 (2022): 60–72.

reaches six thousand years in age (Barnabas 15:1–5). These allegorical interpretations are supplemented throughout with statements from the prophets
that are critical of the behavior of Israel. Thus, Jeremiah's call to circumcise
the heart (Jer 4:4) becomes a prooftext for Barnabas's circumcision of the ears
(Barnabas 9:1), and Isaiah's critique of hypocritical Sabbath keeping and prediction of an eschatological temple (Isa 1:13; 66:1) are transformed into total
rejections of Sabbath and temple (Barnabas 15:8; 16:2–4). Prophetic rejections
of improper sacrifices, fasting, and prayers (2:4–10; 3:1–6) are likewise taken
as proof that God rejected the Jewish expression of these in totality. Barnabas
thus attacks many of the religious practices and beliefs of Jews most visible to
outsiders: Sabbath keeping, temple worship, dietary restriction, fasting, prayer,
torah observance, and circumcision.

Barnabas and Anti-Jewish Discourse

Barnabas's handling of two common questions in early Christian literature
illustrates more fully how anti-Jewish discourse works in the epistle. The first
question concerns the identity of Abraham's true heirs, a subject addressed in
several New Testament documents. As an extension of the aforementioned
argument that circumcision refers to understanding and not flesh, Barnabas
claims that Abraham himself demonstrated who his true heir would be:

> Learn abundantly, therefore, children of love, about everything: Abraham
> who first instituted circumcision, looked forward in the spirit to Jesus when
> he circumcised, having received the teaching of the three letters. For it says,
> "And Abraham circumcised ten and eight and three hundred men of his
> household." What, then, is the knowledge that was given to him? Observe
> that it mentions the "ten and eight" first, and then after an interval the "three
> hundred." As for the "ten and eight," the I is ten and the H is eight; thus you
> have "Jesus." And because the cross, which is shaped like the T, was destined
> to convey grace, it mentions also the "three hundred." So he reveals Jesus in
> the two letters, and the cross in the other one. The one who placed within
> us the implanted gift of his covenant understands. (Barnabas 9:7–9)

Since Greek did not have separate characters for numbers, it simply used
letters of the alphabet instead and relied on context to make clear that a number was meant. In this case, Barnabas noticed the Greek letters that represent

10 and 8 are the same as the first two letters of Jesus's name in Greek. *T* likewise is used to represent the number 300, and its shape is understood as a reference to the cross. This practice of finding significance in the numerical value of words or seeing numerical values as coded messages is known as gematria and was common in the ancient world. In this passage, we see a typical example of how the dynamics outlined above intersect in the interpretation of Genesis. This allegorical theologizing of numbers was an intentional act on the part of Abraham, who had proper understanding because he preceded the loss of the covenant. Barnabas and his community are able to understand what Abraham intended because the covenant has been implanted in them by the same Spirit, granting them the wisdom to see the true meaning.

Barnabas is arguably most vitriolic when he turns to the question of Jesus's mission. Through a dizzying complex of images from various parts of Isaiah, numerous psalms, Genesis, and Zechariah, Barnabas outlines the necessity of Jesus's fleshly existence in starkly Judeophobic ways. Barnabas sets up the discussion by contrasting Israel's response to the wonderworking of Moses (4:14) and the wonderworking of Jesus (5:7–8). Though Moses performed miracles, they still doubted and thus "they were abandoned" by God (4:14). Barnabas warns his audience not to make the same mistake with Jesus's work, outlining in the process the split purpose of Jesus's death. On the one hand, Jesus's sprinkled blood serves as a means of cleansing his followers of their sins that fulfills Isaiah's prediction that he would be "wounded because of our transgressions" and that "by his wounds we were healed" (Isa 53:5–7). This prophetic prediction of Jesus's death, however, "relates partly to Israel and partly to us" (Barnabas 5:2). The dual fulfillment of Isaiah's prophecy thus occurs through Christ's defeat of death and resurrection (5:5–6) but also in God's rejection of Israel:

> Therefore the Son of God came in the flesh for this reason, so that he might complete the full measure of the sins of those who persecuted his prophets to death. It was for this reason, therefore, that he submitted. For God says that the wounds of his flesh came from them: "When they strike down their own shepherd, then the sheep of the flock will perish." But he himself desired to suffer in this manner, for it was necessary for him to suffer on a tree. For the one who prophesies says concerning him: "Spare my soul from the sword," and "Pierce my flesh with nails, for hands of evil men have risen up against me." (Barnabas 5:11–13)

The same idea is repeated elsewhere in the letter in slightly more explicit form:

And he was made manifest in order that they might fill up the measure of their sins and we might receive the covenant through the Lord Jesus who inherited it, who was prepared for this purpose, in order that by appearing in person and redeeming from darkness our hearts, which had already been paid over to death and given over to the lawlessness of error, he might establish a covenant in us by his word. (Barnabas 14:5)

For Barnabas, then, Jesus's earthly existence fulfills a divine plan to provide not only the means of atonement, the guarantee of resurrection, and the foundation for his return but also to magnify the sins of Israel and make manifest God's selection of a different covenant people.

The reason for Barnabas's harsh rejection of Judaism is a matter of scholarly debate, but the author claims to be writing at least in part "in order that we might not shipwreck ourselves as proselytes to their law" (3:6). It is difficult to say if this means that members of Barnabas's community were actually leaving to become Jewish proselytes or whether this happened with any regularity elsewhere among early Christians, but it is clear that many of Barnabas's anti-Jewish arguments begin to appear in even harsher form in later works from the second and third centuries. Scholars cannot be certain that these later texts borrowed their ideas directly from the Epistle of Barnabas, but similar attacks on circumcision, Sabbath, temple, and the like show that that there is some continuity between this early Judeophobic rhetoric and that of later Christianity.[12]

Discussion Questions and Activity Suggestions

1. Clare Rothschild demonstrates that Barnabas's description of the devil as the "black one" (Barnabas 4:9; 20:1) is interpreted by later readers as showing a connection between the devil and sub-Saharan Africans.[13] In what ways might Barnabas's strategy of making Jews the other resemble this attempt to make Africans the other by means of somatic difference? For those later Christians who accepted Barnabas's Judeophobia and also read him as portraying the devil like an Ethiopian, in what ways do these readings intersect?

12. On the difficult question of the relationship between the Epistle of Barnabas and Justin Martyr, see, for example, Paget, *Barnabas*, 240–44.

13. Clare K. Rothschild, "Ethiopianizing the Devil: ὁ μέλας in Barnabas 4," *New Testament Studies* 65 (2019): 223–45.

2. The author frequently justifies the Epistle of Barnabas's point of view by quoting from texts where Israelites are criticizing or attempting to reform the practices of other Israelites and ignoring that this is intra-Israelite discussion. Can you think of other examples from the Bible, history, or even the present day where internal criticism is exploited by external critics? What are the problems with this kind of argument?

3. In the ancient world, religious and ethnic identity were often not distinguished the way they sometimes are today.[14] Some scholars propose that the Epistle of Barnabas's arguments can be more easily understood in ancient context as an attempt to "promote a stable and homogenous Christian ethnic identity."[15] Based on the examples discussed above or on your own reading of the text, what strategies does Barnabas use to accomplish this identity building? How does this constructed identity relate to the ethnic/religious identity of Jews? How does Barnabas's strategy compare to Paul's attempts to expand his own identity to include gentiles?

4. In Barnabas 13:1–7, the author proposes an allegorical interpretation of two sets of brothers, Jacob and Esau and Ephraim and Manasseh, meant to demonstrate the superiority of the followers of Christ to Jews. In Galatians 4, Paul also offers an allegory about two brothers, Isaac and Ishmael, by talking about what their mothers, Sarah and Hagar respectively, represent. Read Barnabas 13:1–7 and trace the logic presented by the argument. Then, read Galatians 4:21–31 and do the same. In what ways are these allegories similar and in what ways are they different? Are these texts making the same claim, a similar claim, or a different claim? If we presume that Barnabas is a gentile Jesus-follower and note that Paul is a Jewish follower of Jesus, should or does that difference in identity make any difference in how we read their respective arguments?

Further Reading

Hvalvik, Reidar. "The Epistle of Barnabas." Pages 268–89 in *The Cambridge Companion to the Apostolic Fathers*. Edited by Michael F. Bird and Scott D. Harrower. Cambridge: Cambridge University Press, 2021.

---

14. The concept of ethnicity could even extend to the gods themselves. See Paula Fredriksen, "How Jewish Is God? Divine Ethnicity in Paul's Theology," *Journal of Biblical Literature* 137 (2018): 193–212.

15. Michael Kok, "The True Covenant People: Ethnic Reasoning in the Epistle of Barnabas," *Studies in Religion* 40 (2011): 93.

Kujanpää, Katja. "Salvaging the Scriptures for Us: The Authoritative Scriptures and Social Identity in the Epistle of Barnabas." *Early Christianity* 11 (2020): 475–95.

Paget, James Carleton. *The Epistle of Barnabas: Outlook and Background.* Wissenschaftliche Untersuchungen zum Neuen Testament 2/64. Tübingen: Mohr Siebeck, 1994.

Soon, Isaac T. "Satan and Circumcision: The Devil as the ἄγγελος πονηρός in Barn 9:4." *Vigiliae Christianae* 76 (2022): 60–72.

33

Martyrdom of Polycarp

DAVID L. EASTMAN

S poradic persecution of Christians was a feature of life in the Roman Empire in the second century. Christians were not systematically persecuted
everywhere at all times, yet the sources—both Christian and non-Christian—
confirm that Christians sometimes ran into trouble with local authorities. Perhaps it was the unpredictable nature of these short bursts of persecution that
contributed to a general sense of anxiety in some Christian sources. According
to a letter from the church in Smyrna, a city in the western part of Asia Minor
(modern Izmir, Turkey), to the church in Philomelium, one such persecution
broke out in their city in the middle of the second century. This letter, authored
by a certain Marcion, focuses on the fate of the city's bishop and is therefore
traditionally identified as the Martyrdom of Polycarp.[1]

The letter opens with a summary of the various trials that the church in
Smyrna had been facing. The author describes the fate of Christians who are
torn apart by whips, exposed to the flames, or thrown to the wild beasts. The
ultimate cause of these persecutions is not the government officials but the
devil. Most Christians endure these torments without complaint, for they are
following the model of Jesus Christ and have their eyes set on their heavenly reward. The text also relates the cautionary tale of a certain Quintus,
who rushes forward to offer himself for martyrdom but ultimately fails in the
moment of trial. Therefore, the text is seeking to teach proper and improper
responses to persecution.

---

1. The most recent edition is Paul Hartog, *Polycarp's Epistle to the Philippians and the
Martyrdom of Polycarp: Introduction, Text, and Commentary* (Oxford: Oxford University
Press, 2013). Translations in this essay are taken from this edition unless otherwise noted.

The shedding of Christian blood does not satisfy the mob of the city, and eventually they demand the death of the bishop, Polycarp. The aged bishop hears that some soldiers are looking to arrest him, so he flees from country house to country house. At last he resigns himself to his fate and willingly surrenders to the authorities.

The text recounts Polycarp's trial and the attempts by government officials to convince the bishop to denounce his faith in order to save his life. The trial takes place in the stadium, an unusual but not unlikely scenario in that period.[2] As Polycarp enters the arena, a heavenly voice charges him: "Be strong, Polycarp, and act like a man." A lively exchange between the bishop and various government officials then takes place. They try to convince him to sacrifice in honor of the emperor, because they seemingly have little interest in executing an eighty-six-year-old man as a public spectacle. They ask him to curse the "atheists," by which they mean Christians, who will not worship the traditional Roman gods. Polycarp responds that they, the Romans, are the true atheists.

A number of the literary elements of the text create a parallel between the death of Jesus and that of Polycarp. Polycarp in some ways is walking in the footsteps of Jesus, as demonstrated by these two examples. (1) The proconsul in Smyrna is named Herod. According to the Gospel of Luke, after Jesus is initially found not guilty by Pontius Pilate, he is sent away for trial to Herod Antipas (Herod the Tetrarch), who had jurisdiction over Jesus's home region of Galilee (Luke 23:1–15). (2) In both the gospels and the Martyrdom of Polycarp, the authors ascribe significant blame to Jewish antagonists who are lurking behind the events described but do not actually carry out the unjust punishments.[3]

The wild beasts have retired for the day, so Polycarp is sentenced to death by fire. An eager crowd, which includes "the Jews," quickly gathers wood to burn the bishop. When the fire does not consume him, a soldier is sent with

---

2. Leonard L. Thompson, "The Martyrdom of Polycarp: Death in the Roman Games," *Journal of Religion* 82.1 (2002): 35–37.

3. For more on the Jesus-Polycarp parallels, see Judith Lieu, "Accusations of Jewish Persecution in Early Christian Sources," in *Tolerance and Intolerance in Early Judaism and Christianity*, ed. Graham N. Stanton and Guy G. Stroumsa (Cambridge: Cambridge University Press, 1998), 288–91; Lieu, *Image and Reality: The Jews in the World of the Christians in the Second Century* (London: T&T Clark, 1996), 64; Candida R. Moss, *The Other Christs: Imitating Jesus in Ancient Christian Ideologies of Martyrdom* (Oxford: Oxford University Press, 2010), esp. 46–47, 56–59.

a dagger to end his life. At that moment "the Jews" enter the story again—although they are truly being controlled by the devil—this time trying to prevent the Christians from collecting the body of Polycarp. The body is burned, and the Christians are finally allowed to gather his bones. The letter states that the church in Smyrna continues to celebrate his "birthday," which in early Christian usage refers to his date of martyrdom, in order to honor him and prepare others for their own possible future dates with persecution and death.

The text ends with final greetings and repetition of praise for Polycarp as a martyr.

The author of the text says that "the Jews" were active, eager participants in the story of the death of Polycarp. Once Polycarp is in the stadium, "the Jews" suddenly appear in the crowd alongside the "godless" pagans, calling for Polycarp's death because he is "the teacher of impiety, the father of the Christians, the destroyer of our gods, the one teaching many neither to sacrifice nor to worship" (Martyrdom of Polycarp 12.2). Later, when it comes time to gather wood for the pyre, "the Jews" are enthusiastic participants, which the text indicates was "their custom." The author therefore paints a picture of "the Jews" as regular and motivated agents in the persecution and death of Christians.

Some scholars point out, however, that this characterization of "the Jews" is rare in early Christianity, even in martyr texts. Jewish villains are virtually absent in martyr accounts.[4] This suggests that one possible stream of Judeophobia—"the Jews" keep killing Christians just as they killed the prophets and Christ—was not popular among the authors of martyrdom accounts. This does not mean that this sentiment was unknown among early Christians, however. Tertullian, writing in North Africa near the beginning of the third century, alleges that the "synagogues of the Jews are the sources ('fountainheads') of persecution" (*Antidote for the Scorpion's Sting* 10.90). Nevertheless, the authors of Christian martyrdom accounts did not follow Tertullian's lead. Christians in martyr texts die at the order of Roman or Persian officials, sometimes ultimately by the work of the devil, and almost never by the actions of Jewish figures.[5]

---

4. Paula Fredriksen and Oded Irshai, "Christian Anti-Judaism: Polemics and Policies," in *The Cambridge History of Judaism*, ed. Steven T. Katz (Cambridge: Cambridge University Press, 2006), 4:995; Lieu, "Accusations," 279–80.

5. Many scholars argue that, in fact, early Christian martyrdom traditions drew extensively from Jewish models, particularly 2 and 4 Maccabees. See, e.g., Marcel Simon, "Les Saints d'Israël dans la dévotion de l'Eglise ancienne," *Revue d'Histoire et de Philoso-*

Tertullian's accusation found new life in the twentieth century with the work of German historian Adolf von Harnack. Harnack's vision of history was a master narrative that linked earliest Christianity with German Protestant liberalism. One of the primary antagonists in his story were Jews, who, according to this telling, from the beginnings of Christianity resented and violently worked against the inclusion of gentiles. Harnack traces this antagonism from the days of Jesus and Paul through the earliest centuries:

> The hostility of the Jews appears on every page of Acts, from chap. xii. on-wards, and it can be traced by the aid even of the evangelic narratives, whose sources go back to the period preceding A. D. 65. The Jews . . . hampered every step of Paul's work among the Gentiles; they cursed Christians and Christ in their synagogues; they stirred up the masses and the authorities in every country against him; systematically and officially they scattered broadcast horrible charges against the Christians, which played an important part in the persecutions as early as the reign of Trajan . . . unless the evidence is misleading, they instigated the Neronic outburst against the Christians; and as a rule, whenever bloody persecutions are afoot in later days, the Jews are either in the background or the foreground.[6]

Although Harnack does not cite the Martyrdom of Polycarp in this context, he comments elsewhere in the same work that "the significance of the Jewish

---

phie Religieuses 34 (1954): 98–127; Margaret Schatkin, "The Maccabean Martyrs," *Vigiliae Christianae* 28 (1974): 97–113; Daniel Boyarin, *Dying for God: Martyrdom and the Making of Christianity and Judaism* (Stanford: Stanford University Press: 1999); David L. Eastman, "Early Christian Martyr Cults," in *The Wiley Blackwell Companion to Christian Martyrdom*, ed. Paul Middleton (Chichester: Wiley Blackwell, 2020), 217–35. On Polycarp specifically, see Gerd Buschmann, *Martyrium Polycarpi—Eine formkritische Studie: Ein Beitrag zur Frage nach der Entstehung der Gattung Märtyrerakte* (Berlin: de Gruyter, 1994).

6. Adolf von Harnack, *The Mission and Expansion of Christianity in the First Three Centuries*, trans. James Moffatt (London: Williams & Norgate, 1904), 1:65–66. For additional studies of the influence of Harnack's antisemitic attitudes on his scholarship, see, e.g., Olivia Stewart Lester, "The Sibylline Oracles: A Case Study in Ancient and Modern Anti-Judaism," in *Protestant Bible Scholarship: Antisemitism, Philosemitism, and Anti-Judaism*, ed. Arjen F. Bakker et al., Supplements to the Journal for the Study of Judaism 200 (Leiden: Brill, 2022), 125–48; Dan Jaffé, "Jesus in the Jewish World of His Time: Reflections on Adolf von Harnack's *Essence of Christianity*," *Études théologiques et religieuses* 92.3 (2017): 587–607; Jean Zumstein, "Le problème de l'antijudaïsme en exégèse du Nouveau Testament à l'exemple d'Adolf von Harnack," *Études théologiques et religieuses* 92.3 (2017): 609–18; Joseph B. Tyson, "Anti-Judaism in the Critical Study of the Gospels," in *Anti-Judaism and the Gospels*, ed. William R. Farmer (Harrisburg, PA: Trinity Press, 1999), 216–51.

element in Smyrna comes out conspicuously in the martyrdom of Polycarp."[7] The death of the bishop certainly falls into the category of "bloody persecutions," and Harnack reads the Martyrdom of Polycarp as placing "the Jewish element of Smyrna" in the "foreground" of the story.

Historical events are always complex, so one is wise to be careful when suggesting direct historical connections. However, it is worth noting that Harnack's presentation of "the Jews" and "the Jewish element" as being antagonistic to Christianity contributed to the intellectual and ecclesiastical context of Germany at the beginning of the twentieth century, a context that later proved fatally hostile to many Jews living there. To be clear, I am not ascribing to Harnack direct responsibility for the events of the Holocaust. Nonetheless, his implicit and explicit anti-Jewish readings of biblical texts and early Christian history served the propaganda that fueled and masqueraded as justification for Nazi antisemitism.[8]

In the middle of the twentieth century, W. H. C. Frend published a book on persecution that shaped much of the scholarly conversation for the half century that followed. He echoes Harnack's instinct: "In the persecutions which were to wrack Asia in the reign of Marcus Aurelius the Jew was often in the background. For nearly another century he continued to stir up trouble wherever he could."[9] Polycarp's story does not appear in this context, but Frend may have this martyrdom in mind. Smyrna was in Asia (Asia Minor), and Marcus Aurelius reigned as emperor in 161–180. The events described in the Martyrdom of Polycarp may fall within that period. While the date of the text remains a source of debate, most scholars agree that the events described occurred sometime between 155 and 168[10] and therefore perhaps within the reign of Marcus Aurelius.

In any event, Frend places responsibility for persecutions on "the Jew." He does not have any particular "Jew" in mind, nor does he blame "the Jews" of antiquity. Instead, his rhetoric is more expansive and potentially dangerous;

---

7. Harnack, *Mission and Expansion*, 3n1.

8. Many other scholars explore these connections; e.g., Eliza McClenagan, "From Replacement to Elimination: Developments in Anti-Jewish Protestant Theology and the Holocaust," *Verges: Germanic and Slavic Studies in Review* 3.1 (2020); Ryan Buesnel, "Adolf Harnack and the Deutsche Christen: A Warning from History," paper presented at "Things That Make for Peace: Sacred Texts and Religious Traditions in a Transforming World" (Sydney, 2018).

9. W. H. C. Frend, *Martyrdom and Persecution in the Early Church: A Study of Conflict from the Maccabees to Donatus* (Oxford: Blackwell, 1965), 259.

10. Hartog, *Martyrdom of Polycarp*, 191–200.

he refers to "the Jew," which could refer to any Jewish person in any context and in any period.

Contemporary scholarly readings of the Martyrdom of Polycarp do not take the literary descriptions of "the Jews" as literally as others have in the past. Close readers of the text understand that while tensions between Christians and Jews in Smyrna may have been a historical reality, "the Jews" as characters in the text serve rhetorical and polemical functions rather than simply historical ones.

Discussion Questions and Activity Suggestions

1. Judith Lieu points out that during the initial discussion of the persecution in Smyrna, no mention is made of the presence of Jews.[11] They appear only when the narrative focus shifts to Polycarp, and then they are found in the arena crying out alongside a pagan mob. What is the impact of placing "the Jews" and pagans on one side of this dispute and Polycarp (and by extension Christians) on the other side?

2. Paula Fredriksen and Oded Irshai highlight numerous passages in early Christian literature in which early Christian leaders complain of relations between Jews and Christians being *too close*: "These sources speak regularly of Christians' frequenting synagogues, keeping Sabbath or feast days with Jewish friends, soliciting Jewish blessings, betrothing their children to Jews, or indeed, marrying Jews themselves."[12] If we read the Martyrdom of Polycarp through that lens, how might it impact our understanding of the author's goals in presenting "the Jews" as an enemy?

3. The story of Polycarp has many parallels to the accounts of Jesus's death in the gospels. If the author was committed to presenting Polycarp as a Christlike figure, would there be any way to tell Polycarp's story without accusing "the Jews" of playing a role? Or does comparing Polycarp to Jesus require such accusations?

4. To focus our attention on the appearance of "the Jews" at the moment of Polycarp's death, read the Martyrdom of Polycarp 17–18 carefully with the following questions in mind: What specific concerns do "the Jews" have in this passage? And would those concerns make sense for members of a

11. Lieu, "Accusations," 285–87.
12. Fredriksen and Irshai, "Christian Anti-Judaism," 997.

Jewish community of Smyrna? Write down specific passages and thoughts related to these questions. Now consider this passage within the broader context of early usage of "the Jews" in texts produced by followers of Jesus. For example, in the Fourth Gospel, traditionally known as the Gospel of John, the author frequently criticizes "the Jews." However, we know that the author cannot mean *all Jews*, because according to the earliest Christian tradition the author of the text is himself from the Jewish tradition. And even if we doubt this tradition of authorship, it is still true that all of the closest followers of Jesus were Jewish, including his twelve disciples and the group of women who followed and supported him (perhaps even financially). Therefore, when the author of the gospel uses "the Jews," he seems to be using this expression to mean "other Jews who disagree with our perspective on Jesus." Along similar lines, several scholars suggest that "the Jews" of the Martyrdom of Polycarp also stand in for Christian theological rivals.[13] In this case, they suggest that the rivals are other Christians who have different perspectives on the veneration of holy people and their bodily relics. From this reading, "the Jews" could be a literary substitute for "other Christians who we think are wrong." With this in mind, reread this passage about the end of Polycarp's life. If we consider "the Jews" as literary characters standing in for Christian theological rivals, how might this impact our interpretation of the passage?

Further Reading

Fredriksen, Paula, and Oded Irshai. "Christian Anti-Judaism: Polemics and Policies." Volume 4/pages 977–1034 in *The Cambridge History of Judaism*. Edited by Steven T. Katz. Cambridge: Cambridge University Press, 2006.

Gibson, E. Leigh. "The Jews and Christians in the Martyrdom of Polycarp: Entangled or Parted Ways?" Pages 145–58 in *The Ways That Never Parted: Jews and Christians in Late Antiquity and the Early Middle Ages*. Edited by Adam H. Becker and Annette Yoshiko Reed. Minneapolis: Fortress, 2007.

Lieu, Judith. "Accusations of Jewish Persecution in Early Christian Sources." Pages

---

13. Lieu, *Image and Reality*, 66–67; Thompson, "Martyrdom of Polycarp," 50; Serge Ruzer, "Reasonable Doubts of the 'Other': Jewish Scepticism in Early Christian Sources," in *Expressions of Sceptical Topoi in (Late) Antique Judaism*, ed. Reuven Kiperwasser and Geoffrey Herman, Studies and Texts in Scepticism 12 (Berlin: de Gruyter, 2021), 69–84.

279–95 in *Tolerance and Intolerance in Early Judaism and Christianity*. Edited by Graham N. Stanton and Guy G. Stroumsa. Cambridge: Cambridge University Press, 1998.

———. *Image and Reality: The Jews in the World of the Christians in the Second Century* (esp. pages 57–102). London: T&T Clark, 1996.

Ruzer, Serge. "Reasonable Doubts of the 'Other': Jewish Scepticism in Early Christian Sources." Pages 69–84 in *Expressions of Sceptical Topoi in (Late) Antique Judaism*. Edited by Reuven Kiperwasser and Geoffrey Herman. Studies and Texts in Scepticism 12. Berlin: de Gruyter, 2021.

34

Gospel of Peter

SHAILY SHASHIKANT PATEL

The Gospel of Peter is an apocryphal gospel, meaning it does not appear in the New Testament. The text offers a brief depiction of Jesus's trial, crucifixion, and resurrection. Though incomplete, the Gospel of Peter is rich in terms of illuminating a variety of Christian beliefs in the postapostolic period.[1] It is also striking for its Judeophobia, which is heightened in comparison to the Synoptic Gospels of Matthew, Mark, and Luke.[2] Intensified Judeophobia was characteristic of many Christian texts from the second century onward. In the Gospel of Peter, Jews are blamed for Christ's crucifixion—a Judeophobic ideology that lingers still.[3] Additionally, this text describes the destruction of the Jerusalem temple as God's punishment meted out against the Jewish people for their role in Jesus's death. These two ideas of Jewish blame for Jesus's death

---

1. Among them include a variety of Christian theology called "docetism," the beginning of the "harrowing of hell" traditions, and the nature of Jesus's resurrected body. These issues will not be discussed here. For an accessible introduction, see Bart D. Ehrman and Zlatko Pleše, *The Apocryphal Gospels: Texts and Translations* (New York: Oxford University Press, 2011), 371–77.

2. I use the term "Judeophobia" here to describe language deployed against Jewish people in the text. For an explanation of this terminology, see Sarah E. Rollens, Eric Vanden Eykel, and Meredith J. C. Warren, "Confronting Judeophobia in the Classroom," *Journal for Interdisciplinary Biblical Studies* 2.1 (2020): 81–106.

3. Joel Marcus argues that the Gospel of Peter is both Judeophobic and Judeophilic. This ambiguity with respect to Judaism is characteristic of other "Jewish Christian" texts. See Marcus's "The Gospel of Peter as a Jewish Christian Document," *New Testament Studies* 64.4 (2018): 473–94. Given the scope of this volume, I focus exclusively on Judeophobia, but we must be careful not to assume coherence within our texts. Texts, like the people who write them, can be inconsistent.

and God's righteous anger at the Jewish people have had devastating historical consequences.

The Gospel of Peter was discovered in the late 1880s in a manuscript of four texts buried with a Christian monk at Akhmîm, Egypt. The manuscript itself is not fragmentary or damaged, but the texts in it are incomplete. For example, the Gospel of Peter begins midsentence with the legendary story of Pontius Pilate washing his hands (1). Likewise, it ends midsentence as Simon Peter sets off on his apostolic mission after Christ's resurrection (60).[4] This suggests that the scribe who copied the Akhmîm manuscript was working from an incomplete original.

The author claims to be Simon Peter (60), but this cannot be the case. The Gospel of Peter bears heavy resemblances to the synoptic passion stories even though it does not have verbatim agreements with these accounts.[5] Probably, our unknown author composed the gospel from early oral traditions.[6] Most scholars offer a late-second-century date based on the church father Eusebius's mention of a "Gospel of Peter" in use around Syria near the end of the second century.[7] This date is not firm, though; it rests on the accuracy of Eusebius's own dating and whether our Gospel of Peter is the same Gospel of Peter used by the Syriac Christians he describes.[8] Nevertheless, the heightened Judeophobia within the text is quite at home among Christian texts of the second and third centuries, lending support to scholars' proposed date.

Judeophobia in the Gospel of Peter

Reading the Gospel of Peter is much like hearing the synoptic passion narratives secondhand. While the larger story remains intact, many of the details

4. There are two numbering systems used for the Gospel of Peter; I use that of J. A. Robinson, "The Gospel according to Peter," in *The Gospel according to Peter and the Revelation of Peter*, ed. J. A. Robinson and M. R. James (London: Clay, 1982), 13–33.

5. The Synoptic Gospels are the canonical gospels of Mark, Matthew, and Luke, so called because they share sources and therefore can be "seen together" (hence: *syn-* meaning "together," and *-optic* having to do with seeing).

6. Ehrman and Pleše, *Apocryphal Gospels*, 375.

7. Eusebius, *Ecclesiastical History* 3.3.2; 3.25.6; 6.12. See the discussion in Ehrman and Pleše, *Apocryphal Gospels*, 371–72, 374–75.

8. The problems of relying on Eusebius for dating are discussed in Pablo M. Edo, "Citing or Doctoring the Sources? Serapion and the *Gospel of Peter* in Eusebius's *Historia Eccelsiastica*," in *Beginning and End: From Ammianus Marcellinus to Eusebius of Caesarea*, ed. Álvaro Sánchez-Ostiz (Huelva: Universidad de Huelva Press, 2016), 107–22.

have changed. These small shifts open a window onto the text's Judeophobia and are therefore worth considering in detail. Take, for instance, the very first verses (1–2): the famous story of Pontius Pilate washing his hands. This story is also found in Matthew 27:24. In Matthew's version, Pilate washes his hands and says: "I am innocent of the blood of this man" after the Jewish crowds demand Jesus be put to death. And although Pilate warns the crowd that they bear responsibility (27:24), *he* is the one who gives the order for Jesus to be crucified (27:26). In contrast, the Gospel of Peter has Herod give the order for Jesus's death (2): "Then King Herod called for the Lord to be taken away, and he said to them, "Do that which I ordered you to do [to him]."[9]

Herod, or Herod Antipas, was Rome's appointed tetrarch for the region of Galilee.[10] He is sometimes referred to as "King Herod" in the New Testament and other Christian texts, but he was a client ruler for the Roman Empire.[11] Herod may have had some autonomy in the administration of Galilee, but it is unlikely that he ordered Jesus's death, simply because crucifixion was a characteristically Roman form of execution. The Roman Empire regularly crucified criminals like insurrectionists in order to make examples of them. Here, the Jewish Herod orders Jesus's execution instead of the Roman Pilate, implicating Jews, not Romans, in Jesus's death. Similar ideas of Jews bearing responsibility for Jesus's crucifixion appear in earlier Christian texts, too (e.g., 1 Thess 2:14–15; John 19:14–16; Acts 2:22–23). Yet the Gospel of Peter takes great pains to repeatedly remind its audience how the Jewish people and *only* the Jewish people bear the full blame for this tragedy.

9. All translations of the Gospel of Peter are my own, based on the Greek in Ehrman and Pleše, *Apocryphal Gospels*, 378–87.

10. For more information on Herod, see Morten Hørning Jensen, *Herod Antipas in Galilee: The Literary and Archaeological Sources on the Reign of Herod Antipas and Its Socio-economic Impact on Galilee*, Wissenschaftliche Untersuchungen zum Neuen Testament 2/215 (Tübingen: Mohr Siebeck, 2006).

11. Several figures named "Herod" appear in the New Testament. They are members of the Herodian dynasty, a family of client-rulers who administered the territory in and around Judea on behalf of Rome. The Herod deemed responsible for the "slaughter of the innocents" in Matt 2:16–18 is Herod the Great, who was made king of Judea by the Roman Senate in 40 BCE. Herod Antipas, one of Herod the Great's sons, features prominently in the passion narrative. Herod Antipas orders the execution of John the Baptist (Mark 6:27), wishes fervently to execute Jesus (Luke 13:31–32), and is the man to whom Pontius Pilate sends Jesus for trial (23:6–12). Herod Agrippa, son of Herod Antipas, reportedly imprisons Peter (Acts 12:1–19) and executes James (12:2). For more information on the many Herods of the New Testament, see Nikos Kokkinos, *Herodian Dynasty: Origins, Role in Society, and Eclipse*, Journal for the Study of the Pseudepigrapha Series 26 (Sheffield: Sheffield Academic, 1998).

Other verses contribute to this Judeophobic theme. The Gospel of Peter 4–9 mirrors the New Testament story of Jesus's humiliation at the hands of Roman soldiers.[12] In our text, however, Jesus's tormentors are Jewish. The author is explicit: Herod "handed Jesus over to the people on the day before their Feast of Unleavened Bread" (5). These "people" were to crucify and bury Jesus before the Sabbath (5). Bizarrely, *Pontius Pilate* asks Herod for Jesus's body, subordinating the Roman administrator to a client-king of the Roman Empire. This minute detail is especially jarring since Pilate was notoriously violent, even by Roman standards.[13] And so, in the Gospel of Peter's retelling, it is Herod's men who drag Jesus around, dress him in purple, mockingly call him the "King of Israel," give him the crown of thorns, and physically abuse him (6–9).

A careful reader will note how the Gospel of Peter leverages every opportunity to tell its audience that Jesus's enemies are Jewish. The text refers to Jesus's executors with stereotypical markers of Jewish identity like the Feast of Unleavened Bread mentioned above or "their Scripture" (15). When Jesus dies, the Gospel of Peter says those who crucified him "fulfilled everything and completed every sin upon their own heads" (17). The language of sin is critically important for understanding Judeophobia in the text. According to this author, the Jewish people did not crucify Jesus out of misunderstanding or fear of Roman aggression against them; rather, Jesus's crucifixion is classified as a sin. In other words, it is a transgression against God.

Because they committed such a grave sin, the Gospel of Peter insists the Jewish people will face God's judgment. Shortly after Jesus's body is given to Joseph of Arimathea for burial, our author writes: "Then the Jews, the elders, and the priests knew how much evil they had brought upon themselves. They began beating their breasts, saying: 'Woe to us sinners. The judgment and the end of Jerusalem are near'" (25). This one verse encapsulates the bulk of the Gospel of Peter's Judeophobic agenda. And here too, the author's design lies in how the story is told when compared with earlier texts. The Gospel of Peter blames "the Jews" as a whole group, alongside their elders and priests. This is a departure from the Synoptic Gospels, where Jesus's enemies are certain groups of Jews and Jewish leaders as opposed to the whole of the Jewish people.[14] In

---

12. Matt 27:27–31; Mark 15:16–20; John 19:1–16. Luke's Gospel mentions that Herod's men (as opposed to Pilate's) clothed Jesus in shining garb and mocked him (23:11), but this is a brief gloss. In contrast to Luke, the mockery Jesus faces in the Gospel of Peter 4–9 is modeled after the more involved accounts of Jesus's treatment by Roman soldiers.

13. For more information, see Helen K. Bond, *Pontius Pilate in History and Interpretation* (Cambridge: Cambridge University Press, 1998).

14. A possible exception is Matthew's Gospel, where the Jewish crowd, roused by "chief

essence, our author makes a distinction between its own version of Christianity and a version of Judaism that bears the blame for Jesus's crucifixion. Such a distinction moves beyond inter-group antagonism and makes *all* Jewish people enemies of believers in Christ. The Gospel of Peter 25 further implies that Jewish people *knowingly* transgressed, since they call themselves "sinners" and lament the evil they have wrought. In the Gospel of Peter, Jews are characterized as bloodthirsty hypocrites who cannot see or follow the wishes of their own God. Their condemnation of Jesus causes God to condemn them.

Finally, this short verse lays out an idea that would become commonplace in subsequent Christian literature, namely that the Jerusalem temple was destroyed as divine punishment for Jesus's death. In the Gospel of Peter 25, the Jewish people know the "judgment and end of Jerusalem is near." Later, we are told they witnessed signs when Jesus died, leading them to believe he was divine (29). This text was written after the Romans destroyed the Jewish temple in 70. Yet here, our author clearly attempts to spin the story of the temple's destruction, ironically blaming the Jewish people for an injustice committed *against Jews* by the Romans.

The Gospel of Peter's Continuing Judeophobic Influence

This short survey of the Judeophobia in the Gospel of Peter only scratches the surface of a notion that only grew more virulent with time. Indeed, in later Christian traditions, Pontius Pilate and Rome are exonerated, with Pilate becoming something of a hero in the "Pilate Cycle," a group of texts dating from around the fourth century, well into the Middle Ages. These texts depict the passion from a perspective sympathetic to Pilate and Rome. While Pilate is absolved, however, more of the blame is apportioned to Jews. Like the Gospel of Peter, the Pilate Cycle is apocryphal. But "apocryphal" hardly means without influence. The geographical and temporal range of these texts alone suggests an uneasy fact: Christians accepted and spread the pernicious lie that Jews, not Romans, were responsible for Jesus's death and consequently deserved divine punishment.

The legacy of this Judeophobic narrative remains with us today. In 2020, the Anti-Defamation League found that 27% of US residents believe "Jews

---

priests and elders" (27:20), insists that Jesus's blood "be on [their] heads and the heads of [their] children" (27:25). Matthew's text assigns blame to *all* Jewish people in perpetuity, despite the crowd being persuaded by certain group leaders.

killed Jesus."[15] Such beliefs do not occur in historical or cultural isolation; they result from the repetition and solidification of stridently Judeophobic rhetoric stretching over two thousand years. Beliefs are not *deployed* in isolation, either; they cause real-world harm. In 2021, the Anti-Defamation League recorded the highest rate of antisemitic incidents since the organization began tracking such occurrences in 1979.[16] Hate crimes against Jewish people are rising precipitously, fueled in part by historical conspiracy theories like those found in our text. If we would destroy these dangerous and inaccurate notions of Jewish culpability for Jesus's death, we should begin with early texts like the Gospel of Peter. By showing how ancient Christians rewrote history in a Judeophobic mold, we can interrupt centuries-long processes of mistaking these writers' Judeophobic rhetoric for historical truth. Only then might we dismantle modern misconceptions that lead to anti-Jewish violence.

Discussion Questions and Activity Suggestions

1. The Gospel of Peter is an apocryphal text, meaning it is not in the New Testament. Despite this, can you think of reasons this text ought to be studied alongside our canonical gospels? What does it tell you about how Christianity developed in the first several hundred years?

2. If the Gospel of Peter's Judeophobia is so stark, how does that relate to the text's understanding of Christianity? What implications might defining Christianity against Judaism have for modern readers?

3. How can we understand the historical significance of the Gospel of Peter while simultaneously recognizing its contribution to Judeophobic ideas that have stood for thousands of years? Would it be better simply to ignore the text altogether?

4. Joel Marcus claims that the Gospel of Peter is a "Jewish-Christian" document with resemblances to other Jewish-Christian texts and reflects a love-hate attitude toward Judaism. What do you make of Marcus's argument? How could such an argument help undermine the Judeophobic myth that arose from texts like the Gospel of Peter?

5. Carefully read through the Gospel of Peter. Now choose one or more of

15. Anti-Defamation League, "Press Release: Antisemitic Attitudes in the U.S.A: Guide to ADL's Latest Report" (27 January 2020) (https://tinyurl.com/msxth9ur).

16. Anti-Defamation League, "Audit of Antisemitic Incidents 2021" (https://tinyurl.com/3ta2ruct).

the following New Testament passion narratives: Matthew 26:30–27:66; Mark 14:26–15:47; Luke 22:39–23:56; John 18–19. Compare and contrast the canonical story or stories with the Gospel of Peter. Pay close attention to the details that have shifted from the canonical gospel(s) to the Gospel of Peter. What do these shifts tell us about Judeophobia in the development of early Christian literature? You can also choose to focus on other aspects of the Gospel of Peter. For example, how does the depiction of Jesus differ among the texts you have chosen? What do these differences tell us about the nature of Jesus in both the canonical gospel of your choice and the Gospel of Peter? Most importantly, discuss *why* your authors would make the choices they make. Think about how each text might be received by ancient audiences. What particular appeal would each version of the passion story have for a specific audience?

Further Reading

Combs, Jason Robert. "A Walking Talking Cross: The Polymorphic Christology of the Gospel of Peter." *Early Christianity* 5.2 (2014): 198–219.

Foster, Paul. *The Gospel of Peter: Introduction, Critical Edition, and Commentary.* Boston: Brill, 2010.

Marcus, Joel. "The Gospel of Peter as a Jewish Christian Document." *New Testament Studies* 64.4 (2018): 473–94.

Nicklas, Tobias. "The Gospel of Peter between the Synoptics, Second Century, and Late Antique 'Apostolic Memoirs.'" Pages 43–69 in *Apocryphal and Esoteric Sources in the Development of Christianity and Judaism.* Edited by Igor Dorfmann-Lazarev. Boston: Brill, 2020.

Schaeffer, Susan E. "The Gospel of Peter, the Canonical Gospels, and Oral Tradition." PhD dissertation. Union Theological Seminary, 1991.

Standhartinger, Angela. "'What Women Were Accustomed to Do for the Dead Beloved by Them' (Gospel of Peter 12.50): Traces of Laments and Mourning Rituals in Early Easter, Passion, and Lord's Supper Traditions." *Journal of Biblical Literature* 129.3 (2010): 559–74.

35

Protevangelium of James

ERIC VANDEN EYKEL

The Protevangelium of James is an early Christian text that chronicles the conception, birth, and early life of Jesus's mother, Mary. It was written in the second or third century, probably in Syria, and is the work of an anonymous author claiming to be James the brother of Jesus (or stepbrother, in this case).[1] While it has never been part of any New Testament canon that we know of, the impact that the Protevangelium has exercised on Christian art and theology gives it an almost quasicanonical status. Scenes involving Mary's parents are standard features in churches around the world, and these characters make their first appearance not in the New Testament, but in the Protevangelium.[2] Similarly, many Roman Catholic Christians adhere to the doctrine of the "immaculate conception," which is the belief that Mary was protected from original sin from the moment of her conception. While this doctrine grew and

1. Translations of the Protevangelium of James are from Lily Vuong, *The Protevangelium of James*, Early Christian Apocrypha 7 (Eugene, OR: Cascade, 2019). A detailed discussion of this text's date can be found in Eric M. Vanden Eykel, *"But Their Faces Were All Looking Up": Author and Reader in the Protevangelium of James*, Reception of Jesus in the First Three Centuries 1 (London: T&T Clark, 2016), 23–24; also Lily Vuong, *Gender and Purity in the Protevangelium of James*, Wissenschaftliche Untersuchungen zum Neuen Testament 2/358 (Tübingen: Mohr Siebeck, 2013), 32–39. Vuong makes a compelling case for the text's Syrian provenance in *Gender and Purity*, 193–239.

2. The fourteenth-century frescoes in the Scrovegni Chapel in Padua, Italy, depict a number of scenes and characters from the Protevangelium, including the presentation of Mary in the temple and a number of scenes involving Anna and Joachim. One can see the influence of the Protevangelium even earlier than this, in the fifth-century annunciation mosaic in the Basilica di Santa Maria Maggiore in Rome, where Mary is pictured as spinning thread while she receives news of her impending pregnancy.

developed over time, it may find its earliest expression in this text.[3] As further evidence of the text's popularity and influence, the Protevangelium survives not only in Greek (the language in which it was written) but also in Arabic, Armenian, Coptic, Ethiopic, Latin, and Syriac translations.

The Narrative of the Protevangelium of James

The narrative of the Protevangelium begins with Mary's parents, Anna and Joachim, whom the author describes as pious and infertile (1–2). As they lament their childlessness, an angel announces that Anna has become pregnant and that her child will be extraordinary (3–4). Mary appears a short seven months later, and from the moment she is born, she is carefully sheltered from anything that might compromise her purity. Anna refrains from breastfeeding her until she is able to cleanse herself from the blood of parturition, for example, and she constructs a sanctuary in her bedroom where Mary is entertained and looked after by virgin women (5–6). Mary's parents transfer her to the Jerusalem temple when she turns three, and she lives in that space for nine years (7–8). When Mary turns twelve, the priests select Joseph as her husband and guardian. In contrast to the gospels according to Matthew and Luke, which describe Joseph and Mary's marriage in more conventional terms, Joseph in the Protevangelium is an elderly widower with no interest in his young bride (9). Not long after she returns home with Joseph, Mary sets to work spinning thread for use in a new temple veil and also receives a visit from an angel announcing her impending pregnancy (10–12). Controversy arises when temple officials discover Mary's pregnancy, but after being interrogated and tested, she and Joseph are cleared of any wrongdoing (13–16). Mary gives birth to Jesus in a cave outside Bethlehem while she and Joseph are traveling to register in the census (17–20). The story draws to a close with the arrival of the Magi, Herod's slaughter of children in Bethlehem, and the murder of John the Baptist's father, Zechariah (21–24).

The stories in the Protevangelium rose to popularity through their various depictions in art and use in later Christian theology and tradition. The text

---

3. A primary theme of this text is on the purity of Mary, and we see an early expression of this in the story of her conception. When Anna and Joachim lament their childlessness, they do so in separate locations; Anna is in her garden and Joachim is fasting in the desert. Both of them are visited by angels. Anna is told that she will become pregnant (Protevangelium 4.1), and Joachim is told that Anna *has already become pregnant* (4.4). This pregnancy is therefore best understood as the consequence of sexual intercourse, but as the product of divine intervention.

itself is lesser known, and so in this respect it is difficult to speak of it as directly engendering Judeophobia in the same way that, say, the New Testament gospels have. And yet there are a number of unsubtle Judeophobic elements in the Protevangelium that warrant highlighting and careful discussion. Scholars of the Protevangelium often disagree on when, where, and why this text was written, but one of the more interesting and heated debates about it concerns its relationship to Judaism in the first and second centuries. Some argue that the Protevangelium's author betrays an intimate familiarity with Jewish practices and institutions and that they are possibly even writing from within a Jewish context.[4] Others maintain that the author's knowledge of Judaism is peripheral, fragmentary, and characteristic of someone writing as an outsider.[5]

Without pretending to solve this debate, I want to suggest another way of thinking about the author's positionality with respect to Judaism, one that seeks to move beyond the usual language of insider versus outsider. My argument is that the author of this text conceives of Judaism in mostly positive terms, but that they unintentionally amplify and propagate Judeophobic tropes related to purity and legalism. In what follows, I suggest that this is the consequence of three interrelated facets: (1) the author's reliance on the New Testament gospels for their knowledge of first- and second-century Judaism, (2) the author's preoccupation with the purity of Mary, and (3) the author's penchant for hyperbole and exaggeration.

Storytelling, Hyperbole, and Judeophobia

Many of the episodes that make up the Protevangelium's narrative are reproduced from the New Testament gospels, and with minimal changes. The angelic annunciation of Mary's impending pregnancy (11.5–8) and the census that forces Mary and Joseph to travel to Bethlehem (17.1–4) are both based on stories from the Gospel of Luke (1:26–38 and 2:1–4, respectively). The story of the Magi (Protevangelium 21) and Herod's slaughter of children (22)

---

4. Tim Horner argues (in "Jewish Aspects of the Protoevangelium of James," *Journal of Early Christian Studies* 12 [2004]: 313–35) that the specific ages mentioned in the story of Mary's being brought to the temple indicate that the author may have been familiar with certain mishnaic traditions.

5. One of the more systematic and impassioned refutations of the notion that there are Jewish elements in the Protevangelium can be found in Michael Mach, "Are There Jewish Elements in the 'Protevangelium Jacobi'?," in *Proceedings of the World Congress of Jewish Studies, Jerusalem, Aug. 1985* (Jerusalem: World Union of Jewish Studies, 1986), 215–22.

both come from the Gospel of Matthew (2:1–18). But in addition to copying and adapting stories from the New Testament, the author of the Protevangelium also builds new narrative material by taking stories from the New Testament and Hebrew Bible and populating them with new characters and details. The story of Mary's parents lamenting their childlessness is patterned off the tale of Elkanah and Hannah, the parents of the prophet Samuel (in 1 Sam 1). Aside from having quite similar names, Hannah and Anna are also unable to have children. Both become pregnant when they petition God to intervene (1 Sam 1:20; Protevangelium 4.1), and both commit their children to a life of service to their God (1 Sam 1:22; Protevangelium 4.2); Hannah brings Samuel to the sanctuary at Shiloh (in 1 Sam 1:24), and Joachim and Anna bring Mary to the temple in Jerusalem (Protevangelium 7.4–6). Another instance of the author's appropriation of biblical narrative occurs after Jesus is born, when Mary is assaulted by a woman named Salome who seeks to "test" Mary's body in order to confirm that it has remained "virginal" even after having given birth (20). This episode is adapted from the story of Doubting Thomas in the Gospel of John, in which Jesus's disciple Thomas seeks to test Jesus's body in order to confirm that he is no longer dead, but alive (John 20:24–29).

The Protevangelium's narrative is filled with overly dramatic and exaggerated elements, and even a cursory skim leaves little doubt that hyperbole is one of the author's favorite storytelling techniques. Mary isn't just sheltered as a child; she grows up in a sanctuary where she's entertained by virgin women (6.4–5). Mary doesn't just live in the Jerusalem temple; she lives in the holy of holies, the most sacred location in the temple (15.11). Mary isn't just a virgin *before* the birth of Jesus; she remains a virgin even *after* Jesus is born (19.18). Hyperbole, of course, is not problematic by definition. It becomes problematic in the Protevangelium because of the author's heavy reliance on the New Testament gospels, whose portrayals of Jews and Jewish leaders are already caricatured, especially with regard to their legalism and concern for ritual purity. The Pharisees are but one example of this. Throughout the New Testament gospels, they seek out Jesus and his disciples and antagonize them ruthlessly for eating with the wrong people (Mark 2:15–17), for picking a bit of grain or healing on the Sabbath (Matt 12:1–8 and Luke 6:6–11), among other things. And because these texts are prominent among the Protevangelium's reservoirs of source material, this means that the author's hyperbolic readings are often exaggerations of characters and narratives that are already themselves exaggerated. The consequence is that the Protevangelium often presents portraits of Jews and Jewish concerns that are caricatures of caricatures.

When the reader first encounters Joachim, for example, he is in the Jerusalem temple preparing to offer sacrifices. There he is told by one of the temple officials that he must wait his turn because he has no children. Joachim is distraught and goes to a record book to confirm whether it is true that he *alone* is childless, and he finds that "all the righteous had raised children in Israel" (1.7). There are a few aspects of this story that stand out. No law in ancient Israel specifies an order for offering sacrifices on the basis of whether one has produced offspring. And certainly there was no detailed, exhaustive ledger by which Joachim would be able to confirm that he was the *only* childless person—righteous or not—in Israel's history. These features were created by the author in order to paint a bleak picture for Anna and Joachim, thus priming the reader for the soon-to-come divine intervention that will result in Anna's pregnancy with Mary. But the result is that the Jewish temple official who tells Joachim to wait his turn appears in this text to be overly and irrationally legalistic, not unlike the Pharisees in the New Testament gospels.

Another example is the story of Mary's childhood in the Jerusalem temple. As noted, Anna's dedication of Mary to temple service is meant to invite comparisons between Mary and Samuel. But the way that the author speaks of Mary's childhood in the temple goes above and beyond simple literary allusion. Mary not only lives in the temple; she lives in the holy of holies, the most sacred location in the temple complex (15.10–11). And of course, the idea that any individual—much less a young girl—would live in the holy of holies is clearly not rooted in any sort of reality. This hyperbolic detail exists in the story to further highlight the exceptional nature of Mary's purity. When Mary turns twelve, however, the priests determine that it is time for her to depart, presumably because she will soon begin to menstruate and because according to Leviticus 15:19–33, the blood of menstruation causes ritual impurity. "What should we do with her," they ask, "lest she defile the temple of the Lord our God?" (Protevangelium 8.4). The author of the Protevangelium does not cast the priests in this episode in a negative light because of their deliberations, but it becomes clear as the narrative progresses that readers are meant to interpret their conundrum as driven by ignorance. Mary's purity in this text is comprehensive and secure, and the notion that she herself could become a source of ritual defilement is unthinkable. Just as the caricatured Pharisees in the New Testament gospels are accused of misunderstanding the true nature and purpose of law observance, the priests in the Protevangelium have no clue what actually constitutes the ritual purity that they are allegedly experts in. In short, the author of this text depicts these Jewish leaders as wholly ignorant of their own statutes and traditions.

It is unlikely that the author of the Protevangelium aims to portray Jews or Jewish concerns in a negative light. In fact, I suggest that this author conceived of Jews and Judaism—or, at least, their understanding of Jews and Judaism— in mostly complimentary terms. Mary's parents are Jews, and of course so is Mary, and these characters are wholly positive. As the discussion here shows, one of the central themes of the Protevangelium is the purity of Mary, and in nearly every episode, the author's attention is directed toward spotlighting Mary as the purest creature who has ever lived. The author understands this concept of purity within a Jewish framework, albeit a caricatured and probably incomplete one. While the author may not *intend* to cast Jews in a negative light, however, this is one of the unfortunate consequences of the way that they chose to tell their story.

Discussion Questions and Activity Suggestions

1. This chapter discussed hyperbole in the Protevangelium of James. What are some other exaggerated episodes in this text, and what function do they serve in the broader narrative?

2. Why do you think that this author chose to tell Mary's story in this way? Wouldn't it have been possible to simply declare, outside of all the messiness, that Mary was unquestionably and invincibly pure?

3. Can you think of any ways that the author's hyperbolic treatment of Judaism has a positive effect in the story? Or is it always negative?

4. Watch Chimamanda Ngozi Adichie's TED talk, "The Danger of a Single Story" (https://tinyurl.com/4hr39azx). In small groups, discuss how Adichie might answer the question behind this talk's title: What *is* the danger of a single story? Together, brainstorm a list of familiar stereotypes and talk about how Adichie's concept of the single story may have given rise to them. A brainstorming exercise like this can be uncomfortable because of the profound harm that stereotypes have caused and continue to cause. In that regard, keep in mind that this exercise presumes that stereotypes are false (or "incomplete," as Adichie puts it).

Further Reading

Foskett, Mary F. *A Virgin Conceived: Mary and Classical Representations of Virginity*. Bloomington: Indiana University Press, 2002.

Kelto Lillis, Julia. "Paradox in *Partu*: Verifying Virginity in the *Protevangelium of James.*" *Journal of Early Christian Studies* 24 (2016): 1–28.

Mach, Michael. "Are There Jewish Elements in the 'Protevangelium Jacobi'?" Pages 215–22 in *Proceedings of the World Congress of Jewish Studies, Jerusalem, Aug. 1985*. Jerusalem: World Union of Jewish Studies, 1986.

Vanden Eykel, Eric M. *"But Their Faces Were All Looking Up": Author and Reader in the Protevangelium of James*. The Reception of Jesus in the First Three Centuries 1. London: T&T Clark, 2016.

Vuong, Lily. "'Let Us Bring Her up to the Temple of the Lord': Exploring the Boundaries of Jewish and Christian Relations through the Presentation of Mary in the *Protevangelium of James.*" Pages 418–32 in *Infancy Gospels: Stories and Identities*. Edited by Claire Clivaz et al. Tübingen: Mohr Siebeck, 2011.

———. *The Protevangelium of James*. Early Christian Apocrypha 7. Eugene, OR: Cascade, 2019.

Mean, Angry Old Testament God versus Nice, Loving New Testament God

. . . **not so fast.** This is a common stereotype! Yes, parts of the Hebrew Bible (Old Testament) depict divine wrath, while parts of the New Testament show divine love and forgiveness.

But there are *three* reasons this stereotype is wrong.

1. **It emphasizes some texts, but ignores many others.**

IT'S VERY EASY TO USE TEXTUAL EVIDENCE TO MAKE THE EXACT OPPOSITE ARGUMENT!

We can find plenty of love and mercy in the Hebrew Bible / Old Testament, and lots of violence and vengeance in the New Testament:

Handout prepared by Eva Mroczek with sources suggested by Matt Rindge, Ethan Schwartz, M. Adryael Tong, and Meredith Warren, in collaboration with James Barker, Chance Bonar, Adam D. J. Brett, Aaron Brody, Greg Carey, Julie Deluty, Angela Roskop Erisman, Chaya Halberstam, Diane Fruchtman Hannah, Martin Kavka, Sarah Kleeb, Barbara Krawcowicz, Lennart Lehmhaus, Shelly Matthews, Kelly Murphy, Sara Parks, Elliot Ratzman, Annette Yoshiko Reed, Kelsie Rodenbiker, and Larry Wills. Special thanks to Mika Ahuvia for "Us versus Them: Challenging Stereotypes about Judaism in the Wake of the Pittsburgh Shooting." Please retain this credit list if you use the handout, and indicate if it has been adapted. Used here with permission.

Divine love and mercy in the Hebrew Bible / Old Testament	Divine wrath and violence in the New Testament
Jesus says he has come to sow violence:	*Jesus says he has come to sow violence:*
The Lord, the Lord, the compassionate and gracious God, slow to anger, abounding in love and faithfulness. (Exod 34:6)	Do not think that I have come to bring peace to the earth; I have not come to bring peace, but a sword. For I have come to set a man against his father, and a daughter against her mother, and a daughter-in-law against her mother-in-law; and one's foes will be members of one's own household. (Matt 10:34–36 NRSV)
God gently cares for all plants and animals:	*Jesus curses a fig tree because he's hangry:*
[God] makes springs pour water into the ravines; it flows between the mountains. They give water to all the beasts of the field; the wild donkeys quench their thirst. The birds of the sky nest by the waters; they sing among the branches. He waters the mountains from his upper chambers; the land is satisfied by the fruit of his work. He makes grass grow for the cattle, and plants for people to cultivate— bringing forth food from the earth: wine that gladdens human hearts, oil to make their faces shine, and bread that sustains their hearts. The trees of the Lord are well watered, the cedars of Lebanon that he planted. (Ps 104:10–16)	[Jesus] was hungry. Seeing in the distance a fig tree in leaf, he went to see whether perhaps he would find anything on it. When he came to it, he found nothing but leaves, for it was not the season for figs. He said to it, "May no one ever eat fruit from you again." And his disciples heard it. (Mark 11:12–14)

Divine love and mercy in the Hebrew Bible / Old Testament	Divine wrath and violence in the New Testament
God is a gentle shepherd who carries people in his arms like baby animals:	*God will torture sinners forever even after death:*
He tends his flock like a shepherd: He gathers the lambs in his arms and carries them close to his heart; he gently leads those that have young. (Isa 40:11)	When the Lord Jesus is revealed from heaven with his mighty angels in flaming fire, inflicting vengeance on those who do not know God and on those who do not obey the gospel of our Lord Jesus. These will suffer the punishment of eternal destruction, separated from the presence of the Lord and from the glory of his might. (2 Thess 1:7–9)
God requires love and equal treatment for all, regardless of where they are from:	*Sinners are like yard waste—they'll be burned:*
The stranger who resides with you shall be to you as one of your citizens; you shall love him as yourself. (Lev 19:34)	[Jesus's] disciples approached him, saying, "Explain to us the parable of the weeds of the field." He answered, "The one who sows the good seed is the Son of Man; the field is the world, and the good seed are the children of the kingdom; the weeds are the children of the evil one, and the enemy who sowed them is the devil; the harvest is the end of the age, and the reapers are angels. Just as the weeds are collected and burned up with fire, so will it be at the end of the age. The Son of Man will send his angels, and they will collect out of his kingdom all causes of sin and all evildoers, and they will throw them into the furnace of fire, where there will be weeping and gnashing of teeth." (Matt 13:36–42)

Divine love and mercy in the Hebrew Bible / Old Testament	Divine wrath and violence in the New Testament
God heals, protects, forgives, and does not judge people based on their sins:	*On judgment day, God will condemn some people to suffer in a lake of fire forever:*
Bless the LORD, O my soul, and do not forget all his benefits— who forgives all your iniquity, who heals all your diseases, who redeems your life from the Pit, who crowns you with steadfast love and mercy. . . . The LORD works vindication and justice for all who are oppressed. . . . The LORD is merciful and gracious, slow to anger and abounding in steadfast love. He will not always accuse, nor will he keep his anger forever. He does not deal with us according to our sins, nor repay us according to our iniquities. For as the heavens are high above the earth, so great is his steadfast love toward those who fear him. . . . As a father has compassion for his children, so the LORD has compassion for those who fear him. (Ps 103:2–13)	Then I saw a great white throne and the one who sat on it; the earth and the heaven fled from his presence, and no place was found for them. And I saw the dead, great and small, standing before the throne, and books were opened. Also another book was opened, the book of life. And the dead were judged according to their works, as recorded in the books. And the sea gave up the dead that were in it, Death and Hades gave up the dead that were in them, and all were judged according to what they had done. Then Death and Hades were thrown into the lake of fire. This is the second death, the lake of fire; and anyone whose name was not found written in the book of life was thrown into the lake of fire. (Rev 20:11–15)

Yikes! **Does this mean that God is actually loving and merciful in the Hebrew Bible, but vengeful in the New Testament?**

No. These examples are meant to illustrate that the "angry Old Testament God versus loving New Testament God" stereotype ignores lots of anger and violence in the New Testament and lots of divine love and care in the Hebrew Bible. **Both** anger and love are present in **both** the Hebrew Bible / Old Testament and in the New Testament.

Identifying the Hebrew Bible / Old Testament with anger and the New Testament with love doesn't reflect what's really there in the texts—**it is a result of preexisting assumptions, commitments, and prejudices.**

But there's more!

2.   The stereotype overlooks the *reasons* why God is often depicted as angry in the Hebrew Bible / Old Testament:
God is angry when vulnerable people are being oppressed.

God's anger is often directed at people who pretend to be pious, but **get rich by exploiting the poor or unjustly manipulating courts of law.**

Take this example from the Covenant Code in the book of Exodus:

> You shall not mistreat any widow or orphan. If you do mistreat them, when they cry out to me, I will surely heed their cry; my wrath will burn, and I will kill you with the sword, and your wives shall become widows and your children orphans. If you lend money to my people, to the poor among you, you shall not deal with them as a creditor; you shall not exact interest from them. If you take your neighbor's cloak in pawn, you shall restore it before the sun goes down; for it may be your neighbor's only clothing to use as cover; in what else shall that person sleep? And if your neighbor cries out to me, I will listen, for I am compassionate. (Exod 22:22–27)

Here, God is very angry with those who take advantage of the poor and vulnerable, including predatory moneylenders, but is compassionate toward those they have harmed.

Or this one, from the prophet Amos:

> They sell the innocent for silver,
> and the needy for a pair of sandals.
> They trample on the heads of the poor
> as on the dust of the ground
> and deny justice to the oppressed.
> Father and son use the same girl
> and so profane my holy name.
> They lie down beside every altar
> on garments taken in pledge.
> In the house of their god
> they drink wine taken as fines. . . .
> There are those who hate the one who upholds justice in court
> and detest the one who tells the truth.

You levy a straw tax on the poor
and impose a tax on their grain.
Therefore, though you have built stone mansions,
you will not live in them;
though you have planted lush vineyards,
you will not drink their wine.
For I know how many are your offenses
and how great your sins.
There are those who oppress the innocent and take bribes
and deprive the poor of justice in the courts. . . .
Therefore this is what the LORD, the LORD God Almighty, says:
There will be wailing in all the streets
and cries of anguish in every public square.

(Amos 2:6–8; 5:10–12, 16)

Here, God is angry at those who enrich themselves by exploiting the poor through imposing fines, levying taxes, repossessing their goods, and taking advantage of them in court. Here, God's anger will cause these oppressors to lose their wealth.

These same things elicit divine wrath and vengeance in the New Testament!

In the Gospel of Mark, Jesus condemns religious leaders who act pious, but get rich and famous by exploiting the poor—the same reason God is angry in the book of Amos:

They like to walk around in flowing robes and be greeted with respect in the marketplaces, and have the most important seats in the synagogues and the places of honor at banquets. They devour widows' houses and for a show make lengthy prayers. These men will be punished most severely. (Mark 12:38–40)

Here's a different example from the community of Jesus-followers in the New Testament book of Acts. Members were required to sell their possessions and pool all their money together. One wealthy couple, Ananias and Sapphira, sell their land, but give only *part* of the money to the collective, secretly keeping some of it for themselves. Both are immediately struck dead:

Then Peter said, "Ananias, how is it that Satan has so filled your heart that you have lied to the Holy Spirit and have kept for yourself some of the money you received for the land?" . . . When Ananias heard this, he fell down and died. . . . [Then] Peter said to [Sapphira], "How could you conspire to test the Spirit of the Lord? Listen! The feet of the men who buried your husband are at the door, and they will carry you out also." At that moment she fell down at his feet and died. . . . Great fear seized the whole church and all who heard about these events. (Acts 5:3–11)

And finally:

3. **Jesus did say the greatest commandments are about love: to love God and love your neighbor!**

   But Jesus did not make this up—both come from the Hebrew Bible / Old Testament, and love of God and neighbor are key for Jews as well.

You shall love your neighbor as yourself. (Lev 19:18)

As for the love of God, the book of Deuteronomy says:

Hear, O Israel: The LORD our God, the LORD is one. Love the LORD your God with all your heart and with all your soul and with all your strength. (Deut 6:4–5)

In later Jewish practice, this became a prayer called the Shema ("Hear"), and is still recited daily by many Jews today.

Jewish teachers around Jesus's time taught the same thing about the most important teaching of the torah. When the famous Rabbi Hillel was challenged to explain the whole torah while standing on one foot, he said:

What is hateful to you, do not do to your neighbor. That is the entire Torah. The rest is commentary—go and learn. (Babylonian Talmud, tractate *Shabbat* 31a)

Pharisees Flowchart

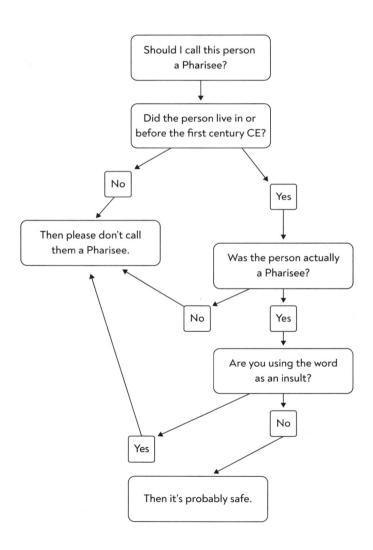

About the Contributors

Matthew R. Anderson holds a Gatto Chair of Christian Studies at Saint Francis Xavier University, Nova Scotia/Mi'kma'ki. He studies Paul and the New Testament in Jewish and Roman context, with particular focus on masculinity, Aware-Settler biblical studies, and decolonizing pilgrimage. Recent books disrupting anti-Jewish readings of biblical texts include *Prophets of Love: The Unlikely Kinship of Leonard Cohen and the Apostle Paul* (McGill-Queens, 2023) and *Pairings: The Bible and Booze* (Novalis, 2021), in French as *Apocalypse et gin tonic* (2022).

Jeremiah N. Bailey completed his doctorate at Baylor University in 2021 with a dissertation on class conflict in First Clement and its occasion. He is series editor for "Classic Studies on the Apostolic Fathers" (Pickwick Press) and the "Baylor Handbooks on the Apostolic Fathers" (Baylor University Press). His main research areas are second-century Christianity, Paul's Letters, Second Temple Judaism, and reception history of early Christian literature.

Mary Ann Beavis is professor emerita of religion and culture at St. Thomas More College. Her recent research interests are in the area of slavery in early Christianity, parable studies, goddess studies, and religion and popular culture. She is the founding editor of three academic journals, most recently, *S/HE: An International Journal of Goddess Studies*. She currently resides in Winnipeg, Manitoba.

Chance E. Bonar is a postdoctoral fellow at the Center for the Humanities at Tufts University. His research and teaching focus primarily on early Christian literature, slavery in the ancient Mediterranean, Christian anti-Judaism, and the concept of the author in antiquity. He is the coeditor of *Authorial Fictions and Attributions in the Ancient Mediterranean* (Mohr Siebeck, 2024) and has a forthcoming monograph entitled *God, Slavery, and Early Christianity: Divine Possession and Ethics in the Shepherd of Hermas* (Cambridge University Press).

Tom de Bruin (he/they) is assistant professor of New Testament and Early Judaism at Radboud University, The Netherlands. They taught New Testament for several years at a Christian seminary and have worked for several LGBTQ+ charities. He is the author of several articles and a book on Satan and demons in early Christianity, with a particular interest in the noncanonical work the Testaments of the Twelve Patriarchs. De Bruin's most recent book is *Fan Fiction and Early Christian Writings: Apocrypha, Pseudepigrapha and Canon* (T&T Clark/Bloomsbury, 2024).

Christy Cobb is associate professor of Christianity at the University of Denver. She is the author of *Slavery, Gender, Truth, and Power in Luke-Acts and Other Ancient Narratives* (Palgrave Macmillan, 2019) and a coeditor of two volumes: *Sex, Violence, and Early Christian Texts* (Lexington, 2022) and *Ancient Slavery in New Testament Contexts* (Eerdmans, 2025). A member of the editorial board for the *Journal of Feminist Studies in Religion*, Cobb's research and teaching interests include slavery, gender, sexuality, early Christian families, Acts, and the Apocryphal Acts.

Cavan Concannon is professor of religion at the University of Southern California. He is the author of *Profaning Paul* (University of Chicago Press, 2022) and *Assembling Early Christianity* (Cambridge University Press, 2017) and codirector of the "Mediterranean Connectivity Initiative."

David L. Eastman is the Joseph Glenn Sherrill Chair of Bible at the McCallie School, a research fellow at the University of South Africa, and a fellow with the "Beyond Canon" project at the Universität Regensburg. His research employs archeological, textual, liturgical, and artistic evidence in analyzing early Christian constructions of martyrdom traditions, sacred space, the cult of the saints, and the reception and expansion of apocryphal apostolic traditions—in particular, those related to Peter and Paul. He is the author of four books and a cofounder and coeditor of the "Inventing Christianity" monograph series with Pennsylvania State University Press.

Scott S. Elliott is a professor in the Department of Humanities at Adrian College. His work centers on literary analyses of biblical narratives and adaptations of those narratives in film, graphic novels, and other works of fiction. He is the author of *Reconfiguring Mark's Jesus* (Sheffield Phoenix, 2011) and *The Rustle of Paul* (T&T Clark, 2020).

Sarah Emanuel is assistant professor of theological studies at Loyola Marymount University. Her research attends to the diversity of early Judaism, including its relations to the early Jesus movement, as well as how diverse reading strategies showcase the ways in which biblical sources function as sites for the negotiation of power, meaning-making, and identity. She is the author of *Humor, Resistance, and Jewish Cultural Persistence in the Book of Revelation: Roasting Rome* (Cambridge University Press, 2020) and *Trauma Theory, Trauma Story: A Narration of Biblical Studies and the World of Trauma* (Brill, 2021). Her next book on Paul, Judaism, and Christian anti-Judaism is forthcoming with Fortress.

Emily J. Gathergood is a postdoctoral fellow in New Testament at the University of Nottingham, England, where she was awarded her PhD in 2022. Emily's research focus is on divine and human embodiment in early Jewish and Christian writings. Her doctoral monograph *The Midwifery of God* (forthcoming with Oxford University Press) is a winner of the Manfred Lautenschläger Award for Theological Promise. Her master's thesis on the material Pauline corpus is published in the journal *New Testament Studies*. Emily serves on the editorial board of the *Journal for the Study of the New Testament*.

Mark A. Godin is a minister of The Presbyterian Church in Canada. He has served congregations of the Church of Scotland and the United Reformed Church and is now based in northern Sweden. He has written articles and chapters on interfaith relations, ecclesial repentance, theology and literature, and practical/liturgical theology; his research interests include the theology of translation and institutional structure.

Jill Hicks-Keeton is associate professor of religion at the University of Southern California. She is the author of *Arguing with Aseneth: Gentile Access to Israel's Living God in Jewish Antiquity* (Oxford University Press, 2018) and *Good Book: How White Evangelicals Save the Bible to Save Themselves* (Fortress, 2023), as well as coauthor of *Does Scripture Speak for Itself? The Museum of the Bible and the Politics of Interpretation* (Cambridge University Press, 2022) and coeditor of *The Ways That Often Parted* (SBL, 2018) and *The Museum of the Bible: A Critical Introduction* (Lexington/Fortress, 2019).

Meira Z. Kensky is senior assistant dean and director of undergraduate advising for the University of Virginia College of Arts and Sciences. Previously she was Joseph E. McCabe Professor of Religion and director of advising at Coe College. Kensky is the author of *Trying Man, Trying God: The Divine Courtroom in Early Jewish and Christian Literature* (Mohr Siebeck, 2010) and is working on a book on the Apocalypses of Peter and Paul and Early Christian tours of hell (to be published by Eerdmans). Recent publications include articles on Paul and apocalypticism, the Acts of Timothy, and John Chrysostom's Homilies on 1–2 Timothy. She has served as codirector of the ACM Newberry Seminar in the Humanities and as Coe's director of first-year experience, and she has served as an inaugural ACM/Mellon academic leadership fellow for 2023–2024.

Kyu Seop Kim is associate professor of New Testament studies at Asian Center for Theological Studies and Mission. He has written numerous articles on Hebrews and Pauline letters in light of papyrology and early Judaism. His first book is *The Firstborn Son in Ancient Judaism and Early Christianity: A Study of Primogeniture and Christology* (Brill, 2019). He has completed his second book, which explores the concepts of covenant, high priesthood, and inheritance in Hebrews.

Brian Yong Lee is assistant professor of New Testament and early Christianity at Loyola University Chicago. His research focuses on early Christian origins in the context of late Second Temple Jewish and Greco-Roman intellectual and cultic discourses. He is currently working on two monographs: one on Paul's use of philosophy in 1 Corinthians, and the other on the origins of early Christian interpersonal forgiveness.

Harry O. Maier is professor of New Testament and Early Christian Studies at Vancouver School of Theology and senior fellow at the Max Weber Center for Advanced Cultural and Social Studies, University of Erfurt, Germany. He is author of several books, including *New Testament Christianity in the Roman World* (Oxford University Press, 2018) and *Picturing Paul in Empire: Imperial Image, Text, and Persuasion in Colossians, Ephesians, and the Pastoral Epistles* (T&T Clark, 2013), as well as edited volumes, including *Encountering the Other: Christian and Multifaith Perspectives* (Wipf & Stock, 2020), coedited with Rabbi Laura Duhan Kaplan. For several years he was cochair of the

Vancouver Jewish Christian Dialogue hosted by the Center for Jewish and International Affairs and coordinated with Vancouver School of Theology.

Shelly Matthews is professor of New Testament and director for the Carpenter Initiative on Gender, Sexuality, and Justice at the Brite Divinity School, Fort Worth. She is the coauthor, with Barbara Reid, of the Luke commentary published in the Wisdom Commentary Series by Liturgical Press; the coeditor, with Tat-Siong Benny Liew, of a volume on race, pedagogy, and biblical studies published by SBL Press; and author of several articles and monographs on anti-Judaism and other forms of violence in Luke-Acts. She is currently finishing a monograph with the working title *A Feminist Politics of Early Christian Resurrection: Justice, Authority, Flesh.*

James F. McGrath is the Clarence L. Goodwin Chair in New Testament Language and Literature at Butler University. His work has spanned early Christology within the context of Jewish monotheism, the historical Jesus, John the Baptist, and the Mandeans, as well as the Bible and religion in popular culture. He is the author of numerous books and articles, including *What Jesus Learned from Women* (Cascade, 2021), *The A to Z of the New Testament* (Eerdmans, 2023), and *Christmaker: A Life of John the Baptist* (Eerdmans, 2024).

Hugo Méndez is an associate professor of religious studies at the University of North Carolina at Chapel Hill, where he teaches New Testament and early Christianity. He is the author of *The Cult of Stephen in Jerusalem: Inventing a Patron Martyr* (Oxford University Press, 2022) and coauthor of *The New Testament: A Historical Introduction to the Early Christian Writings* (8th ed., Oxford University Press, 2024).

Mark D. Nanos (PhD, University of St. Andrews, Scotland) is a Jewish scholar whose research focuses on reading Paul's letters as mid-first-century Jewish correspondence, which generates new historical constructions for the movement that offer more promising options to pursue for contemporary issues, not least Christian-Jewish relations, than the legacy interpretations of Paul's voice have generated. His publications include *The Mystery of Romans* (Fortress, 1996—winner of the 1996 National Jewish Book Award in Jewish-Christian Relations), *The Irony of Galatians* (Fortress, 2002), and several volumes of collected essays, beginning with *Reading Paul within Judaism* (Cascade, 2017). For a full list of publications and speaking engagements, see https://www.mark nanos.com/.

Sara Parks is assistant professor in religious studies at St. Francis Xavier University. She researches competing streams of Judaism in the Hellenistic and Roman periods, with a focus on the New Testament, gender, and Christian anti-Judaism. She has two books: *Gender in the Rhetoric of Jesus: Women in Q* (Lexington/Fortress, 2019) and *Jewish and Christian Women in the Ancient Mediterranean* (with Meredith Warren and Shayna Sheinfeld; Routledge, 2022).

Shaily Shashikant Patel is assistant professor of early Christianity at Virginia Tech, where she teaches courses on demonology, orthodoxy/heresy, and magic. She researches discursive genealogies of magic in early Christian literature and is the author of *Smoke and Mirrors: Discourses of Magic in Early Petrine Traditions* (Oxford University Press, forthcoming).

Adele Reinhartz is Distinguished University Professor at the University of Ottawa, where she is also a professor in the Department of Classics and Religious Studies. She is also a research fellow in the Department of Old and New Testament Studies at the University of the Free State. Her main research contributions have been in the study of ancient Jewish/Christian relations, as well as religion and film. Adele served as the general editor of the *Journal of Biblical Literature* from 2012 to 2019 and as the president of the Society of Biblical Literature in 2020. Adele was inducted into the Royal Society of Canada in 2005 and into the American Academy for Jewish Research in 2014. Her most recent books are *Cast out of the Covenant: Jews and Anti-Judaism in the Gospel of John* (Fortress Academic, 2018); *Bible and Cinema: An Introduction* (2nd ed., Routledge, 2022); and *Jousting with John: Essays on Jews, Gender, and Ethics in the Fourth Gospel* (de Gruyter, 2024).

Michael Scott Robertson is a postdoctoral researcher at Universität Regensburg, Germany. In 2023, he was awarded a Deutsche Forschungsgemeinschaft Eigene Stelle for the project "The Social Locations of the Acts of Titus: How a Minor 'Apostle' Affected the Identity of a Big Island." He is the author of *Reading the Letter to Titus in Light of Crete: Dynamics of Early Christian Identity Formation* (Brill, 2023).

Sarah E. Rollens is the R. A. Webb Associate Professor and chair of the Department of Religious Studies at Rhodes College in Memphis. Her research concerns the social formation and the production of literature among early Christ-followers; this research focuses specifically on the Synoptic Gospels and the Q source, as well as on the letters of Paul. She is the author of *Framing Social Criticism in the Jesus Movement: The Ideological Project of the Sayings Gospel Q* (Mohr Siebeck, 2014) and is the coeditor and contributor to *Worth More Many Sparrows: Essays in Honor of Willi Braun* (Equinox, 2022).

Justin P. Jeffcoat Schedtler is associate professor of religion at Wartburg College in Waverly, Iowa. His research focuses on early Jewish and Christian apocalyptic literature with special interest in the book of Revelation. He has published *A Heavenly Chorus* (Mohr Siebeck, 2014) and *Royal Ideologies in Revelation* (Cambridge University Press, 2023). With Kelly Murphy, he is coeditor of *Apocalypses in Context* (Fortress, 2016).

Nathan Shedd earned his PhD in theology and religious studies from Liverpool Hope University in 2020. He is the author of *A Dangerous Parting: The Beheading of John the Baptist in Early Christian Memory* (Baylor University Press, 2021). He is also the coeditor (alongside Joan Taylor) of a forthcoming volume on the early reception history of John the Baptist (T&T Clark).

Shayna Sheinfeld is assistant professor of religion at Augsburg University in Minneapolis. Her research emphasizes the vast diversity of Judaism in antiquity, including ancient constructions of gender, apocalypses, and the afterlives of ancient texts in popular culture. Sheinfeld is the author of numerous books and articles, including coediting *Constructions of Gender in Religious Traditions of Late Antiquity* (Lexington, 2024) and *Gender and Second-Temple Judaism* (Lexington, 2020). Sheinfeld published *Jewish and Christian Women in the Ancient Mediterranean* (Routledge, 2022) with Sara Parks and Meredith J. C. Warren.

Ekaputra Tupamahu is associate professor of New Testament at Portland Seminary. He has a broad range of academic interests, including the politics of language, race/ethnic theory, postcolonial studies, immigration studies, critical study of religion, and global Christianity (particularly Pentecostal/Charismatic movement). All these interests inform and influence the way he approaches the texts of the New Testament and the history of early Christian movement(s). His first monograph was *Contesting Languages: Heteroglossia and the Politics of Language in the Early Church* (Oxford University Press, 2022).

Eric Vanden Eykel is associate professor of religious studies at Ferrum College in Virginia. His research focuses on Christian apocryphal literature, with a special emphasis on texts and traditions about the infancies and childhoods of Jesus and Mary. He is the author of *"But Their Faces Were All Looking Up": Author and Reader in the Protevangelium of James* (T&T Clark, 2016), coeditor of *Sex, Violence, and Early Christian Texts* (Lexington, 2022), and author of *The Magi: Who They Were, How They've Been Remembered, and Why They Still Fascinate* (Fortress, 2022).

Alana M. Vincent is docent in history of religion at Umeå University. She is an expert in modern Judaism and post-Holocaust Jewish-Christian dialogue, and the author of *Making Memory: Jewish and Christian Explorations in Monument, Narrative, and Liturgy* (Pickwick, 2014) and *Culture, Communion, and Recovery: Tolkienian Fairy-Story and Inter-Religious Exchange* (Cambridge Scholars Publishing, 2012).

Meredith J. C. Warren is senior lecturer in biblical and religious studies at the University of Sheffield, where she directs the Sheffield Centre for Interdisciplinary Biblical Studies. She is the author of numerous books and articles on gender in early Christianity, food and meals in ancient literature, and anti-Judaism and the New Testament. Her most recent book, coauthored with Sara Parks and Shayna Sheinfeld, is *Jewish and Christian Women in the Ancient Mediterranean* (Routledge, 2022).

Taylor M. Weaver earned his PhD in theology and religious studies at the University of Kent in the United Kingdom, where he specialized in New Testament studies (specifically Paul), reception, and continental philosophy. His current research interests include the use of Marxist criticism and critical spatial studies for constructing early Christian communities. He is the author of *The Scandal of Community: Pauline Factions and the Circulation of Grace* (Lexington/Fortress, 2021), has published numerous articles and chapters in edited volumes, and is working on his second book. Currently he is an assistant professor in library science at East Texas Baptist University, which he took on after his 2023 postdoctoral fellowship in Det Teologiske Fakultet at Universitetet i Oslo in Norway.

Index of Authors

Index of Subjects

Index of Scripture and Other Ancient Sources